FORTY YEARS

IN A

MOORLAND PARISH

REMINISCENCES AND RESEARCHES IN
DANBY IN CLEVELAND

BY

REV. J. C. ATKINSON, D.C.L.

INCUMBENT OF THE PARISH

AUTHOR OF
'A HISTORY OF CLEVELAND,' 'GLOSSARY OF THE CLEVELAND DIALECT,' ETC.

EDITOR OF
'THE WHITBY CHARTULARY,' 'THE RIEVAULX CHARTULARY,'
'THE FURNESS COUCHER BOOK,' ETC.

WITH MAPS

London

MACMILLAN AND CO.

AND NEW YORK

1891

First Edition, April 1891.
Reprinted from standing type, with corrections and additions, May 1891.
Stereotyped and reprinted, with additions, July 1891.

Printing Statement:

Due to the very old age and scarcity of this book,
many of the pages may be hard to read due to the
blurring of the original text, possible missing pages,
missing text and other issues beyond our control.

Because this is such an important and rare work, we
believe it is best to reproduce this book regardless of
its original condition.

Thank you for your understanding.

CASTLETON BOW BRIDGE.

BUILT 1175-85 ; DESTROYED 1873 (see p. 443).

TO

MY LOVING FRIEND

G. A. M.

BUT FOR WHOM THESE PAGES WOULD

NOT HAVE BEEN WRITTEN

PREFACE TO THE SECOND EDITION

THE Author desires to acknowledge the kindly reception accorded to his book, alike by the Public and the Press; and, although it be but in few words, to do so both fully and gratefully. And to these words of acknowledgment he would fain add a few others suggested by more than one of the friendly notices adverted to.

In each of these cases, and in divers private letters besides, the fact has been noticed that terms and idioms identical with, or precisely similar to, those instanced as belonging to the Cleveland, and especially to the Dales vernacular, are in use elsewhere, notably in the Lowlands of Scotland, in Lancashire, parts of Cumberland, West Yorkshire, and so on. This is a circumstance which the Author has not only never lost sight of, but has put forward and enhanced, as probably few others have done. He has always regarded the Cleveland folk-speech as a survival from the tongue of (speaking generally) the great Northumbrian kingdom; and it would be contrary to the nature of things if there were not other like survivals in various different districts embraced by the said kingdom.   But, at the same time, he holds that, while *a priori* the remoteness and seclusion of the Dales-district especially, and of a great part of the Cleveland division at large, favoured the survival there to a singular degree as well as in a singular manner, the copious constituents of the folk-speech, as it continued to be up to half a century ago, have actually rendered. it more conservative of the ancient type of the tongue than is perhaps true of the folk-speech of any other district in the kingdom.   Indeed, what the writer has himself observed and registered has led him on to the recognition of the fact. that, to all practical intents and purposes, the people of his own district continued for ages to be a Danish-speaking people ; and little as this principle has hitherto been acknowledged, it would be strange indeed if the influential bulk of the people in these northern parts of the Danelagh had been anything else.

The Author is quite aware that, in such matters as local nomenclature, such an allegation as this almost amounts to the statement of a revolutionary principle. The absolute fact, however, is that after forty years of systematic study of the folk-speech in most of its applications, connections, and developments, he has been compelled to fall back on this conclusion by the utter impossibility of accounting for or explaining the local terminology on the old theory of its imposition by the original " Danish " colonists, or native Scandinavians, as they mainly were.   Conceding fully that such principal or cardinal names as Danby, Ormsby, Normanby, Asolfsby (Aislaby), Ugleberdesby (Ugglebarnby) were given by native Northmen, it is yet impossible to suppose that of the scores of subordinate local names found in those several divisional areas (all with a traceable, and most of them with a distinct Scandinavian character belonging to them), the preponderating amount could have been given by any other than a folk continuing to speak Danish for generation after generation. Nay, the literary-Danish expression *at pladske paa söen* lives still in the current Whitby phrase descriptive of a seaman's life, namely, that he " blashes for his living "; while our Cleveland saying of a man, like Pharaoh's dream-kine, " fat-fleshed and well-favoured," that he " does not look as if he had lived on ' deaf nuts,' ". is but the South Jutland *han lever int' ved dövv nödr*, still living on this side the North Sea. And when such instances can be given by the page at this, the far end of the nineteenth century, what about the language of the folk generally, before the era of the printing-press ?

DANBY PARSONAGE, *May* 1891.

PREFACE TO THE FIRST EDITION

THE writer of the following pages, from a calculation made now several years ago, must have walked more than 70,000 miles in the prosecution of his clerical work only; and much more than as many again for exercise, relaxation, or recreation. Far the larger proportion of these miles were walked alone. But none of those (as they seem now) endless miles, however companionless, were really lonely. The birds and the beasts, especially in the hardly-awake hours of the morning, or the stiller shades of evening; the scenery far and near with its ever-varying aspects; the atmospheric changes and effects, never twice alike; the material objects, natural, or modified or made by man's hand; with all the infinite speculations and inquirings prompted by such matters, never permitted him to feel that he was "alone." And least of all has he been able to feel alone as these pages have been penned and revised, and he has had to recall the familiar figures, the well-remembered features, the unforgotten though long-silent tones of so many old friends long since reverently and lovingly consigned by himself to their silent homes in the churchyard.

Personal as such reminiscences as these last must be, the others are scarcely less so, albeit in another sense. There might be no palpable companionship in all those hours and leagues of daily walking; but there was perpetually so distinct a personality in the matters which passed in succession through the mind, that the effect was rather one of conversation than of solitary reflection. Sixty miles from any collection of books worthy to be named a library, with few neighbours, clerical or otherwise, who could offer intellectual sympathy, the need for something to converse with in those long hours—half of them spent on the lonely moors—was constant. And some of the "conversations" thus held are recorded in the pages which follow.

Some of the views put forward three-and-twenty years ago in the Cleveland Glossary, as well as previously elsewhere, have been contested or made light of, but seem to be generally, even if sometimes tacitly, admitted now. Others are advanced below which may quite possibly be questioned in their turn; but, as before, they are advanced only for what they are worth. Let the thoughtful reader decide.

DANBY PARSONAGE, *March* 1891.

CONTENTS

Contents

DESCRIPTIVE AND GEOLOGICAL

MANNERS AND CUSTOMS

WEDDINGS—BURIALS—HALIKELDS AND THE MELL-SUPPER— THE DOG-WHIPPER

HISTORICAL

MISCELLANEOUS

APPENDICES

ILLUSTRATIONS

MAPS

DANBY AND ITS SURROUNDINGS

London: Macmillan & Co.

INTRODUCTORY

B

INTRODUCTORY

"FORTY years in a Moorland Parish." Forty years is a long time to have spent anywhere, and I have been nearly forty-five years in this parish; and during the whole of that time it is not simply that I have been learning something more yearly about the place or its people, or its characteristics, but that, for long spaces together sometimes, I have been almost (like Cato) *quotidie addiscens.*

Much that I have thus learnt may be of little or no interest to any besides myself. Much of it might not be worth reproducing under any circumstances; and it may truly be added that none of it would have been reproduced in any form had it not been that strong pressure has at divers times been put upon me.

The publication of the Cleveland Glossary, followed as it was by that of the major part of a History of Cleveland, made my name known to many who otherwise would never have heard of my existence, and of these several from time to time paid me visits during their stay at Whitby or Scarborough (the former especially), or sought my acquaintance in some other way. By a considerable proportion of these, after I had been handing out to them from my "stores, things new and old"—facts, theories, investigations, conclusions, or what not—the question has been asked in some form or other, but literally again and again, "Is that in print?" And up to two or three years ago I could and did not only make answer, "No," but add besides, "Nor ever likely to be."

However, about that time since, I was induced to alter such decision, and the following pages are the issue of the change.

If it had been an autobiography I had undertaken the task would have been a comparatively easy one. There would have been the string of time, in its ordered flow of sequence, to connect the varied pages of the records of my life and experiences. But much of what follows has been thought out or worked out at intervals of many months, and even, in some cases, years, and there is no possible bond of tangible connection between one section or subject and another. Things that were matters of speculation twenty years ago, which became matters of conviction, or even certainty, ten years later, are here recorded as matters of knowledge now ; and the records have to stand with as little mutual connection or interdependence as the articles in a magazine. They may be compared with a score or two of old coins which were handed over to me some ten or fifteen years ago, some Roman, some Saxon, and the rest more recent English, a few silver, the rest copper, the only trace of connection between them being that they were contained in the same small metal box.

But forty-five years, it may be said yet once again, is a very long time, and surely the changes in the place, in men and in manners, must have been considerable, and more or less noteworthy, and there can be but little difficulty in giving details of them in sequence, if not in actual successional order.

Yet even here the annalist is not without his difficulties ; for the changes are less striking, and lend themselves less to description, than the permanent stability of not a few of the habits and usages of the Dales dwellers. It is true, the young people have learnt to dance within the last twenty years or so, and dance with great enjoyment and quite proportionate vigour. It is equally true that the young women (rather remarkable always for their prevailing comeliness) have learned, like other young women in other places, to study the fashions of female dress somewhat more than was customary forty years ago. It is true also that, in the language of a leader in the *Standard* of only yesterday's date (24th September 1890), "much has been quietly and unostentatiously done by the Church in the discharge of her mission to elevate the tone of society and to raise the standard of comfort as well as of conduct among the people," and that it is many years indeed since I heard the remark, once so common, made about the mother of an illegitimate child, "Ay, poor gell, she's had a misfortin; but she's nane the warse for't." And it is quite equally true that hereditary leather breeches are gone out of fashion, and that drab breeches and continuations are no longer looked upon as the *de rigueur* clothing for the lower limbs of "t'priest," or, as the personage in question is more usually termed, "our parson." Neither do the old folks call me "bairn" any longer; but it is because almost all those who knew me forty-five years ago are laid in their last beds, and I am too old myself for the application of that something more than friendly vocative case, although there were some still who called me so years after I was turned of sixty.

But still there is a singular amount of old and unchanged custom, habit, feeling, among us. It is not long since that I was asked by some who proposed to gather a large party of the Dales folks together for objects all of a social nature, "But will it do to ask masters and mistresses and their farm-servants to meet one another?" My answer was an unhesitating "Certainly"; and I went on to illustrate rather than explain my dictum by a descriptive reference to the universal custom of the country. The master—the farmer himself, whether he be tenant-farmer or yeoman—and his wife, their children (whether under age or adult), and the servants, male and female (the large proportion of them engaged in the farm-work), all live together. They sit down to the same table and partake of the same dish. At least, with one exception: the mistress prepares the food—in the local vernacular, "mak's t'meat"—sets it on the table, and in one word "waits," getting her own meal afterwards. When the labours of the day are over, all gather in the same room, kitchen, or house, or whatever other term may be used ; and in a truer sense than as the word is customarily used, they are all "one family."

Nay, in ninety-nine cases out of the hundred the masters and the mistresses, the male servants on the farm, and the female workers in the house, the dairy, the fields, all went to the same school and imbibed the same amount of the three R's at the lips of the same teacher. I hardly think that during all my forty-five years of residence and intimate acquaintance with the households throughout the parish I have known anything like twenty-five instances in which boys or girls belonging to the farmers' families have been sent to schools other than, or over and above, the village school. True, it has been a good one, and "under inspection" for forty-four years ; and in the days when Blue Books were issued bearing on the character and condition of the schools of the kingdom, when one inspector held the field now occupied by a score or two of the said officials, it stood among the half-dozen or half-score best country schools in the Riding. But still that does not affect the principle I am speaking of. None of our young folks have been what their parents express by the term "high-learnt" ; and there has been almost no desire among the folk that they should be. Certainly, I have myself, in several instances, given friendly assistance, in the way of Latin or arithmetic and accounts, to lads of promise who wished to "better themselves," and so have helped to swell the ranks of "professional men." But that exception assuredly proves the rule I state. Forty-five years ago it was not unusual for a farmer to be unable to read or write, sometimes both. The then tenant of far the largest farm in the parish was compelled to "make his mark" for this reason, and so was my nearest neighbour, the tenant of one of Lord Downe's largest farms ; and it was a very common thing for the parish clerk, who held the office of parish schoolmaster as well (and so was "qualified to know "), to say to me when I was preparing to register the newly solemnised marriage, that one or more of the parties—sometimes all four, or the newly wedded pair and the witnesses—were "marksmen"; in other words, could not write their names. All that is altered, it is true; but not the fact that the education aimed at and possessed by the great majority is still strictly "elementary."

Again, the farms are all, as they have always been, small. Lord Downe has taken the one that exceeded 200 acres into his own hands, paring off a field or two on the outskirts that could be laid with advantage to the adjoining farms. But with the exception of that farm there is no other in the parish with so much as 145 acres of arable land in it. In all, there may be now six or eight farms of more than 100 acres; all the rest, in number hardly if at all under seventy, and exclusive of small holdings or cow-keepings, scarcely average seventy-five acres each.

As compared, in the matter of such statistics, with the Danby of two centuries and a half ago, there has been un-doubtedly a very considerable change. When the entire estate, comprising Glaisdale as well as Danby, changed hands in 1656, it would appear that there was a total of not less than 165 tenements, all, with very few exceptions, involving some land, however little. The preponderating majority of these tenements were farmholds, and of the sum total more than two-thirds were in the Danby township. But this is tantamount to saying in other words that the farms in Danby now are less in number than they were two hundred and fifty years ago, by something like 25 per cent. And that is certainly so. I am quite aware, from the testimony of the old conveyances themselves, that in divers cases two farms of moderate dimensions have been laid together to make one comparatively large one; and that, in several instances again, a larger farm has absorbed, so to say, one small one, or more, that lay contiguous. And even within my own time I have known at least half a dozen small farms dealt with in this way. Partly in order to raise his farms to an average size, and

partly with a view to do away with the expense of maintaining
buildings which could, without any prejudice to land or tenant,
be dispensed with, the landlord has found himself more than
justified in adopting such a policy. But admitting all this,
still it is absolutely true that Danby is a district of small
holdings ; and if the greater landlords are wise, it will always
remain so. The holdings are suited to the Dales farmers, and
the Dales farmers are suited to their holdings, and alike by
their means, their experience, their hardihood, industry, and
energy, and by the simplicity of their habits and manner of
life. And what I mean by that is that they depend mainly
upon the produce of the farm, in kind, for their subsistence.
Forty years ago I hardly suppose that the average consumption
of butcher's meat per week throughout the parish amounted
to half the carcase of a beast or a couple of sheep. The
butchers killed once a week, and sold the little that was called
for by the requirements of the parish, and carried the remainder, far the largest proportion of the whole, down to
the Whitby market on the Saturday. And even still, although
there are four or five resident butchers in the place, the same
statement with only a little qualification may be made. The
bacon, bread, potatoes, and milk produced by the land supply
by far the chief part of the sustenance of masters and servants
alike.

That there are changes in relation to the management of
the land may be almost assumed ;[1] and these changes
mostly in the line of improvement. But the general
system remains totally unaltered. The land is held from
year to year, and I hardly suppose there is an extant lease

[1] Notably the introduction of "mowers" and "reapers." Improved
or modern ploughs, harrows, rollers, are more frequent than they used to
be. But the drill is comparatively rare still. The introduction of artificial manures, when concomitant, as it oftener than should be is, with a
much lessened application of lime, is hardly a step in the march of improvement ; especially as viewed in connection with the nature and needs of no
small part of the Dales land.

throughout the parish. Neither is there apparently any desire
to have the system altered. On the principal estate the farms
in a certain sense may be said to go by descent. I mean
that if a tenant dies leaving a son, or even a widow, capable
of conducting and managing the farm suitably and efficiently,
the preference, to say the least, always rests with such successor.
There is one farm in the parish which has descended from
father to son in this way for two centuries at least, and when
the last male "heir" died, ten or twelve years ago, the preference fell on the husband of one of his sisters, by whom it is
still held. It is not so very long since a tenant-farmer, holding of one of our freeholders, on asking me to use my interest
with the landlord of the estate in question on his behalf,
added, "Why, every one knows, sir, that being 'on the estate'
is next best to being a freeholder." And the land as held
from year to year is for the most part well and efficiently
managed, and dealt with in a husband-like way.

The system of management, or rotation of crops, remains
practically unaltered in every particular throughout the entire
period of my acquaintance with the district. Beginning with
the fallow, a large breadth of potatoes is grown, and the area
occupied by Swedes and turnips is by no means a small one.
But little wheat is raised, hardly more than enough in most
cases to supply the household with flour. Of the rest of the
land occupied by corn, a moiety (or nearly) is taken up with
the growth of a mixed crop of barley and oats, which grains
are ground as well as grown together, and the meal mixed
with the potatoes just named (when duly boiled) and served
to the pigs, a large head of which is kept, part being used at
home in the form of fat bacon, and the rest disposed of to the
bacon-factor. I have sometimes seen as many as a dozen up
to twenty large carcases of pigs going from one farm to the
purchasers in the farm waggon, and had reason to know that
not so very many fewer had been kept at the farm for consumption by the family, constituted and fed as above noticed.

The corn-crop which succeeds the fallow is itself succeeded by a crop of hay springing from mixed grass-seeds and clover-seed, sown in the spring when the young corn is two or three inches above the ground. After the hay is secured and the aftermath—locally called the "fog"—has grown, it is fed off by the stock of the farm, and not infrequently the land lies in grass a second year. But whether it be so or no, the sward is then ploughed up and a crop of oats is taken; after which the fallow, and so on *de novo*.

As to the stock on the farms: besides the pigs already named, our farmers have considerable flocks of sheep, a few of them Improved Leicester, but the great bulk Blackfaced, or so-called "moor-sheep." Connected with each farm, and I think with hardly an exception (if indeed there be an exception), is what is called a "common right," in virtue of which the tenant is privileged to enjoy the liberty of free sheep-stray for a number of sheep proportionate to his acreage, besides taking what quantity of peat and turf he requires for his own use from the "peat-moor," or the available surface. And besides this, he may take what ling he wants for "kindling," subject to the same rule.

After the sheep come the cattle and the horses. Most farmers with a hundred acres of land keep nine or ten cows for dairy purposes, some of them making cheese of excellent quality, and the rest producing butter, which is bought up by the "badgers" who go round the parish week by week, collecting the eggs and spare poultry as well, and who find ready sale for them at Middlesbrough, Stockton, and other centres of population.

Much of the stock kept is of a very good type, and the proportion kept, inclusive of horses, is a very large one. On a farm which maintains eight or nine dairy cows there will be, inclusive of calves, yearlings, and two-year-olds, a total of hardly less than thirty head of "cattle"; and, inclusive of foals, yearlings, and two-year-olds, at least nine or ten horses.

And in speaking on this head it must be broadly stated that there has been a great and marked change in the district generally. Forty-four years ago, at the rent-dinner given to Lord Downe's tenants, reference was made to the desirability of something of the nature of a Show of live stock in the district. I took the opportunity of offering, if the farmers were really wishful to organise such an association, to undertake the secretary's part; and in no long time an Agricultural Association was formed, of which I became secretary and treasurer, giving whatever assistance in other directions I could, or as far as my experience and ability permitted; and I remained secretary for thirty-one years. The Society still exists, and is as flourishing as ever; and the proofs and tokens of its efficiency and success are everywhere apparent.

I remember at the first, or perhaps the second, Show we held being myself in attendance on the judges, recording their decisions and bestowing the premium tickets as they were awarded, on having a class of bulls brought into the ring for adjudication, hearing one of the judges, as he cast his eye over the lot as they arrived, and noticed a strange-looking, brindled, breedingless animal, say to the other, " I say, S——, what breed is this?" The answer was, " Well, I don't know. I should say a cross between a bear and a jackass!" But our Show soon altered all that; especially as Colonel Duncombe, the owner of most of the land in the adjoining parish of Westerdale, had already interested himself in the improvement of the stock kept in the district, and with an eye to it had introduced some good blood from the Duncombe Park herd of the day. For many years past our farmers have been able to show really fine stock, and a good head of it; and only half a dozen years ago one of the tenants on the Estate exhibited a shorthorn bull which not only carried off more than thirty premiums in local and other more important or provincial exhibitions, but " took a second" at the All-England Show held at York.

But whatever the change in the way of a better class of cattle may have been, I think the change in the same direction in the matter of horses has certainly not been less marked. Not only has the number of horses bred in the district been on the increase, and steadily so, but we have now, in place of the two classes of Cart-horses and Cleveland bays, the same two classes with the additional classes of Hunters, Roadsters, and Coaching-horses. At our recent Show in August last, the horses shown in the several classes were not only about five times as numerous as in the shows held during the earlier years of the existence of the Association, but such in quality as to elicit the highest commendation from very many good judges of a horse who had come from a distance to attend our Dales Show.

Recognising, then, and as fully as possible, the change that is implied in the statement that better stock, and as much of it, is kept now than was actually kept forty-five years ago, and the still more important change involved in the alleged fact that there is far greater regard for moral decency, that there is distinctly more respect among the younger folk both for themselves and for one another, than there used to be, still it may, perhaps it must, seem strange that so much should remain still unaltered. It may be that, growing old with my elder parishioners, and seeing my younger ones grow up around me and becoming middle-aged men and women, with their families (and no longer only children) about them, I have been in a measure insensible to the changes passing over men and things; and even yet, though my attention is awakened, continue in the same condition. But I do not think it is so. We have no more class-differences among us than we had half a century ago. The master lives and works with his men, and the mistress with her maidens. We have no rich men in our midst, nor any who live the life of idleness, save only those whose work is done, or the few lazy ones who have not sufficient self-respect to be ashamed of sponging upon others. I think, indeed, that if a rule could be laid down in such matters, it would rather be that the farmer, or other "master-man," works harder, and at things wanting more nicety or care or skill, than any one else merely in his employ; and his sons are hardly exceptions to the rule as long as they remain at home with their father. I remember, nearer forty years ago than thirty, when just beginning a long pastoral walk into some one of the many far parts of my parish, seeing three lads of from thirteen up to sixteen or seventeen working away at a bit of toilsome clearing which had been made necessary for "mensefulness," and indeed for the plough, by the recent erection of a new dry-stone-wall. Their father I knew was ill, unable to leave the house, and, hard-handed son of toil as he had always been, always laborious and "endeavouring," would never leave his house again save once. When I came back, five or six hours later, they were still there, still at work, and with goodly piles of material moved to be a record that they, boys as they were, and with no one to set them their task and see that they did it, had "worked with a will" while I had been gone. Those same three are all still living and are all that their father was before them, steadily and enduringly industrious, and bringing up their families to tread in the same steps they have trodden in before them. The eldest too, poor fellow, has been sorely stricken by disabling attacks twice, and he who was the strongest man in the parish, or nearly so, is now but a crippled wreck; and still he is never idle, never negligent, the condition of his farm being such as to show that he must farm well and work hard who would fain be George's "master" in farming and all that belongs to it. We may have—I suppose with our small farms and somewhat capricious seasons we can have—no scientific farmers among us; but we have what the scientific farmer cannot do without, the steady, persistent industry and energy which lies at the root of all real success in the multitudinous ways in

which men's heads and hands are occupied. And so our
farmers, our master-men, are as much workers now, and with
and among their men, as they have ever been.

And what is true of the men is not less true of the females.
I remember, when I first took up my abode in the place, discovering after a week or two that there was a piano in the
parish, old-fashioned and jangly, but still a pianoforte; and I
remember the young lady to whom (together with the three
farms left her by her yeoman father) it belonged, in obedience
to her mother's injunction, "Now, sit thee down, Hannah, and
mak' the minister some music," sitting down accordingly and
playing "The Battle of Prague." And beyond that I remember how this solitary Danby piano became supplemented in
less than a score of years by some fifty or sixty other pianos
and harmoniums, and how one of our old inhabitants, on my
noticing this great increase in musical instruments, gravely
shook his head, and misdoubted how it would work; whether
or no the farm-daughters and others who were learning to play,
or had already learnt, would not become too fine-fingered,
and too much given to other new-fangled ways, to attend as
they ought to the dairy, with its cheese-press and butter-
runner; and the household work, with its dainty cleanliness;
and the "mak'ing the meat" and its thrifty hospitality. But
our butter is as delicate and sweet as it used to be, and
our cheeses still take the best premiums at the shows of
agricultural produce; and I am sure that no one who has
partaken of the hospitality of one of our extant farms, and
much more has sat down to a real "Yorkshire tea" as provided (for perhaps hundreds of guests) by our Dales house-
wives, can do so without being forced, and even admiringly,
to admit that the cunning has not left the hands of those who
provided such pastry, such cakes, and such and so varied other
delicacies.

But while, as it seems to me, our social relations have, in
all essential matters, submitted to but very little variation

during the last half-century, I cannot but think that very
much the same remains to be said as to any very apparent
change in matters pertaining to politics or religion. Shortly
after my acceptance of the incumbency the patron wrote to
me, " You will find the Wesleyans worthy of much consideration. Indeed I think that if it had not been for them and
their influence, religion would practically have died altogether
out in these Dales." And I am very much inclined to think
there was more truth in the remark than a stickler for the
influence of the Church would find it pleasant to have to
admit. The days were but lately passed away when one
" minister " (or " church priest," as he was quite as often called)
found himself charged with the burden of three, in one or two
cases I knew of, even four parishes ; and where parishes are
such as this moorland district necessitates in point of area,
that is equivalent to saying that even one service in the week
and a proportionate amount of visiting was a thing to be
desired rather than statedly enjoyed. My immediate predecessor had Danby (of 13,600 acres) and Westerdale (of about
9000) on his hands, and was neither strong nor good at reading, let alone preaching. One of his predecessors had Danby,
Rosedale, and Farndale. Another parson in the same district,
and not a century ago, had Glaisdale, Egton, and Goathland.
And I have reason to think that even thus the pittance earned
by such men was barely up to the proverbial wealthiness of
" forty pounds a year." Thus, the Wesleyans with their
admirable organisation were an important factor in the conditions of religious life in the Dale, and had more than merely
a claim to consideration. And they are still a strong and
influential body. And I think they will continue to be so
yet awhile, although they are but barely holding their own
at present. The religious fervour and earnestness of the old
days seems to have lost warmth and energy, and to have been
in part replaced by more secular feelings and objects. And
the change will be fatal in the end. Nor do I think that the

Primitive Methodists, who constitute another strong element in the religious life of the parish, quite reach the point of making up what is missing. There is one defect in the organisation of both bodies, the weakness of which is already becoming more than apparent, and which will be but the more evident as time rolls on and the advancing tide of information, knowledge, and especially inquiry, more than keeps pace with the times. They can multiply chapels, but the local-preacher system will not supply the teachers that are, and will increasingly be, wanted. "Men of light and leading" do not grow up like mushrooms in remote places like these, and will be slow of growth even where the culture can be and is attended to.

For the days are upon us when such things are, and will be. Forty-five years ago there were, I believe, about three newspapers brought into the Dale. Fifty years ago, certainly not more. I myself remember the *Yorkshire Gazette* passing on from one farmer to another, and its circulation hardly ceasing until it was three or four weeks old. But all that is strangely altered now. Newspapers abound, and comprising those statedly taken and others of more casual introduction, all classes of opinion, religious, non-religious, agnostic in a greater or lesser degree, sectarian and unsectarian, and of many different shades of political opinion, are to be met with. Other literature also, over and above the Parish Magazine class, or the authorised publications of the Wesleyan body, is freely introduced, and although the qualified readers may be by some assumed to be few, still the fact remains that there *are* some, and they not the least thoughtful or the worst informed in the parish. Many years ago I was not a little astonished by a call from one of my parishioners, a yeoman (or freeholder cultivating his own farm, one of our principal ones in point of size), who came with a book in his hand, which he said he had lately bought, and he thought it was hardly a book he cared much for ; maybe I might think it worth looking at, and I could keep it if I liked. The book was Colenso's volume on the Pentateuch. There are difficulties in store for the local-preacher system in such facts as these. For my own part, I have been in the habit, now for several years past, of touching from time to time on matters of doubt or debate, such as are mooted perpetually by agnostic or free-thinker writers or speakers, in my pulpit work, and I have not found any apparent want of attention, much less evidences of indifference, among my hearers. Perhaps, speaking generally, the very reverse.

As to changes of a political complexion, I should speak with very considerable diffidence, even if not hesitation. As a rule, I have abstained from any active participation in political matters, and the rule has never been broken through but on one occasion, and that was the candidature of a man whom I had known and loved from his childhood, one of the noblest of a noble family, namely, the late Guy Dawnay. Apart from this, my overt interest in politics has never been displayed, and I have had but few opportunities of observing any very pronounced manifestations of political feeling. But judging by what I have seen, and from the casual facilities afforded me in my continued intercourse with all the sections of my own parishioners and the people of the neighbouring Dales district, I should say there was but little change in the political views or feeling or bias generally. It is very seldom that direct reference is made in my presence to the subject in any company, or on any occasion, except when local or general elections are pending, and there is of necessity more or less excitement stirred in the country-side. More than forty years ago, on occasion of the first general election which took place after my arrival here, the then agent of the late Lord Downe was desired to notify to the tenants at large that their landlord wished every man among them to vote according to his own views, and without the slightest reference to any supposed feeling or views of his; and I was requested privately to confirm the same on any or every occasion of personal application to myself on the subject. But I had no doubt whatever, either then or since, that the majority, perhaps the large majority, of voters, whether freeholders or tenants on the Estate, voted, and continue to vote, as Conservatives.

I have used the word "feeling," because I think it more descriptively suitable than any other term would have been. Hitherto there has been but little agitation, and the works and ways of the schoolmaster have not diffused any great amount of the materials out of which political principles are supposed to spring, or of the methods by which such conclusions as go to the formation of principles are evolved. I have not always been able to suppress a smile at the simplicity with which I have heard almost startlingly Radical sentiments propounded by a staunch Conservative, or admissions made by a pronounced Liberal which would have sounded well from the lips of a through-and-through Tory of the old school.

But however inconsiderable, in comparison with the great mass of unchanged usage and habit among the people at large, such changes as I have referred to above may actually be, still there is one particular as to which a very great and significant change has taken place, which if not effected literally within the last half-century, yet surely has experienced its most marked development within that specified term. What I mean is a matter that may be regarded as a revolution rather than simply an alteration, and one affecting private morality rather than decency only, and connecting itself as well with the simplest experiences of health as of comfort. I refer to the altered conditions characterising the dwellings of the people. No doubt the change has been advancing for several generations; but it is only within a very measurable space that it can be assumed to have attained its completion—even if it can be positively affirmed even yet that there is nothing left to admit of improvement.

Some twenty years ago or thereabouts, on occasion of some official inquiry as to the ways in which the working classes were housed, I received an invitation from the then Vicar of Egton (Ishmael Fish) to go down thither to meet the Commissioner, and to assist in the inquiries he wished to make. Besides myself and Mr. Fish, at least one other neighbouring incumbent was present, and two or three of the most intelligent of the Egton farmers and office-bearers. We first went to a small farmhouse, which has since been entirely rebuilt by the present owners of the estate, wherein the commonest rules of decency were not, and could not be, attended to as regarded the sleeping arrangements. We then went to two cottage dwellings in the main street of the village or (one of them) hardly out of it. As entering from the street or roadside, we had to bow our heads, even although some of the yard-thick thatch had been cut away about and above the upper part of the door, in order to obtain an entrance. We entered on a totally dark and unflagged passage. On our left was an enclosure partitioned off from the passage by a boarded screen between four and five feet high, and which no long time before had served the purpose originally intended, namely, that of a calves' pen. Farther still on the same side was another dark enclosure similarly constructed, which even yet served the purpose of a henhouse. On the other side of the passage opposite this was a door, which on being opened gave admission to the living room, the only one in the dwelling. The floor was of clay and in holes, and around on two sides were the cubicles, or sleeping-boxes—even less desirable than the box-beds of Berwickshire as I knew them fifty years ago—of the entire family. There was no loft above, much less any attempt at a "chamber": only odds and ends of old garments, bundles of fodder, and things of that sort. And in this den the occupants of the house were living! And the other place we went into was no better. The Commissioner seemed "satisfied";

at least he did not desire to carry on his investigations any farther.

This was at Egton. Now let me tell some of my experiences nearer home. I made a fierce onslaught, when I first came to the place, on the shameful immorality of the usages and manners I found prevalent here. The resident Wesleyan minister wished me God-speed, and hoped I would persevere, adding that his own hands and tongue were tied by reason of certain relations affecting his position. One of my most respectable inhabitants, himself a leading Wesleyan, also came to me, equally wishing me God-speed, but adding, "But you must not stop here, Mr. Atkinson; you must go a bit farther yet," and when I pressed him to speak out, and explicitly, he said, "You must go in at the landlords and put it upon them to give us better-arranged houses to live in. I want to keep my servants decent. But how can I when, doing all I can, I have to let my men farm-servants go through the women-servants' room, or else, just the other way, the girls through the men's apartment?"

Nay, one day, when as little expecting anything of the kind as to be called upon to say "Nolo episcopari," on occasion of a visit to Kilton Castle, I entered the farmhouse on the Liverton side, to greet my old friends who lived there and permitted the stabling of my horse, and the woman of the house said to me (in direct reference to my "onslaught" aforesaid), "Would you mind coming upstairs with me, and seeing for yourself how our sleeping-place is arranged?" Of course I went, and what I found was one long low room, partitioned off into four compartments nearly equal in size. But the partitions were in their construction and character merely such as those between the stalls in a stable, except that no gentleman who cared for his horses would have tolerated them in his hunting or coaching stable. These four partitioned spaces were no more closed in the rear than the stalls in an ordinary stable, and the partitions were not seven feet, hardly six and a half in height, while the general gangway for all the occupants was along the open back. The poor woman said to me, as she showed me the first partition, allotted to her husband and herself and their two youngest children, the next to their children growing rapidly up to puberty, the third to the farm-girls, and the fourth to the man and farm-lad, "How can I keep even my children clean when I can only lodge them so?"

But the hopeful thing in these cases, and in one or two others like them, was that the people themselves were awake to the shame and the indecency and the certainty of moral degradation involved in such usages and arrangements as these. And yet the state of feeling and sentiment so illustrated was by no means universal thirty or forty years ago. I remember —and the date was subsequent to 1857, though not much— the then great lady of the place coming to me one day in great displeasure. Much had been done to a certain house in Danby Head with a view to the observance of the ordinary rules of decency and classification in the sleeping department; and on looking to the way in which the directions given had been complied with, she had become aware that the very object of the alterations made had been nullified, and ignored by the arrangements made and carried out by the tenants. The apartment which had been practically added to the accommodation of the house for the very purpose of reliev- ing the plethora of sleepers in the other available chamber (or chambers), had been converted to the use of a guest- chamber, and the abuses themselves—many of both sexes and divers ages having to sleep together in the same limited area—deliberately continued. True, there was a bed in the new room; but it was a bed not in use, and not intended to be used save on the very few and far-apart occasions when they had an honoured guest to be put up for a night or two. To all intents and purposes the new room had been made a reception room, and the family had to huddle together as

before. And this was no uncommon case. I knew of a
dozen or more instances in which a room with a bed in it, and
needed as well as intended for a bedroom, was in use only
when a "party" was being entertained. It was "the best
room," and never profaned by homelier use, notwithstanding
the fact that such use would have done very much indeed
towards a decent separation of the sexes, and of the married
from the single, in the rooms used as sleeping apartments.

That all this regardless commingling of the young lasses
and lads of the family, whether sons and daughters or hired
farm-servants, and of the married heads with children (old
enough to need to be kept apart), was simply and solely a
survival from older and strangely less refined days is a matter
that hardly needs assertion. I hinted above that the entire
completeness of what I spoke of as a "revolution" might
perhaps be a matter open to some question. What I meant
was this. There are two of the old-fashioned, as well as old,
cottages, once the rule in the district, still remaining in one
part of the parish. In one of these, when I first came, the
Dog-whipper (named elsewhere), his brother (and successor),
and their sister lived together. The hut contained one room
(with a floor sunk beneath the level of the ground), of perhaps four yards square, and no pretence at a separate room
for the woman, there being no loft even. In the other, much
the same in point of area and arrangement, lived a married
couple with their family; and when the Dog-whipper family
died out, their cottage was occupied by another married
couple and their offspring. The united population of these
two one-roomed, loftless dens at one time reached the trifling
total of twenty-three souls! They are still occupied, the one
by a widow woman and two or three of her children, and the
other by the occupant of the old days, now a widower, and
one or more of his progeny.

But these cottages are but modified types of what the old
dwellings of the district used to be. Some four or five years

ago I was walking between my residence and the station, when my attention was arrested by the then proceeding demolition of a very old, and latterly unused, tenement close by the road-side. The roof was gone, one gable-end was down, the side next the road was a mass of fallen material and *débris*, and what was left of the farther wall seemed to require but a moderate thrust to fall over bodily too. But the striking thing was what is here called "a pair of forks"; in other words, one of the principal pairs of rafters of the old roof; and I noticed that the old walls had been so built as to admit or receive and enclose the rafters, and not the rafters so pro-portioned and shaped as to be supported more or less directly by the walls. I drew the attention of the elderly tenant who was "siding up" some of the ruinous mass of material, to the circumstance, adding the information (as I intended it to have been) that in the old days the houses had customarily been built with the forks resting on the ground, and not on the side walls. "Ay," said he with a good-humoured but somewhat meaning smile, "I wur born in just sikan a yan." And again, but a week or so since, I was told of just such other houses as now or lately extant more in the Kirby Moorside direction.

But the bare mention of these houses, without some ade-quate measurements and plans as well as mere letterpress description, hardly serves the purpose I had in view when reference was just now made to them; and it so happens that the wrecks of several of them, or rather their ramshackle, shattered, imperfect skeletons, still remain for delineation, measurement, and close examination, down to the present moment. In fact I have within the last three weeks had four photographs of one of them taken, and three of another, besides noting all the salient features of the same. In one of these the two original pairs of forks remain *in situ*, and in the other one pair is still extant. Their ends rest still on what was once the ground-floor, meaning the actual or natural surface of the ground. In the one case large flat stones, as nearly flush with the level of the soil as may be, were placed for the forks to rest on; in the other the accumulation of fallen stones and rubble, with infinite and majestic nettles growing thickly among them, makes it difficult to ascertain whether the base of the rafter rests on stone, wood, or earth. But it is obtrusively plain in either case that the side-walls were an afterthought, and entirely foreign to the idea and the construction of the original dwelling. When those rafters, of scantling sufficient to furnish forth half a dozen pairs of such as are used in the construction of modern houses of much greater pretension than these under mention, were first set up, the roof (a fairly high-pitched one), with the gable-end walls, was all there was to constitute the exterior shell of the house, and the door was in one of the ends of course. Whether originally there was a chimney in the primitive structure, cannot be asserted with distinctness. For myself I incline to think there was not; that the fire was on the hearth, and the smoke escaped from a hole in the roof. Certainly there are no very apparent indications in the gable-ends of the existence of a chimney of however primitive a type, and it is scarcely possible that some trace of smoke or fire should not be observable if there had ever been one.[1]

With respect to these pairs of forks it may be remarked that they have evidently been carefully selected for the pur-

---

[1] I was examining the interior of a very old house still standing at Ainthorpe but a few days before writing this, and abutting on the inner side of one of the ends were the remains of the fireplace and of the chimney which had formerly suffered the escape of the smoke. Both the cheeks or jambs of the fireplace projected from the flat surface of the wall between two and three feet into the room, and the chimney had been constructed on a similar principle; there had been no tunnelled passage in the substance of the wall. A chimney of the same character may still be remarked in one of the lofty chambers in Danby Castle, one of the massive tie-beams having been cut away for some distance on either side (to allow for the safe passage of the chimney), and supplemented by the insertion of another between the next pair of rafters—a measure made all the more remarkable by the fact that the roof is a fine specimen of hammer-beam construction. See Appendix H.

RUINS OF RAFTER-BUILT HOUSE IN DANBY DALE.   [*To face p. 24.*

pose. They fail of being quite rectilineal throughout their length. At about four feet from the surface on which they stand is a curve, such as may be seen in the timber designed to be the stem of a boat, and such also as to allow of a much steeper slope upwards from the ground than could have been possible if the whole had been in one and the same straight line. From this point of curvature, however, the rafters are straight all the way to the ridge piece, and with the old tie-beam would form an almost exact equilateral triangle.

The deflection thus noticed would allow for more and somewhat more available space within, than if the rafters had reached the ground in a straight line unbroken from the ridge. But allowing for this, still the space within must have been inconceivably cramped; for the interval between the two pairs of forks longitudinally was scarcely more than eighteen feet, and the total width within the perpendiculars from the point of curvature of the rafters was barely as much. In other words, the dimensions of the one room in which the family had to live, work, cook, sleep—fulfil all the functions of human existence—were just about eighteen feet square; and, as a woman who had lived in one of these very houses down to less than twenty years ago (enlarged as it had been by later additions), remarked to me in connection with the dimensions of the original dwelling, "Ay, there was not much room for fancy there"—"fancy" in her mouth meaning the simplest dictates of decency.

I have referred to later additions made to the original dwellings of such contracted dimensions. The evidence of this is apparent enough in the still extant side-walls. In one of the two houses under notice three successive additions, each to the end of its predecessor, are noticeable; in the other, two.

I connect these old, old habitations with a very early and a very interesting period in the economical history of the parish. From the dates still remaining on most of the wrecks

that are left, it is assured that the side-walls are, in each
several case, not earlier than 1656.   That date still stands on
one of these old-fashioned houses, and on such a part and in
such wise as to show incontestably that the part of the house
on which it is cut was a secondary, and by no means a primary,
alteration in the original fabric.   It marked a much later
innovation on old fashions and habits.   First there had
grown up the side-walls enclosing within their embrace the
"forks" of the first house; then this side-wall had had a projecting insertion introduced, such as to give a little more width
inside and to admit of the intrusion of a window, the fashion of
which attests the age as well as does the inscribed date, 1656.
Here are thus two distinct periods of building-work both
subsequent to the epoch of the rafter-built dwelling the
remains of which are still extant.

But this throws us back into the sixteenth century, and,
beyond doubt, into an early period of the same; and, if so,
what about the date of the original rafter-built house? And
quite possibly this inquiry may prove to be a suggestive one.
But as there is at least an equal possibility that it might be a
thought tedious if introduced here, the reader who is interested
in such matters is referred to Appendix A.

Passing on to our more general survey of dwelling-
houses as they were, I would remark that the replacement
of these ancient, incommodious, comfortless, hovel - like
dwellings by new and substantial and decently arranged
houses, or at least the substitution of such for them,[1] did not
begin, certainly was not in full progress, much, if at all,

[1] In some cases at least the old house was not destroyed or entirely
removed; but such part of it as was available and in sufficiently good
repair was incorporated in some or other of the new farming offices.   Thus,
in listening to the Stormy Hall legend [see Note, p. 293, and end of
Historical Section, *infra*], the auditor is assured that part of the old house
honoured by the king's presence may yet be seen in the stable: and surely
there are parts of the old mullioned windows, which characterise all these
old ruins, perfectly evident in the buildings referred to.

before the last quarter of last century.   There are dates
on some of the existing (or what were till lately) freehold
farmhouses which warrant such an assumption.   And I should
be inclined to put the more general progress of rebuilding or
replacing later still; and, if that be so, the change for the
better in the habits and manners and morals of the people,
which is seen to be involved in such sweeping alterations
in the mode of living as the rule is now, can scarcely be
looked upon as a full century old yet, even in its active
inception.

   That there may be rowdyism among us still, it would be
absurd to dispute; but, at least, it is limited rowdyism, and
of a mitigated character.   Time was, unquestionably, when
such an assertion could not truthfully have been made.
But that time had passed before I had ever heard of
Danby.   But there were men I had a personal acquaintance
with soon after I came into residence, who were the last
of an expiring class; men whose pastime it had been, if not
whose object and desire, to provoke a row or a scuffle, and
to fight it out then and there.   One of these persons, a stout-
built muscular man, even in his old age—he must have been
turned of seventy—was described to me as literally the "hero
of a hundred fights."   Poor old William was quiet enough
when and after I began to know him; but those who had
known him in the elder days said he had, in the days of his
strength and vigour, been the most turbulent of a turbulent
group.   Rows, scuffles, scrimmages had been the rule then,
and William, with another still then living, was never out of
them.   Hardly-contested boxing-bouts, with a cruel amount
of "punishment," were of continual occurrence, and truly
William's scarcely lovely countenance looked as if it had
been sorely battered.   From all I could hear, the stranger
whose devious footsteps brought him to Danby in those old
days, was likely to experience something of the "Heave 'arf
a brick at 'im" treatment recorded by George Stephenson as

the customary welcome extended by north-country natives to unlucky explorers of the country wilds.

As to drinking habits and usages, I must not say they are extinct. But the evil is not so great as it once was. I have seen but too much of it and its unhappy influences and results, and know too many victims (many of them innocent victims) of intemperate habits and indulgences. Five-and-forty years ago all the business of the parish, inclusive of vestry and other public meetings, was transacted at the public-house, and it was far more customary than not to find pipes and glasses the accompaniments of the business ; and to a great extent the same rule, barring only the pipes and the drink, prevails even yet. The church, a mile, and indeed much more than a mile, away from the bulk of the people, affords no facilities for even the vestry meetings themselves, and there is no public building that is available for such purposes. Thus the parishioners were driven to such resorts as were open to them. As having to attend divers of these meetings, inclusive, of course, of those connected with the operations of the Agricultural Association, I had to go where the meeting was. But I took neither tobacco nor a "glass," merely paying my sixpence for the use of the room—an implied charge which was supposed to be covered by the "custom" in the case of the rest of those present. Very shortly the natural courtesy of the farmers led them on to dispense with the pipe and glass until all business was out of the way; and even then, if I remained for a space, I often had to suggest the lighting of the pipes, which had been laid aside on my account. In the old days, on all such occasions, and on the days of the rent audits, and also after the markets and fairs, and those very undesirable things, the hirings, much liquor was consumed, and many went home the worse for it. Some became uproarious, and others were only able to sit their steady old galloways in a mysterious manner. I could tell much as touching this matter. I knew men who rarely went home sober from either

market, fair, or meeting, or who never missed their daily
potations, and carried on so for so many years—two of them
lived to be over eighty—that many notes of admiration were
employed in speaking of their marvellous endurance. But
many, sadly too many, came to grief in either body or substance, or in both, in consequence of their indulgences of this
kind; and more than one I have known whom drink excited
to such a degree that the lives of their wives and children
were hardly safe on their return home drunk.

But I think that all of this is mainly, though not quite
entirely, a thing of the past. Of course there is excess, and
some of it habitual, still; but I think that sobriety is, on the
whole, steadily advancing, and that the movement is not one of
yesterday only.[1] Of course we have our Temperance Societies,

---

[1] I do not think the extravagance, the absolute "intemperance" of
ideas, words, language, which too many advocates of even temperance,
and much more total abstinence, indulge in with respect to those who do
not go entirely with them, can be, or is, anything but repellent, certainly
deterrent, to many who might be influenced by gentler methods and
milder figures of speech. I remember being asked by a strong advocate of
temperance principles (who afterwards, by the way, became the victim of
his own excesses) for the loan of my schoolroom, and that I would add
to that favour the further one of presiding, and acting as judge of the
merits of certain essays on Temperance which were to be composed and
read (or recited) by lads or quite young men resident in the parish, and
for the best of which he had offered certain premiums. One of them,
rather a clever fellow, but odd in some of his ways during his continuance
at the school, had "committed" his composition, and hopelessly broke
down. What he had said up to the time of his failure was sensible and
good. Most of the others delivered themselves of a series of platitudes
and stock phrases, and their essays were distinctly below mediocrity.
One or two, however, distinguished themselves by a voluble outpouring of
blatant intemperance in connection with all who were not total abstainers.
And as I sat there and heard myself and at least three-fourths of the
steady, respectable, sober members of the meeting denounced under the
designation of "little-drop-drinkers" in the most scathing terms, sent
without respite, and before our proper time, to a very warm place, and
described as the guides, if not the drivers, of all such as were not
teetotalers to the same hot residence, I admit I did not feel the least like
"taking a pledge" which committed me to the countenancing any such

our total abstainers, our Bands of Hope, and what not, and I
do not doubt for a moment that their operation and influence
are beneficial. But at the same time I cannot help thinking
that there are other influences at work which, quiet and
gradual as they may be in their nature and operation (and of
which it may well be that much of the influence of the
various temperance societies, if not the societies themselves,
are but consequences), are, and have been for years, becoming
more real day by day. I am old enough to remember when
the "social gatherings," the dinner-parties of the day, met at
2 P.M., and sat with the wine before them, after the removal
of the cloth, until six or seven o'clock in the evening, and
sometimes later still, the guests being the country gentlemen, the parsons, and other "professions"; some among
whom were pointed out to my young mind for admiration
as "three-bottle men"; when "going to the ladies" meant
more or less inability to drink any more, possibly even
to remain on their chairs; and when nobody, not even
the parson, was thought much the worse of because of such

ideas, or the language in which they were conveyed, on any future
occasion. In fact, I was forcibly reminded of one of my experiences at
Scarborough before I had ever heard there was a place called Danby. I
had taken the Prayers at Christ Church, a very noted ultra-Protestant
preacher having been announced as the occupant of the pulpit that evening. The sermon, professedly in aid of the interests and objects of a well-
known society, was throughout one virulent, unreasoning, unreasoned
attack on the Roman Catholic Church and Roman Catholics generally.
I "sat under" him sensible of mental and moral creepiness, and was glad
indeed when the senseless, most unlovely exhibition was over. Two or
three days after I met the Roman Catholic priest then stationed there (no
unfriend of mine, by the way), and he congratulated me on the vigorous
sermon we had had the previous Sunday evening. "I like such sermons
as that," he said ; "they do us no harm, but the contrary. For they set
reasonable people thinking, and there is generally a little reaction when
it is found we have been unjustly bullied and baited." And I think it is
so too with the intemperate effusions of ultra-temperance orators and
writers. Even non-callous "little-drop-drinkers" don't seem to see themselves or their doings or shortcomings in quite such lurid lights or in
such highly coloured pictures ; and it "reacts."

debauches (as they would be called now) as these. Less than three-quarters of a century ago that was the state of public and private feeling both within and touching the class of society customarily spoken of as "the clergy and gentry." I need not waste space in describing what it is now. All that is altered indeed. In other words, public opinion has spoken out on such matters, and her utterance is respected.

And, as it seems to me, precisely the same may be said of the class to which the people I am most interested in belong. It is growingly felt and admitted among them that intemperance carries a stigma with it; that it is not a fine thing to be a drunkard, even occasionally; that a man can be a good fellow without being a sot; and that it is a thing to be regretted and apologised for if such a lapse occurs. I have had men come to me bitterly resenting the supposed or gossip-born statement that they had come home from market or rent-dinner "changed," in other words, not quite sober; and others hoping, if I had heard such things about them, that I did not believe them. But what had been, or was supposed to have been, imputed to them, would not have been felt as tending to their discredit, either with themselves or others, fifty years ago, and I know that such "opinion" is of steady growth still.

But there is one change, and a great one, which I cannot help remarking upon, and in a tone of real regret, which is not lessened because I myself have been "art and part" in it to so great an extent. I mean the decay of the old pure Yorkshire speech. Time was when I heard it all round me, and from the mouths of all my old parishioners. Time has been when I have seen a southerner who had chanced to be by during a colloquy between myself and one of the "old school"—literally *lucus a non lucendo*—after showing more and more perplexity as the dialogue proceeded, at last break out into a laughing inquiry, "What language it was we were speaking?" Time was when, after a talk with old George Coverdale, or his wife Esther, or with old John Plews, or indeed half a score others I could name,

I could go home and lengthen my list of old outlandish terms and phrases, and enlarge my note-book with memoranda for recollection or inquiry. But all that is different now. The schoolmaster and the Inspector of Schools have been the ruin of the so-called "dialect." During my five-and-forty years of acquaintance with the Inspector I have of course seen and known almost every conceivable species or variety, from the gentleman who left his boots in his bed and his night-shirt underneath it, to the other who crossed every *t* and dotted every *i* religiously ; or from him whose eye twinkled with enjoyment of a racy bit of Yorkshire in a child's answer to his question, to the other who set his face, as well as his ear, against a northern tone or a non-"Elementary Education" vowel or consonant sound. I thought the latter mistaken. The vernacular, with all its suggestiveness over and above its racy peculiarities, was doomed, and he might have let it die with simple quietude. But he wanted to "worry" it. One day a poor shy, slim slip of a girl was set to read in due course, and she read the "Standard English" of the Standard Readers fluently enough, but with the unmistakable intonation and pronunciation of a child who did not speak as the Dales children speak, and it was this that drew his attention really. He made her read the sentence over again, and she read as before ; for she knew no other way. A second time and a third she had to repeat the reading, and then he lost patience, and spoke a little sharply to her, adding that she had never heard her mother speaking so. It was the worst shot he had ever made in his life ; for, if I had been blindfolded, I could have told whose child Annie P—— was, the tones and accents she had employed being just those her mother had used all the days of her life. But as illustrative of the dictum that the dialect is doomed, I may mention two circumstances. The first is that, as the author of the Cleveland Glossary, I was asked a few years ago to adjudicate on the merits of certain descriptive essays written by the children of the upper classes of an East Riding parish school. The conditions were that, over and above any merit they might have in the way of good spelling, tolerable composition, and fair descriptiveness, they were to be couched in the English of the folk-speech ; they were to be as " good Yorkshire " as the competitors could write. Not quite a dozen essays were sent to me, and although the writers in one or two cases had gone a little out of their way to get a " Yorkshire word " in, it was like an ill-assorted square in a patchwork quilt. The essays, one and all, were not " Yorkshire " in any sense. The other circumstance is more suggestive still ; for the influences tending to conservatism in such matters as words, phrases, idioms, are surely more operative in a comparatively retired place like Danby, than in the Bridlington and Driffield district. During the past year, in the hope of encouraging observation, thought, efforts to describe, and so forth, I offered a series of premiums to the boys and girls of the three higher standards in the Danby School for the three best papers on " All about Danby," following that subject up, and on the same principle and conditions, with " All about Birds," and " All about the Cow." As I write these lines I have from thirty-five to forty of these essays before me, some very good for such children, some fair, many mediocre, and a few disappointing. But throughout there is no " Yorkshire," let alone " good Yorkshire," in them. One or two of them occupy three sides of a foolscap sheet, with never a true " dialect-word " or idiom in them. Thirty years ago I disinterred a longish series of words which had become obsolete, and were buried in practical forgetfulness. But now, at the end of these thirty years, I puzzle the men and women of the day, baptized by myself the most of them, by the use of words their grandparents regularly employed in their everyday intercourse with their fellows. " Ill-gotten gear has nae drith with it," is not now understood by the very sons and daughters of the good old friend who one day produced the saying for my behoof and edification out on the wild moor.

D

Nor is this decay of the ancient tongue the only change in the same direction which we have to bewail. Previously to the decadence of the dialect there were not only a great number of quaint, forcible, pungent sayings current,—not all of them perhaps remarkable for the absence of what was not, when they were framed, counted free or indecent, but is so reputed nowadays,—which for point and brevity were not easily to be beaten; but, besides this, there was a proclivity among not a few of my elder parishioners forty years ago to express themselves, in the ordinary flow of their talk, in the same sharp, sententious manner. I was at a largely attended parish meeting one day, when reference was made to a man who was giving himself over to immoderate smoking, and an octogenarian present described his habit in the sentence, "Ay, he reeks like a sod-heap." This man it was who was one of the "company" taking in the *Yorkshire Gazette* forty-five years ago, and who, with a canny twinkle in his eye, when the old question as to the right pronunciation of the word "neither" came up for comment at some small gathering of Dales folks, with a happy reference to the only sound of the word ever heard in the Dales, remarked, "Weel, now, Ah s'ud seea, 'twur nowther." It is very nearly forty years ago since I buried that dear old friend, so that his saying was not a recent plagiarism on Joe Miller.

Another impromptu saying, in the nature of a retort, struck me much, especially taking all the circumstances into account, as really somewhat telling. Our local medico was visiting an old lady, an old acquaintance of mine, who always had a "gey gude dish" of "my Lady Tongue" ready for instant production. She was in peril of her life with hæmorrhage, which the doctor had had much difficulty in staying, and which might come on again at any moment, and was almost safe to recur if she began her usual voluble chatter. However, talk she would, and at last the doctor, out of patience with her, addressed her sharply in her own tongue: "Ho'd thah noise, thee blethering au'd feeal, or Ah'll tie thah toongue ti thah teeath;" the instantaneous rejoinder being, "Thee caan't, doctor; fur Ah ha'e na a teeath i' mah heead!" But much of this readiness seems a thing of the past now, and I think it is because the stiffness of the "New English" instilled in the Elementary School lends itself both less familiarly and less well to the ready expression of quaint conceit or incisive repartee.

As further illustrative in the same connection, I may perhaps mention the following. Making inquiry one day about a person who, I had supposed, was no longer single, I was answered as follows: "Neea, neea, he's nane married. He still trails a leeght harrow: his hat covers his household." And from an old note-book I extract the next: "He's ower mickle a feeal to ken how many beans mak's five." Of a miserly skinflint, "He wad skin tweea deevils for yah pelt." Of an emaciated man, "He's that thin, he's lahk a ha'porth o' soap efter a lang day's weshing." Of a woman newly but not wisely married, "Ay, she's tied a knot with her tongue she'll be matched to unloose wiv her teeath." And lastly this, of a man without brains or 'gumption,' "Ay, there's t' heead an' t' hair; but there's nowght else."

MY INTRODUCTION TO DANBY

THE way in which I came to find myself planted in Danby was as follows. A letter, written with the intention that it should be read by me, was shown me, in which this parish, with its ecclesiastical income of £95 a year, was described as one affording a fine field for work to any one so inclined. There was a church in it, it was true, but distant from the overwhelming majority of the parishioners—exceeding 1500 in number—by from one and a quarter to four miles, upwards even of that in some directions. There was a clergyman, too, but he had not been famed for strength of body nor energy of mind and purpose; so that, while there were Wesleyan Methodists and Primitive Methodists, in numbers and organisation alike considerable, Churchmen were not conspicuous in either the one respect or the other; a condition of matters which of course need occasion no surprise under the circumstances. But even this was not all; for when I mentioned to a shipowning friend, who had been a seafaring man in his earlier days, that I had thoughts of going a-prospecting, and looking at the place, in consideration of the offer of the living made to me, his view of my wisdom, and of the eligibility of the place itself, was expressed as follows : " Going to see yon place ! Why, Danby was not found out when they sent Bonaparte to St. Helena ; or else they never would have taken the trouble to send him all the way there !"

However, I had my own reasons ; and one fine afternoon,

six-and-forty years ago, I found myself riding along the not
too traffic-worn road to Whitby from Scarborough.   Born
and reared a South-countryman, and not as yet conversant
with the wild solitary tracks and the deep pitches and steep
ravine-banks of the North Yorkshire moors, I was but little
prepared for some of the sights and sounds that greeted my
unaccustomed perceptions.   One might sometimes see an
eagle in those days still;[1] and two or three large hawks
might well be seen on the wing at once; and the curlew
skirled as he crossed, far above your head, from the wild
moors of Goathland or Glaisdale, where he bred then and
breeds still, to the sea-coast on the east.   Hitherto, moreover,
I had been accustomed to regard the sheep as a quiet, un-
impulsive sort of creature, with unstartling habits, much
given to the pursuits of growing wool and developing the
masses of fat not loved by boys at school; but during the
experiences of this ride my preconceived notions were exposed to a very rude shock.   For I saw a sheep—there could
be no doubt that it *was* a sheep—deliberately,—no, I must not
use that word, for there was no deliberation about the act,—I
saw it jauntily skip up a six-foot-high bank, steep as a wall-
side, and rugged with rock and brier, which rose from the
road I was riding along to the foot of a five-foot-high rough
mortarless stone wall or dike, and proceed incontinently to

[1] On one occasion, not so very long after the date of the ride mentioned
in the text, I saw, from near the eminence called Danby Beacon, an eagle
on the wing, which doubtless was the bird which was taken or shot—I
forget which—some few days after, at no great distance away, with a
rabbit-trap attached to one of its feet.   This was an erne or white-tailed
eagle, from which the Arncliff of the West Arncliff woods in Egton parish,
and the Arncliff of Ingleby Arncliff in West Cleveland, had both taken
their names in the old Anglian times.   On the same day, and in the same
part of the moor, I saw a pair of hen harriers, and another large hawk,
which might have been a buzzard, but was too far off to be identified.
Once too I have seen the kite here; and in the older days ravens used
to breed in the parish, and might be seen or heard any day, or almost
every day.

leap up part of the height and scramble the rest with cat-like activity and hoofs that clung like claws, and disappear in the enclosure on the other side. Other denizens of the moor too, besides these athletes among sheep, were there, and were noted by me as creatures to be much observed. For grouse and golden plover—a good pack of the one, or a large flock of the other—claimed my attention; or a series of symmetrical mounds, dotting the moor on either side of me—the intent and contents of which have been familiar enough to me since—were like the "little star" to the child, and made me "wonder what they were."

Three hours' riding brought me to Whitby, and the quaint, picturesque old town—there were no lodging-houses there then; the Royal Hotel itself was not so much as projected—with the setting autumn sun gilding and glorifying its red roofs and quaint gables, impressed an image on my retina which has never faded away, and which has stirred the eye and the heart of many a one besides the artist with a longing for some lasting memento of its beauty.

The following morning saw me still farther on my journey of exploration. I was told I should find but few on the road to make inquiry of as to the route I was bound to pursue. After the first three or four miles, a rough moorland road would have to be traversed, and I might not see a passenger for miles and miles together. Nor did I. The heights of Swart Houe once attained, with the bare moor on either side of me, I passed on to Barton Howl without seeing a soul. Thence to Stonegate, according to the directions obtained at the little roadside inn just passed, and there the solitude of my way was singularly broken. I was no longer the sole traveller on this rugged lonely roadway; for there was a cavalcade such as I had never before imagined, much less realised. What I met was a stone-waggon with a team—a "draught" we call it in our North Yorkshire vernacular—of no less than twenty horses and oxen attached to it, half of either kind. They were drawing a huge block of fine freestone up the terribly steep "bank," or hill-side road, which rises like a house-roof on the eastern side of Stonegate Gill. At the foot of the bank, on the limited level space available, there were standing four other waggons similarly loaded. The full complement of animals dragging each of these "carries" was a pair of horses and a yoke of oxen; and when they reached the foot of one of these stupendous hills, the full force of animal power was attached to each of the carriages in succession, and so the ponderous loads—five tons' weight on the average—were hauled to the top; and then, when all were up, the cavalcade proceeded on its slow march again. I had seen oxen used in the plough in Suffolk, but never before had I seen such a spectacle as this on the highroads of England.

At last I reached the Beacon, the highest point, houe-crowned, of all that part of the North Yorkshire moors, and the site of a beacon in Armada times, and on many subsequent occasions when it was thought or feared that invasion might ensue. Before me, looking westward, was moor, so that I could see nothing else. On either side was moor, with a valley on the left, and on the right, to the north, an expanse of cultivated land beyond. Across the valley just named there was moor again; and the valley was, it was clear, but a narrow one; while behind me, as I knew, lay three good miles of moor, and nothing but moor. It was a solitude, and a singularly lonely solitude. The only signs of life were given by the grouse, or the half-wild moor-sheep, whose fleeces here and there flecked the brown moor with white spots. It was a wild as well as a lonely solitude; and yet not dreary, nor could one well feel altogether alone. For there, from the south-east round by the north to Tees mouth on the north-east, and thence on again straight out to the north along the coast of Durham and Northumberland, was the great wide open sea; and no one feels alone in sight of the sea, any more than under the clear canopy of a starry

heaven in a bright cloudless winter's night. Nay, the stillness
of such a night, far more than the wild wailings of the rushing
blast, is instinct with the wisht, weird creatures of the
imagination; far too much so for the superstitious or fancy-
led to be able to feel themselves alone; and more so yet to
one fairly cognisant of his inner life and its connections.
And the sea, even at a distance, is a creature—a being—full
of a great vitality, and with many voices; and by aid of one
of them at least, whatever the mood of the listener, there is
an inner and most real communion with the unseen.

But I was at the Beacon, and with a choice of roads—at
least of tracks—before me; and beyond a general idea that I
was too much to the north to be in the right way, I had
nothing to guide me. A direction-post there was, but the
arms which had once borne the names of the places the
various tracks led to were gone. There was nothing in sight
but moor, to the west, and to the north and south of the
same; while the track or rough road that appeared to lead
downwards towards the farther part, if not the termination,
of the valley on my left, was grass-grown and little used.
My suspense and uncertainty were terminated in an unforeseen way. A woman, riding a strong pony, had come up
unseen and unheard behind me, the hoofs of her steed giving
out no sound on the grassy sward at the edge of the road.
I asked her the way to Danby; but whether she misunderstood my Southern English, or I misunderstood her Yorkshire vernacular—a mighty easy thing to happen, as I knew
right well before long—or whether she did not like the look
of me, and preferred solitariness to company—for she was
herself bound for Danby Dale-end—the direction I took
led me away from the place I wished to reach, instead of
directly towards it. A mile and a half more of nothing but
heather—or, in Yorkshire speech, "ling"—convinced me of
what I had but suspected before, namely, that I was too far to
the north, and now too far to the west, to be right for Danby

Dale. So the first road I came to bearing south was taken, and a mile ridden along it brought me in sight of one of the loveliest scenes it had ever been my lot to behold. There was the long valley, running east and west, which had seemed so narrow when beheld from the grudging heights above, and which was now seen to be from a mile to a mile and a half broad, and with dale after dale, not wide but long and deep, opening into it from its southern side. High on either side of each of these dales towered the moorland banks, and along each dale I could trace the course of a minor stream, with its fringe of trees, running its descending race towards the main stream in the longer or medial valley. There was verdure everywhere, with plentiful signs of careful tillage, and the luxuriant growth springing from a grateful soil. It might be that, having had the wild wilderness of the brown moor around me for so long, the eye was doubly grateful for the fresh greens of the beck-side pastures and the widely-spread green crops. But with colour, contrast, and contour, soaring hill and deepening dale, abrupt nab-end and craggy wood, all claiming notice at once, rather than in their proper turn, the scene spread before me was something more than simply beautiful.

Ten minutes now brought me to a little country hostel, as clean as it was plain and unpretending, kept by two sisters known far and wide as "Martha and Mary," and wherein, some two or three years after, I heard propounded the doughty question, "Gin Adam had na sinned, how wad it ha' stooden then?"—and commending my horse to the care of the blacksmith, who officiated as ostler, I betook myself to a hamlet half a mile distant, where I was told I should find the "minister." The house I was told to look for was found without difficulty, but to find the "minister" in it did not seem quite so easy. It was a long low gray building, on a sort of grassy terrace by the roadside, and with nothing between it and the roadway. At one end were a cow-house and other like premises, and at the other a low lean-to shed appearing to give access to some sort of a back-kitchen or scullery. Beyond the one window which looked out upon the highway was a door, twin to the one opening into the cow-house, and quite innocent of any such appendage as a knocker or a bell,—innocent even, one would have said, of any nascent suspicion that such things existed. But seeing no other door and no way that seemed to lead to any other, I made up my mind to knock at this one. I knocked once, twice, and again, with no response. I learned in after days that I ought to have gone to the door in the lean-to, the only one in use by all the members of the family; for there in the kitchen, which was also the living-room, as it presently appeared, I should have found father and mother, son and four daughters, who, together with the daytal-man [1] (who was working for the father, and with the son), were just sitting down to dinner. Not suspecting this, I went on knocking; and at last I heard a slow step evidently sounding from an uncarpeted floor of stone approaching the door. Slowly the door was unlocked and the bolts drawn, and as slowly was it opened; but not for more than a few inches. As well as I could see, the person who opened it was an old man, clad in a rusty black coat, with drab breeches and continuations, and with a volume of what was supposed to be white neckcloth about his throat. I asked, "Does Mr. D—— live here?" and the answer was, "Mr. D—— does live here." I rejoined, "Can I see Mr. D——?" I was asked in return, "What do you want with Mr. D——?"—"Well," I said, naming the patron of the living, "Lord Downe asked me to call on Mr. D——." My interlocutor responded, "Lord Downe sent you to call on Mr. D——! Why, last week he sent a Fowler Jones to call on Mr. D——." My reply was, "I am not Mr. Fowler Jones; my name is so-and-so. And Lord Downe told me he

---

[1] That is, a day-labourer; a man reckoned with by the day, in contradistinction to one reckoned with by the term; a man the "tale" of whose wages, or work, is from day to day.

had written to Mr. D——, mentioning my name, and not without reference to helping him in the parish. Can I see Mr. D——?"—"Why, yes, I suppose you can. I's Mr. D——." After this the door was opened a little more widely, and I was requested to walk in and partake of what I afterwards found was the dinner prepared for the family at large, who were meantime left hungry and expectant in the kitchen without.

In due time I was asked, Would I like to go and see the church?—a proposition to which I gave a willing assent. After a walk of a mile and a half it was reached, the door unlocked, and we entered. There is no need to dwell on what I saw of the condition of the said edifice. It must suffice to say that my conductor, the "minister," entered without removing his hat, walked through the sacred building and up to the holy table with his hat still on. Although I had seen many an uncared-for church, and many a shabby altar, I thought I had reached the farthest extreme now. The altar-table was not only rickety, and with one leg shorter than the others, and besides that, mean and worm-eaten, but it was covered with what it would have been a severe and sarcastic libel to call a piece of green baize; for it was in rags, and of any or almost every colour save the original green. And even that was not all! It was covered thickly over with stale crumbs. It seemed impossible not to crave some explanation of this; and the answer to my inquiry was as nearly as possible in the following terms: "Why, it is the Sunday School teachers. They must get their meat[1] somewhere, and they gets it here." It may be thought I am romancing, drawing upon my imagination. But indeed I am not;

---

[1] This is the term in universal use throughout the district in order to convey the sense of food in general. What is usually termed meat, is here spoken of as flesh, or perhaps flesh-meat. In the old days a daytal man—day labourer in ordinary English—used to be spoken of as "addling" (earning) half a crown a day and his meat. And there was, and is, a verb to correspond. So-and-so is *meated* in the house is quite the customary manner of expression.

I am but detailing the literal fact. And everything was in hateful harmony with what I have thus described. There lay the dirty shabby surplice, flung negligently over the altar-railing, itself paintless and broken, and the vestment with half its length trailing on the dirty, unswept floor. The pulpit inside was reeking with accumulated dust and scraps of torn paper. The font was an elongated, attenuated reproduction of a double egg-cup, or hour-glass without the sustaining framework; and in it was a paltry slop-basin, lined with dust, and an end or two of tallow candle beside it.[1]

Such was the parish church and its reverend but hardly reverent minister. And he was but one of a pair; for his brother was parish clerk and parish schoolmaster as well; and the first time I had to take a funeral, on arriving at the church a little in advance of the hour fixed, and entering the basement of the tower (which in the days of the barbarous re-edifying of the poor old church had been made to subserve the purposes of a porch), I became aware of a strong perfume of tobacco smoke; and there inside the church I saw the clerk sitting in the sunny embrasure of the west window, with his hat on of course, and comfortably smoking his pipe. A good harmless man enough, but one who might as happily be described by the effective Scottish word " feckless " as by any more laboured attempt to convey an idea of him. He

---

. [1] The explanation of this fact lay in the circumstance that, as the rule, baptisms were not solemnised in the church. When, some months after the time of the incidents mentioned above, arrangements had been made for the transference of the incumbency to myself, Mr. D—— said to me one day, " I hope you will be kind to my people ; " my reply being to the effect that I had no thought of being anything else. But the old gentleman went on to explain more fully what was in his mind, and very much in the words which follow : " I must say I have been very kind to them, but they have not been very thoughtful or considerate about me. I mean," he continued, " that when a child is born, they send for me to baptize the bairn ; and I go. A fortnight afterwards, they send for me to ' church the mother '; and I go ; and I think they might be content with that. But they are not, for a fortnight later they send for me to ' christen ' the child. And that is surely a little too much."

had begun his independent life not so ill provided for as a
Dalesman of those days. His elder brother had had a uni-
versity education, and he himself had received the patrimonial
land, subject, I daresay, to some small burden on a sister's
account. He had muddled through this in some way or other,
but nobody knew how, and he himself least of all. He had
smoked his pipe and played his 'cello, and I suppose done
nothing much besides. And then, when at the end of his
resources, mental and other, he had had the parish honours
above named almost literally "thrust upon him." For, a little
later in the course of my connection with the parish, I asked
the worthy old gentleman who was then the senior church-
warden, why this very incompetent person had been put, of
all places, into the onerous as well as responsible office of
schoolmaster; and his answer was significant, as well as
graphic. It was, "Wheea, he could dee nowght else. He
had muddled away his land, and we put him in scheealmaster
that he mou't get a bite o' brëad." A sort of Free School it
was, with a small endowment furnishing the fees for about
twenty children "put in free." The rest of the scholars paid
weekly fees at the rate of threepence for reading only, four-
pence for reading and writing, and sixpence for all "the three
R's" combined. Some two years and a half after the date of
this smoke in the church, the rector of a parish some seven
miles distant from Danby, a friend of longer standing than
my residence in the parish, with another beneficed clergyman
from the same neighbourhood—now the Archdeacon—came
over to call upon me, and to see how the house, which was
then in process of building with a view to its becoming the
Parsonage house, was getting on. The rising buildings duly
inspected, the rector said he would like, as we returned to my
temporary dwelling, to call upon the aforesaid minister of the
parish; and to this his companion added that he would like
to pay the Free School a visit of inspection. I dissuaded him
from this project as forcibly as I could, knowing but too well

what must of necessity await him there. However, he still continued bent upon the visit, alleging that, as he was Diocesan Inspector, it was after all no more than his duty. Of course there was nothing that could, with propriety, be urged against this view, and I was silent. Well, we arrived at the school-house, a low thatched building of some antiquity, the door of the schoolroom being reached at the end of a narrow, long, dark, roughly-paved passage. Here the noise, which had been plainly audible outside, became very pronounced ; but somehow seemed to harmonise better with the idea of a jolly good game of romps than of severe study. I knocked at the school door. I might as well have knocked at the door of a smithy with half a dozen blacksmiths plying their vocation in full swing. I knocked again, taking advantage of a partial lull within ; and this time I was heard. Silence ensued. At least, a sort of comparative silence ; for the shuffling of feet and the scraping of wooden soles, strongly tipped with iron, upon the stone floor could be heard only too plainly. I knocked a third time ; but there was still no response, nor any that answered, "Come in." So I opened the door, and motioned the "In-spector" to enter. The school was still enough now ; for most of the boys and girls were in their places. Only three or four small figures could still be seen struggling under the desks, or into the places that should have been occupied by them. But meanwhile, where was the master ? Fast asleep, and again with his tall hat on, in a large high wooden-backed chair by the fireside. But the unwonted stillness did for him what all the preceding hullabaloo had failed to do :—it woke him. Rubbing his eyes with a half-comprehending consciousness, he presently recognised the presence of strangers in his abode of the Muses. His first action was to pull off his hat; unfor-tunately, however, leaving a black skull-cap on, which he was wearing under his hat. To remove this also was his next attempt, while he staggered up to make a show of receiving his visitors. By this time the "Inspector" had found an opportunity to whisper to me, "Let us get away as soon as we can;" and thus terminated the first "inspection" of the schools of this parish of Danby.

But I find myself wandering far away from the special matter I was describing, namely, my "prospecting" visit to the parish of which I have so long been the incumbent. After my interview with the "minister," and my visit to the church, with all the concomitant circumstances, I was at no loss to comprehend the derogatory description, given in the patron's letter, of the state of the parish as regarded from a "church work" point of view. I could understand the slovenly, perfunctory service once a Sunday, sometimes relieved by none at all, and the consequent sleepy state of church feeling and church worship.[1] I could well understand how the only religious life in the district should be among and due to the exertions of the Wesleyans and Primitive Methodists. I could easily understand too, how the spirit of a good, right-thinking, earnest-minded man like the patron of the living, one largely interested, moreover, in the welldoing and wellbeing of the many tenants who held under him, as well as more generally of the parishioners at large, would be, or rather had been, affected by finding what he, in common with so many others set in high places as to position, intelligence, and earnest zeal for the true elevation of the people, held to be one of the chief energies of improvement, so sadly in abeyance. And I hope I thought that, while I felt no great dread of the seclusion, any more than of the work I needed no one to tell me would lie before me in such a field, things might be so ordered that I might be enabled, at least in part, to become a fellow-helper in the good work which I knew right well this good and noble man wished to organise and see carried out.

[1] One of the freeholders, a steady churchman, told me not long afterwards, that within a given period—a little more than a year, as I remember his information—he had himself been to church four times oftener than the minister himself. The latter, besides being a man uninterfered with by any superfluity of energy, either bodily or intellectual, was an old and infirm man, and did not care to face the elements in bad or stormy weather.

FOLKLORE

SURVIVALS OF "FAIRY," "DWARF," "HOB"
NOTIONS

I WAS once paying a visit to one of my elderly parishioners who was not exactly "bed-fast," for she could get up from time to time, but being far past "doing her own tonns" (turns), or little odds and ends of household work, was still house-fast, or unable to leave the house, even for the sake of a gossip at the next door. I found her, with her husband—a man who died a couple of years since at the age of ninety-seven—just sitting down to tea. As a rule, I carefully avoided meal-times in all my visiting from house to house; but on the occasion I refer to there was some deviation from the customary hour for the meal just mentioned, and the old couple were going to tea at the timely hour of about half-past two in the afternoon. On finding them so engaged, I was going to retire and call in again later, or perhaps some other day. However, this did not suit the old lady's views at all, and I had to sit down and wait until their tea was satisfactorily disposed of. Naturally we fell into talk, and as the old woman had lived in the district all her life, and most of it in the near vicinity, I began to ask her questions about local matters. Within a quarter of a mile from the house we were sitting in—one of a group of three or four—was a place commonly known by the name "Fairy Cross Plains." I asked her, Could she tell me why the said place was so called? "Oh yes," she replied; "just a little in front of where the public-house at the Plains now stood, in the old

days before the roads were made as they were now, two ways
or roads used to cross, and that gave the 'cross' part of the
name. And as to the rest of it, or the name 'Fairy,' everybody knew that years and years ago the fairies had 'a desper't
haunt o' thae hill-ends just ahint the Public.'" I certainly had
heard as much over and over again, and so could not profess
myself to be such a nobody as to be ignorant of the circumstance. Among others, a man with whom I was brought into
perpetual contact, from the relative positions we occupied in
the parish—he was, and is, parish clerk—had told me that his
childhood had been spent in the immediate vicinity of "the
Plains," and that the fairy-rings just above the inn in question
were the largest and the most regular and distinct he had ever
seen anywhere. He and the other children of the hamlet used
constantly to amuse themselves by running round and round
in these rings; but they had always been religiously careful
never to run quite nine times round any one of them. "Why
not?" I asked. "Why, sir, you see that if we had run
the full number of nine times, that would have given the
fairies power over us, and they would have come and taken
us away for good, to go and live where they lived."—"But,"
said I, "you do not believe that, surely, Peter?"—"Why, yes,
we did then, sir," he answered, "for the mothers used to
threaten us, if we wer'n't good, that they would turn us to
the door (out of doors) at night, and then the fairies would
get us."

But to return to the old woman with whom I was con-
versing. I admitted that I had both heard of and seen the
fairy-rings in question; but what about the fairies themselves?
Had anybody ever seen them? "Ay, many a tahm and
offens," said she; "they used to come down the hill by this
deear (door), and gaed in at yon brig-steean," indicating a large
culvert which conveyed the water of a small beck underneath
the road about a stone's throw from the cottage. A further
question elicited the reply that it was a little green man, with

a queer sort of a cap on him, that had been seen in the act of disappearing in this culvert. Just here the old woman's husband broke in with the query, "Wheea, where do they live, then?"—"Why, under t' grund, to be seear (sure)." "Neea, neea," says the old man; "how can they live under t' grund?" The prompt rejoinder was, "Why, t' moudiwarps (moles) dis, an' wheea not t' fairies?" This shut him up, and he collapsed forthwith. His wife, however, was now in the full flow of communicativeness, and to my question, Had she ever herself seen a fairy? the unhesitating reply was, "Neea, but Ah've heared 'em offens." I thought I was on the verge of a tradition similar to that of the Claymore Well, at no great distance from Kettleness, where, as "everybody used to ken," the fairies in days of yore were wont to wash their clothes and to bleach and beat them, and on their washing nights the strokes of the "battledoor"—that is, the old-fashioned imple- ment for smoothing newly-washed linen, which has been superseded by the mangle—were heard as far as Runswick. But it was not so. What my interlocutor had heard were the sounds indicative of the act of butter-making; sounds familiar enough to those acquainted with the old forms of making up the butter in a good-sized Dales dairy. These sounds, she said, she had very often heard when she lived servant at such and such a farm. Moreover, although she had never set eyes on the butter-makers themselves, she had frequently seen the produce of their labour, that is to say, the "fairy-butter"; and she proceeded to give me the most precise details as to its appearance, and the place where she found it. There was a certain gate, on which she had good reason to be sure, on one occasion, there was none overnight; but she had heard the fairies at their work "as plain as plain, and in the morning the butter was clamed (smeared) all over main part o' t' gate."

But her fairy reminiscences were by no means exhausted, even by such a revelation as this. She had known a lass quite

well, who one day, when raking in the hayfield, had raked
over a fairy bairn. "It was liggin' in a swathe of the half-
made hay, as bonny a lahtle thing as ever yan seen. But it
was a fairy-bairn, it was quite good to tell. But it did not
stay lang wi' t' lass at fun' (found) it. It a soort o' dwinied
away, and she aimed (supposed) the fairy-mother couldn't deea
wivout it any langer." Here again I was a little disappointed.
I had expected to get hold of a genuine unsophisticated
changeling story, localised and home-bred. But the termination was as I have just recorded.

From fairies the old lady got on to recollections of what
clearly was a survival of dwarf folklore. For she told me
of certain small people who used to dwell in the houes (grave-
mounds) that years ago were to be found in the Roxby and
Mickleby direction, but which had been dug into and afterwards ploughed over, so that the former denizens had clearly
been evicted and forced to retire. But it was only imperfect
recollections of what she had heard in her own young days
that my informant was dealing with now; and the lack of
feature and detail consequent on her lack of personal interest
in the subject was quite evident. But it was quite different
when I began to ask her if in her youth she had had any
knowledge of the Hart Hall "Hob." On this topic she was
herself again. "Why, when she was a bit of a lass, everybody knew about Hart Hall in Glaisdale, and t' Hob there,
and the work that he did, and how he came to leave, and all
about it." Had she ever seen him, or any of the work he had
done? "Seen him, saidst 'ee? Neea, naebody had ever seen
him, leastwise, mair nor yance. And that was how he coomed
to flit."—"How was that?" I asked. "Wheea, everybody
kenned at sikan a mak' o' creatur as yon never tholed being
spied efter."—"And did they spy upon him?" I inquired.
"Ay, marry, that did .they. Yah moonleeght neeght, when
they heared his swipple (the striking part of the flail) gannan'
wiv a strange quick bat (stroke) o' t' lathe fleear (on the barn

floor)—ye ken he wad dee mair i' yah neeght than a' t' men
o' t' farm cou'd dee iv a deea—yan o' t' lads gat hissel' croppen
oop close anenst lathe-deear, an' leeak'd in thruff a lahtle hole
i' t' boards, an' he seen a lahtle brown man, a' covered wi'
hair, spangin' about wiv fleeal lahk yan wud (striking around
with the flail as if he was beside himself). He'd getten a
haill dess o' shaffs (a whole layer of sheaves) doon o' t' fleear,
and my wo'd! ommost afore ye cou'd tell ten, he had tonned
(turned) oot t' strae, an' sided away t' coorn, and was rife for
another dess. He had nae claes on to speak of, and t' lad, he
cou'd na see at he had any mak' or mander o' duds by an au'd
ragg'd soort ov a sark." And she went on to tell how the lad
crept away as quietly as he had gone on his expedition of
espial, and on getting indoors, undiscovered by the unconscious Hob, had related what he had seen, and described
the marvellous energy of "t' lahtle hairy man, amaist as
nakt as when he wur boorn." But the winter nights were
cold, and the Hart Hall folks thought he must get strange
and warm working "sikan a bat as yon, an' it wad be sair an'
cau'd for him, gannan' oot iv lathe wiv nobbut thae au'd rags.
Seear, they'd mak' him something to hap hissel' wiv." And
so they did. They made it as near like what the boy had
described him as wearing—a sort of a coarse sark, or shirt,
with a belt or girdle to confine it round his middle. And
when it was done, it was taken before nightfall and laid in
the barn, "gay and handy for t' lahtle chap to notish" when
next he came to resume his nocturnal labours. In due course
he came, espied the garment, turned it round and round, and—
contrary to the usual termination of such legends, which
represents the uncanny, albeit efficient, worker as displeased
at the espionage practised upon him—Hart Hall Hob, more
mercenary than punctilious as to considerations of privacy,
broke out with the following couplet—

> Gin Hob mun hae nowght but a hardin' hamp,
> He'll coom nae mair, nowther to berry nor stamp.

I pause a moment in my narrative here to remark that this old jingle or rhyme is one of no ordinary or trifling interest. It seems almost superfluous to suggest that up to half a century ago, and even later, there was hardly a place in all Her Majesty's English dominions better qualified to be conservative of the old words of the ordinary folk-speech, as well as of the old notions, legends, usages, beliefs, such as constitute its folklore, than this particular part of the district of Cleveland. The simple fact that its Glossary comprises near upon four thousand words, and that still the supply is not fully exhausted, speaks volumes on that head. And yet this couplet preserves three words, all of which had become obsolete forty years ago, and two of which had no actual meaning to the old dame who repeated the rhyme to me. These two are "berry" and "hamp." "Stamp" was the verb used to express the action of knocking off the awns of the barley previously to threshing it, according to the old practice. But "berry," meaning to thresh, I had been looking and inquiring for, for years, and looking and inquiring in vain; and as to "hamp," I never had reason to suppose that it had once been a constituent part of the current Cleveland folk-speech. But this is not all. The meaning of the word, and no less the description given of the vestment in question, in the legend itself, throws back the origin, at least the form-taking, of the story, and its accompaniments, to an indefinite, and yet dimly definable period. There was a time when the hamp was the English peasant's only garment; at all events, mainly or generally so. For it might sometimes be worn over some underclothing. But that was not the rule. The hamp was a smockfrock-like article of raiment, gathered in somewhat about the middle, and coming some little way below the knee. The mention in *Piers the Plowman* of the "hatere" worn by the labouring man in his day serves to give a fairly vivid idea of the attire of the working-man of that time, and that attire was the "hamp" of our northern parts. For the word seems to be clearly Old Danish in form and origin. But although the form and fashion and accessories of our old lady's stories were of so distinctly an old-world character, it was impossible to doubt for a moment her perfect good faith. She told all with the most utter simplicity, and the most evident conviction that what she was telling was matter of faith, and not at all the flimsy structure of fancy or of fable.

EVIDENCES OF LATENT FAITH IN ARCHAIC
FOLK-TALES

THE subject adverted to at the close of the last section was the simplicity, the—to all appearance—absolute personal faith, which characterised all the deliverances or forth-tellings which my old parishioner favoured me with. Neither the fairies of Fairy Cross Plains nor the Glaisdale Hob were unrealities to her mind. They might not be now; but they had been, as certainly as her own remote fore-elders, and much more certainly than Oliver Cromwell or Julius Cæsar. And I have noticed the same sort of underlying implicit faith in more than one or two of my hard-headed, shrewd, matter-of-fact Yorkshire neighbours, dwellers in these deep, retired, and, fifty years ago, almost out-of-the-world dales of ours, when once I had succeeded in breaking through the outside husk of semi-suspicion and reserve instinctively worn as a shield by the mind of the unlearned when newly roused by the prickings of doubt or the questionings of incredulity. I have often found it very difficult to get them to speak with any approach to unreserve on the topics which lie nearest to the very core of our most interesting folklore. One old man in particular, as simple-minded, honest, truth-loving, and, I always believed, as good and God-fearing a man as I ever met with, who had a great personal regard for me, and besides was drawn to me by my connection with the place of his birth and the people of his father's house, as well as by the official intercourse which

his position as master of the Union House at Guisborough,
and mine as guardian of the poor for the parish, had involved
during a period of several years, was, with the greatest difficulty, led on to speak at all, and much more to talk freely,
about such matters.   I knew from many sources and circumstances that he was a veritable storehouse and magazine of
folklore subjects and experiences—I use the latter word
advisedly—and recollections.   In the course of our business
relations there was too much on his hands and on mine to
admit of our "hoddin' pross" (holding a gossiping talk) about
such matters as "wafts" (Scottice, wraiths), or "wise men"
(Anglice, wizards, soothsayers, or conjurers);[1] but some little
while after he had ceased to wear the official dignity just

---

[1] This is a word which had some few years ago, if it has not still, its
full and true sense in this part of the world.   Some forty years ago, when
country-parsons, or, as we were called throughout this district, "Church-
priests," were not so distinguished by their clerical attire, or clerical
pursuits, or clerical activity, either Sunday or "war-day," as they have
come to be since, and when I was seldom walking less than thirty-five or
forty miles weekly in my church and house-to-house work, an elderly
woman living about half a mile from my house, and who had been used
otherwise than well in her younger days, and in consequence was not
quite sound as to some particulars in her intellect, sent to me urgently
one day to go to her house, for she was in much trouble.   I had seen her
often, both at my residence and her own, and had a shrewd suspicion as
to the nature of her trouble, and that it was spiritual, in a sense, although
perhaps not quite within the province of the parish priest.   On going to
her house I found poor old Dinah was much troubled indeed.   She told
me the house was fairly taken possession of by spirits, and that, turn
which way she would, she was beset by them.   She told me what spirits
they were, and in some instances whose spirits, and what their objects
and efforts were ; and she had sent for me that I should "lay them."   I
tried to soothe her, and talked to her in the endeavour to divert her
thoughts into a more reasonable channel.   She was perfectly clear and
reasonable on every other topic ; but do what I would, and represent what
I could, her mind continually reverted to the one subject that possessed
her, namely, the actual presence of the spirits.   I told her at last I could
not, did not profess to "lay spirits" ; and her reply was, "Ay, but if I
had sent for a priest o' t' au'd church, he wad a' deean it.   They wur a
vast mair powerful *conjurers* than you Church-priests."

named, having been pensioned off in consideration of long and faithful service, I rode over to his abode, partly to pay my old friend a visit, and partly to try if I could in any way induce him to talk to me freely about the matters which were of interest to me as a folklore inquirer, and which I knew had greatly occupied, and perhaps exercised, his mind through years of his long life. It was long before I could get him to enter upon the subject at all. His scruples were partly of a religious nature—there was so much that seemed uncanny in his recollections, so much that his unsophisticated mind could not but refer, directly or indirectly, to the agency of something unhallowed, if not to " t' au'd Donnot " himself—but partly they were due to the fear of being thought credulous or superstitious ; and partly, no doubt, to a suspicion that many or most among his questioners and interlocutors on such topics would most likely be trying to draw him out on purpose to make fun of his old-world tales, and treat him as an object of ridicule and mockery. His anterior knowledge of me, and personal respect and regard for me, combined with my already well-known and unquestionably sincere interest in what I wanted him to tell me about, prevailed at last, and he began to discourse freely. He soon warmed to his subject, and there came a flow of reminiscences, personal experiences and impressions, reflections, considerations, and remarks, that kept him occupied as the chief speaker for well on to a couple of hours. And all through, from beginning to end, there was not a word or a look or a gesture to even suggest a doubt or a question, I must not say as to the entire truthfulness of his narratives, for that was transparent, but of his own implicit but unconscious conviction that he was relating to me the plain unvarnished tale of what had actually taken place under his own observation, or within the scope of his own personal knowledge. He told me much that he could not explain, much that was quite beyond his comprehension, much that he clearly looked upon as very questionable in its origin or inspiration, but which he had seen or heard, and no more thought of questioning than his own being, present and future, because no doubt either of one or the other had ever suggested itself to his simple mind.

Another case of the same sort was that of one of the worthiest of my many worthy parishioners, a man sensible, clear-headed, intelligent, one of my best helpers in all good and useful things as long as he was spared for this life's works, a man with the instinctive feelings of the truest gentility, but who always seemed averse to entering on any folklore talk or inquiry, and was, even admittedly, on his guard lest he should be led on to speak of them inadvertently. Twice, and twice only, I got him into conference with me on the, by him, tabooed subject-matters; and on both occasions it was equally a surprise both to him and to me. In either case an accidental remark was like a spark by chance firing a train ready laid, but not laid for the special purpose of firing that special mine. And on both occasions not only did I succeed in collecting some of the very most interesting details it has ever become my good fortune to meet with, but I saw that my usually recalcitrant informer was strangely impressed with what he was telling me in the connection in which I had put it.[1] One of these subjects was the careful ceremonial to be observed in the obtaining of effectual "witch-wood" for the incoming year; and the other, one that led on to the discovery of an original act of Odin-worship in one of the commonest, most every-day practices of all the farmers and occupiers of the district, as they were five-and-twenty or thirty years ago, not a few of them doing the same thing to this day.

But perhaps the most striking illustration that can be given of the tacit, unsuspected, but still implicit faith, in the

---

[1] This was my friend William Robinson of Fryup Head. What he told me about the care necessary in obtaining effectual witch-wood is recorded at p. 97. John Unthank's communications touching the Wise Man will be found pp. 114 *et seq.*

Dales folks' minds, in old folklore usages and customs is as follows. This used to be, and still is to a considerable extent, largely a dairy district. The farms are none of them large, there not being half a dozen in the parish much over a hundred acres in extent. Nevertheless, dairies of ten or twelve cows each used to be the rule on these larger farms. And it is alleged as a fact, and by no means without reason or as contrary to experience, that if one of the cows in a dairy unfortunately produces a calf prematurely—in local phrase, "picks her cau'f"—the remainder of the cows in the same building are only too likely, or too liable, to follow suit; of course to the serious loss of the owner. The old-world prophylactic or folklore-prescribed preventative in such a contingency used to be to remove the threshold of the cow-house in which the mischance had befallen, dig a deep hole in the place so laid bare, deep enough, indeed, to admit of the abortive calf being buried in it, on its back, with its four legs all stretching vertically upwards in the rigidity of death, and then to cover all up as before.[1]

Now, I had good reason for feeling assured that this had been actually done on a farmstead no very great way distant from my dwelling, and almost within the term of my own personal acquaintance with the place; as also I had reason to believe that it had been done more than once, within the same limit of time, in more than one of the adjacent dales to the south of us. Wishing to be fully assured of the first-named circumstance as a fact, I took the opportunity afforded by a casual meeting with the occupant of the farm just referred to —in point of fact a son of the alleged performer of the said rite or observance, and a regular hard-headed, shrewd, inde-pendent-willed Yorkshireman, now dead, poor fellow—to ask him if he knew of the continued existence of the said usage, adding that I had heard of it as still practised in Farndale. "Ay," he said, "there's many as dis it yet. My au'd father

[1] See Appendix I.

did it. But it's sae mony years syne, it must be about wore out by now, and I shall have to dee it again." Poor George Nicholson's faith needed no greater confirmation as a still living faith than this. But the like characteristics were not merely present, they were palpably evident in the case of each of the other persons I have mentioned. The old woman in Fryup, the ex-Union-House master, my much regretted old friend, all spoke of the matters they talked to me about as things that had been, and were real, and not as creations of the fancy, or old-wives' tales and babble.

THE HOB AND OTHER MATTERS, AND HOW
RECEIVED IN THE FOLK'S MIND

BUT we left our old lady in the midst of her "Hob" reminiscences, which, as I have said, and emphasised in the last
chapter, she told with a sort of personal recollection of them,
rather than as what had been told her by others, or handed
down from one teller of the old, old story to another. One
of her tellings was that the people of the farm in question, or
Hart Hall in Glaisdale, had been leading—that is, carting—hay
in a "catchy" time, when every load got was a load saved, as
if by snatching from the wilfulness of the weather; and
another load had been won, and was creeping its slow way
towards the "staggarth," when, as ill-luck would have it, one
of the wheels of the wain slipped in between two of the
"coverers of a brigstone,"[1] and there remained fast and

---

[1] A brigstone is a kind of rough conduit for water across a gate-stead, or
even a road of greater pretension, made by paving the bottom of a transverse
trench or channel, dug on purpose, with flagstones, setting up other flags
on either side as walls, and covering all in with other slabs of stone of
sufficient solidity to upbear any loaded vehicle likely to be driven across
the said conduit. The "coverers" are the slabs just mentioned, laid
over all ; and, from wear and tear, or natural decay, it not infrequently
happens that the interspace between two coverers widens by degrees,
however closely the edges may have been laid at first, until, on some
unlucky occasion, a wheel a little narrower than usual, or grinding along
under a load heavy enough to break a bit from the attenuated edge, forces
its way down and betwixt, and remains a fixture, even if it does not
occasion an overthrow.

inextricable by any easily applicable force. Extra horse-power
was fetched; men applied their shoulders to the wheel; gave-
locks were brought and efforts made to lever the wheel out of
its fix; but all equally in vain; and there seemed nothing for
it—awkward as such a place was for the purpose, for the
brigstone lay across a gate-stead—but to "teem" (empty) the
hay out of the vehicle, and liberate it when thus lightened of
its load. But it was too late in the day to do that at once,
with prudence, even had the weather been much less uncertain than it was. And so, with whatever unwillingness,
the load was left for the night under its detainer, and all
hands were to be set to work the first thing in the morning
to effect its liberation. But there was one about the place
who thought scorn of waiting for the morrow for such a
trifling business as that, and when the wearied and worried
household had retired to bed, Hob went forth in his mysterious might, made no difficulty about extricating the locked-in
wheel, and trailing the cumbersome load up the steep, broken
road to the homestead, putting the hay in beautiful order on
the stack, and setting the wain ready for the leading that
would of course be renewed early in the morning.

This was but one of the many exploits of a like nature
achieved by this well-willed being in aid of the work on that
favoured farm. In the barn, if there was a "weight of work"
craving to be done, and time was scant or force insufficient,
Hob would come unasked, unwarned, to the rescue, and the
corn would be threshed, dressed, and sacked, nobody knew
how, except that it was done by the Hob. Unaccountable
strength seemed to be the chief attribute ascribed to him.
One did not hear of him as mowing or reaping, ploughing,
sowing, or harrowing; but what mortal strength was clearly
incapable of, that was the work which Hob took upon himself.
Another thing to be remarked about this Hob—at least in all
the stories about him and his doings—was that there was no
reminiscence of his mischievousness, harmless malice, or even

F

tricksiness. He was not of those who resent, with a sort of pettish, or even spiteful, malice, the possibly unintended interference with elfish prerogative implied in stopping up an "awfbore" or hole in deal-boarding occasioned by the dropping out of a shrunken knot, and which displayed itself in the way of forcibly ejecting the intended stopping, in the form of a sharply driven pellet, into the face, or directly on to the nose, of the offender. Neither was he like the Farndale Hob told of by Professor Phillips (among other chroniclers), who was so "familiar and troublesome a visitor of one of the farmers of the dale, and caused him so much vexation and petty loss, that he resolved to quit his house in Farndale and seek some other home. Early in the morning, as he was on his way, with his household goods in a cart, a neighbour meeting him said, 'Ah sees thou's flitting.'—'Ay,' cries Hob out of the churn, 'ay, we'se flittin'.' On which the farmer, concluding that change of abode would not rid him of his troublesome inmate, turned his horse's head homeward again."

I am sorry that it has never fallen to my lot to hear this last story from one of the people—one of the "folk" themselves. In that case, I am certain it would have assumed a very different aspect. I have not given an exact copy of Professor Phillips's version, and for this reason—that the whole story is in reality a mere travesty. The story never was, and never could be, told in that form, and with such "properties" as are given by the author in question. He speaks of the neighbour who meets the flitting farmer as "addressing him in good Yorkshire." It would be a strange thing indeed if a Farndale farmer even now spoke anything else except "good Yorkshire." He makes him carry all his "household goods and gods" on one cart. He causes him to suspend and reverse all his flitting proceedings, quite regardless of what a flitting is, and how subject to a set of sufficiently fixed and stated rules, as to period or term, succession of one tenant to another, and so forth. He seems to me entirely unaware that a "flitting" is, like matrimony, "not to be lightly or wantonly taken in hand"; and, still less, abandoned after the said fashion. And besides, he makes a "play on the vowel" in the words, "Ay, we are flutting," which he puts into the mouth of the Hob, and which is simply nonsensical when all is taken into account. Such a play on the vowel is alien to the district; and. a Farndale man would be fully as likely to say "hutting" for "hitting," "sutting" for "sitting," or "mutten" for "mitten," as "flutting" for "flitting." Reference is also made to the Scandinavian version of the story. But that, as told by Worsaae himself, is reasonable and to the point; and is true as to the characteristics in which Phillips goes astray. Certainly the Danish professor calls the being of whom the story is told "Nisse," instead of "Hob," as he calls the human actor in the drama by his Danish epithet "bonde" instead of English "farmer"; but he steers clear of the mistake of calling the Nisse "a dæmon," which is the term applied by the English professor to poor soulless Hob. "In England," says Worsaae, "one may hear many a tale told, just as in Danish lands, about the tricksiness of the Nisse (Nix). On one occasion during my stay in England, it occurred to me to tell our northern story about a 'bonde' (a word nearly equivalent to our English 'yeoman') who was teased and annoyed in all sorts of ways by a Nisse. At last, he could not stand it any longer, and he determined to quit his holding, and to go to some other spot. When he had conveyed nearly all his movables to his new farm, and was just driving the last load of all, he happened to turn round, and what was the sight that met his eyes? Nothing less than Master Nisse himself, red cap and all, calmly perched on the top of the load. The small chap nodded with provoking familiarity, and added the words, 'Ay, here we are, flitting.'" But there is no play on the vowel in Worsaae's Danish. It is just the ordinary Danish phrase, "Nu flytte vi," which is employed.

Worsaae adds that the English counterpart—almost word

for word (*næsten ord til andet*)—was found by him localised in Lancashire ; and it is possible Phillips's version is not really of Yorkshire origin at all, although localised by him in Farndale. For I do not doubt that, misconceived and mistakenly coloured as the features of the story as told by him are, the change of the vowel may have a significance. Times without number I have heard the word "bushel" sounded "bishel"; the personal name "Ridsdale" is commonly "Rudsdale" in Cleveland at the present day ; and I have many instances in which the bishopric (of Durham, namely) is written "busshoprick" in the first James's time and later, and written so, moreover, in the official Records kept by the Clerk of the Peace of the time. It is possible, therefore, that, if the story as given by Professor Phillips is not in reality derived from a Lancashire, a County of Durham, or a Scottish Border source, the presence of the form "flutting" in it may be of antiquarian significance, and betoken that such form of the tale indicates an antiquity of not less than from two to three centuries, and quite possibly even much more than that : that, in other words, the terms "hamp," "berry," and "stamp" of the couplet given above, and the "flutting" of this Hob story, are correlative as to the inference we are, in either case, more than simply enabled to make as to the hoary antiquity of the Hob legends.

And yet our communicative old lady told forth her tale as of things that had happened under everybody's cognisance, and as it might be only the other day ; and of which she had only just missed personal cognisance herself by coming a little too late on the scene. She told her story of the doings and disappearance of Hob, and of the fairy dancing, of their retreat to their underground habitations, and "bittling" their clothes, of the finding of the fairy-bairn, in precisely the same tone and manner as I was told in after years by divers of the folks in the same vicinity, who only had not been actual eye-witnesses; of the marvellous escape of a child sleeping between two adults in their bed in a cottage no great way distant, and yet coming forth scatheless, although both his companions had been struck dead in a moment by lightning; and she told her story of the butter-making as of a thing the actuality of which was so assured that it never entered her imagination to suppose it could be questioned.

Of course such an unpremeditated, unintended assumption of personal experience, such a spontaneous disclosure of personal conviction, made the telling very effective; and if it could be appropriated and employed at will by the *viva voce* story-teller, would forthwith make his fortune. But that is a point by the way, which need not be dwelt upon. The thing really worth notice is the deep hold these divers matters of overtrow had gotten, and had continued to hold, not only on the imagination, but on the uncultured mind of our dale-dwellers of even less than a century ago. But if, in saying this, or in anything that I have previously advanced, I have led on to the idea that I hold these people to be, in any true practical sense of the word, a "superstitious" people, I shall have conveyed a wrong impression. I have met with any number of educated, cultured people who devoutly believe that suffering the sun to shine freely upon a fire in the ordinary grate puts it out; that setting a poker vertically up against the fire grate in front of it, causes the smouldering, nearly extinct fire to burn brightly up; that the changes of the moon influence the changes of the weather; that even the coincidence of certain phases of the moon with certain days of the week exercises a disastrous influence upon the weather of the ensuing days of the week, or month; that a great profusion of hedge-fruit—"hips and haws" especially—betokens, not a past favourable fruiting season, but the severity of the coming winter; and so forth. Now all this is what I would willingly call "overtrow," or believing overmuch, not "superstition": which word, as Professor Skeat tells us, is due to the elder French *superstition*, which is derived from *superstitionem*, the accusative of Latin *superstitio*, and means "a standing still over or near a thing, amazement, wonder, dread, religious scruple." Now there was no more dread, nor even wonder or amazement, in the simple minds of these worthy parishioners of mine, than there is in the mind of the refined and cultured lady who leans the poker against the top bar of her drawing-room grate to draw the fire up, or puts down the venetian blind to prevent the sun extinguishing the fire that seems to be dulled by the superior brightness of his rays. The nearest approach to the feeling—I must not say of dread, or even apprehension, so much as—of precaution that I have ever met with was in the case of a farm-lass in Farndale, who, hearing the "gabble-ratchet"[1] overhead, as she was coming in from the fold-yard to the house in the dusk of the evening, rushed hastily indoors, slammed the door to, bolted it, and flung her apron over her head. On being asked, "What was the matter?" her answer was, "I heared t' gabble-ratchet; but I lay I've stopped it fra deeing me any ho't (hurt)." Or I might quote another and entirely analogous instance. In the days when there was no lime procurable here otherwise than by sending waggons with their full teams over the moor to Hutton le Hole, or some such place, the journey was often one which, beginning at four o'clock in the morning, was not concluded until eight at night. It was at the close of just one of these tedious, wearisome expeditions that the farm-servant on one of the farms in Fryup Head was loosing out his weary "draught" (team), and the willing farm-lass was lending a helping hand, when they saw in the swampy, undrained "swang" lying some quarter or third of a mile below the house on the border of the beck, a will-o'-the-wisp, or in local nomenclature, a "Jenny-wi'-t'-lant'ren." The man turned his jacket inside out and the girl turned her

---

[1] A name for a yelping sound at night, like the cry of hounds, and probably due to flocks of wild geese flying by night. Taken as an omen of approaching death. See my *Glossary of Cleveland Dialect, sub voce.*

apron; after which they proceeded placidly with their occupation, troubling themselves no more about the misleading
propensities and powers of the assumed personal entity just
named.

Not that I suppose there was any real or deep-seated
dread or apprehension, or any feeling allied to either, which
led to the adoption of these precautionary measures in these
last two instances. I don't believe for a moment that the
Fryup Head man and lass supposed the Jack o' Lanthorn
would actually come up from the swamp and try to bewilder
and mislead them where they were; nor that the Farndale
maiden believed that the omen would have a personal application to herself had she omitted the ceremonies named in her
case. The feeling in action in either case may be difficult to
analyse, but I do not think it is hard to comprehend. I was
walking one day, many years ago, with a very old and a very
dear friend of mine, only just out of this immediate neighbourhood, when a magpie flew across the line of our path. My
friend, a solicitor in large practice, and holding the position of
Deputy Clerk of the Peace, as well as that of Clerk to the
local Bench of Magistrates, a wise and a good man, with
such opportunities of insight into the workings of human
nature as such a position forced upon him, took off his hat
with the greatest ceremony, and so saluted the bird in its
passage. On my remarking on the circumstance, "Oh," said
he, "I always take off my hat to a magpie." And I myself
was always in the habit of turning all the money I had in my
pocket on the first sight of the new moon, until one day
another old friend of mine completely disillusioned me by
remarking, when he saw me busy in the accustomed way,
"Why, what's the use of doing that? You always see the
moon through glass," in allusion to my invariably-worn
spectacles. And it is but a week since I saw a lady stoop
down in one of the most frequented streets in York, deliberately
pick up a horse-shoe which lay by the side of the flags of the

foot-pavement, as deliberately deposit it in the natty lady's light basket she was carrying, and I was quite well aware that it would be heedfully borne off home, and hung, as I knew nearly a dozen predecessors were already hung ; but fruitlessly and in vain, as I had often told her, because they were hung as they could be hung on a nail—and that is, with the toe upwards ; and not, as everybody ought to know, with their hinder ends or heel upwards—a matter which, unless it be attended to, completely invalidates the efficiency of the prophylactic power of the accidentally found but observantly picked up horse-shoe.

And yet it was not "superstition," in either of its graduated senses as tabulated by Professor Skeat, which induced any of the three actors above mentioned to do as they did. It was not even "overtrow." For no one of the three for one moment believed or imagined, entertained so much as the initial germ of a conception, that we should be advantaged in reality, even by the mass of a mote in the sunbeam, by what we did ; or, on the other hand, disadvantaged by its omission. There was a sort of "use and wont" in it, which, though in a certain sense "honoured in its observance," it was felt in some sort of indirect, unmeditated, unvolitional sort of way, would not be dishonoured in the breach.

And something of the same sort, as I take it, was the condition or attitude of mind in these old friends of mine who, divers of them, and on divers and manifold occasions, have told me such stories and traditions as the above with so much *empressement* and apparently evident conviction of the reality of what they were relating. I do not say that I think it was so always ; that there had never been a time when there was absolutely a faith of a sort in that which furnished the basis of all these narratives, a superstition really, and not a mere harmless exhibition of overtrow. Thus, for instance, I have no doubt at all of the very real and the very deep-seated existence of a belief in the actuality and the power of the witch. Nay,

I make no doubt whatever that the witch herself, in multitudes of instances, believed in her own power quite as firmly as any of those who had learned to look upon her with a dread almost reminding one of the African dread of fetish. Fifty years ago the whole atmosphere of the folklore firmament in this district was so surcharged with the being and the works of the witch, that one seemed able to trace her presence and her activity in almost every nook and corner of the neighbourhood. But this is far too wide and deep and intricate a subject to be entered upon at the close of a section already quite sufficiently long.

THE WITCH NOT ALWAYS OR NECESSARILY AN IMPOSTOR

AT the end of the last section I made reference to the omni-presence of the witch and the persistency of witch-tales or legends throughout the Dales district. It would indeed be difficult to exaggerate the dimensions of that element of folk-lore. I can but give an illustration or two of the position thus laid down.

It is not yet twenty-five years since a member of the Society of Friends, himself a very shrewd and observant man, as well as a successful tradesman in a considerable market-town in Cleveland, when talking to me about some of the different matters which he knew were of interest to me, touched not only on the general subject of folklore, but on the specific branch of it furnished by witchcraft, and the extensive and, in some part, still current belief in it; and he gave me the following anecdote in illustration of what he was advancing. "Not long since," he began, "a woman very well known to me as a neighbour and more than a merely occasional customer, came into my shop, and after making her purchases, took out her purse for the purpose of paying for the goods bought. In doing so she dropped something which had been in the pocket together with the purse. A close and very diligent search for the object that had fallen ensued immediately. But it was apparently in vain, and it continued to be in vain for so long that I asked her what she had lost. For a space she seemed shy of telling me; but at last she replied, 'I have lost my witch-wood; and it will never do to be without that.'—'Why, Mally,' I said in reply, 'surely you don't believe in witches!' 'Not believe in witches, saidst 'ee? Wheea, Ah kens weel there's eleven in G—— at this present tahm (time)! Neea, neea, it will na dee to be wivout my witch-wood!'" But not only was there this still current and widely-spread faith in the witch, in her influence as well as her malevolence, but not a few of the stories current were such as to imply absolute conviction on the part of the witch herself of the actual possession of the powers she was credited with. I do not mean that under terror of possible application of some modified sort of "question" or torture, or the pressure of actual cruelty, they admitted the imputation of witchcraft, nor even that for sinister purposes they laid claim to the possession of the powers implied;[1] but that, whether under the influence of an excited credulity, or possibly a condition allied to if not identical with that spoken of as "magnetic," "hypnotic," or "mesmeric," they might verily and really conceive themselves to be possessed of the alleged powers,[2] and adopt both the

[1] As to the matter here adverted to, note the following extract from the preface (p. 30) to *Depositions from the Castle of York* (S. S.), the immediate subject being certain depositions illustrative of the history of this remarkable superstition, witchcraft: "And yet some of these weak and silly women had themselves only to thank for the position they were placed in. They made a trade of their evil reputation. They were the wise women of the day. They professed some knowledge of medicine, and could recover stolen property. People gave them money for their services. Their very threats brought silver into their coffers. It was to their interest to gain the ill name for which they suffered. They were certainly uniformly acquitted at the Assizes, but no judge, jury, or minister could make the people generally believe that they were innocent. The superstition was too deeply rooted to be easily eradicated."

[2] In illustration of this point the following paragraphs translated from Hylten-Cavallius's *Wärend och Wirdarne* will be found not without their interest. Speaking on the general subject of what we call "witchcraft," and adverting to the special subject of spells, written charms, incantations, etc., he mentions the collection of books on the so-called Black Art, which had been accumulated in the course of the witchcraft

language and the action consonant thereto. Indeed I can hardly conceive that it could possibly be otherwise. It is not long since I was reading a series of very able and, some of them, very striking essays and addresses by Rev. J. M. Wilson, one of which might be looked upon as, in a certain sense, an "Apology for the Christian Miracles," or some of them. The immediate subject of his remarks is the "interpretation to be put on St. Paul's words touching the miracles wrought by him according to his own account." This interpretation is, says he, "that certain highly unusual phenomena repeatedly took place, which the agent and the witnesses agreed in considering as in some sense supernatural ; that these phenomena consisted in an exalted spiritual condition, which developed extraordinary spiritual and intellectual gifts, such as those of exposition, speaking with tongues, or extraordinary physical power, such as that of healing certain unspecified classes of disease. . . . It further appears that these phenomena

investigations carried out in some parts of Sweden in the earlier half of the eighteenth century, and which were seen by Linnæus in 1741, and by him described as full of jargon and gibberish, of idolatrous notions, superstitious prayers, devil-worship, and the like, and mainly in verse and rhyme ; and then proceeds : "The same irregular rhyming forms are also the peculiarity of nearly all spells or incantations which are yet to be met with. The very form itself, as the natural mode of expression for an excited condition of the senses, carried with it also the implied certainty that the incantations of the old times would be uttered with a deeply perturbed spirit, just as the remarkable vagaries of the understanding which are so characteristic of the entire category of 'trolldom,' or witchcraft, can only be psychologically explained or illustrated on the assumption or supposition of the strongest excitement of the imagination and inner consciousness. Take, for instance, the confession made by Ingeborg Boge's daughter before the King's District-court in 1618, in which she set forth how she, in order that her husband might not detect her nocturnal expeditions to Blaakulla (the witches' place of meeting), without using any definite form of words or spell, employed for the purpose certain good devices, such as that taking her sark she blew into it till it was filled out with air, when she laid it by her husband's side, making it so completely in her own image and form, that, if he looked at her, he could not detect any difference from her actual self. From such a statement as this no of healing consist in the action of mind upon mind or mind on body; and the conditions plainly include a highly exalted spiritual condition in both agent and patient. The class to which the phenomena alluded to by the agent himself belong, is that obscure class of mental actions of whose existence we have now ample evidence, but of the details of which we are still at present very ignorant, from lack of a sufficiently wide and accurate observation of facts to serve as the basis of induction. Such phenomena need not be regarded as in any sense miraculous, nor evidential of anything else except of those highly wrought spiritual conditions which an induction from experience may show are inseparable from such phenomena. . . . That these powers would in such a society" as that contemplated by the circumstances of the case "be often misunderstood, the limits of them unperceived, the exercise of them misreported and exaggerated, is certain. In St. Paul's letters, however, I think it will be admitted by any candid reader, there is no trace of their mis-

one can draw any other conclusion than that in this imaginary night-trip to Blaakulla the real state of the case was that she was in a strangely visionary and most likely spontaneously magnetic condition. In the case of other individuals, that same condition of nervous non-natural excitement has been induced by the application of unguents impregnated with strong narcotic or narcotico-soporific drugs, whence also the ointment horn (*smörje-horn*) is looked upon as part of the witch's equipment ; such a horn being preserved among other like matters in the High Court of Gothland. In some way or other, however, whether called into play by incantations merely, or by the use of some other means, have an unnatural and pervading straining or tension of the nerves, and psychical delirium, closely united with an aberration of an imaginary nature, always found admission as a fundamental condition in the original and archaic development of the witchcraft system, whose most remarkable expression or manifestation, together with journeys through the air, and so forth, thus find their readiest psychological explanation. . . . Yet further, and without recourse to any, even the simplest spell, witchcraft has provided itself, under diverse circumstances, with equally various means and resources, among which, and in the midst of other articles of the same general nature, is preserved in the court-house just named a little horn pipe, which was used by the witches when they desired to exercise their art or summon their familiar to their presence."

representation; he was himself an agent, and speaks of them without exaggerations and without surprise. Let us repeat, therefore, that St. Paul possessed an astonishing power over the minds, and through the minds over the bodies, of men; that such powers were regarded both by himself and others as miraculous, so abnormal were they; and that we may regard them as exceptional powers produced by certain conditions of mind and will, primarily highly exalted and intense spiritual conditions, and therefore evidential of those conditions."

These powers, the lecturer goes on to say, "produced effects of at least two kinds"; on the one hand, in really wonderful spiritual results, both in the agents themselves and in the masses of men to whom they addressed themselves; and "on the other hand, in power over men's bodies through their minds and emotions; in other words, gifts of healing; and both of these were appreciated by contemporaries."

Now, it would seem to me that, on collation of these extracts with the translation from the Swedish inquirer and author given in the last long note, there is really no valid reason why whole sentences from the former, with only slight verbal alteration, should not be transferred from the subject of the Christian miracles (or some certain section of them) to the question of the actual possession by the reputed witch of two hundred years ago, and of later periods still, of some very actual power or active influence. I am quite satisfied that some of those phenomena of witchcraft might and did "consist in the action of mind upon mind or mind upon body," and that the conditions plainly include "a highly exalted or excited mental and nervous condition" in both "agent and patient." Quite apart, moreover, from the possible, or more than possible, use or application of powerful drugs, there must have been cases, of by no means rare occurrence, in which the witch not only produced given and remarkable effects upon both the minds and bodies of her "patients," but knew that she could do it, and both intended and expected to produce them. In fact, the annals of animal magnetism go infinitely beyond anything here postulated, in hundreds and hundreds of facts which are of the most ordinary and everyday occurrence. I remember being told by one of the then leading medical men in one of the principal watering-places in the north of England, nearly fifty years ago, that being a mesmerist himself and having a case in which he believed that the influence then known as "mesmeric" would be beneficial, he applied it daily; but finding it often inconvenient to have to attend his patient at the precise hour at which the inducement of the mesmeric slumber most conduced to her benefit, he resolved to try whether he could not induce it otherwise than by personal attendance and operation. For this end he, as the phrase was, mesmerised a bottle of water and also a handkerchief, and gave them to her with orders to use them, or one of them, at the proper season. Somewhat to his own surprise—for it was somewhat nearer the birth of animal-magnetism than this present year of grace 1891—the experiment was a complete success. I myself knew the patient, and visited her, both as a friend and as a clergyman; and I had the means of verifying the statements made to me, if I had had any doubt, which I had not. Finding his initial experiment so far successful, Dr. W—— tried others also, and found that it was possible in this patient's case to bring on the slumber without entering her presence, or even giving her any tangible token of the influence he had established upon her. What he did was to make the "passes," which in those days were the recognised means employed for inducing the slumber, as he passed along the street in which her residence was situated, and the passes were found to be efficacious. All this is mere everyday experience now, and indeed is very much short of many of the experiences detailed in any memoir or treatise on the subject of electro-biology or animal-magnetism. What is possible in the way of action of mind on mind or of mind upon body, the nervous and mental

conditions of the patient and the agent being in fitting correlation, is in point of fact almost astounding. Is it possible to
deny, or rather, is it not imperative on us to assume, that in
some quite sensible proportion of the hundreds of persons
credited with the power of the witch, there may or must
have been an exact analogy to the examples afforded in the
experience of the magnetic or biological professor?

And so, I believe that in multitudes of cases the witch
herself was a believer in the reality and the efficacy of her
own powers. No doubt, "these weak and silly women made
a trade of their evil reputation." No doubt, fraud and
imposture were rife among them. But still there must have
been many a member of the sisterhood who was, as regards
a belief in the power or influence of the witch, to the full as
"superstitious" as the silliest and weakest of her dupes or
the victims of her craft. And it is thus that I account for
the existence of that class or phase of witch-story or legend
which was so very far from uncommon some forty years ago,
when I was gathering up the fragments that remained of a
witch-lore which must have been singularly rich, and in which
phase or class the witch herself was the principal or prominent
agent rather than simply the witch's patient, victim, or dupe.

THE WITCH: LOCAL LEGENDS OF HER DOINGS, AND ILLUSTRATIONS

AT the time indicated at the close of the last section, or more than forty years ago, a very noteworthy proportion of these witch stories were not only localised, but the names, the personality, the actual identity of the witches of greatest repute or notoriety were precisely specified and detailed. I have had houses in three or four of the townships of this immediate district pointed out to me as the abodes of this or that "noted witch." In Danby, Westerdale, Glaisdale, Farndale, as well as farther afield, this place or that, and sometimes to the number of two or three in a single one of the parishes named, has been indicated as the scene of this or that strange experience springing out of witchcraft, or of some stranger exploit in the same connection. Here the witch was baffled by the employment of an agency more potent than her own (of which more at a future page); here she was irresistible or triumphant; there she came to grief, perhaps through the use of silver slugs fired at her, perhaps through some other of the accredited means for neutralising her power or damaging her person. In one of these stories, perhaps as graphic as any I have met with, and which to my regret I am unable to give in detail by reason of the nature of the means, or at least the effect of the means, employed for the purpose of bringing the witch to book, her name and abode as well as those of her victim being given with all precision, she is brought on the scene as forced to confess her misdeeds, and constrained to remain in a condition of sheer bodily purgatory until she had removed the spell laid on her victim and his goods, and besides that remedied its baneful effects. Another, in which the self-same uncanny old lady is the principal actor, and eventually the actual sufferer, runs thus : A party of freeholders,[1] mainly

---

[1] It is not without interest to observe that this legend accommodates itself with accuracy to the actual sporting circumstances of the district at the period alleged—at least assumed—by the names of the men mentioned. Even to the present day I sometimes meet with an old inhabitant who recalls the time when the exclusive right of sporting over the common or moorlands was not as yet claimed, or at least not as yet exercised, by the lord of the manor. There was a man living here when I first knew the district, at that time "well on in his seventies," who was described as having possessed a singular species of skill or dexterity in the use of a peculiar missile, such as I had never heard of before. This was a short straight cudgel of some eighteen inches in length, which he could hurl with such unerring aim that a grouse or partridge within the range of his weapon—not a very wide one, it may be noted—had but small chance of escape. John S—— never missed. It so happened one day that three or four of our Danby freeholders had taken their guns in quest of a hare, but in vain ; every shot had been missed, and they were coming home without the game, when they met our friend John with his cudgel. Being told of their want of success, with the utterance of a gibe or two, he offered to go with them to the moorside they were leaving, and procure them the hare they wanted. A short time only elapsed before one was found, and John's cudgel rolled her over before she had gone half a dozen yards. Over and above this feat of marksmanship, the matter of interest to me was that these freeholders, whose names and histories and successors were all quite familiarly known to me, should be sporting, apparently quite at their own will and discretion, over what was, at the time of narration, and had been for many years, the jealously preserved and exclusively enjoyed sporting ground of the lord of the manor. A word or two of inquiry sufficed to convey to me the fact that, up to the time of such and such a predecessor of the present lord, the freeholders had exercised the right of sporting at their own discretion over the entire moor, and even of shooting the sacred grouse exactly as they pleased. But the lord aforesaid had instituted a suit at law with the view of proving that such right was vested in him and his successors only, and had won his cause. There is, therefore, in the story in the text observance of an historical fact which serves to illustrate the fidelity of the legend in a case where modern invention would infallibly have gone astray.

if not exclusively belonging to Westerdale, were out coursing, but had met with no success, not having found a single hare in the course of their long morning's quest. When thinking of giving up their pursuit as hopeless, they fell in with old Nanny ——, the most "noted witch" in all the country-side. No long time passed before she was made aware by the dis-appointed sportsmen—and some thought she knew it all before —of their failure to find a hare, and much more of getting a course. "Oh," says the wrinkled, hook-nosed, crook-backed old dame, "I can tell you where you will find a hare ligging, and a grand one and all. I'se ho'd ye (I will undertake to you) she'll gi'e ye a grand course. Only, whativver ye deea, minnd ye dinna slip a black dog at her! That wad be a sair matter for ye all." They gave their word to attend to this injunction, and proceeded to the locality the old dame indi-cated. There, sure enough, they found a noble hare, which went away gallantly before the two dogs slipped at her. I ought to mention that the names and abodes of all the party were mentioned to me in detail by my informant; the place at which the interview with the witch took place, the place where she told them to seek the hare and found her, and the line of country taken by the quarry, with the places where the grey-hounds "turned" her, and all the particulars of a most exciting and, to sportsmen, interesting course. In short, the hare led them a chase of several miles over parts of the Westerdale moors, over the Ingleby boundary, circling back by Hob Hole till she had nearly reached the spot where she was originally met with. Here, as luck would have it, a black dog, not belonging to any one of the party, and coming no one knew whence, suddenly joined in the course, and just as the hitherto unapproachable hare made a final effort to get through a smout-hole at the foot of the wall of the garth in which the cot of the reputed witch was situate—and the habitation in question is a habitation still—the black dog, according to the expression used, "threw at her," but succeeded in little more

than tearing out some of the fleck of her haunch, bringing
with it, in one place, a bit of the skin. That was the end
of the course, but not of the story. It continued thus:
The party after a pause, due, as it would seem, in part to
apprehension, and, in the case of one at least, to suspicion,
went to Nanny's door, and, although it was fast, succeeded
eventually in obtaining admission. The apprehensive members of the party, having a wholesome fear of witch-prowess
in general, and of Nanny's in particular—especially in consideration of their live stock—desired to excuse themselves
for the inadvertent violation of her injunction as to the colour
of the dogs which were to be permitted to join in the course.
One of them, however, as just intimated, more suspicious or
better informed than his comrades, wished to satisfy himself
as to the presence and the condition of old Nanny herself.
Finding admission to the dwelling, in the cots of the time,
was finding admission to the sleeping apartment and all. For
there were no chambers upstairs then. There was the living
room, with a sort of boxed-off place or two for sleeping
arrangements, and perhaps a roost for the fowls; but nothing
beyond in the way of more modern refinements. And when
the party entered, there was old Nanny stretched on her bed,
disabled and in pain. "What was wrang wiv 'er? She had
been weel eneugh but a bit afore."—"Eh, she had happened
an accident, and lamed hersen." But the suspicions of the
suspicious one were allowed to prevail, and the old woman's
hurts were overhauled, and it was found she was rent as if
by a dog's teeth on the haunch, exactly where the hare, which
had run through the smout into Nanny's garth, had been seen
to be seized by the unlucky (and unwelcome) black dog.

There was another Nanny, of Danby celebrity, who lived
in a house of precisely the same character as the Westerdale
Nanny's, situate about half a mile to the east of the house
in which this is written. I have no doubt that she was
really an "historical" character, and that the plain English

of many of the stories that have been told me about her is
that she was an object of persecution by the "young bloods"
of the day and district,—young fellows of the farming
persuasion, the sons of freeholders, or possibly freeholders
themselves. But the story I would relate came to me in much
the following form. "Au'd Nanny" used to lie *perdu* in the
evenings in a certain whin-covered bank—a regular gorse
covert in those days, as I was made to understand. Here
these young fellows beat for her as they would for a hare, and
for the same purpose—namely, for sport's sake—and expecting
to find her in her *quasi* form there. When found, she always
"took the same line of country," namely, up the hill from the
side of the basin low down in which her hut was placed, and
then along the slope from the moor-end down towards the
hamlet called Ainthorpe, and so down the steeper part of the
same descent to where a run of water used to cross the road
on its surface, but is now bridged over in a substantial, if not
a showy, manner. Down this steeper descent there was
and is a flagged path or causey—the survival of what had
once been the veritable highroad, or king's highway, up and
towards the eastern part of the parish. Down this causey
it was the witch's custom, when she was thus chivied, to run
at headlong speed, and as she wore clogs, or rough shoes
with wooden soles, fortified at the extremities with iron
tips and heels, the clatter of her footsteps could be heard long
before she arrived near the foot of the slope, and the water,
at which perforce the chase ceased. One evening one of the
customary starters and pursuers had not been present at the
"meet," nor consequently at the "find." However, he was
near the lower part of the causey when the clatter of the
wooden shoes at the highest part warned him that the hunt
was up. His first thought was to stop the quarry in her headlong race for the running water, and see what would happen
when she was headed and forced to turn back, or away from
her refuge. So he set himself firmly right across the causey

aforesaid, with his legs necessarily a little apart, in order to stop the gangway effectually. Onwards came the chase ; the footsteps sounded nearer and nearer, and sharper and sharper. But there was nothing to be seen. Thomas P—— began to be in a fright, rather : it was uncanny to hear what he heard, and as he heard it, and to know that the witch he had so often harried and hunted was the author of it, and yet not be able to see a hair of her. But he had no time for deliberation ; and before he had made up his mind about the best thing to be done, he felt something rush full force between his legs, himself carried on unresistingly for a yard or two, and then hurled over on one side like a sucked orange, hearing a weird sort of chuckling laugh as the being he had expected to baffle reached the point beyond which pursuit was impracticable.

The idea in this case, as also in the story last given, was that of the witch becoming the object of pursuit, and under the form of a hare. In the one case, certainly, she spontaneously offers herself in that capacity, while in the other it hardly seems possible to assume entire willingness on her part ; while, besides, there is a sort of a jumble between the silent pads of the hare [1] and the noisily resonant clatter of the iron-

---

[1] There is also in this story another discrepancy or inconsistency, as collated with the ordinary witch-lore deliverances, and as regards one of their most customary features. What I refer to is the idea that the witch could not cross running water. Every one "kens" Tam O'Shanter's adventure, and the apostrophe to his gallant mare—

> Now, do thy speedy utmost, Meg,
> An' win the key-stane of the brig ;
> There at them thou thy tail may toss,
> A running stream they darena cross ;

and in one of the most graphic of the witch stories known to me as told in this district, the convicted witch remains in acute suffering because she is unable to cross a stream and undo the spell which is torturing her. And yet, in this story of the hunted Nanny, her flight is always directed to the running water at Ainthorpe, once beyond which she was no longer the victim of her persecutors' malice or mischief. But this is nearly the only, if not the one single, striking incongruity of the kind that I have detected.

shod wooden clogs. But it is to be observed that the witch, under the form of a hare, is of perpetual recurrence in all the copious witch-lore of the district : most often, perhaps, as the sufferer, but by no means invariably so. And what is interesting, especially in connection with the Scandinavian repertories of the same kind, there is reference to the witch as taking that form in relation with the abstraction of milk from the cows in the field by night. One story of the kind, in which moreover the witch did not come off second-best, may be worth recording, especially as there was—what was not true of the general run of these stories—a kind of anachronism, as it would seem, introduced into the telling of it. That milk-stealing was a common offence from two to three centuries ago there is no manner of question ; milk-stealing, I mean, from the cows in their pasture. The entries in the Quarter Sessions Records alone would be sufficient to establish that fact. But it may not occur to a modern reader to consider how it was that such a practice became feasible. Our idea is naturally of the cows belonging to any given farmer being all duly milked in the evening, and turned out into the safe pasture to browse and provide another " meal of milk " by the morning. But down to the time when the Enclosure Act was obtained in any particular parish, the cows of the village community all pastured together in one common field (or in one of them, if, as usual, there were more than one within the vill) ; and it is obvious that under such circumstances, when the cows of perhaps thirty to forty owners were all mixed up together, dishonest milking would be much more difficult of detection than under the modern arrangement. And, doubtless, many cases of apparently mysterious failure of milk would be referred to the witch, when the witch and her wicked works were commonly in men's minds, and almost as currently in men's mouths. One thing, however, is quite certain ; and that is that not only was the witch accredited with the abstraction of the milk from the neighbours' cows, but that she was supposed, if not believed, to do the deed by aid or by means of the "witch-hare." In the Scandinavian "trolldom," or witch-lore, over and above other means employed by the witch in this unrighteous process, such as tying a rope to the cross-beam of the barn (or other out-building), and manipulating it (after due employment of the appropriate spells) as one does the paps of the cow in the act of milking, the calling into being and despatching of the witch-hare is constantly referred to or described. A log of wood, a three-legged stool, a bit of hair rope, and the like, might, either or each of them, be utilised, and, once the incantation was spoken, the hare rose up and was ready to be sent on its dairymaid errand. Here, however, in this district, I have never been fortunate enough to come on any scrap of tradition, or any feature in a story, leading on to the identification of the means or the mode by or in which the hare was evoked and pressed into the witch's service. But still, the hare was the vehicle by which the neighbour's milk was conveyed from his cow to the witch's dairy, and, among many other stories, I heard the following, in which, as I said, the "witch did not come off second-best." The scene was laid in Commondale, part of which valley lies in this parish and part in the parish of Guisborough. A farmer there was perpetually finding that his cows gave very much less milk to the milker's fingers than they ought; and the loss became so considerable that it was deemed necessary to try and put a stop to the cause of it. There were witches *galore* in the neighbourhood, and their well-known nefarious practices in the way of diverting the flow of milk from the right channel were also only too well known. But how to discover if this were the right explanation of the loss complained of, and, if it were, how to obviate its continuance, were both matters the solution of which was not unattended with difficulty. In the issue it was settled that the best and most feasible plan would be to watch the field in which the cows were turned out to pasture during the night, and to take further

means or measures according to the result of the watching
process. Accordingly the farmer set a trusty hand to keep
the necessary watch. An uneventful night, a second, a third
passed. . The sentinel declared nothing had passed into the
field, the cows had never been approached by a soul, and least
of all by crone or maid with pail and stool complete. And
yet the morning meal of milk was as deficient as ever, there
being nothing in the condition of the cows, or in the circumstances of the pasture, or what not, to account for the vexa-
tious fact. At last one of the neighbours, "mair skeely
'an t' ithers," or perhaps, like the Westerdale yeoman, a little
more suspicious, on cross-examining the watcher, elicited the
fact that it was not quite accurate to say that nothing whatever had gone into the field where the cows were pasturing,
for that each night he had noticed a hare that came in through
a gapway in the dike, and that seemed to be feeding about, and
mostly right in amongst the cows where they were feeding or
standing the closest together. Asked whether the hare
always came from the same side, and entered the field through
the same broken way, he answered, "Ay, for seear (sure),
and wherefore not? Hares allays gaed the seeam gate, as a'
folks kenned." But the said gap happened to be on the side
that was handiest of access to a certain "Au'd Mally," who
had an uncanny reputation, and the "skeely" (or perhaps
suspicious) neighbour suggested that "Au'd Mally might
lik'ly ken whilk weea t' milk gaed." Hereupon followed
another deliberation, the upshot of which was that the farmer
himself should watch the next night, armed, and with his gun
loaded—not with leaden pellets, but—with silver slugs; and
as it was not easy to come by silver slugs in an out-of-the-way
place like Commondale,—and besides that, it was highly
expedient to keep their plans as quiet as possible, which could
not be if they went to a town to buy such ammunition,—it
was resolved to cut up an old silver button or two, and charge
the gun with the pieces. Well, all was duly done according

to programme; the farmer, with his "hand-gun" charged
according to rule, took up his position near the gap aforesaid,
and in such a place that, while he was well concealed himself,
he could have a good sight of the hare as she entered, and
also of the pasturing cows; for he did not want to "ware"
(expend) his costly charge on a mere ordinary long-eared
pussy, but wished to catch "Au'd Mally"—if it were she—
flagrante delicto, and shoot at her in the very act. Midnight
passed and nothing came; but as the small hours drew on
the hare was seen approaching with stealthy step, and sitting
up on her haunches every minute or two to listen for
suspicious sounds, as natural as life. With sheer expectancy
the farmer's heart began to beat much faster than usual, and
the palpitation did not decrease when, just at the verge of
the gap, it stood up again and glowered at the very spot
where he lay concealed. Apparently reassured by the stillness, pussy resumed her leisurely advance, and entered the
enclosure; but instead of approaching the feeding cows, she
came deliberately on with direct course to the farmer's ambush,
her eyes getting bigger and bigger with each lope she took,
until almost upon the startled watcher, when she reared herself up, growing taller and taller, and "wiv her een glooring
and widening while they war as big as saucers," and with
their glare directed full upon the terrified skulker the form
stalked straight up to him! With a scream of utter, horrified
terror, he sprang from his hiding-place, flung his gun far from
him, and rushed headlong away, "rinning what he could," and
never halting even to draw breath until he had got himself
safely within his own door, and doubly locked and bolted it.
And so ended that attempt to bring the milk-stealing witch
to book; and certainly hardly either to her complete discomfiture, or even to her complete conviction.

WITCH STORIES AND WITCH ANTIDOTES

OUR last story ended with something very like a somewhat telling *coup* on the part of a grievously suspected witch. But such incidents are decidedly rare. It was very much otherwise with many of the "noted witches" who had the credit of doing so much mischief that remedial measures had to be taken, shooting at them with silver shot or silver slugs seeming to be the only, at least the readiest, means available. Thus, in Glaisdale Head the trees in a young plantation were continually eaten off. If replaced, still the same fate awaited their successors. It was easy to say there was nothing new in having young sapling trees gnawed completely off by hares and rabbits; or, if of larger size, barked by the latter if not by the former. But there were circumstances in this case which showed—so it was said —that no mere ordinary hare was the cause of the damage complained of. "Hares might have been seen in the nursery (plantation), leastwise, one particular hare, a bit off the common to look at : but common hares did not cut the tops of the young trees off, ommost as gin they had been cut wiv a whittle, and leave 'em liggin' about just as they were cut, as if nobbut for mischeef. Hares was reasonable creatur's eneugh, and i' lang ho'dding-storms, when ivvery thing was deep happed wi' snow, and they could na get a bite ov owght else, they'd sneap t' young trees, and offens dee a canny bit ov ill. But they did not come, storm or nae storm, and just knipe off tweea or three score o' young saplings, any soort o' weather, as if for gam' or mischeef." So the usual consultation was held, and with the issue that watch was to be kept by the owner concerned, with a gun loaded with silver shot—which, by the way, was procured as in the last case—and the moment he saw the suspicious hare beginning its nefarious practices, he was to take steady aim and shoot. The watch was set, and at the "witching hour of night" of course, the hare put in an appearance—"a great, foul au'd ram-cat ov a heear t' leuk at—and began knepping here and knepping there as if 't wur stoodying how best t' deea maist ill i' lahtlest tahm. Sae t' chap at wur watching, he oop wi's gun, and aiming steady he lat drive (discharged his gun). My wo'd! but there was a flaysome skrike! An' t' heear, sair ho't (badly wounded), gat hersel' a soort o' croppen out o' t' no'ssery, and ho'ppled (hirpled, limped, hobbled) away as weel 's she could, an' won heeam at last at Au'd Maggie's house-end, in a bit o' scroggs at grows on t' bank theear." Inquiries, however, were made next day, not among the brushwood on the bank (steep slope or hillside), but at the cottage of the old woman called "Au'd Maggie"; and unluckily for her reputation, already more than sufficiently shaky in the witch connection, she was found in her bed "sair ho't in many spots," she said with splinters of a broken bottle she had fallen down upon; but her visitors thought "mair lik'ly wi' shot-coorns o' some soort."

Another story, essentially of the same character, but varying in some of the details, runs as follows: A farmer in Farndale was terribly unlucky with his live stock. "Stirk and heifer, yearlings and two-year-au'ds, he had lossen yan efter anither, and naebody kenned what ailed 'em; and now at last t' cauves wur gannan' too. And it had coomed to be notished that, whenivver a lahtle black bitch wur seen i' t' grip o' t' cow-'us, or i' t' cauf-pen, then, for seear, yan iv 'em took bad and dee'd." So the customary consultation ensued, and the accustomed advice was sought, and the prescription was: "Charge your gun with silver shot, watch for the black bitch —but be sure you don't shoot your neighbour's black cur-dog (collie)—and when it gets out of your garth, let drive." All was arranged accordingly. The black "female dog" came in due time; it was noted that it was black all over, off forefoot and all—the neighbour's cur-dog had that foot white; it was in the grip (the groove or channel in the floor behind the cow-stalls), but it could not win into the calves' pen; and as it was leaving the farmstead garth the fatal shot was fired, followed by the "skrike" as aforesaid; the domiciliary visit, not of condolence but of detection, was paid next day, and the suffering witch found groaning in bed, with a terrible series of shot-wounds in the hinder part of her person.

There were other modes, besides those recorded in these stories, of bringing an offending witch to book; as there were divers offences and shades of offence alleged against the offender; but the majority of the tales did not record such eventual proof of the justice of the suspicion, or overwhelming testimony that the punishment had fallen on the actual transgressor. Indeed, in a very considerable class of stories the punishment inflicted on the particular witch proceeded against was rather left to inference than specified, or even indicated. Nay, there were even cases in which modes of permanent or sustained annoyance or mortification of the witch were resorted to; measures calculated and intended to defeat or frustrate her malice, and to nullify her power. Thus, I have before me now a spell or charm the object of which was to hamper and hinder the witch in her attempts (possible or anticipated) to injure the stock of the person employing it. And this said charm or spell was in process of application much within the period of my personal residence here and acquaintance with the said person. He was the largest farmer in the parish, a right good sort, and a fair specimen of the old untutored, unschooled Yorkshire yeoman, with a large amount of natural shrewdness at the bottom, and with any amount of credulity in some directions, and obstinate incredulity in others, mainly on the side where reason and knowledge lay. He could neither read nor write —by no means an unknown thing among the Dales farmers of fifty years ago; but he was as honest as the day—in horse-dealing even. Perhaps I need hardly say he had a lively sense of the actuality of the witch, of her power, of her malice, and not least, of the ascertained direction of it against himself and his belongings. He never assigned any reason he had for supposing himself a special object for the malevolence of the uncanny old crone. But why, or how, could he doubt it? Were not his beasts continually affected with the red-water, when his neighbours' were not? Was there ever a year when he did not lose a yearling or two, or may be more, with some mysterious languishing illness? Were not his calves afflicted above other men's calves, so that he scarcely ever was able to rear more than a part of them? Of course, to one like him, this reasoning was irrefutable, and he "went the entire animal" in his appreciation of what the witch—whether it were one or several—could and did do day by day continually. Prejudiced people might say that bad management, insufficient food and shelter, pasturage on sour undrained lands, with an alternation of scraping for bare subsistence on dry, parched, shaly banks, might have something to do with the unluck of his stock generally; but my old friend Jonathan knew a vast better than that. "There was more than one witch in the Head (Fryup Head), and there was more than him as kenned it." Well, among other ways and means, Jonathan employed a standing charm; and when he died it was found in (as was to be presumed) full operation, in his standing-desk or bureau, with a white-handled penknife, half open, laid in front of it. It consisted of a half-sheet of letter-paper, folded in the fashion of those days when as yet the envelope was undiscovered, and sealed with three black seals, inserted between each two of which was a hackle from a red cock's neck. This, when opened, was found to have a pentacle, inscribed within a circle, drawn on it. It is somewhat difficult to make out which is top and which is bottom. But from such indications as there are, I assume that the point from which the passage from the Psalms, which surrounds the circle just named, begins to read is the bottom. The said extract is, "In Him shall be the strength of thy hand. He shall keep thee in six troubles, yea, even in seven shall no harm come to thee,"—the "thee" being interlined over the word "come." In the central hexagonal space formed by the mutual intersection of the three triangles which form the figure, is what is meant for a short sentence of three words in the Hebrew character, but is really a mere rough imitation, such as might be made by an ignorant impostor, who knew the general characteristics of the Hebrew as printed. There are then six triangular spaces formed by the cutting off of the apices of the composing triangles by the intersecting sides of the same; and beginning with the lowest—as we are regarding the diagram—and proceeding to the right, round the circle, in the first (or lowest) is the word "Agla"; in the next, the letters or the word "El"; in the third, "On"; in the fourth, and upside down, as we are regarding it, the word "Nalgah," with a cross above it; in the fifth, "Adonai"; and in the sixth, "Sadai." Besides these triangular spaces, there are six other spaces formed by the segments of the containing circle cut off between the several apices of the constituent triangles and the sides of the small vertical triangles, already noted. Taking as the first of these that on the left of the triangular space numbered as the first, just above, the words inscribed are, "Caro verbum factum est;" and proceeding in the same order as before, in the second the inscription is, "Jesu Christi Nazarenus Rex Judæorum;" in the third, the word "Permumaiton"; in the fourth, "Amati schema"; in the fifth, "Sadai"; and in the sixth, "Adonai." Turning the charm the other way up, nearly underneath the cross above named, as it now stands, begins the sentence, "Ye are everlasting power of God theos;" and then, at the bottom of all, in a straight line, the words "Hoc in vince," all run together, as was the case also in the sentence previously noticed. This last, doubtless, refers directly to the sign of the cross made immediately above in the small triangle containing the word "Nalgah."

Surely a formidable-looking weapon of defence is here, and, as it is reasonable to suppose, one likely to occasion Jonathan's unfriends among the uncanny crew of witches more than a mere occasional miscarriage of some of their nefarious, however craftily laid, schemes and intentions.

But there were other and less elaborate, and beyond question less costly, means available for frustrating, or at least in some measure enervating, the witch's maleficent energy. I say "less costly," because a spell like the one just described involved a visit to the nearest, or possibly the most renowned, "wise man" (of whom more at a future page) in the district; and he, like the doctor and the lawyer, and other learned professors, naturally expected and took care to secure his *honorarium, quid pro quo,* or fee. But of these simpler and more inexpensive safeguards more in the following section.

THE WITCH AND WITCH ANTIDOTES (*continued*)

ONE of the simpler and more inexpensive resources adverted to at the close of the last section, and which, in point of fact, has been already mentioned at a former page, is the use of the "witch-wood," that is, of portions of the rowan or mountain-ash tree, duly obtained and selected ; for, as I think, all was not "witch-wood" that was of the rowan-tree. The "witch-wood," to be effectual, was not to be lightly or unconsideringly come by. It must be cut in due season, and in due season only ; and not only that, but it must be cut in due place, and with due observances. But by way of illustration, it may be best to introduce here a little story told me by one of my parishioners of the days that are gone, and to whose normal unwillingness to talk to me on such matters reference has been made at a previous page. The story was on this wise : He was out and about his farm one day, several of the fields belonging to which lay far up towards the Head of the dale, where the surroundings, however rugged and picturesque, were quite sufficiently lonely. Rarely indeed, when I have been—as I have been scores of times, whether with my gun or with only my walking-stick for my companion—in that part of my parish, have I ever seen a human being in these wild solitudes, except attracted by the sound of my gun, or perchance in quest of some stray sheep. Naturally, then, my old friend was a little surprised, not to say startled, at seeing one day a woman he

H

knew, and knew as somewhat quaint in some of her ways, coming by an unfrequented route into the loneliest part of this lonely wilderness; and not only that, but casting anxious and inquiring looks all about her, as if wishing to be assured she was neither followed nor under observation. She was carrying some bright object in her hand, which, as well as he could see from the distance at which he stood, might be a "gully," or large domestic knife. His first thought, he told me, on recognising the female in question, and connecting her queer suspicious ways with the fact of her being in such a peculiarly lonely and, for her, strangely out-of-the-way place, was that she might be meditating making away with herself. A little consideration seemed to be sufficient to dispel that notion, and after watching her with some little wonderment for a few minutes, he went about his business. A little later in the day he met her full face, and apparently bending her steps towards her own home. But the way she was pursuing involved a considerable circuit, as leading from the place at which he had last seen her, and particularly as connected with the route by which she had entered on the scene when he had first noticed her. "Hie, Hannah," he said to her, "what mak'st t' here?"—"Wheea," says she, "Ah's just gannan' yam (home) t' gainest (nearest) way Ah can." And then he told her he thought it was a strange sort of "gainest way home" for her to be taking, considering where he had seen her an hour or so before, and the way he had seen her arrive there by. And then he went on to tell her how her goings on had perplexed him, and how for a minute or two he had thought perhaps he ought to follow her, and prevent her doing herself a mischief. The poor woman seemed a little taken aback by the discovery that she had been thus under observation, when she had fondly imagined that all her doings were unseen, at least unnoted by any mortal eye; but presently, recovering herself, she uttered the explanatory sentence, "Wheea, I was nobbut lating my witch-wood" (only seeking my wood-charm against witches). Well, but why go all the way into the Head, and that far into the Head, moreover? In reply to this, and a series of other questions, the old woman gave the following mass of information: To be effectual, the requisite pieces of rowan-tree,—for many were wanted: one for the upper sill of the house-door, one for the corresponding position as to stable, cow-byre, and the other domiciles of the various stock, one for personal use, one for the head of her bed, one for the house-place, etc. etc.,—must not only be cut on St. Helen's day, but, in order to be quite fully efficacious, they must be cut with a household knife: they must be cut, moreover, from a tree which not only the cutter had never seen before, but of the very existence of which he must have had no previous knowledge or suspicion; and that, on the tree having been found in this blindfold sort of way, and the requisite bough or boughs having been severed and secured, they must be carried home by any way save that by which the obtainer of them had gone forth on his quest. And so, as she had known all the rowan-trees in the nearer neighbourhood of her cottage for years, she had been obliged to go farther afield, and all her proceedings had been regulated according to these various conditions.

Whether these conditions were always and punctiliously observed by the devout believers in the power of the witch and in the prophylactic efficacy of the witch-wood, I am not able from positive knowledge or information to affirm; but I am quite well aware that the consumption of the article in question was by no means small, and that, too, even within the period of my personal acquaintance with the district.

But there were other means of anticipating or obviating such harm and loss, and not a few, besides these already mentioned. Thus, I knew an old lady, a dear, canny old body she was, who, before she proceeded to churn, invariably took forcible measures to expel the witch, or any witch-emissary, who might, in the malice of her intention, have lodged herself

in the churn. And this she did by proceeding to throw one
pinch of salt into the fire and another into the churn, re-
peating the alternate sprinkling until the mystic number of
nine times for each had been completed. Another and not in-
effectual method on the like occasion was—in order, I suppose,
to make the place too hot to hold the witch—to take the
kitchen poker, heated to an unmistakable red heat, and,
inserting it at the opening or bung-hole, to turn it slowly
round, sweeping as wide a space as possible within the said
utensil, nine several times. Witch-wood too had its allotted
station in the dairy, and in connection with the various
dairy vessels.

So that, on the whole, the witches must have had a hard
time of it to get in, and it would almost seem, having somehow
or other got in, a harder time still to maintain the position
they had won. But, on conning over the old woman's recipe
for the gathering of effectually serviceable witch-wood, we see
there was a good deal to think of, and a good deal to be very
punctilious over, and that a lapse in any one of the particulars
named might easily be fatal to the virtue of the whole season's
stock of the article in question. I remember when I was a
schoolboy in Essex, with youthful ambitions stirring within
me, how the being able to do some day what the old statute
terms "shooting in a gun loaded with powder and hail-shot,"
with the said "tormentum" or "hand-gunne" pressed to my
own individual shoulder, seemed a consummation most devoutly
to be wished for. What a jolly life I used to think the
little village boys who were set to "keep the crows" in that
then wheat-growing county of Essex must lead. No tiresome
school, dame or boarding, no multiplication table, or, worse
still, pence-table, to learn, no work of any kind—for bird-
nesting and cutting the bark off long switches in alternate
rings clearly was not work—but just to halloa *ad libitum* from
time to time when the crows might be coming, or the master
or the foreman be within hearing—and what boy does not

like kicking up a hullabaloo of that kind when it suits him?—
but over and above all the rest, and over and above with a
towering pre-eminence, the privilege and the opportunity to
fire the real gun, and then to recharge it one's own glorified
self! Certainly, creeping round those huge thirty- or forty-
acre fields, and duly peeping into every fork in the old thick
hedge, and scrutinising every moss-covered stub, and every
half-hidden but suggestive hollow in the bank, all took time,
and when you were doing your "work" of this kind on one
side of the wide field, the crows might perchance find their
way in at the other, and pick up a few stray grains of the
scattered seed-corn. Again, sitting down and ringing those
bonny long straight sticks required a good deal of attention
and care, and even measurement, and when one was intent on
such rightful occupation, of course a cunning, cautious, keen-
eyed crow might seize the chance afforded by such pre-
occupation. Besides, a boy, even a brazen-throated one,
cannot always be halloaing, especially on market-days or
sales-days, when both master and looker are safe to be away,
"minding their business" there. Lastly, too, the gunpowder
is dealt out in such graduated doses, like physic that is not
bad to take, that you cannot in the nature of things keep up
an all-day-long fusillade, and so, some way or other, the
crows that our small friends in rough boots which smell of
stale oil, and ragged jackets that tell of past rather than future
wear, are set "to keep," find as many loopholes as a rabbit in
the fence enclosing its natural covert, or as the proverbial
coach-and-six in the proverbial Act of Parliament.

And just so, I think, it must have been with the sadly
peccant witch of the days not so very long gone. At least
this is quite certain, that, from time to time, not only our old
friend Jonathan's young stock and so forth "went wrong,"
and, of course, by reason of the malice and the uncanny might
of the witch, but many and many another besides him were
sufferers too. But were they to continue sufferers, tame,

unresisting, uncomplaining, resourceless, almost acquiescent sufferers? Were they not to stir hand or foot in self-defence, in defence of their hapless, witch-abused calves and yearlings and beasts and milking-cows? Could not they in any way oust the witch after she had gotten possession,—at all events, carry the war into her quarters, and make her feel and understand that the motto which accompanies the heraldic thistle may be the practical motto still of the North Yorkshire owner of "neat stock, sheep, and pigs"? The thought was one not to be entertained for a moment by a canny, considering, and devoutly believing farmer of three-quarters of a century ago. If the witch had got in in spite of all his forethought and precaution, what was to hinder her being driven out? Nay, what was to hinder her being made to feel, and sensibly too, that if she had the power, and used the power, to make the farmer suffer through the suffering of his stock, even if not in his own person, still there were means available, by the application of which all her malicious intentions, all her mischievous plottings and workings, might be made of none effect, and she herself be reduced to the condition of being the personal sufferer, in place of the unlucky stock belonging to the object of her envy, hatred, or malice?

These means, or some of them, may well become the subject-matter of the succeeding section.

THE WISE MAN

" Ay, the witch might have—there's not yan that kens, but kens that she *had*—a vast o' power; but the Wise Man he had a vast mair; he was mair 'an a maister over sike as her."

And great was the resort by our old friend Jonathan, and many and many another of his day and school, to the said Wise Man on the occurrence of troubles of the class and kind indicated. And, as became a wise man, many and various were the resources at his command; but, being a wise man, he did not take everything for granted, even when related with a strange quaint fulness of detail, enforced by a heap of stranger imaginations and more marvellous amplifications of suspicions as to person and motive. " Ay, maybe your beasts are 'witched.' What you tell me looks like it. And Au'd Betty may be at the bottom of it. She's a noted witch— we all ken that. And as like as not she has a bit of a grudge against you. Nay, even if it bean't as bad as that, still some folks can't keep themselves quiet, even if they'd like. They mun be doing, or him that gies them the power might not be weel suited. Still, ye ken, we mun be canny, and ken what we're efter. I mak' no doubt that somebody has 'witched' your stock, and maybe 'wished you' (invoked some evil thing upon you) as well. But that is what we have got to find out. And if we mak' sure o' that, why then we'll see who's done it." Some discourse of this kind, there is no doubt, passed between the Wise Man and the seeker unto him. And one

not uncommon recipe furnished by him—for a consideration
always; that goes without saying—was as follows, due instruc-
tions as to time and mode of provision of the requisites named
being first of all given: "Take nine bottry (boretree, common
elder) knots, and put them on a clean platter all close together,
but without too much care about arranging them in regular
order; only let them be all in a bunch. Then cover them—
exactly at midnight is the right time—cover them with a clean
cloth, set the whole on a table near the window, and take
tent that no one goes nigh-hand them while (until) the morning. And if, when you take the cloth off in the morning, you
find them all squandered (scattered in confusion) about the
platter, well, it's a safe thing that your stock is really witched."
Then, in some cases, especially if the symptoms were not very
urgent, came a further inquiry as to the identity of the wrong-
doing hag, who was the active cause of the trouble in hand.
But in cases of emergency, where the stock was grievously
afflicted, and perhaps death was already busy among them,
more summary measures were resorted to, and without delay.
One course, of which I heard from more informants than one,
and which I had unquestionable reasons for being assured had
been put in practice, twice if not three times, by the Jonathan
mentioned above during his occupation of the farm he held in
this parish, was much if not exactly as follows: He took the
heart of one of the animals which had died under the male-
volent witch's maleficent practices, and having provided
himself with all the various requisites, proceeded to stick it
carefully with nine new pins, nine new needles, and nine new
nails. Then a fire was to be made as the "holl time of the night"
(the depth of the night) drew on, yet not with ordinary or
any haphazard kind of fuel; but with bottree wood—in one
or two of the stories rowan-tree wood, or even ash-wood, was
specified—and such wood only was to be used. And the fire
was to be kindled and kept up so that there might be the
hottest possible bed of bright, clear-burning embers exactly

at midnight. But before lighting the fire all the doors and windows of the house were to be made fast, very safely fast; and besides, the utmost care had to be taken to darken the windows, and even cover the cracks in the door (if there were any), so that no ray of light should by any possibility be seen from the outside, and no curious eye from without be able to penetrate to the mysteries within. And on no account, whatever happened, whatever noise or disturbance occurred without, was any one to look out or do anything to interfere with the precautionary barriers against external observation or interference. All this duly attended to, the prepared heart was to be placed on the glowing bed prepared for it at just such time that it might be dried to a coal and ready to take fire, and blaze away and fall into ashes, at the very hour of midnight; at which precise moment two verses of a certain psalm were to be read aloud by the principal operator. On one occasion when this uncanny ceremonial was carried out to the very letter, the concomitant circumstances outside, according to the statement of the narrator, were more than sufficiently startling; and he told me with all the apparent simplicity and sincerity of a person who believed it all himself, and had no sort of doubt he was telling an "ower true tale." He described the house and its situation to me, with all the circumstances of local feature and character. It was a house with a door in the front, there being the parlour on one side and the "house" or living room on the other, into which, moreover, the door opened. Between it and a roadway which ran past it lay a bit of garden-ground separated from the roadway by railings, through which a wicket-gate gave admission to a flagged pathway leading directly to the door just now mentioned. As the witching hour drew on, cries and moans as of one in pain were heard outside. As the heart began to shrivel and blacken, these increased in intensity. As it began to blaze, and the reader commenced the reading prescribed, steps as of a person shod with the wooden clogs of the district, iron-tipped and iron-heeled, clattered loudly down the flags,—a loud lumbering noise was heard as of heavy wheelbarrows driven hastily over a pavement of cobble-stones, unearthly efforts such as might have been made by some boneless and yielding body, against the barred and darkened doors and windows, and then, just as the heart blazed up with a final leap of flame and collapsed into darkening ashes, a prolonged wail, like that of one in bitter agony, and after that only still silence.

In another case, all the details of which were given me with even minute exactness, embracing the names and residences of witch and victim, the mischiefs enacted, the mode of conviction employed, the scene of the final ordeal— all appertaining to the neighbouring parish of Westerdale— the new pins, new nails, new needles, nine of each again, were to be put into a clean bottle, which was then to be very securely corked, so that by no ordinary means could the cork be extracted; and then it was to be buried in a hole dug for the purpose with much secrecy, and not without due observance and ceremony, and, besides that, on the other side of a small stream which ran along the foot of the steep bank on the side of which the spell-detected witch's rudely and anciently fashioned hut-cottage stood; and buried, moreover, with the neck and cork downwards, the filling in of the hole being very carefully done, and all made as like an undisturbed bit of ground as could be. The witch—no other, in fact, than the old carline who had changed her shape into that of a hare, as detailed in a former narrative—soon began to feel the effects of the spell laid upon her, then began to be sorely uneasy, tried all her arts, all her power, to reverse it or make it of none effect; but all in vain. Indeed, she ascertained what the spell was, and where in its sensible potency it was acting; but though she was able actually to move the bottle in its mysterious hiding-place, she could not reverse it, or tamper with the security of the cork, or in the least degree impair the efficacy of the charm. At last, in the extremity of her suffering, which was becoming more than she could bear, she wandered down to the place where the bottle was hid, regardless of the implied confession, at least disclosure, of her guiltiness, with the intent of doing by manual agency what she found herself unable to do by aid of witchcraft—namely, tear the bottle out of its hole. And then came in the power of the running water, and the superior craft of the Wise Man, who had been duly consulted, and under whose direction every one of the preceding steps had been taken. She could not cross the running stream! There, within arm's reach of the active instrument of her pitiful misery, she was remediless and help-less altogether. Just then, as previously instructed by the doughty discoverer of witches, the sufferer under her malice and unhallowed practices enters on the scene. A short colloquy ensues, the issue of which is that the witch, in the extremity of personal suffering, surrenders unconditionally, reverses her evil spells, and promises to undo all the mischief then in pro-gress, and never to injure him and his again. The victim of her spells then proceeds to take up the bottle out of the hole, and finds it, of course through the potency of the spells the unlucky witch had exercised in her desperate efforts to medicine her pains, almost drawn up to the surface of the ground, and thinks to himself he has had but a narrow escape after all. The sequel of the story is that he breaks the bottle, and so dissolves the charm, and the poor suffering, baffled hag obtains relief and escapes with her life, which had come in sore danger through what the Wise Man had laid upon her.

THE WISE MAN (*continued*)

I DO not know how it may be with others, but to me, when thinking over such legends and narratives as those above given, it appears that the conception of the Wise Man is not only extraordinary, but also exceptional and anomalous—himself a wizard, and the chief of witches, and yet the foe of witches, the counter-plotter and confounder of the whole malignant crew. That the conception is a very old one, as old, or nearly as old, as that of the witch herself, it is hardly necessary to remind ourselves. But there are other matters in the conception which call for a measure of attention. The witch was supposed to derive her power more or less directly from the evil spirit himself. The Wise Man, however, was scarcely credited with commerce with "T' au'd un," either personally or indirectly. The witch again was credited with malignity more or less pronounced. Not so the Wise Man, but rather the reverse. The one went about not exactly like a roaring lion seeking his prey, but still seeking victims, some to maltreat, injure, and destroy; others of whom an evil-gotten gain might accrue. The other stayed at home to be consulted, and always ready for a consideration to do the good he was asked to do. And yet this jelly-fish sort of beneficence and benevolence was scarcely assumed by the devotees, or even too forcibly declared by the Wise Man himself, to be altogether celestial in its origin, any more than it was purely unselfish in its application and utility. I look upon the conception of the Wise Man as a survival, and a survival only—that is to say, as I found it still extant here some forty odd years ago. And, like other survivals, it had both lost and gained in divers particulars. The conception in reality would seem to be a compound arising out of a confusion of the characters and credentials of three or four original creations of the imagination, aided by overtrow and superstition. In other words, I think the Wise Man part wizard or witch, part sorcerer, magician, or enchanter, and part "conjurer" in the true and full sense of the word. But I think there was more of the conjurer, and of the sorcerer and enchanter, in him than of the wizard or witch. And if any one tries, he will find it harder than perhaps he anticipated to keep these characters and their special attributes apart in the character under notice. Perhaps some illustration of this position may be obtained by collation of the two following quotations from Brand. Grose says, "A sorcerer or magician differs from a witch in this: a witch derives all her power from a compact with the Devil; a sorcerer commands him and the infernal spirits by his skill in powerful charms and invocations; and also soothes and entices them by fumigations." The difference between a conjurer, a witch, and an enchanter, according to Minshew, on the other hand, is as follows: "The conjurer seemeth by praiers and invocations of God's powerful names to compell the Divell to saie or doe what he commandeth him. The witch dealeth rather by a friendly and voluntarie conference or agreement between him (or her) and the Divell or familiar, to have his (or her) turn served, in lieu or stead of blood or other gift offered unto him, especially of his (or her) soule. And both these differ from inchanters or sorcerers, because the former two have personall conference with the Divell, and the other meddles not with medicines and ceremonial forms of words called charmes, without apparition." The confusion is manifest. The character and some of the attributes of the witch are fairly distinct and clear, however vague and blurred, as well as imperfectly delineated, the general character may be. But can anything like that be said as to the ideas or conceptions of the conjurer and the sorcerer? And surely the fundamental idea in the word conjurer—one whose tools or implements, material instruments of operation, are invocations, exorcisms, spells or forms of words instinct with power—is totally different from that involved in the word magician or enchanter; one, that is, who works by the exercise of occult arts, magic arts, the black art, or whatever other name may be, or may have been, applied to his supposed supernatural enginery.

But I am in danger of being led away from the Cleveland conception of the Wise Man of less than a hundred years ago. I have heard much of him, and, as I suppose, the ideal of him is preserved in the hundred and one stories told of "Au'd Wreeghtson, t' Wahse man o' Stowsley." And in all the stories I have heard of him, and whoever chanced to be the narrator, I never once heard him spoken of as a man of mischief, or as an evil-liver, or as extortionate, or as a man who had, it was likely or possible, made a compact with the devil; or even as one with whom the less people had to do the better. No doubt, by some he was spoken of with a kind of involuntary or unconscious awe; and by all he was evidently credited with the possession of extraordinary insight, knowledge, and power.

More than one or two of the most remarkable and the most graphic of the stories I used to listen to came from one who had himself visited the Wise Man of Stokesley. He was the man to whom pointed reference was made at an earlier page (p. 58), a good, sensible, simple-minded old man, who had up to quite recently held an office of trust and much responsibility, when I obtained from him the details about to be given. And I would observe that the terms employed by him in speaking of Wrightson were simply terms of respect, not unmingled with a sort of wondering awe. And certainly nothing that I heard either from him or any other of my informants was such as to prepare me to read such a notice of him as that which is conceived in the following terms. The narrator, it should be said, is described as a Yorkshire gentleman, and the date given is 1819. "Impostors who feed and live on the superstitions of the lower orders are still to be found in Yorkshire. These are called Wise Men, and are believed to possess the most extraordinary power in remedying all diseases incidental to the brute creation, as well as the human race; to discover lost or stolen property, and to foretell future events. One of these wretches was a few years ago living at Stokesley in the North Riding of Yorkshire; his name was John Wrightson, and he called himself the seventh son of a seventh son, and professed ostensibly the calling of a cow-doctor ('cow-leech,' it should have been). To this fellow people whose education, it might have been expected, would have raised them above such weakness, flocked; many came to ascertain the thief, when they had lost any property; others for him to cure themselves or their cattle of some indescribable complaint. Another class visited him to know their future fortunes; and some to get him to save them from being balloted into the militia,—all of which he professed himself able to accomplish. All the diseases which he was sought to remedy he invariably imputed to witchcraft, and although he gave drugs which have been known to do good, yet he always enjoined some incantation to be observed, without which he declared they could never be cured. This was sometimes an act of the most wanton barbarity,[1] as that of

[1] In all my many inquiries and all my continued listenings I never heard one single syllable leading me to suppose, or even to suspect, anything of this kind. Had the charge been true, I must have heard of it— at least have met with some trace or evidence, however slight. But I never did, and I entirely doubt the accuracy of "this deponent"; and not in respect of this particular statement only. Both the next succeeding allegations require much more to prove that they are true than the fact that they are thus made.

roasting a game-cock alive, etc. The charges of this man were always extravagant; and such was the confidence in his skill and knowledge, that he had only to name any person as a witch, and the public indignation was sure to be directed against the poor unoffending creature for the remainder of her life" (Brand's *Popular Antiquities,* vol. iii. p. 34).

My own view of this statement is that much of it is exaggeration, and no small proportion of it gratuitous misrepresentation. My old friend John Unthank did not speak of Wrightson in such a way as this; and the story of the extravagant fees is, on the face of it, absurd. He did not do what he was asked to do for nothing, undoubtedly; but anybody who knows the country and the people, and their means, and the saving, thrifty [1] life they lead, knows that the payments actually made to professional men, parsons, lawyers, and doctors, even down to the middle of the present

---

[1] Perhaps I might as well mention an anecdote in illustration of this point here as defer it to a future page. On occasion of the first show of live stock held under the auspices of the Danby Agricultural Association, two among the elders of the people, each much respected both in the parish and out of it, were among the after-dinner speakers. Both delivered themselves sensibly and well, and both with more than a mere touch of native humour. One of them, by name William Hartas, was an old Quaker, whose judgment, experience, and probity were equally well known, and caused him frequently to be appealed to as arbiter in cases of dispute or valuation. Among other things pithily and tersely—albeit a little quaintly—said, he addressed some remarks to the subject of, as he conceived, the apparent declension of habits of thriftiness and careful, not to say rigid, economy. He said, and I wish I could give it in his own inimitable Yorkshire, "I aim (think, assume, believe) folks are not so saving and careful as they used to be. You must look to it. Farmers' daughters are not content with good calico, but want something smarter for their dresses; and dressing and dairying won't go together, no ways you can frame it. And the young chaps, why, they're almost as bad as the lasses; they want cloth trowsers and smart waistcoats. Why, when I was a lad there was a vast still sitting in their fathers' leather breeches, and more than one I kenned had breeks their grandfathers had had for their best, and there was a vast o' good wear in 'em yet. Mak' things last what they will, is my advice to this meeting; and old-fashioned homespun and good leather breeks is baith very lasty."

century (and in some cases even still), are such as to laugh
that part of the statement to scorn. I have known men personally whose clerical stipends had not exceeded £40 a year
at the earlier date alleged, and the medical and legal fees
were in strict accordance therewith. But, quite apart from all
this, the impression I was unconsciously led on to receive of
Wrightson was—setting aside the inevitable circumstance
that, like all others of his class, he was, up to a given degree,
a charlatan and an impostor—that of a man of a not unkindly
nature, with a pungent flavour of rough humour about him,
shrewd and observant, and with wonderfully well-devised
and well-employed means of information at his command.
I say "a charlatan and an impostor up to a certain degree";
but by no means an impostor *pur et simple*. A grudging
admission that he "gave drugs which have been known
to do good" is made in the extract given above. By the
light of what I think I may say I know, I should read that
thus: he possessed, in common with many others then and
since, wide and deep acquaintance with herbs and simples,
and he used his knowledge with skill and judgment. No
doubt also he knew the properties and uses of what we more
usually speak of as "drugs," and employed them accordingly.
No doubt either that he possessed the power of influencing
men's minds and imaginations, and knew it right well, and
used it of set purpose and intention; and heightened it, moreover, by the mystic means he had at his command, and knew
how to render serviceable on occasion and with sufficient
impressiveness. But, grant these particulars frankly, it must
yet be admitted that he had much and effectual machinery
available, other than what is implied when we style a
man a "rank impostor." The unjust steward's lord "com-
mended" him for the sharpness or cleverness of his trick,
detected though it was. I am sure that the attitude of my
mind when I had heard what Unthank had to tell me about
his own personal intercourse with Wrightson (after I had

I

heard so much about him and his doings from others) was
something of the same sort as that with which the lord of
the steward is accredited in the parable. I said to myself,
This Wise Man must have been, no doubt, part knave; but
all the same one of the cleverest, not to say ablest, fellows
of his craft.[1] He must have known the district as if it
were a map, and the people in it as the master knows his
scholars. He must have had channels of information such
that he could depend upon what they supplied him with, and
yet such as not to be known, or even suspected. That some
of these sources or origins of information were local, I have
no doubt at all; that some of them were simply personal I
have as little; and that some of them depended on confederates
I regarded as established. But his confederates were they of
his own household : namely, as described to me, an elderly
housekeeper-servant and an odd man about the house. I
have been told too that an ostler at one of the inns at Stokesley
was an ally. And there was a code of signals whereby much
general information about a visitor and the cause of his
application might be and was given to the master, without
any personal passages between himself and his dependants.
But all this will possibly be better illustrated after producing
one or more of the stories to which reference has been made
at an earlier page.

One of the most telling of these narratives, and possibly
the most illustrative of them all, was that told me by old
John Unthank. At the time of the occurrence of the
incident he was living with his uncle, who held the post
of gamekeeper to the then Viscount Downe, and lived at
what was then called Dawnay, but now Danby, Lodge.
The uncle held some pasture land of his lordship, and
kept sundry cows and other stock. Among these was a

[1] Except Dawson, mentioned in the popular talk as Wrightson's
nephew as well as successor, I have heard of no other local wise man *by
name*. That there had been many another before him goes without saying.
But he was as the sun among stars.

beast (a stot or bullock) grievously afflicted with some mysterious disorder—an "indescribable complaint," as the above extract phrases it. The symptoms were altogether unusual, the sufferings of the poor brute seemed to be very great, and no local cow-leech was able to make anything of the case, or hold out any prospect of cure. So the uncle decided to apply to the Wise Man, and sent his nephew to Stokesley, a ride of about eleven miles over a rough, wild, lonely road, the greater part of it. Unthank went as directed, and on reaching Stokesley proceeded first to stable his nag at one of the "publics" there, and this done repaired to the Wise Man's abode. After some little delay he was admitted. The Wise Man was seated in his consulting room, dressed in some sort of long robe or gown, girded round him with a noticeable girdle, and with a strange-looking head-covering on. There were some of the accustomed paraphernalia of the character assumed and its pretensions—a skull, a globe, some mysterious-looking preparations, dried herbs, etc. etc. Unthank, who was then quite a young man, and to whom a journey to Stokesley formed an epoch in life, and who knew but little indeed of what went on in the world outside the lonely, half-inaccessible dale which was his home-place, was naturally impressed alike by the strange garb and the strange objects, and by his preconceived ideas of the personage he beheld. Before he had time, or perhaps presence of mind, to open the cause of his coming and explain what he wanted, Wrightson addressed him with the words, "Well, John, thou's come to ask me about Tommy Frank's black beast, that is carried on in yon strange way." Unthank told me he was taken quite aback by this unexpected greeting, and was too astounded to be ready with a word in reply; and without giving him time to collect his ideas, the Wise Man went on— "Why, it is little use your coming to me for advice, or to ask me for something to mend the beast, if I can't tell you why you've come, and what you want. And maybe you think I

can't do that.   But I'll let you see that I ken more than you
think. What was it the last thing your uncle said to you
before you left to ride to Stokesley ?"   Unthank told me he
stopped a moment to recollect, and before he had recalled the
parting words, Wrightson continued, "Ay, I see you have
forgotten.   But I'll tell you.   The last thing he said to you
was, 'Now, John, you mind and see t' galloway gets her
whoats and eats 'em afore you leaves t' stable.'"   "And, by
gum," said the old man to me, "them was the very words my
uncle said to me as I rode away out of the yard."   Wrightson
then went on to tell his visitor divers particulars touching the
sick animal.   He described the position it occupied in the
cow-byre—the door opened right on to its rump, only a much
coarser word was employed; it made a very peculiar and
unusual noise; it was continually shifting its position; the
spasms or fits of pain came on at such and such times, and
the manifestations were variable, and so forth.   It was all
accurate and true, and Unthank seemed to think he could not
have told the Wise Man about the beast so clearly and descriptively as Wrightson had told him.   The end of the interview
was that Wrightson said he could do nothing that would be
of any good; that the affection under which the beast was
suffering was past his skill; that the poor beast would die;
and that when it was dead, they had better open it—in politer
language, hold a post-mortem examination—and then they
would find some abnormal growth which was the cause of the
illness and pain, and would be, with scarce any delay, the
cause of the death.   Unthank further stated that when the
beast died it was opened accordingly, that the strange growth
inside was found, and, in fact, that everything the Wise Man
had said was verified.

Now, I have no hesitation in admitting that I believed the
story as the old man told it me from point to point.   He told
it with great clearness, and as he went on with it seemed
almost to be living the scene over again.   He grew quite

animated, and told it all with readiness and fluency as if it had been something he had witnessed but a day or two before. And besides believing it to be an essentially true story, I thought I could see the explanation of much which seemed the most striking, and which at the time had, to Unthank himself, seemed the most startling. It was, of course, a piece of Wrightson's business, nay, of his very "wisdom," to keep himself *au courant* of all such extraordinary cases as this. His system of information, well organised, as I have already said I think it must have been, would provide him with early notices of all such matters; and his code of home signals would acquaint him with much that remained to be known. Given that he had a canny old housekeeper and an inquiring man about the house, and an ally at the inn stables, there would be no great difficulty in fishing out of the comparative novice, as Unthank was, such minor matters as the position of the creature in the byre even, and much more the general way in which it was "handled," or "carried on"; and even the parting caution of old Tommy Frank, whose peculiarities, moreover, were well known to less shrewd and observant people than the Wise Man himself, was one which might easily have been forecasted.

Another characteristic story which I had from Unthank, as also an independent counterpart from my other great informant in such matters, was given me with great precision of detail, as well as with the names, families, and abodes of the actors—or rather the acted upon—in the transaction as described. Two men, both belonging to, or at least connected with, this parish, were on their way to Stokesley on some particular occasion,—the "Hirings" there, I think I am right in assuming,—when it occurred to one of them, just as they were going down the bank or steep moor-side, lying above West House—a singularly lonely farm on the road from Castleton to Stokesley, and within a mile or so of Kildale— to propose to the other, as his idea of a joke—"Let's gan and

have a bit o' spoort wiv Au'd Wreeghtson." They were to
go to him as if in earnest, with some imaginary case, I forget
what, even if it were mentioned in the narrative; but his
wisdom was to be tested by asking his advice about a matter
which existed in imagination rather than in reality. In due
time they reached his house, and were before long admitted
into his presence. But there was no long robe or headgear
with mystic symbols; no grinning skull or stuffed creatures
of strange or gruesome look. The sage was in the house-
place, with his pipe in his mouth, sitting in his own comfortable high - backed chair, with a cheery fire — for it was
Martinmas time, when the days are raw and cold—and with
something to drink quite handy. The Wise Man made his
visitors kindly welcome, made them draw in their chairs to
the fire, provided them with pipes and tobacco, and no doubt
the requisite moisture also, and, in short, "behaved hissel'
real menseful wiv 'em." The day was cold, and he heaped on
fuel, and kept them "weel entertained wi' pross an' talk."
Presently, as the fire began to blaze up higher and higher,
and the glow to become ruddier and hotter, the visitors began
to find they were over near the glowing coals for comfort,
and they were for setting their seats a bit back. But try as
they would, not only the said seats would not move, but they
themselves were quite fast in their seats ! The heat continued
to become more and more unbearable, and what with the
roasting they were getting, and the perturbation of spirit
which had come upon them on realising their position, they
were undergoing the experience of the inner fat of the newly-
slaughtered pig when being "rendered" (melted down) in
the process of conversion into lard. After quietly enjoying
their discomfiture and their discomfort for a space, and when
nature could have endured no further continuance of melting
moments such as theirs, Wrightson quietly but sardonically
said to them, "Ay, ye cam' to ha'e a bit o' spoort wiv Au'd
Wreeghtson. Au'd Wreeghtson aims it's a spoort 'at differs fra

what ye considered (settled on, fixed) coming down West House bank. Anither tahm, mebbe, ye'll think tweea tahms afore making spoort wiv Au'd Wreeghtson. And noo, Gude deea tiv ye!" and as he spoke those last words, they found themselves freed from their previous helplessness, and losing no time in elaborate leave-takings, they got themselves away from the uncomfortable presence of such a joker as "t' Wahse Man o' Stowsley."

Here again, with all the features of a very uncanny insight into men's thoughts and intentions, it seems to me by no means impossible to give an intelligible account of the whole affair. Thus, it is hardly possible to think of a couple of young men, bent on a spree of the kind in question, keeping their scheme religiously secret. It is far more likely that, whether with a sort of bravado, or with an idea of the great original wit involved in their purpose, they would talk about their intention, and the where and when and how of its original conception. And as to the fixing them in their chairs, the simple supposition that he possessed certain so-called mesmeric powers—a supposition that accredits itself as soon as suggested—is enough to account for it, and there certainly would be nothing marvellous in an experiment of that description.

But still, there are other stories about this personage and his doings, the explanation of which must be of an entirely different cast—namely, that we have a good deal of embellishment, addition, exaggeration, perhaps even fiction, connected with them. Certainly these were told me by my two principal and most trustworthy informants with the same amount of apparent faith, often assuming the aspect of thorough conviction, as any of their other recollections or experiences. But then there were elements in them which claimed a very confiding receptiveness, or a very well-grown credulity, in order to accept them all, chapter and verse, just as they were told. One of these was touching the recovery of some stolen weights, and another, of the same general character, as to the

recovery of a stolen shirt. Perhaps I ought to state at once
that, according to the legends I had so many occasions to
listen to, no small part, and, no doubt, the most lucrative part,
of the Wise Man's "practice" seems to have been connected
with the recovery of stolen or otherwise lost goods. Indeed,
that is one of the items in the indictment laid in the extract
from Brand. The stories I specially refer to were on this
wise. The weights belonging to one of the water-mills on
the Esk in this parish were found one fine morning to be
missing, and it was at once concluded that they had been
stolen. After vain search and inquiry, a messenger was sent
to the Wise Man. On his arrival, and after giving in his
information, and answering all the questions put to him by
the wizard, he was told to go straight home, and, it was added,
"Thee'll find the weights back again afore thou wins sae far,
and they'll be all clamed wiv (with) ass-muck,"—in other words,
smeared over with peat-ashes and such other refuse as is
thrown into an ordinary moorland ash-pit. And the final
direction was, "Thee'd best not ask any questions. Ah kens
all about it, and when thee gets t' weights back, thee'll be
nane the warse. Sae, just ho'd yer noise (make no outcry)
about the matter." [1]

The other story was of a like nature. A man living at
Danby End was engaged as one of the miners employed at

[1] By the kind permission of Sir Joseph Whitwell Pease, I add the
following story, belonging to the same class with this just told, and
which he narrates himself: "As to old Wreeghtson, I recollect my grandfather telling several stories about him. Some hams belonging to
his mother, hanging in the wool warehouse at Darlington, were stolen.
The mill-hands were much disturbed lest any of them should be suspected.
They sent a deputation to the Wise Man at Stowsley, the members of it
necessarily staying the night there. They saw the Wise Man, who said,
'Them that's gotten the hams is tired of them: they'll be fund before
you get back to Darnton.' They left Stokesley at daybreak, arriving at
Darlington at dinner-time (noon). The mill-hands were crossing the bridge
over the dam when, just as the ambassadors arrived, one of the workmen
saw the mistress's hams in the water. No doubt the dread of discovery
by the supernatural wisdom of the Wise Man had alarmed the thief."

the Fryup Head (or Fryup Trough) coal-pits, the said pits being more than four miles from his house. A wilder scene can hardly be imagined; the Trough being a ravine, and the pits themselves in the midst of the brown, almost trackless expanse of the moor, with no human dwelling within almost half an hour's walk. The miners had a difficult time of it, as the coal is not only inferior and impure, and of but small value compared with the coal of commerce, but it is in such thin seams as to make the winning of it a matter of no small labour in proportion to the mass won. A seam of fully eighteen inches in thickness is, I should say, almost a thing unknown. Consequently the miners have to work a great amount of the adjacent strata to spoil, in order to obtain room in which to work the coal itself. A man can scarcely work in less space than four feet from floor to roof; and thus the labour is made additionally burdensome. Necessarily the men undress before descending into the pits, which, however, are none of them of any great depth. The man of whom the present story is told had left his clothes above ground as usual, but on coming to bank again he missed his shirt. All inquiry proving fruitless, he made up his mind to go directly away from the pit-mouth to Stokesley, in order to consult the Wise Man about his loss, and the possible recovery of the abstracted garment. He went off accordingly, was admitted after the usual manner, detailed his loss and the circumstances of it, answered the various interrogatories put to him, and in due course was told to go straight back home as directly as he could, and to rest comforted with the assurance that the shirt would be safely in his wife's hands before he got back himself. And then came the customary rider: "You may think it strange I know more about this shirt than you do yourself; but if I didn't know that, and a vast more like it, it would be to no use you and such as you coming to me to find how to get back what you have lost, or maybe what folks have thieved from you. Well, I'll tell you this about your shirt; it

was made by a left-handed woman. And I'll tell you one
thing more. When you get home, you tell your wife not to
give salt out of the house to anybody, unless she wishes the
witches about to get sair ho'd on her."

The man went home as directed, found that the shirt had,
as the Wise Man had said it would, got home before him, and
that it was a fact that the seamstress who had made it actually
was a left-handed work-woman. This put him in mind of
the Wise Man's injunction about the salt, and the danger of
giving it away from the house. " Who's been here to-day ? " he
inquired. " Well, nobbut so-and-so, and t' strange chap as
brought the shirt, and wad say nought about it but that a
man had gi'en it him to hug (carry, bear as a parcel or
package) on to me."—" What, no one else ? no one of the
neighbours ? "—" Wheea, au'd Elsie Green wur in, axing me
to lend her a bit o' salt, as she said sho wur out " (had none
left). We can imagine the rest, and one might venture to
conclude that the wife, on hearing the husband's story, would
not be too easy in her mind at thinking of what she had
unwittingly done, and the possible consequences of the gift so
unwisely bestowed.

But our very attempt to imagine all this very possibly goes
part of the way in illustrating the process of mind in the
thief himself in either of the cases just detailed, or indeed
in any like case whatsoever. The Wise Man's commonly
believed-in marvellous insight into hidden or obscure matters,
the country-side persuasion that there was scarce ought but
what he knew, the reputation he had, and which it is perfectly
evident, from what I have called the "riders" to these narratives,
it was his object to consolidate and keep as well as obtain,
must, in the very great proportion of cases, have affected the
thief's mind, and powerfully too, when once he knew that the
inquiry into the theft and as to the perpetrator of it had been
referred to such a detective ; and in quite as pronounced a
manner and degree as the telling of this miner's tale and

experience would affect his wife's imagination, would it impress the many neighbours to whom the narrative, and very likely with ever-increasing accentuation, came to be in due course repeated ; and the thief must at once feel that detection was inevitable, and that his best plan would be to restore the plunder, and, if in such a way as to avoid exposure, so much the better. And no doubt this was one reason why the Wise Man so often enjoined a "calm sough" about the offence and the offender upon those who went to consult him. No doubt, too, the wizard's domestic confederates would easily contrive to fish out of such people as the miller in the one case, and the miner in the other, the main points of the matters which had brought them over to consult the "master." It is even quite supposable that Wrightson might have become acquainted with the circumstance of there being a left-handed seamstress in some sort of connection with the shirt-loser's female belongings.

But still, when we get beyond these considerations, we are at a standstill as to any probable or reasonable hypothesis. The salt incident can only be explained away. Was the incident one of real occurrence at all? Or was it a telling addition to a tale in other respects really founded on fact? Such suggestions will present themselves, and it is impossible to avoid the conviction that they are quite reasonable and fairly satisfactory. And the story of the recovered mill-weights may perhaps be dealt with upon the same principle.

But there is yet another solution possible with a case presenting such features as these. What I mean is that the whole affair might have been a "put-up" concern. Wrightson might have planned it, arranging all the details in such a way as to lead on to the desired result—that is to say, increased *prestige* accruing to himself. Such an assumption would explain every detail given ; but I must admit that, to myself, it is utterly and entirely unsatisfactory. And certainly I never heard of any such insinuation being made against the man's doings. On the contrary, the faith in their reality as well as authenticity was a robust faith ; and it would have been but to little purpose to suggest to either of my principal " contributors " any doubt as to the *bonâ fide* nature of the things they told about the Wise Man's exploits, however strange and marvellous they may have been.

Before taking final leave of the Wise Man and his doings, I will add only the following copy, made *verbatim et literatim*, with the capitals and stops (or the want of them) precisely as in the original, of a prescription or recipe to be followed or put in practice in the case of an animal affected with some mysterious kind of malady, which formula is in my possession, and is, as I have reason to believe, in Wrightson's own handwriting. It is written on a half-sheet of letter-paper, such as I remember in use nearly sixty years ago. It is folded in four, and yellow with age, and is, moreover, somewhat soiled, as if often touched with warm but not dirty hands. I cannot be quite positive that it emanated from Wrightson himself ; as there is a bare possibility that Wrightson's successor, a man said to have been his nephew, and to have inherited his books, but not, I fear, his native shrewdness and ability—if any other of his better qualities—may have been applied to by the former owner of this paper. But Dawson's—the nephew's—occupation of the office or position of Wise Man was but a short one ; and it was so, I was led to suppose, by reason of his utter incompetency to fill the post ; and no long time elapsed before he died a wretched death, that of a drunken, miserable, beggarly outcast, "like a dog by the roadside," as the man who told me about him expressed it. Thus I have no doubt in my own mind about the authorship of this noteworthy manuscript. It reads thus : " Bleed the Sick animall and Clip in amongst The Blood som hair Cut of the animals mane Tail and 4 Quarters Then put in 3 spoonfuls of Salt Then have a Sheeps heart stuck with 9 new pins 9 new needles 9 small nails Then rool The heart well in the blood and at 12 at night put The heart on a Good fire of Coals and ash Sticks and as it Burns Read Those Psalms 35—104. 109—56—77 Read Them 3 times over and let all be done by one Oclock make doors and windows fast keep all very Secret and have a Strong faith if this do not answer you must do it twice more at the full and Change of the moon Just as you did the first time with fresh Things should This fail you need go to no one else as Thay will nor Can not Cure your Beast."

This precious formula is written in a firm, bold, unfaltering hand, very plain and legible. The occasional misspelling may be noticed, as also that the numeral preceding the words "new pins" is 59, which, as I have no doubt the number intended was 9 and not 59, I have altered to the former figure. The direction as to the psalms to be read is altogether perplexing. I assume that what is meant is that the psalms so numbered are to be read in the sequence indicated; but it is somewhat difficult to understand the principle upon which the selection was made—assuming, that is, that there was a principle and also a selection.

It only occurs to me further to remark that the use of this formula appears to be very greatly variant from that, resembling it in several particulars, described at a former page. There the intention and the anticipated result were both of the most pronounced anti-witch description. She, the witch, was to be baffled, foiled, defeated, and made to suffer for her misdeeds past. Here the entity even of the witch is not so much as glanced at. The animal, whose illness is supposed, is ill of a lingering disorder; but no imputation as to any person or party's connection with the illness is so much as hinted at, and the formula seems intended to be used with a curative intention only. Just as the witch-wood was understood to be a prophylactic against witches in general, with no personal application, so, it would seem, was it the intention of the present charm to reverse or baffle the malicious practices of some or any witch unknown.

BEE CUSTOMS AND NOTIONS

THERE is yet one topic among the many suggested by the comprehensive term "Folklore," on which I would willingly add a few remarks. I mean the curious and interesting subject of Bee Notions. They are very various, and some, at least, among them are still very persistent. Such are the ideas that bees bought by the exchange for them of the sterling coin of the realm never thrive with the purchaser; the swarm or hive dwindles and dies out, or perhaps it takes its departure to settle elsewhere than in the place destined for it in the ill-omened trafficking; that a swarm which comes to the bee-keeper adventitiously is lucky, but if claimed by its proper owner, no money must pass for its surrender, or, on the other hand, in consideration of its retention; that if a swarm settles on dead wood, such as a post or rail, or a dead tree or shrub, it surely betokens the imminent death of some member of the household visited; and so forth.

But I think one of the most curious notions is that connected with the manner of dealing with the bees when a death occurs in the household they belong to, and especially when the death in question is that of the master or head of the household. I remember when I was a schoolboy in Essex, my father being then curate of a country parish not far from Colchester, the news came that the rector was dead, which of course implied the consequent removal, after a space of weeks or months, of the curate. But that did not affect me or fix

itself on my attention as did the proceedings taken in connection with the bees, of which a large stock belonged to the
rectory. I cannot remember who the person acting on behalf
of the rectorial family was, or by what authority the said
person acted; but I do remember the key of the main door
of the house being taken, together with sundry strips of
some black material, and a kind of procession organised for a
formal visit to the bee-stand. And when it was reached the
bearer of the key proceeded to bind a black strip round each
hive—this was called "putting the bees into mourning"—and
as each strip was knotted, three taps with the key were given,
and each hive severally informed that the master was dead.
There was a sort of weird solemnity about the whole proceeding which produced a lasting impression on my young mind.

In after years many things conduced to the retracing and
deepening of such impression. I will not enter into details of
them, but simply say I was led to notice and collect as well
as inquire. While my interest was still fully awake I happened to receive a long letter from the then rector of Sessay,
in which, among a variety of other matters, all more or less
illustrated by classical quotations, he gave me an account of
a recent experience of his when he had been called upon to
bury one of his elder parishioners, and had accordingly been
"bidden" to the house where the deceased man was lying,
some hours before the "body was to be lifted" and taken to
the churchyard. He told me he had partaken of the accustomed hospitality, and had retired to the garden to smoke his
pipe in quiet, and had seated himself accordingly in a sort of
arbour or summer-house. Presently his attention was aroused
by the passage of a woman, the wife of the eldest son of the
deceased man. She was carrying a tray, on which he saw
there were piled a variety of eatable and drinkable matters.
She went straight to the beehives, and he heard her address
the bees themselves. Naming the late owner, she said, "John
G—— is dead, and his son is now master. He has sent you

something out of every dish and jug on the table, and we hope you will be content to take him as the new master."

Founded on this were divers inquiries of mine prosecuted in Danby and the Dales district generally, and from my old and helpful friend who was my right hand in most of my barrow-digging undertakings, I ascertained that at no less than four recent "buryings" he had noticed some observances more or less tallying with those recorded by the Sessay rector. He had seen the bees put into mourning; he had never known the intimation of the death of the late owner and the accession of the successor omitted; and the offering of food and liquor had been, and to some extent was even yet, much more than simply prevalent. And he gave me more than one illustration of the formula employed when the offering was presented. One was, "So-and-so is dead, and So-and-so is the new master. He has sent you a bite and a sup of whatever there is on the tables, and he hopes you won't be offended."

I do not think I am acquainted with any part of England in which these bee observances have not obtained, and in the days of my youth I met with them in a still flourishing condition. Of late years they may have not unusually fallen into a condition of decadence, but I have met with some or other among them in different parts of Lincolnshire and in the north in such vigorous existence, within the last ten to fifteen years, that my interest in them has never been permitted to die away. And all the less because at an earlier period still I had been able to connect modern English notions and usages with certain analogues undoubtedly as archaic as they were non-English.

For years ago I had gone through a course of Folklore reading, very copious and equally curious, mainly (though not exclusively) Danish and Swedish, in which I had met with quite unanticipated illustrations of a great variety of our Yorkshire superstitions and practices founded upon them;

and among others, these bee notions and usages received no little illustration.

It would be tedious to detail the various steps and stages by which I reached my conclusions, and it must suffice to say that after a long course of other reading, mainly Danish, I became acquainted with Hylten Cavallius's *Wärend och Wirdarne*, which not only enabled me to co-ordinate matters derived from various sources, but in many instances gave me lively illustrations proceeding from origins hardly a century old (and some of them much younger still), of many things which had hitherto seemed altogether obscure. It was in this way I was led on to perceive what an important factor, not only in explaining the conceptions involved in the old legends about fights in the old grave-mounds for the possession of the buried sword of a mighty hero, but in clearing up much of the obscurity involving many folklore principles and practices, both ancient and modern, the old animistic theory as propounded by Tylor and others really becomes. Why should we hear as we do of the burial with the dead of articles of food as well as weapons of war and the chase? There is no answer to the question until one remembers that what may be called the animistic entity of the man might be conceived as being in a position to utilise and employ the animistic principle of the food or the weapon. I think there are four if not five constituents, according to Egyptian philosophy, going to make up the complex idea or entity involved in the human being, and although our far-away ancestors may not have realised those subtle definitions and half-metaphysical conceptions, still they were able to realise something as to the fact, and conjecture something as to the particulars, of a state of existence after the mortal life had ceased, and to fashion their own beliefs and practices accordingly.

It is not a little curious as well as interesting to notice the way in which the old popular notion of the ghost or haunting spirit lends itself to the illustration of the matter in hand.

K

When the old lady of the " Mark's e'en watch," mentioned else-where, threatened to "come again" if her directions touching her burial were not faithfully attended to, or when Jonathan F——'s funeral procession was detained and delayed by reason of the discussion of the church-road notion, and its sequel, it was not merely because the old woman herself, or even the witch-fearing old farmer, had held certain well-defined super-stitious notions, but far more because all the survivors principally concerned were themselves, however tacitly and unsuspectingly even, under the influence of exactly analo-gous feelings and fears. The expressed conviction of the mourners that Jonathan would not "rest easy in his grave" if borne otherwise than along the church-way—the "Hell-way" of the old mythology—to his last resting-place, meant neither more nor less than what was not only implied in the old wraith-seer's open threat, but acknowledged by her friends. But it is important to observe what a wide and impassable gulf lies between the crude conception of the rest-less entity breaking through the prison-walls of the grave, or the vindictive coming-again-being (*gengångare* of the Swedish folklore tellings), and that of the "spirit" of our Christian faith—the one as essentially non-immaterial as the other is impalpable, like "the baseless fabric of a vision."

The step from a non-immaterial "ghost" to an "animistic principle," a quasi-*umbra* of the dead, who, in such condition of being, might need the corresponding substitutes for his weapons of the old life, for the food and drink by which the old life had been sustained, is not a far or a difficult one, and the conception of the daily-renewed fights and slayings of the Valhalla bit of mythology, with the nightly-renewed banquet-ings on the as regularly revivified and re-slaughtered boar which furnished the staple *pièce de résistance*, with the equally recurrent bowls of mead and new ale, is one which, when considered in its concomitants and consequences, involves a singularly effective illustration of these singular bee notions and bee usages. The departed bee-owner, in his new condition of being, would require his appropriate arrows, axe-hammer, sword, what not. He would require his appropriate "victuals and drink." But much of his drink had depended on the produce of his bees. All the mead that washed down the boar-meat must depend still on the honey they produced. What wonder then that he should be idealised as wanting the busy makers, and, being even more and more actively non-immaterial than the old woman's "ghost," should be likely to prefer his claim, and make it good moreover by actually "coming again" and taking possession, if not formally and effectually prevented? The suicide, the executed malefactor, down to not so very far back even in enlightened England, was staked down in his grave, sometimes had his legs or arms strangely hampered with cord or by twisting, simply to prevent his "coming again," while in parts of Sweden the precautions taken were even of a stranger and (to modern ideas) far more revolting character. Nay, when the corpse was just newly taken from the dwelling-house, scarcely a century ago, the use was to scatter live embers just beyond the threshold, avowedly to bar the road back thither against the *gengångare*; and for the same reason, and with equally little reticence as to the object, the bee-skeps were visited, and a formal intimation conveyed to the occupants that the old owner was departed, and that no summons to wait on and serve him for the future was to be heeded.

In fact, the more one really enters into the story of the folklore still surviving in these dales of ours, until lately so little accessible and so little intruded upon by the people and the opinions of the outside world, the more one finds to suggest how hard has been the struggle between the old paganism and the new Christianity. Survivals of this form or that of the old nature-worship, of the old cults of hero, demigod, traditional divine ancestor, of this or that quaint, dim, blurred, obscure conception of man himself, and his mysterious constitution and attributes, meet one at every turn. The burial of the abortive calf suggests the propitiatory offering to the earth-spirits almost as sensibly or strikingly as the pins cast into the halikeld, or the votive rags tied to the adjoining bush, do that to the spirits of the water, or of the special spring in question. The dead lamb, or other portions or remnants of animal matter, thrown up into the berry-bearing tree have as much to impart to the inquiring observer tracking the once prevalent Odin-cult as has the strangely significative name of the accustomed weather-presage in the clouds which we call "Noa-ship." There are places, but not with us in "thoase deeals," where the name has been biblicised into Noah's Ark; but the old dalesman still abides by the old "Noa-ship." And in the homes of our Old Danish fore-elders the equivalent "Noeskeppet," wherein the final *et* is the postfixed Scandinavian definite article, and the prefix is the easily traced corruption of Odin, tells us an equally plain and (to some) over-true story of the place held a thousand years ago (and who can tell how much earlier or how much later ?) by the old northern god of the seas and the weather in the thoughts and notions of the men who went before us in Danby and near.

Truly the ghost notions and the bee notions and bee practices are not hard to comprehend when reviewed under such side-lights as these.

ANTIQUARIAN

BARROWS—EARTHWORKS—BRITISH VILLAGES

BARROW-DIGGING

I REMEMBER, on one occasion when my father came to pay me a visit here, making arrangements with two or three men to be present the next morning at a large tumulus, grave-mound or houe, known as Herdhowe, and situate at no great distance from the top of the steep hill on the road leading to Guisborough from Whitby, called Gerrick Bank. My object was to show my father what sort of work barrow-digging really was. One of the men I had sent to, a shoemaker by trade, a strong resolute worker, by no means imaginative, but shrewd, hard-headed, "Yorkshire" through and through in the matter of a bargain, or a deal in horse-flesh, had been a "pal" of mine in every houe-digging enterprise I had yet undertaken. He it was who, in my maiden essay in that line, when I was creeping carefully, and with cautious scrapings and anxious probings of the soil—for I felt sure we were near a deposit—tiring of my tardy approaches to the centre of expectation, reached forward over my bended back and lowered head, and with his shovel firmly grasped in his nervous hands, made a fell scoop into the thick of the little mound I was delicately shaping; and by his action disclosed the deposit, it is true, but at the expense of shearing off one-third part of a perfectly entire and uninjured cinerary vase. His concern and regret at the consequences of his impatient act were really rather distressing to witness; and his shame at having misunderstood and undervalued my careful and cautious approaches helped to make him one of the most careful as well as most vigilant workers any barrow-digger could possibly be blessed with.

He became also a diligent and effectual helper in a different kind of grubbing or digging, namely, in the search after the "dialect" or provincial words which it had long since become an object to me to collect and record. No one could exceed him in zeal in this pursuit, and not many in discretion; and it was "as good as a play" to mark the manner in which, when he remembered or thought he had secured a "good word" for me, he brought it out; often in the course of a digging, when there was no excitement from an expected or imminent "find," and almost always set in a very characteristic saying; so that frequently I had the sentence to record, and not just the new word itself only. Such was the case, for instance, with the fine old saying, "Ill-gotten gear has nae drith (pronounced dreet) wi't"; and again, with a remark touching an old mare of his own, "She mayn't be ower good at gannin', but she's a maister to eat."[1] He's still alive, but no longer the man he was. His "record" as walking postman would be "bad to beat"; but the unsparing use he has

[1] I may perhaps be pardoned for mentioning one other instance of the same kind. My old friend was driving me one Sunday when I had taken a duty at a place several miles away from home—and he was always my driver on such occasions—and as we were coming home he told me of a recent experience of his. The occasion had been an attempt to put rings in the noses of two "gilts" (sow-pigs of any age short of maturity), which had been suffered to remain unringed far too long. He described their intromission into the pig-cote, not effected without difficulty, and the entrance of another man and himself to effect the decoration in question. The pigs were disinclined to submit, and in their disinclination did more than simply resist: "they spanged aboot t' cote a' weeas (all ways) at yance; an' for hoddin'-on tiv 'em, 'twarn't to be deean." One of the two would-be operators was floored and "left liggin', an' t' gilts, they spanged and they louped, while ower t' cote-deear they gaed clean! Ay! We's heared at 't' Aud un' wur sent intil t' swahne when t' Loord wur walkin' t' yarth, an' Ah aims he's nivver getten oot in 'em (out of them) syne."

made of his bodily powers has paved the way for worse than
mere gradual bodily decay. Still, however, the old interest in
our joint diggings remains; and he listened with sympathetic
eagerness to the details I gave him a short time ago as to
the digging I had been directing in Skutterskelf Park.

On the morning referred to above, I fell in with this man
on his way towards the scene of our intended operations, but
at some little distance from it still. He was always ready for
a "bit o' pross," or "to ho'd talk wiv a body," on any topic
of common interest; but this morning he was even eager to
talk, for he had something to tell me. He began much as
follows: "Ah nivver could understand what pleasure folks
could finnd in fox-hunting; men and hosses and dogs all
rinnin' like gaumerils after a nasty, stinking, lahtle beast like
yon! But Ah've coomed to see different sin' Ah got to come
diggin' wi' you in thoas houes. You'll maybe hardly credit
it, but sin Ah gat word fra you yesterday at e'en, Ah framed
as if Ah could settle to nowght, only thinking it lang o' t'
moorn to come. Well, I gat me to bed middling early, aiming
it wad nae be sae lang while moorn, gin Ah could only get a
gay good sleep. But bless you, bairn, there wa'n't nae sike a
thing as sleeping. Ah tonned (turned) and Ah toommled,
and tahms Ah sloommered (dozed) a bit, but wakkened oop
again iv a minnit or tweea, while (till) Ah was as wakrife as
a backbearaway i' t' glooaming (a bat in the evening dusk).
Towards moorn Ah gat me to sleep some mak' (make, way,
fashion) or ither, but it wa'n't for lang. Ah began to dream
all mak's and manders o' fond things. But all at yance, Ah
foonn (found) mysen digging for bare life in this houe we's
boon for now, and we coomed on a finnd, a soort of a lile
(little) chamber made wi' steean. And in't there was a main
big pankin (pancheon, cinerary vase or urn), and it wur near
hand full o' bo'nt beeans (burnt bones). Some way—Ah
deean't ken how—it gat whemmled ower, and a skull rolled
out, nearlings a haill yan (a whole or entire one). And it

looked to be splitten all across the top; and then it oppened,
and out cam' a elephant—and a greeat foul beast it wur!
And Ah warsled (wrestled, struggled) to get out o' t' rooad,
and wiv a skrike and a loup (a shriek and a leap) Ah gat me
out iv the houe, and that minnit Ah wakkened i' truth; and
if you'll believe me, Ah fun (foon, found) myself raxing
and striving o' t' fleear (straining and struggling on the
floor) as gin Ah had gaun clean wud (stark mad). And
Ah've considered thae foxhunters 's nae sike feeals as Ah
aimed 'em."

I do not wonder the man enjoyed those days on the moors
among the grave-hills as he did. We all enjoyed them. I
seldom had more than four men at work at once; they were
as many as I could fairly supervise and direct. Once or
twice I had five or six. But, all save one, who was casually
impressed one day (and whom I never in the course of years
saw smile, or otherwise than grumpy), made almost a gala-day
of a day's digging on the moor with the parson. But the man
just noted seemed to find no more excitement in and preceding
the finds than "a gowk in finnding its gorpins" (a cuckoo in
feeding its fledglings). To be sure, he relaxed a little over
what he called the grub; and no wonder, for what appetites
we all had! It was a veritable picnic, with all the *abandon*
and enjoyment of a picnic, and with excitement of a
very pleasurable sort superadded. My wife and a friend
or two, together with two or three of my elder lads—boys
from ten to fourteen years old—besides the working men, were
the party. And we all of us worked. The boys had their
small spades. I marked out the work, and directed it; and
when there was no near likelihood of a find, took my place
among the working "navvies." Two of my men were so well
trained and so trusty that I could, to some considerable
extent, leave the supervision of the work done by the others
to their vigilance. But the moment any of the recognised
signs of an approach to what might prove to be a deposit were

observed, the vicar was warned ; and all the work of localising
the deposit precisely, and of carefully groping and feeling for,
and finally extracting, the precious and probably broken or
crushed, as well as frail, earthen vessel was his exclusive
province. And the eager faces grouped around as the interment began to be defined, especially if it were a "pankin" of
some dimensions ! And the theories that were broached as to
what the contents would prove to be ! And then, when it
was finally taken from the place it had occupied for perhaps
two thousand years, possibly even for many more than that,
the speculations were renewed, and the value or the interest
of the find compared with that or those of some other day.

The measure of success attending these diggings was of
course a variable quantity. Speaking generally, however, a
"blank day" was a thing we hardly knew. And this is a remarkable fact. For in the grave-hill researches I have personally conducted—in several cases begun and carried through
with my own unassisted labour—with about two exceptions,
the mounds we examined had been previously tampered with
and opened. Indeed, in every case but one they had been
excavated from the apex or summit, and very often terribly
mutilated and blundered.

The one exception from the rule of digging down to the
centre from above, was in the case of the largest grave-mound
in the entire district. The basin-shaped hollow at the summit,
betokening the former disturbance, was there ; but the height
of the hill—originally not less than sixteen feet—had frustrated
the efforts of the explorers, and they had opened a drift into
the side of the houe. Another, the Herdhowe already named,
had been broken into by the menders or makers—or marrers
—of the highways for the sake of its stony constituent parts ;
and in consequence the ugliest-looking gaps and cavities had
been left. I believe that this previous work expended on our
barrows had been systematic—organised and carried out by
treasure-seekers. It is a matter of record that in different

parts of the kingdom treasure-hunts of this kind were arranged
and effected under the authority of a written permission, duly
signed and sealed, from the sheriff of the county.   Such documents are still extant, and copies are given in more than one
book dealing with the prehistoric antiquities of such and such
a district.   And although there is no record of any such
authority given in this county, so far as I have been able to
ascertain, still the idea has been proved to be quite livingly
extant down to a very recent period.   Once I asked permission from a Moorsholm freeholder, a wealthy rather than
merely well-to-do man, to open a very fairly perfect-looking
barrow on a part of the moor which had lately been enclosed
in virtue of an apportionment which allotted it to him as his
own absolute property.   My first request was met with a
demur, the grounds of which were not stated.   The second
time it was made on my behalf by a near connection of the
owner's, and permission was ultimately conceded; but with
the condition attached, that I should make over to him all the
silver and gold I might chance to meet with in the course of
my excavations.   And again, to quote another instance illustrative of the same particular, being one day, with my party
of diggers, occupied in the examination of a houe at no great
distance from a trackway across the moors leading to Guisborough, one of a small party who were crossing in that direction, after watching us in silence for a few minutes, called out
to us, " What is it you are after there ?   Are you laiting gou'd
(seeking gold) ? "

But to return to what I was saying, namely, that it was
remarkable that, dealing with grave-mounds which all, with
scarcely an exception, had been opened before, still we were
almost invariably successful.   In fact, the success was so great
that in the issue my workmen became a little demoralised by
it; and, failing the excitement of the accustomed finds, after
digging vainly for a while they began to lose spirit, and to
work languidly and listlessly until such time as something

happened to brighten them up a little. And indeed there was some justification for their excited anticipations; for on one occasion we carried home no less than eight sepulchral vessels of one kind or another; and one of them was found on examination to contain, over and above the usual complement of burnt bones, a very beautiful and finely polished axe-hammer of fine-grained granite. A total of two or three urns from the same barrow was by no means unusual; and while some houes yielded only one interment, or at the most two, others produced three or four. Herdhowe, indeed, yielded in all, counting the distinct evidences of previously rifled and ruined deposits, no less than the extraordinary number of sixteen. There were nine entire urns—including a so-called food-vessel and three small vases such as are usually described under the general but misleading term "incense-cups"—all added to my collection from that one single source.

And I pause here to notice one particular group of four among the rest of this great find, which was such as to constrain one, entirely against the dictates of his soberer judgment, to hazard a sort of wild-goose guess of what might have been the antecedent reason for their deposit, grouped as they were. For two of the vases in question (small ones all of them) contained each the calcined bones of a child of very tender years; another, the largest of the set, was inverted as well as empty; and the remaining one, besides the bones of an adult of small stature, had in it a perforated bone-pin, or quasi-needle, with the fragments of what had most evidently been a fine cutting instrument of flint, which had flown to pieces in the burning. These four, as I have said, formed a group. The empty—was it a cenotaph?—vessel was a little in the rear. Advanced a few inches were the two urns with the children's remains; and on a stone, thin and flat and some twenty inches in length, laid over them, stood the fourth vase, containing the needle and cutting-flint.

What theory will my readers devise for themselves touching such a group? For I think the vessels could not have been placed as they were without thought, intention, or object.

Again, another day I went, with only my two eldest boys, lads of twelve and thirteen years of age respectively, and set to work on a tumulus which I knew had been opened before on two different occasions; on the latter, by a party of gentlemen from Whitby, now fifty years ago or more, who left a precise memoir of the results of their investigation, which memoir has since passed into my possession. In this document they speak of the evidences of former opening from above, and of the discovery of the fragments of two large urns which had been found by the previous explorers, broken up (as the manner was) and the sherds thrown carelessly on one side. It was recorded, too, that, though they had carried their trench right through from north to south, they had met with nothing to recompense their labour and pains; and that they were assured there was nothing left beyond the traces of former spoliation as described.

Knowing only too well how utterly unscientific and unthorough all such investigations then were, and having the good reason of considerable experience for thinking that the part of the houe they had left untouched was almost certain to prove the most prolific, I began, after my usual system, on the eastern side of their bootless cutting, at its southern end, working inwards from about a yard within the south-eastern rim of the mound towards the centre. About half-way between the circumference and the centre, and within a few inches only of the eastern edge of the abortive cutting from north to south, my spade suddenly passed through no less than four thicknesses of "Ancient British" pottery. To say that I was vexed, annoyed, discomfited at such apparent proof of reckless rather than unconsidered working, would be to convey a wrong impression, for I knew I had been working as carefully and as watchfully as usual, and that there had not been any, the slightest, indications of proximity to a deposit

hitherto afforded. Besides, the section of material obtained
by that one application of the sharp edge of the spade was in
itself astounding to an old digger. As described above, my
energetic friend with his trenchant shovel shore off at one
stroke one-third part of a rather large cinerary vase, but he
had only cut through one thickness of the luckless vessel,
while I had just cut through four thicknesses! Now we have
all seen oranges peeled for the amusement of children by passing a skin-deep incision round the greatest circumference, and
proceeding carefully to raise each half of the peel by the use
of a spoon or what not, so as to get two cups or bowls (so to
speak) each of them comprising half the skin of the orange.
Treat two oranges thus, and fitting the one half of the peel of
each into the other half, bring the two double cups thus obtained
into contact, hollow to hollow, and, more or less roughly, edge
to edge. Then press them together so as somewhat to flatten
the resulting globe (but without bursting the peel), and pass
some sharp cutting instrument transversely through the four
thicknesses. The section that will be obtained will be precisely
the kind of section just spoken of as effected by my spade,
two curvilinear concave edges opposed to two other concave
curvilinear edges precisely like. I need not say that curiosity
was stirred, or that close and careful investigation was
prompted. With every possible care and delicacy a space of
more than two feet square was laid bare, and then the mystery
stood revealed,—at least a certain measure of it did, not quite
all. Over the whole area exposed, portions of a large urn
were dispersed, and with them the calcined bones which it
had once contained. In that particular part cut through by
the spade the chief part of the said vase had been laid (or
thrown), one concave piece within the other, and two such
composite pieces opposed to other two like, just as with our
supposed orange peel. In the very middle of this medley of
burnt human bone and sherds of the old imperfectly baked
vessel stood a small delicately moulded and decorated vase of

the type usually called "incense-cups," with its own proper
deposit of incinerated remains and accompanying flints. I
described it as follows in the *Gentleman's Magazine* at the
time : "One inch in height and under one inch and a half in
greatest diameter, of red ware, and scored with lines crossing
one another diagonally, but so as to leave a space of three-
eighths of an inch all round, nearest to the bottom, untouched.
It was placed mouth upwards, in the centre between four
flints laid east, north, south, and west, and comprising a very
flat leaf-shaped arrow-point, another of the same description,
but thicker, a thumb-flint or scraper, and some other imple-
ment; but all of them coarsely or rudely fashioned and
chipped,—that is, as compared with many others found by
the writer."

These were both, and quite obviously, what are called
"secondary deposits." The houe had not been originally
built or piled over them. They were later—and who shall
say how much later?—than the mound itself as originally
fashioned. Perhaps even the original mound had been
added to or enlarged on purpose to qualify it for receiving
these later interments, each in its own proper sequence. For
again it is perfectly obvious that there were two insertions in
succession,—the disturbed or desecrated one, and that which
had led to or caused the disturbance or desecration. For the
present I leave the idea suggested by the alternative terms
employed for a little consideration.[1]

[1] I may mention here that by very far the largest proportion of all
such objects as those mentioned in the text, that I have at any period
found in Cleveland, are preserved in the British Museum. Among them
are forty-three cinerary vases of one description or another, inclusive of
the minute cup described on the preceding page, as well as of the 16-inch,
18-inch, and even in one case 24-inch high cinerary vase proper, or "urn."
Besides, there are the few and roughly wrought jet beads found with an
inserted interment, the polished axe-hammers found in two of the larger
urns, with sundry bone pins, arrow-points, and other objects of flint. But
it seems to be a matter for a little regret that they are not all grouped
together as a collection belonging to one definite and strictly limited
Yorkshire district.

BARROW-DIGGING (*continued*)

THERE is a good deal of speculation involved in the alternative terms made use of at the close of the last section. Was what had been observed the result of disturbance, or was it accidental only? Or had it been desecration, intended, systematic, effectual? I remember well what I felt rather than thought as I opened out that questionable deposit. For the time being I entertained no doubt of the intention and the object, namely, that desecration, reckless and purposed interference with the remains of one departed, was the end sought. I had been doubtful in divers other cases. I had thought the interference with, or the displacement of, a previous burial which had come under my notice in earlier explorations might be best and most easily explained as accidental and unintended. Thus there had been an examination of a large howe on the Skelton Moors, sixty-three feet in diameter, in which, at a point twenty feet south of the centre, I had found an inserted cairn, or conical pile of stones, of very considerable size for only an "insertion," and which covered incontestable evidences of disturbance of a previous burial, if not of more than one. The pile had flat stones laid slopingly round and over it. They were of considerable size, and when they were removed they left the appearances of hollow spaces within, which led one to expect the speedy discovery of deposits. Half an hour spent in careful work disclosed the site of the main deposit intended to be protected or signalised by the cairn, and near it a small incense-cup of red clay inverted and quite without ornament. "There were many stones of

L

the pile still to be removed, several of them below the exact
place where the cup had just been found ; and at a level lower
by at least a foot, numerous fragments of another red urn,
accompanied by portions of calcined bone, which had assumed
a clay colour, and were much decomposed as well as scattered
about, were met with, and under such circumstances that
there could be no reasonable doubt that they belonged to a
deposit anterior in point of date to that found just before, and
disturbed in the process of excavating the bed on which the
cairn enclosing that had been raised.   This urn was completely
disintegrated, and its various mouldering portions found in
divers different parts of an area of fifteen or eighteen inches
square." And my contemporaneous commentary on all this
was as follows : "This barrow was a most interesting one,
and certainly wonderfully illustrative of the custom of burying
continuously in a barrow already formed.   No less than nine
interments, clearly, and ten urns were discovered ; besides
which, the distinct chronological connection of three of them
is clearly indicated.   First, the tumulus was raised over the
remains of some one of note or importance.   Then, and one
cannot even guess how long afterwards, a secondary deposit
was made on the southern flank.   Then again, and doubtless
after many years, a third interment was made on the very site
of this last mentioned, causing the entire demolition of its
accompanying urn and the dispersion of the incinerated
remains enclosed."   It is clear, then, that I did not then think
—it is now twenty-six years ago—of anything but a chance
or accidental disturbance of the previous burial.   Years and
years in that dim far-away past had come and gone, and the
precise locality of this secondary interment had been forgotten,
or lost sight of.   That was what was in my mind when fresh
from the contemplation of the circumstances.   But how about
this other, where the entire previous deposit had been
deliberately spread, or rather scattered about, in order to
make room for, and, as it were, wait in degraded subjection
upon, the latter deposit of the bones of a deceased superior—

and superior, it might be, in virtue of a stronger arm, or of a greater and overwhelming force?

In truth there were many things in the interior of these old-world burying-places to set the thoughtful man thinking, and the speculative man imagining, guessing, reconstructing. No two of those of the larger size were built of the same material, or planned on precisely the same principle. In one I found a circular platform of symmetrically piled stone. It was twenty feet in diameter, nearly six feet in vertical depth, with a cist neatly constructed in the centre, and the entire level surface of it covered, six inches deep, with the whitest, snowiest sand. It was years upon years—twenty-four or twenty-five, I should say—before I ascertained where that sand could have been procured from. I knew of its existence, but not in anything like sufficient purity to supply a tithe of what I saw bestrewing that platform. And the place at which, as I at last ascertained, it could have been obtained in the requisite whiteness and quantity, was at least seven miles distant in a linear direction!

Not perhaps that that would make any difference to those devoted builders. For, in one large and still symmetrical houe at the foot of Freeburgh Hill—the very grave-mound in which I obtained the conditional permission to dig recorded above— I found, on the natural surface, and concentric with the mound itself, a cairn or conical pile of stones, many of them as heavy as, putting forth all my strength, I could lift, the base of which was sixteen feet in diameter and the height six. And every one of those stones was so marked in character that I had no more uncertainty about the place of their origin than I had about the dwelling-places of the men who were working with me or merely looking on in wondering curiosity.

Everybody has heard of the "whinstone dike" that runs transversely across Cleveland, entering the district no great way from Yarm and running a south-easterly course of nearly thirty-five miles, only slightly deflected from a perfectly direct line. It was this whinstone or basaltic dike which had furnished every individual block in the whole of that very considerable cairn ; and the nearest point at which it could have been obtained in the quantities employed was at least three miles and a half away, and across the untracked moor, with swamp and morass to cross and recross on the route.

In the case too of another grave-hill nearer home, the great constituent mass thereof consisted of clean water-worn pebbles and nodules of half a dozen different varieties of stone, such as could have been derived only from the bed of a beck running its course to the sea through a moor-valley some two miles and a half distant.

As a rule, I should say that the constituent materials of all the largest houes—and some of them are very large, one being ninety-five feet in diameter at the base, and even still thirteen feet in height—were brought from a distance.   There are no signs of excavation, or even of removal of the former surface, anywhere in their vicinity ; I have ascertained that by direct personal examination.   I am inclined to think too that the work was done not only very carefully but very systematically, whether merely for the due preservation of symmetry, or (it might be) under the direction of some chief, or the personal oversight and engineering of some skin-clad "clerk of the works," with curiously tattooed body and limbs.

For, in divers different hills, when I had succeeded—often at the cost of some sensible amount of personal labour— in obtaining a good clean section of the interior of a grave-hill, I have observed a significant regularity of stratification, always following the outline of the mound, as that outline must have been in the early days of its being.   And this stratification was such in its character as to show con- clusively that the material was not only derived from diverse localities, involving different colours and various qualities, but also deposited, when obtained and brought to the site of its destined application, with the steady regularity which characterises systematised and methodical, as well as graduated, accretion.   By way of illustration of what I mean :

One often sees a railway embankment in process of construction. Coup-cart after coup-cart is tipped at the edge of the slowly growing and lengthening mound, and the contents of each go streaming down the sloping face in intermingling and irremediable confusion. There is no such thing as stratification there, even though sand and gravel, clay and peat, loam and vegetable soil are all being brought up in unfailing supply. In the houes, on the other hand, there is often well-defined stratification. Not that there was not an unfailing supply also in those days of houe-building, as long as the demand lasted at least; but what was brought was carefully strown and neatly evened over the whole surface of the rising mound.

But to turn to quite another topic, and matter also for some little attentive consideration. I hardly think that on these wide and wild moors in this division of the district of Cleveland the custom as to the actual placing of what remained of the body after cremation—for no one actual instance of inhumation simple has so far been met with—varies at all, except in the rarest instances. The incinerated remains were simply laid on the natural surface, whether with the protection or accompaniment of an urn or without, and then covered over with earth, and whether with or without the protection of some sort of rough or rude stone-work. Once, and once only, have I found a platform of stones, in a cist wrought in which the body had been placed; and once, and once only, a platform of earth on which the accompanying urn had been placed; and once, and once only, a shallow excavation or grave, which had been the receptacle of the original deposit—speaking, of course, of the "original deposit" only.

As to the "secondary burials," they seem to have been made, at least occasionally, in excavations hollowed out in the side of an existing grave-mound. Perhaps, even, that was the rule. But there can be no doubt that in many cases these secondary interments led on not only to very considerable additions to the existing grave-hill, but to additions of such magnitude as entirely to remodel the grave-mound dealt with.

Thus, in one instance—that of the mound, about his adventures in which my faithful helper dreamed his dream, and in which I ascertained that, from first to last, no less than sixteen cinerary vases had been deposited—what I had no doubt had been the original work of the hill, namely, a shallow pit of sixteen feet in length by something less in width, filled in and piled over with a cairn of stones, had been thrown some eight feet out of the centre by subsequent additions, chiefly on the southern and eastern flanks.

But whatever the alteration on the original pile, or the deviation from the original ground-plan, there was no departure from the rule of symmetry. Wherever enough of the mound stands as when it was left as finished by its builders, to guide one's conclusions, the base is regularly circular, and the sides slope up with the graceful lines of the accurately-shaped cone. And not unseldom there are as evident signs of careful and diligent pains expended over the exterior as in the general and consistent construction of the whole great mass of the barrow. In many instances the more considerable among these remnants of antiquity are girt in at the base with large containing stones, laid slopingly, so as not to interfere with the even outline of the sloping sides. Sometimes even an exterior ring of encircling stones, sunk deeply enough into the earth to have remained firm fixtures during the long wear and tear of five-and-twenty or thirty centuries, is found.

Truly these men of the past, whoever they were, and whatever they were, and whencesoever they came, wrought great and abiding memorials, leaving traces behind them that but few are disposed to notice without a sort of sneer for those who care for them, but which yet are more full of material for thought than five-sixths of the books which cumber the modern bookstall.

I go into a graveyard of the day that now is—into this quiet, remote, reposeful one around my own parish church, if you will—and I see there headstones by the hundred, all of them, with the exception of a scant half-dozen, tasteless, ill-

shapen, ugly, meaningless, hopeless, wretched erections; with
an occasional equally unprepossessing monument—"thruff," as
it is termed here,—and one or two plain slabs lying flush with
the turf.   If I examine them with some care and attention to
date, and so forth, I find two or three that record the burial
of persons who were still living in the latter part of the seventeenth century.   If I want anything of the sepulchral "in
memoriam" type, I have to look in the walls of the churchyard, or in the lintel of the door out of the basement of the
tower (which does duty as the porch to the right modern
church of to-day), and there I can see bits of floriated crosses
on portions of the original coffin-covers, or perhaps a stray
entire one, just saved from utter demolition because they
admitted of being employed in the mason-work of the alteration!   These once covered the remains of men of position in
the parish, perhaps of knightly rank; but we know no more
of them than we do of the builders of the grave-mounds on the
moors.   And those great imposing grave-mounds will survive,
as durable as ever, if left only to the hand of time, when the
crosses on those grave-slabs shall have mouldered away ages
before; while, as to the headstones which disfigure as well as
crowd the churchyard, whereon the pagan "urn" contends for
supremacy as an emblem—of what?—with the Christian cross,
they are already put to self-invited shame by the enduringness
of the piles which were raised to cover the urns they feebly
mimic, the urns that enclosed the still enduring ashes of those
who had no cross to cling to!

One thing else.   I am told that it is a shameful thing, an
abuse, to violate the graves of the dead, to disinter the
remains of those committed to their "last resting-place," as is
done in barrow-digging.   Many a philippic of that sort I have
had to listen to, and to read.   I suppose that is a part of
the rampant cant of the day.[1]   I am sure I have seen more

---

[1] It has been no unfrequent experience of mine, on showing my church
and churchyard to some stranger or friend from a distance, to hear very
heartfelt expressions touching the feeling of peace and repose stirred by

desecration of churchyards, more interference of the most shameful and shameless kind with "the last resting-places of the dead," in one case of a "restoration" of an old parish church, than has been occasioned by all the excavations of all the barrow-diggers united ! I have actually seen cartload after cartload of mingled earth and human remains—the latter now and then predominating—taken out of the churchyard of one watering-place in the North of England (the church of which was undergoing restoration), and carelessly thrown down on the cliff !

And yet further, let us not forget that there was something to be gained, some knowledge to be acquired, in and by and through every instance of careful and observant barrow-digging properly carried out. The feeling that in and through our work we were trying—and not altogether unsuccessfully—to decipher a partly obliterated page of history, has been sometimes so strong in my own individual case, that it hardly seemed a mere stretch of erratic imagination to try and form a mind-picture of the old dwellers among these wastes, whose abiding memorials I was dealing with. I have long ceased to look upon the groups of pits which have been christened "British villages" as connected, even in the remotest degree, with our "Ancient British" predecessors. But it was otherwise indeed with the old and by no means—at least when properly questioned—uncommunicative grave-mounds of the wild moors.

such a site for one's last resting-place. Again and again people have said to me, "Of all places I have ever seen I could wish to have my grave here." It is now more than thirty years since I succeeded in obtaining the addition of a new piece of land to the existing graveyard ; because I had found that, in the ordinary course of grave-digging, only too many decaying remnants of mortality were exposed. And still, on occasions when people desire to be buried close to or among "their own fore-elders," with all our care such cases occur. Not many weeks since, the sexton, on digging such a grave, in a place where he knew no one had been buried for at least seventy years, came upon a nearly entire skeleton. And if this is so in such a quiet, remote, reposeful churchyard, what about the churchyards of populous places, and cemeteries at large, wherein interments may be legally made in previously used grave-spaces after an interval of time not, or hardly, half that just named ? Yet there is no outcry against this !

EARTHWORKS

ALTHOUGH the last thing I said was that the connection of the groups of pits, so-called "British villages," with our ancient British predecessors was a matter I had long ceased to look upon as probable or indeed reasonable, still I hardly propose to enter into a consideration of the reasons which have led me into such an instance of unbelief as that is, just at present. I can only say now that I believe the object with which they were excavated, and the epoch of the excavation, have to be inquired for in a widely different direction from any indicated by the name they are credited with and made to bear.

But although it may be, and is, idle to look for any traces of habitation amidst these misnamed, or rather misdescribed pits, and especially of such a date, or, perhaps, anywhere in this district, it is not idle to look for traces of occupation—occupation as distinct from habitation. They are to be seen, and seen distinctly, in many different directions. But they are mostly of one character, and the indications they afford are nearly all of the same general nature and bearing.

It is true, I am told of "camps" and "British strengths," and even "castles"; and I regret to see the authority of the Ordnance Survey pledged to such statements. For, while I know that many of them are altogether imaginary, and others utterly suspicious, in very few cases are the accepted designations or allegations to be fully depended upon.

But it is otherwise with the "dikes," "intrenchments," "trenches," etc., many of which are marked, and others left unnamed, if not unnoticed, in the Ordnance sheets, and undescribed or misdescribed by local writers. They all have a legend to be read, if only there be one sufficiently versed in such lore to decipher it. Not that the task is easy, or the interpretation self-suggesting and unmistakable. I take, for instance, the dikes or intrenchments which cross the ridges of moorland, between which lie our dales of Glaisdale, Fryup Dale (Great and Little), Danby Dale, Westerdale, etc. None of these have less than two lines of defence crossing them, and some of them have three, and even four, or at least have had; for the clean stone of which more than one of them were constructed had, since the times of enclosure, and especially of drainage, came in, proved a strong attraction to the farming freeholders to plunder, and eventually entirely destroy them by total removal of their material.

Moreover, all these dikes seem to have one general feature in common, and to indicate one special intention. As defensive works at all, they are defensive against attack delivered from the south, and in no other direction whatever. Wherever the works are left sufficiently undamaged by time or depredation to admit of adequate examination, that is the direct testimony of them. There is one, for instance—one out of two, moreover—across what is named the Castleton Ridge in the one-inch Ordnance map, and therein designated the "High stone-dike," of which a small section is yet so far intact as to permit it to be definitely asserted that the front of it (looking south) has been faced with stone, and had a deep ditch before it. Besides, as it would appear from what is left still standing, stone posts have been set thickly along the crest of it, of nearly four feet in height above the surface, and yet almost flush with the aforesaid stone-faced front.

Granted what is thus premised, of course the question

arises, Against what attacks, directed from the south, against what assailants, were these defences designed and erected? Were they meant for bulwarks against the onset of the men of one tribe or tribelet, dwelling in the Farndale, Rosedale, Wheeldale valleys, or, in other words, the people of the valleys south of the watershed furnished by the line of the Cleveland Hills, delivered upon the inhabitants of the general district lying north of the said ridge line; or had they some totally distinct object and end from any of such a merely local and arbitrary supposition?

For my own part, after walking over and along these ancient earthworks, some of them so elaborate, and all evidently forming a part of a single and individual system, extending several miles in their dale-interrupted course from east to west, I have become less and less able to entertain the view that the tribes on the south—supposing that phraseology can be looked upon as sufficiently admissible, if not accurate— were likely to live in a state of chronic warfare with the tribes to the north. Indeed, I do not in the least believe in such distinction of tribes so sharply defined. I do not think it even possible that there should have been a hard-and-fast line of demarcation between two sets of people of the same general family who could have differed, and did differ only— so far as our means of testing the matter go—in living a few miles north, or a few miles south, of a certain geological "axis."

But if not war between contiguous tribes or tribelets, warfare between what two sets of combatants could have led up to and occasioned the erection of the earthworks in question?

In order to try and answer this question to my own more or less complete satisfaction, I have said to myself: "If General Pitt Rivers's researches and investigations touching the Danes Dyke, the Argam Lines, the Scamridge Dykes, go for anything—and surely the patient, systematic, long-continued inquiries of a military engineer, with all the special advan-

tages in and by that designation implied, ought to go for
something—then surely the results and deductions he has
arrived at in an investigation which more than probably
presents many points of analogy with the question we have
ourselves propounded, not only ought not to be overlooked
by us, but most likely will be found to be by no means without suggestiveness."

His conclusions seemed to be something of this nature :
That the Danes Dyke was a defensive work thrown up, not
by the denizens of the land, but by an invading force, coming by sea necessarily ; that it, the said dike, constituted a
base for their invasive operations, and that having acquired
mastery over a given area in their front, they pushed still
farther forward, protecting their advance by another work,
on the same principle, namely, the Argam Lines ; and that,
pursuing the same tactics, they advanced farther into the
interior from thence, protecting both their front and their
flanks by other earthworks, which still remain in more or
less of their being to attest alike the strategy and the skill
with which the invasive progress was devised and conducted.

And then next came the question, "Who"—or, if that
could not be answered—"What, of what age and period, or
quality, were these said invaders ?"

An answer of some sort, perhaps as satisfactory as,
under the circumstances, could have been anticipated, was
obtained by the process of cutting through the so-called
Danes Dyke in divers places, with the view of ascertaining, if possible, if any, and if so what, indications as to
the people who really constructed those huge works might
possibly be found buried in those old banks of earth and
stones.   And one section in particular—nearly all of them
affording something or other in the shape of indication—one
section in particular might almost be termed communicative
from the nature and amount of the information it conveyed.
For it disclosed the fact that the men who threw up the

fortification not only used flint implements, but made them, and, moreover, made them on the spot.

We find flint chippings, flint flakes, flint implements even (of the commoner sort), in the graves in our churchyards; a fact which just proves that the users and makers of flint objects had once lived in the district. We find scrapers, flakes, drills, knives, arrow-points, all of flint, in and about the barrows so continually and systematically, that we know they were scattered or deposited (as the case might be) of set purpose, by those who raised the barrows as well as used the flint. And I have myself found three places on these moors where the chippings, *spiculæ*, remnants of flint of divers characters, as plainly showed that flint implements and weapons had been manufactured there, as the matters commonly lying about a blacksmith's shop show the vicinity (past or present) of the forge. And just such indications of the manufacture of flint were found in the very thick of the dike, not scattered about as in our grave-mounds, and so much more sparingly in our church-yards, but as thickly spread as you find the shavings and scraps and odds and ends of wood below the joiner's bench. The inference was obvious. While the works, mis-named the Danes Dyke, were yet in progress, while they lacked still some feet of the intended or ultimate height and massiveness, some among the host of the builders were plying their vocation as makers and fashioners of those indispensable flint weapons and implements. There lay the little piles and accumulations of the chips and refuse material, ready to be covered up and preserved by the next course in the building of the bulwark, and for discovery and cross-questioning and interpretation by the modern military engineer.

Yes, the devisers and builders of those massive and skil-fully projected lines of defence were makers and users of flint weapons and flint implements; and yet that is not a fact inconsistent with a knowledge, on their part, and possession of instruments and weapons of metal. On the contrary, all that we know—and it is no little nowadays, thanks to the scientific, accurate, and painstaking researches and records of such men as Greenwell, Pitt Rivers, Rolleston, and others of the same school—of the men who raised the round barrows that stud the high grounds of our country, tends to the assurance that they were possessors and users of bronze for their tools and weapons, as well as fabricators and employers of the more primitive flint. What then is to hinder the inference that the Danes Dyke invaders, wielders of bronze weapons as well as users of flint-headed arrows and javelins, prevailed over the simply stone-weaponed denizens of the land of which they had arrived as the invaders; that, as prevailing, they became occupiers; and that, as occupiers, they left those intelligible, if not communicative, memorials of themselves which have been so abundantly met with in the grave-mounds and earthworks of the district?

But, suppose all this admitted as regards the origin and purpose of the works we know under the name of the "Danes Dyke," the "Argam Lines," and the "Scamridge Trenches," can we for a moment maintain the theory that the only landing-place available to or utilised by such invaders was just that particular point on the Yorkshire coast which afforded ready access to the headland which was made defensible by the casting up of these great lines of defence? The merest consideration of the circumstances in their general significance—to say nothing of the knowledge derivable from what is known of later invasions made from the same side of the North Sea—leads on inevitably to the conclusion, not so much that there may have been, as that there must have been, divers and sundry raids from over the sea upon the old stone-weaponed inhabitants of the land, made at different times and at various places. And it is much more than merely possible that these lines of defence, and of defence, moreover, against possible or menaced attack from the south, to which attention was drawn a little above, may all admit of the same kind of explanation as Danes Dyke near Flamborough Head, and its more inland accessories.

And if this be so, one of the first inquiries to be made must of necessity be, "Where should the base to correspond with the base identified in the Danes Dyke be looked for in this more northerly part of the country? Can any suggestion of even a possible similar site be made?" And I think the answer may not be far to seek.

The very remarkable fortification at Eston Nab, which has given occasion for so many wild guesses and unreasonable hypotheses, remains as yet totally unexplained and totally unappropriated, and might well challenge, at the hands of some competent local antiquary, or some scientific Society in the district, some such careful and scientifically conducted inquiry as that which has resulted in the happy identification of the real origin and purpose of the strong ancient lines near Flamborough, and across the inland route from thence.

At least this much is certain, that while the Ordnance Survey amply suffices, even where the possibilities of personal examination do not exist, to demonstrate that certain lines of communication between the Cleveland seaboard and the interior are cut across and blocked by carefully, often elaborately, devised intrenchments, the only conclusion admissible is that, at the times indicated by the construction of the said lines, the only route or routes available for a body of men to move along on such an expedition were just these lines of way so blocked. For the merest and most superficial examination of the entire Dales district is sufficient to show that even in the earlier historic period, all that was not moorland was a series of swampy marshes, intergrown rather than overgrown with wood and forest. And one has but just to dip into such a book as Green's *Making of England* in order to become aware of what the barriers were that were presented to hinder or forbid the further advance of better equipped as well as better armed invaders of many centuries later, by marsh and swamp, forest and wood, and other such natural defences.

But while firmly believing that all the works which have been referred to afford indications, not of small intertribal scuffles or skirmishes, but of systematic military advances from the seaboard into the interior, and that they can only belong to the same date, and be attributed to the same constructors as the numerous and most instructive grave-mounds of the district (so many of which have been made to yield up their hidden testimony), I still find myself totally unable to agree with those who have had no difficulty in discovering any number of "British villages" almost at command. But this is a subject which deserves to begin a new section.

BRITISH VILLAGES, SO CALLED

I SUPPOSE there must be something very attractive in the British Village theory akin to the delight of castle-building or the weaving of Alnaschar's famous dreams. I have seen pilgrimage after pilgrimage paid to the alleged British Village on the Danby low moors. People used to come up in carriage-loads from Whitby, to see it; and now, in the time of trains, the number of votaries, notwithstanding the distance from the station and the difficulty of the walk, does not fall off; and they look at the holes in the ground, and, I suppose, they go away happy. I remember once on a time taking a learned Greek professor, afterwards Master of his college, to see the said "settlement," warning him first that walking through the ling from the Beacon—as far as which point I had driven him in my pony-trap—and back again, might prove no joke to his professorial legs. As we went down the slope from the hill bearing the said Beacon he smiled superior to the idea of a tramp through the ling proving fatiguing. He smiled also on scanning the instructive line of holes in the soil, with tufts of rushes growing in them. But he smiled no longer when we took the slope the other way on, and had to make our way through ling mid-thigh high. But he smiled again, and benignantly too, when, some three hours later, he was seated at my dinner-table, and felt himself refreshing and in a fair way of reaching the perfect tense of the operation; but this time it was his own simplicity in

M

undertaking such an expedition for such a questionable object that he smiled at.   And veritably the craze is a funny one.

Because it is nothing but a craze, and a most manifest craze, on the face of it, in the great majority of instances ; and it is hard to deal with the way in which the theory is delivered in any other sense.   The preposterous rubbish, for instance, written by Ord in his *History of Cleveland,* touching what he calls "British habitations," might be enough, one would think, to show any thinking person the unstable basis on which the British village theory is made to rest : "Large oval or circular pits, eight to twelve feet deep, and sixty to eighty and a hundred yards (!) in circumference," and "many hundreds in number"—truly any one who can swallow that as the first item in a description of the aggregated dwellings of the scattered and scanty population of half a dozen, perhaps half a score centuries before Cæsar, with whom bronze implements must have been about as common and as procurable as silver dinner-plates and dishes among our village populations now, will have no occasion to "strain at " any "camel" that is likely to follow.   Probably, if Mr. Ord had been set to work with the best and sharpest wood-axe and saw procurable for love or money, to roof over a pit— not thirty yards in diameter, or even twenty, but a modest ex- cavation—of half a dozen yards wide, with poles cut from the forest, and rushes from the marsh, or ling from the moor, and then to maintain his spouse and his progeny with the pre- carious supplies derivable from hunting, and the hardly less doubtful produce of his herds, flocks, or agricultural toil, he might have thought twice before proposing to domicile some hundreds—not of persons, but—of families in such dwellings and on such sites as his absurdly "tall talk" asserts rather than assumes.

For my own part, I am exceedingly doubtful whether, in even one single instance of all the British villages or settle- ments alleged, the claim for such consideration can be shown to have any reasonable, and much more any satisfactory, ground to rest upon. There is no extant record of any really careful and conclusive examination of any one of the pits by competent, qualified, and intelligent investigators. There is no satisfactory proof adduced in any of the accounts or so-called records of such attempts that the true and actual bottom of the excavation operated upon had really been reached, or, indeed, nearly approached.

I remember a great archæological authority telling me one day of the way in which he had had shown to him a series of pits, with a striking local name, some of which had been "opened" under the auspices of a local Scientific and Literary society; and how he was assured that the bottom had been reached in this pit and in that; and with all the particulars or accompaniments of charcoal, stones affected by fire, etc. etc.; and how, in his inexcusable (though latent) incredulity he had craved, and not without some persistence obtained, his desire for further excavation in one of the already (perfectly!) explored cavities. Two feet below the previously "ascertained" bottom unquestionable proofs were obtained that, as old Edie Ochiltree expressed it on a somewhat similar occasion, "the ground had been travelled before," and the assembled science and literature began to feel surprised, and look perplexed. To make a long story short, my archæological friend afterwards instituted investigation on his own account; and the upshot was that he had to go down, with patient, persevering excavation, to the depth of thirty-three feet before he reached the real bottom of the pit, which had been regarded as fully and satisfactorily explored by the local philosophers.

But even that was but a beginning of what knowledge and experience, or, in one word, science, enabled the new investigator to achieve, in the way of ascertained knowledge of facts, as regards the great group of hitherto mysterious pits he was working among. He discovered that all the pits, scattered about

in rude quincunx form, just like the great majority of our so-
called British villages, communicated with one another by a
series of low-roofed galleries at the real level of the ascertained
bottom. He discovered the tools with which the ancient ex-
cavators had worked, and the object for which they had
worked. For just where the sinking ceased there had been
a six-inch layer or vein of flint, such as to be available for
manufacture of flint implements and weapons. This had been
won, not only over the area of the actual bottom of the shaft,
but as far under the encircling sides of it as it was safe to
excavate; and then the sinking of another shaft from the
surface had been commenced, and the same process again
pursued at its bottom as in the previous one, so as to lead
on necessarily to what has been mentioned above as a galleried
system of communication of shaft with shaft.

Now, rejecting altogether Mr. Ord's "hundreds of habitations of from sixty to eighty and a hundred yards in circumference," I do not think that any one pit in all the
hundreds of pits which are ticketed with the name of British
village, has ever been subjected to such an examination as
were these old flint-mines in Norfolk by Canon Greenwell.
Indeed, I do not think that, if there had been a whole
Committee of such inquirers and historians as Ord so abundantly proves himself to have been, the merest notion of what
to look for, or how to look for it, would have so much as
risen in the brain of any one of them. They would have looked
for the charcoal of a foregone conclusion, and found it; they
would have looked for a preconceived bottom, and found it.
But as to ascertaining, actually ascertaining beyond the
possibility of a dispute or doubt, that it really was the veritable bottom, or, being the bottom, why it was so, and how far
all round the circumference it extended, or did not extend,—
why, neither the mode of examination required, nor yet the
grounds on which it was required, would so much as have presented themselves to their imaginations. They would simply

have looked for a preconceived bottom to a preconceived habitation, they would have dubbed the search with the grand names of examination and investigation, but they would have ended as they began, with their own preconceived notions— nothing else.

But what might not have been the results of a systematic and scientific investigation, on the other hand, properly and exhaustively carried on by competent and trustworthy inquirers? It would at least have been ascertained what the noteworthy groups of pits were not, even if nothing very definite in the way of actually deciding their real character had been met with. But my own conviction is that the origin and object of the pits grouped together as they are would, in the majority of cases, if not in all, have been actually and fully ascertained; and that it would have proved identical with the conclusion which is suggested by observation of the geological character of the vicinities wherein they are found, illustrated by a little experimental as well as local knowledge.

What I mean by " the geological character of the vicinity " will be better shadowed forth, perhaps, if I say that I believe that wherever a group of the pits in question in eastern Cleveland and the vicinity of Whitby Strand is met with, a fairly accurate geological map shows also the presence, at or near the surface, of some seam or other of ironstone; and what I think and mean by " local and experimental knowledge and observation " will be best illustrated by the following relation. It was an object with me some six or seven years ago to collect whatever local information I could, bearing in any way on the somewhat obtrusive fact that, at a long-ago time, the reduction, although not the actual smelting, of iron had gone on largely in this immediate district. Quite forty years ago I had become aware from a variety of historical sources, that iron had been worked in various parts of this and the adjoining North Riding divisions; and even before that, I had noted the fact that the traces of the said working still existed in nearly

a score of different places, almost all situate in my own parish
and in what once had been a part of it, and all as striking as
they were numerous.

What I especially refer to were the hills or mounds, many of
them of very considerable, and some of them of very large
dimensions, composed of nothing else than the slag which had
resulted from the obviously very incomplete reduction of the
iron ore.   These hills had the common name of "cinder-hills."
But all tradition, all trace indeed, of any survival of recollection as to the time when, or the way in which, they had been
accumulated had ceased to be, and to all appearance had so
ceased for a long time past.   Still they were unmistakable
indications of what once, in the far-away past, had certainly
been.

As inquiry went on, and I slowly succeeded in gathering
together a series of facts of one kind or another, all bearing
upon the subject of investigation, I became aware that in
one part of the parish, and within the memory of living
men, structural remains had existed, the former object of
which my informant could not explain, but which, from his
description of them, I could only infer had been built and
used in the production of the iron the manufacture of which
had led to the accretion of those huge mounds of slag.   The
size, shape, mode of construction of these remains all tallied
with what I had got to know about the simplest sort of furnaces used in the early epochs of the process of reducing iron-
ore.   And what was almost more, there lay in the close
vicinity a cinder-hill, a large mound, in fact, which had been
much drawn upon by the road-makers of no very distant date
in order to be employed in the making and mending of the
cross-roads in the near neighbourhood of the Fairy Cross
Plains already more than once mentioned above.

Naturally, having satisfied myself that the ancient furnace,
or rather group of furnaces, was here in juxtaposition with the
slag which had resulted from their operation, the next question

was, "Where did the ironstone, which it was apparent had been abundantly used, actually come from?"

No one knew. No one could even hazard a guess.

Eventually, however, I referred the question to one of the gentlemen employed on the Ordnance Geological Survey, who had been occupied in that part of the district, and with whom I had frequently spoken on such topics. His reply was remarkable, for it was to this effect: "You have asked me a question which is, in a sort, a little puzzling; for all I can say in answer is that the ironstone available for a furnace in the position indicated by you ought to show itself at this point and at that point," indicating two recognisable places on the six-inch map, one of them only separated by the modern highway from the site of the furnace and slag-heap which were the subjects of my inquiry; "but," he continued, "it certainly does not show itself at either of these two points."

This was, as I said, remarkable. The geological surveyor knew exactly where to look for the mineral; only the mineral was not there. Only a day or two later a purely fortuitous circumstance enabled me to explain its absence. And this circumstance befell as follows.

I wished to test the accuracy of my recollection of what had been told me about these assumed furnaces by the man who, as a boy, had been, as he had told me, in the habit of playing "hide-and-seek" in them. The narrative, as he proceeded to give it, ran almost *verbatim* as my memoranda recorded it. But as he concluded, he added this: "You remember, sir, my old father-in-law held the farm on which this particular spot is, for some little time after you first came into this country?" Of course I remembered the circumstance and poor old Jonathan equally well. In fact, the spell or charm described on another page was his, and his were the anti-witch proceedings also noticed above. "Well," continued my interlocutor, "when he died, all his papers and such like came into my possession; and among the rest there was a farm-plan of the holding he occupied, and in it every field marked with its own name; and among them, of course, the field just across the road that runs past these old furnaces and the cinder-hill: and the name it was called by was 'Mine-pit Field.'"

Here was an explanation indeed. No wonder my geological friend could not find the ironstone where it ought to have been, seeing it had all been mined away from the immediate vicinity in the manner indicated by the name of the field in question; that is to say, by a series of pits or shallow shafts worked down to the level of the seam, so as to enable the sinkers to win all the ore at the bottom of each shaft, and as much besides as they could reach all round, by the process of undermining the walls of the circular shaft as far as it was safe to do so—a system thoroughly well known in different parts of the kingdom under the name of the "Bell-pit system."

But my purpose in mentioning this incident is not merely to illustrate the connection of furnace, slag-heap, and ironstone seam, but is of quite another nature. I had known that field for near forty years, walked over it, shot over it, speculated even from how great a distance the ironstone which had been reduced just across the road had been brought for the purpose. But there was nothing in or about the field to indicate the former existence of mines or pits, or depressions even, anywhere near. No one remembered anything of the kind. No tradition, however dim, existed. And yet the pits had been there. The old field-name left no doubt of that.

But most likely, if they had remained till our own day we should have had a "British village" the more in the parish.

As a matter of fact, one day when I was prosecuting my inquiries touching the slag-heaps or cinder-hills in Glaisdale, which, in a certain sense, I knew where to look for, because I knew more or less about the limits within which they had been formed during the thirteenth and two following centuries by the canons of Guisborough—these holy men having been empowered by certain definite grants from the great lords of the district, namely, the De Brus barons, to dig mines, build furnaces, and make charcoal to reduce the iron with—I hunted up a certain old friend of mine, whom I had long known as one of the shrewdest dalesmen in the district, and asked him to tell me what his local knowledge enabled him to tell me about the precise locality of any, or as many, cinder-hills as he was acquainted with. He pointed out the sites of five or six; and then he asked me if I was aware of the "Roman village" just on the edge of the moor, about half a mile to a mile from where we were talking at the time. I said "No" in the most natural way I could, and asked him to show me the place. He was delighted to be able to instruct the chief archæological authority of the district, and took me "up the bank," and a pretty steep one it was. On the road thither he showed me one of the cinder-hills he had only indicated by word and gesture previously, and a very nice untampered-with specimen of a slag-heap it was, containing I do not know how many hundred tons of slag.

After examining this and making a few local notes, we resumed our climb, and presently came to a large group of pits dotted about in due quincunx order, and in point of numbers such that they might be counted by scores. "Here they are, sir," said he, "and a biggish village it must have been." I agreed with him. "But," I added, "what makes you call it a Roman village?"—"Why, sir," said William, "there is the 'Julius Cæsar' band of ironstone there," pointing to a line easy to be traced in the upper part of the face of the sweeping curve of the bank of the dale-head we had in sight; "there's the 'Julius Cæsar' band; and that shows the Romans must have known of it, and named it too." True, there was the band—more indisputable than the logic perhaps—and the local geologists have named it the "Julian band"; and tracing the line, it was "good enough to see," as my friend would have expressed it, that its level was some dozen feet or thereabouts below the surface we were standing on, all pock-marked with my informant's special set of assumed hut-pits.

I am afraid I became chargeable with the crime of perverting my friend William's faith alike in the Romans and their village. My remark' was "Why, it's a bleakish spot, William. It must be a deal snugger and more sheltered down yonder," pointing to his own home in the valley beneath,— "especially when it snows and blows in the winter-time; or any time, indeed."—"Ay, you may say that," he replied. "Well," I continued, "but don't you think the Romans were canny enough to have found that out for themselves?" William pondered, perplexed for a while, and then queried with the tone of one "convinced," but somewhat "against his will," "But what do you say them pits is, then, Mr. Atki'son?" The briefest reference to the "Julius Cæsar" band and to the requisite supply of ironstone necessary for the production of the huge mound of slag we had inspected as we came up the hill, lying quite handy, seemed to be enough to convert his lingering doubts into a state of quite satisfactory conviction.

Now had Mr. Ord been taken to this place in Glaisdale Head, and been duly "insensed," as I was, there can be little or no doubt, judging from the way in which he deals with similar "discoveries," that he would at once have discovered another beautiful example of at least a British village; even if the Roman camel was a little in excess of his capacity for absorption. And it is on such foundation, and on no other, that—to mention but two or three of the better-known so-called British settlements—the group of pits above Glaisdale Station, locally known as Holey Intack, the Killing Pits on the verge of the Goathland moors, and the Refholes (as they were called nearly seven hundred years ago) at Westerdale, have been so denominated, or rather nicknamed. So far as I

am aware, no particle of actual evidence has ever been offered
such as to justify the name in question. The very idea that
"evidence" might be wanted seems never to have entered
the mind of the godfathers. Like Cæsar, they came, they
saw, they conquered; but the conquest they won was localised
only in the dreamland of their own fancy. There were the
pits; and the pits were of course the sites of ancient British
habitation. The process was equally short, summary, decisive,
and convincing, so long as no questioning or inquiry was
allowed or desired.

Certainly, there are the pits; and if the fiat of the discoverers of British habitations in them be neither like the
law of the Medes and Persians, nor yet absolutely final, the
question, "What, after all, were they?" may be ventured.
And this is what a very cautious geological writer has to say
about the group last named,—that, namely, at Westerdale,
and situate at no great distance from the village: "On the
northern front of the height called Top End is a considerable plateau constituted of the ironstone and the harder beds
of the upper part of the Middle Lias. On this plateau are
the 'pits' conjectured by some to be ancient British settlements. These are excavated in the ironstone." And again,
a few pages farther on, he resumes: "The earliest discoverers
of the local stores of ironstone are considered by some to have
been the Romans, by others the monks; but we are agreed
in thinking that these early operations were carried on in the
so-called top seams. With respect to the supposed ancient
British settlements in Westerdale, which are pits sunk in the
main seam of the ironstone, a difference of opinion exists as
to the use they may have served." The writer then proceeds
as follows: "Charcoal is said to have been found at the
bottom of some of them, which seems to indicate dwelling-
places, yet their great depth seems to militate against the
idea."

Undoubtedly it does; for they are said to be eleven feet

deep before the ironstone is reached, and the ironstone itself
is two feet thick at the place indicated.   And the objection
thus raised to the habitation theory—for, however easy it may
be to get into a hole eleven or twelve feet deep by as many
wide, it might be much less easy to get out of it; to say
nothing of the advantages (?) attending the presence of a fire
at that depth below the surface—would be quite sufficient to
demolish it, even if the finding of charcoal in them—the only
item of proof alleged of their occupation as dwellings—were
of some little force, instead of being in reality of none at all.

Let me try and illustrate what I mean.   I have, I suppose,
at one time or another, made intimate acquaintance with the
interiors of from one hundred to a hundred and twenty of the
grave-hills, little and large, which dot our Cleveland moors all
over.   But I have never opened one, or seen one opened, in
which — although in the larger half of them there were no
signs whatever of an interment present—there was not charcoal in noticeable quantities, and in some of the larger houes
in such abundance—sometimes in layers covering four or five
square feet—as to force attention rather than merely to invite
it.   And yet I never heard of any one who argued that, simply
because of the presence of charcoal, the houes aforesaid were
old habitations.

But again, there is another consideration by no means
irrelevant to the charcoal incident—and an established fact in
the Norfolk flint-pits—and that is this: that at such a depth,
even on a not very dark day, especially when the workers
had to win the mineral that underlay the circular sides; and
still more, when they had occasion to work out what I have
called "the galleries" from the bottom of one shaft to the
bottom of its newest or nearest neighbour, artificial light not
only may, but must, have been wanted; and it is certainly
conceivable that a resinous pine-branch, for instance, may
have occasionally done duty in that capacity.   And is not this
enough to account for the charcoal in the Westerdale and

other pits of the same class? The artificial light theory, moreover, does not depend on mere imagination, or even deduction; the flint-pits referred to gave up among other things small-sized lamps rudely fashioned out of the chalk— one or more of them, if I remember, with traces of the wick still in its place.

But indeed the argument from the presence of charcoal to the not-to-be-questioned fact of human residence in the place or places wherein it occurs, is too utterly unreasonable to call for detailed refutation.

To return then to our geological writer (Mr. Blake, in *The Yorkshire Lias*): "On the other hand," he continues, and that is as militating against the habitation theory, "there is the remarkable fact of their being excavated on the most considerable outcrop of the ironstone in the dales; and as most other excavations are known to be made for some economical purpose, it would seem probable that these were too. Though the workers would have been very foolish to make such isolated vertical diggings, and not carry their operations horizontally as others have done."

Yes; but that is the very point to be ascertained, and not gratuitously assumed. So too the isolation is a matter to be ascertained, and not merely assumed. This is what a writer, who in dealing with matters of fact was thoroughly careful, observant, and accurate—I mean Dr. Young, the historian of Whitby—had to say about these pits, in a book published just over seventy years ago: "The Hole-pits commence about 500 yards south-west of the church, and extend in that direction about 1000 feet, and in breadth about 300 feet. They are partly on the common, but chiefly in an enclosure. The pits are in many places much defaced by the cattle. The most entire are chiefly towards the south end, where some of them owe their preservation to bushes growing on their sides."

And if some owed their preservation simply to the fortuitous protection afforded by growth of bushes, what about those which had no such protection? And what about the defacing by cattle, and the ploughing, harrowing, scruffling, tillage generally, within the enclosure? Let us recall the fact that our own Danby Mine-pit Field has not had a pit to show within the memory of man, nay, within the date of tradition even. And while the Westerdale Hole-pits or Refholes are of seven centuries of ascertained age, it would require a vast deal more proof than could be adduced that the Mine-pits had not been in process of working as late as the reign of Henry VII, and possibly even later than that.

Mr. Blake winds up his notice of these Westerdale pits in the following cautious terms: "Though, therefore, we incline to the opinion that these may have been early mining excavations, we cannot consider the fact conclusively proved." But, at all events, from personal talk with the writer during the course of his investigations in Westerdale and other parts of the Danby neighbourhood, I had not the slightest doubt what his own personal convictions were. And if, on the last day he was at my house, I could have gone on with him only half a mile farther than the point to which I had guided him in connection with his ironstone quest in Fryup, and have told him all I knew only two or three years later, about Mine-pit Field; or if I could have gone still farther with him, and showed him what I so soon came to know about as the "Roman village" and its accompaniments, I dare venture to say that the sentences quoted above from *The Yorkshire Lias* would have been very materially altered both in tone and definiteness of assertion.

For my own part, if only the opportunity could be achieved, I should go in for an examination of any of these so-called British villages with very definitely preconceived opinions as to what should be looked for, and the way in which the looking for it should be conducted; and, for one thing, I should have no more doubt about finding "horizontal operations" than about the fact that the pits were there. If I did not find the ironstone, it would be for precisely the same reason that my geological friend did not find it where "it ought to have been" just across the road dividing the old furnaces and slag-heap from the—for our purpose—happily named "Mine-pit Field."

With the Geological Ordnance Survey maps before one's eyes, it is impossible not to be struck with the fact that there is either a distinctly marked outcrop of some iron-stone seam or band, or else that it is present at no great depth in the strata marked as those of the surface, in the immediate vicinity of, if not at the precise spot occupied by, every one of the alleged "villages." Even at the British village on our Danby north moors, between the Beacon and Waupley—perhaps honoured with more pil-grimages than any other in the list—the tale-telling map places a seam of "impure ironstone" inconveniently close by. And yet this is the one of all others, the circumstances and surroundings of which admit of most doubt as to their original intention or *raison d'être*. For they are not only not arranged in more or less quincunx order as the rest are (or have been), but they are in two parallel rows, and apparently with an intended outside bank or protection. They have never been properly examined, or indeed subjected to any process of exploration that would satisfy the merest tyro in such inquiries; for the recorded examination already referred to was, as a scientific examination, altogether delusive. True, the inevitable "bottom" and the inevitable "charcoal" were found, and the burnt stones, and so forth. But the full and convincing investigation remains to be made; and from my own personal experience on the spot, I am disposed to think that when the true bottom is found the British village theory will be disposed of for good.

Certainly the extravagant absurdity of Mr. Ord's account (*Cleveland*, p. 111) might be supposed to have done that

already with all thinking readers.   If his own words were not
reproduced, it might be imagined that I was romancing, not
misrepresenting merely ; so I give them : " Our exploration
was amply rewarded by the discovery of the remains of a
complete BRITISH TOWN of vast magnitude . . . stretching
upwards of two miles to the base of Rosebury Topping.   The
remains of these British dwellings are in the form of large
oval or circular pits, varying considerably in size, viz. eight to
twelve feet deep, and sixty to eighty and a hundred yards in
circumference.   These pits commence near Highcliff, stretch
across Bold Venture Gill and the Kildale road, nearly on a
line with Haswell's Hut, run along the lower edge of Hutton
Moor, below the Haggs, Hanging-stone, and White Hills, and
terminate in a deep line of circumvallation round the upper
part of Rosebury Topping.   Of the pits here mentioned there
are many hundreds in single or double lines, of a zigzag
irregular form. . . . On one level spot, right of the Kildale
road, these habitations are extremely numerous ; indeed the
hill is completely scooped out like a honeycomb, sufficient to
afford room for a whole tribe of Brigantes."   Then come the
charcoal, and the burnt stones, and the fortifying, and all the
rest of the marvellous tale ; but not a thought or a suspicion
even of all the strange inconsistencies involved.   A "vast
town," "two miles in length," and—what the adventurous
author does not state—following a tortuous course to which
the erratic vagaries of a frolicsome letter S, with a curlicue at
each termination, would form no unsuggestive parallel, and
yet, "with the comfort of a town," uniting "the security and
protection of a fortified camp " !

But however little our author thought of consistency or
possibility, he thought still less of what the geological map,
with its perverse system of colouring following all those
sinuosities and contortions just noted with a pertinacious
fidelity, would have to reveal to an inquirer after the real
rather than the fanciful.   Even the obliging nomenclators

of the Ordnance maps could not quite digest this marvel among discoveries, and they are unkind enough to prefix the word "supposed" to "British settlement," and to insert in the very thick of the indications of pits the still unkinder cut involved in the two words "jet holes." The simple explanation of course is, that the pits follow the course of the strata containing minerals capable of being applied to economic uses, inclusive of jet as well as ironstone.

Alas for the ruined glory of the "vast British settlement"!

N

DESCRIPTIVE AND GEOLOGICAL

DESCRIPTIVE AND GEOLOGICAL

IN one of the introductory sections of the present book I tried to give some sort of an idea of the way in which I first came to hear of Danby, and under what circumstances I first beheld the place, as well as of some of the impressions produced upon my mind by what I saw and experienced. In few words, I wanted others to see it in some sort or degree as I saw it, and with something of the same preparation of mind and thought as in my own case. And I gave the several details. Now, however, I want rather to proceed with a more descriptive notice of the place, and, perhaps, in part, of the district it belongs to, and so to try and delineate some of the Danby features as they display themselves to the observant eye whether of native or visitor.

I remember, among other "fond"[1] things I have been guilty of, once telling my children a story of "The Last of the Giants," whose habitation I placed in a great cave in our local "Crag Wood," and to whom, jointly with his walking-staff (with a huge knob at the upper end of it), I assigned but one eye with certain remarkable properties, giving him, in

---

[1] This word here means "foolish," "silly." A "fond trick" is what only a foolish or silly person would be guilty of. A "fondy" means a natural, a born fool. Like so many of our so-called "dialect words," it is only a survival of the older English. In Palsgrave, or about 1530, "the word *fond* changes from *stultus* to *amans* (cynics say that that is no great step): *I waxe fond upon a woman* is translated by *je m'enamoure*" *The New English*, vol. i. p. 456).

part-compensation, a hand with five fingers besides the thumb,
the fifth of the right hand having two tips to it, the middle
one being short instead of the longest, and all of them gnarled
and swollen-jointed from such rheumatics as a giant, dwelling
in a very damp cave, would be likely to suffer from. I do not
remember giving this great personage a princess for his housekeeper—princesses having been, I think, scarce hereabouts in
those days—but a regular old crone, of the old-fashioned
sort. Now, had he chanced one day, when the old woman in
question was making bread-cakes for his consumption, and the
solitary eye was in the head of the stick (where it used to
spend a good half of the four-and-twenty hours) instead of in
his own, to stumble as he moved from his place, and in the
attempt to steady himself, put his hand by accident upon the
cake she was moulding, with the rolling-pin lying across it, the
dough would have been impressed with one longitudinal
valley, due to the rolling-pin, and five smaller ones, roughly
at right angles with the long one, and presenting divers
irregularities of form and length, due to the eccentric shape
and make of the impressed fingers, and, most likely, with
some roughnesses and steepnesses here and there, due to the
sticking of the paste to the fingers that had not been duly
floured before the contact with the dough, and so had broken
the smoothness of the edges of the impressions. Now the
mould that would thus have been left might serve to give a
reasonable idea of the configuration of the district of which
Danby forms by far the most considerable part. It must,
however, be remembered that the main or rolling-pin valley
has a general direction of east and west, and that, consequently, the subsidiary or finger-valleys are roughly north and
south. The fifth finger, with its twin tips, will represent
Westerdale; the next, Danby-dale; the third, or short
middle-finger, Little Fryup; the next, longest of all, Great
Fryup; and the remaining one, with its nail rather crushed
out of shape, and bulging on the side towards the left hand,

Glaisdale. The ridges between the impressions, especially if
you bear in mind that the plastic mass of dough, from the
nature and manner of pressure put upon it, as supposed, would
of necessity thicken towards and beyond the extent of the
finger-tips, would represent the moorland ridges which lie
between the dales, and which unite beyond the terminations
—locally "the Heads"—of them, forming one huge area of
moorland, which grows higher each furlong of its progress
towards the south, until, where Danby marches with Rosedale,
it reaches at one point the not inconsiderable height of 1420
feet above the sea. But while the impressions of the fingers,
such as we have supposed them, with knotty joints and
partially distorted configuration, serve fairly well to convey
an idea of what these dales are as to fashion and form, we
must not suffer ourselves to be entirely misled by the rolling-
pin notion. The valley which cuts across the mouths or ends
of the dales is no more straight like the pin itself, or regular
like its impression, in reality, than the dales themselves are,
in proportion as they justify the idea of the impressions made
by gouty fingers. It varies in width as it varies in regularity
of outline. Some of the outstanding moorland ridges project
themselves farther into its area than others do. True, the
northern boundary, a bank which rises with decision from the
general level of the central valley until it reaches the moor
again, and then still goes on ascending until it reaches to
nearly 1000 feet above the sea, is much more regular in the
directness of its outline than the other side, and is but a little
broken in upon by the passage of small streams or "becks,"
none of which are of sufficient dimensions to need or produce a dale to convey their waters to the main stream—
that, namely, which rolls and rattles, winds and twists its
devious course along the slow slope of the central valley.
Still, with all these deviations from directness—and in
places they are so pronounced that the stream, running
past a given point for three-quarters of a mile or so, returns

to within a hundred or a hundred and fifty yards of the said point, only to continue the same vagaries at a somewhat lower level—still, with all this, the direction of its course, on the whole, is always to the east, and though it trebles the necessary distance for reaching the place at which it receives the waters of the Glaisdale stream, it receives them at last. And from the vagrant line of this lesser rivulet, called the Glaisdale beck, to the watershed of the ridge between Danby-dale and Wester-dale, with a wide deep cantle of moor to the south of the dales, reaching across to Westerdale Head, and with a corre-sponding sweep of moorland on the north side of the principal valley (claiming a crow-line length of six miles and a half for the extent of its northern boundary), all lies within the meres and limits of the ancient demesne or district known as Danby. The entire area of this great expanse is nearly 23,000 acres of land, of which 11,600 consist of "undivided moor" belonging to the two townships of Danby and Glaisdale, and 6290 acres represent the enclosed or cultivated land in Danby alone. The following description is given of the parish in *Cleve-land, Ancient and Modern* : "The shape of this tract is that of an irregular five-sided trapezoid, having the least side for the southern boundary. The greatest length is from north to south, and is not less than seven miles; while the medium breadth is scarcely under six, the diagonals being respectively eight miles and a half, and seven and a half. Throughout the entire district thus embraced it is difficult, except, perhaps, for a small space on either side of the main stream, and that with many interruptions, to find a plot which for a hundred yards together lies on a real level. The lowest level in the entire area, as marked on the Ordnance contours, is 250 feet, and the area lying under 300 feet is probably less than a score of acres; while between this practical minimum and the maximum of 1420 feet, which is attained at Loosehow on the south, there is a continual and a continually renewed series of fluctuations and variations. This reiterated sliding scale may

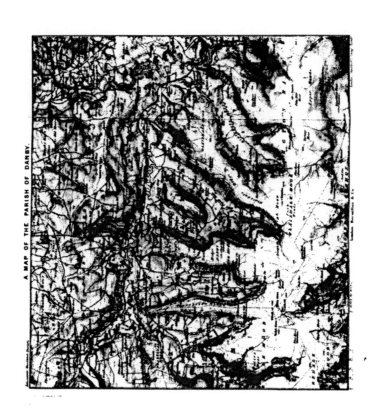

A MAP OF THE PARISH OF DANBY.

be the better imagined, perhaps, if we keep in mind that in the district under notice we have the dales—giving its full meaning to the word, so descriptive in its local use and application—of Glaisdale, Great and Little Fryup, Danby, and Commondale, besides a portion, six miles and a half long, of the Esk valley; and besides, also, several "gills" or rocky picturesque ravines, the most important of which are Stonegate and Crunkley Gill. For it is impossible to think or conceive adequately of what is meant by a "dale" without having brought before the mind's eye the steep or abrupt slopes or "banks" which on either side must aid in its constitution or formation. And the realisation of what is thus implied in the enumeration of so many "dales" and "gills" as combining to constitute the district under notice, necessarily prepares the way for accepting the idea of an endless succession of changing levels and altitudes."

But no amount of letterpress description can give any adequate idea of what the district really is in its physical aspects and conditions. I once heard a very taking and comprehensively descriptive remark made by a man who had seen much in foreign travel as well as in home rambles, in regard to the diversified sections and aspects of these dales of ours and their characteristic scenery. He said: "They differ from all other I have ever seen, and in this particular especially, that elsewhere you have to go in search of the beautiful views; here they come and offer themselves to be looked at." That is true; and necessarily true when the contours and configuration of the district are borne in mind. For the advance or retrocession of a hundred yards or so will remove the obstacle to vision intruded rather than merely presented by some steep nab-end or projecting spur of a hillside outlier, and permit one to gaze at will on some varied or romantic scene alike unexpected and unforeseen.

But even this is but one item in the many which, when united, have the effect of making the Dales scenery what it is.

In the way of illustration of what I have just written, I will
mention one noteworthy matter. Fryup Head (that is, the
upper or higher end of the dale, where it is newest and
narrowest, where it has just begun to be scooped out from
between its steep containing banks) is one of the most picturesque of all the picturesque dale-heads in the district. At the
point at which that division of the dale called "the head"
begins (that is, as you ascend or go up the dale in a southerly
direction) the width of the valley from moor edge to moor
edge is fully a mile and a quarter. On the west side the upper
half of the bank is steep and rocky, and clothed with wood,
mainly pines, extending nearly a mile in length. Where
the wood ends the last rise or upper hundred feet of the
bank becomes more rugged and precipitous, turning round
abruptly about the third of a mile farther on, and taking an
easterly direction instead of the original one towards the south.
And soon after the turn the place or part of the "head"
called "the hills" is come upon, and "the hills" in Fryup
Head are a very singular feature indeed. Of course the
authentic story of the Eildon Hills and the manner of their
formation is in everybody's recollection, as are also their
general aspect and appearance. Remembering all this, one
would be fully justified in assuming that some apprentice of
the great manufacturer implicated there had been at work in
the head, and that his "'prentice hand" had wanted a very
great deal of "trying" indeed. For all along the last half of
the rugged, broken, precipitous bank (as it has now become),
spoken of as running towards the east, and yet onwards still,
when it makes a turn and goes for the south, lie tumbled, in
infinite and most confused confusion, a series of short banklets,
hillocks, mounds, and peaks, with intertwining gullies, slacks,
and hollows—these last with the lush growth of damp or
watery places in them, and the banks with scattered rather
than scanty growth of bracken, juniper, and whin all about
them. Many a question has been asked me by the people,

craving an explanation of this wilderness of confused and tumbled piles of earth and rock. "Had there been mining, perhaps mining for iron, there, and on a large scale, in old times ?" "Had there been an earthquake, and had it thrown 'the hills' up in that strange way ?" "Had they been made and left so by the Flood ?" Such questions have been put forth once and again, and I remember wishing the querists could have been present one day as I was walking with an enthusiastic and much-travelled geologist over the lofty ridge of moorland commanding a full view of a great part of these "hills." As he came suddenly and unexpectingly in sight of the strange waste of broken ground, down dropped his stick and up went both arms in his surprise and admiration, a rapid exclamation following, "Oh, what a lovely undercliff!" There was the explanation in one word—an undercliff—and opening up what a vista into the far past ! A great body of water filling up these depths that are now dales, in its milder moods gently laving the foot of the cliffs which now supply the moor-topped banks of the dale, and in its rougher tempers sapping their stability as surely as rudely. And then when the process had gone forward to the requisite extent, there ensued the falling forward of the upper and undermined portion—veins of rock and deeper solid beds, and thick strata of unconsolidated earth and stones—and the issue of the fall was "the hills."

Strange to say, I once saw these dales—the illusion was so utter, so complete, so perfect, that I can use no other words competent to convey what I want to communicate—I once saw these dales just as they must have appeared in the times —how many tens of thousands of ages ago who shall say ?— when this great water-flood filled them. I had been travelling all night in order to get back, after a pressing call from home, to my duty on Sunday. I had left York by the early train, as the trains ran in those days, and there was a trap waiting for me at Grosmont. In this I began my drive,—over moorland almost the whole way when once I had climbed the long wearisome hill from Grosmont Station to the village of Egton. When we reached the heights from which we could see well into Eskdale, it was—so far as the testimony of actual vision went—full of water as far as the eye could see, and full to such a height that only 100 feet or so of the upper banks was not submerged. No amount of rubbing one's eyes prevailed to corroborate the testimony of my recent conviction that there was no water, save the usual fine-weather supply, in the bed of the Esk when I had crossed Grosmont Bridge a short half-hour before. As the scene expanded itself more and more before me, Eskdale and all its tributary dales were inundated, drowned, submerged, and there was the level of the mighty flood just marking its horizontal line at the foot of what ought to have been the higher banks rising from the dales, but which were in all reality, so far as ocular demonstration went, absolute cliffs on the margin of a mighty sheet of water—inlet from the sea or lengthening inland lake. As I mounted higher and higher towards the Beacon, and looked into what ought to have been, and had been, Danby-dale when last I had seen it, there was nothing but the calm glistening surface in sight as far as the eye could discern, and the point I had attained was high enough to enable me to look into the very head of Danby, a good six miles distant. There was a great sheet of water with deep, narrow, far-reaching gulfs or inlets, and only the moorland heights standing out of it. No stranger to the country and to the actual everyday scene could for a moment have suspected that it was not a sheet of water over which his eye roamed.

By this time the sun was getting well up, and there was no cloud to obscure his rising brightness. Truly it was a wonderfully and mysteriously beautiful scene. But just as Nature had spread before our eyes this mimic representation of one of her ancient phases, so Nature presently supplied the disillusionment. As the sun rose to a greater altitude, and

his rays began to fall on the seeming water-sheet with
incidence at a greater angle, I saw little threads and streaks
of the dissembling surface detach themselves from its face,
rise up and disappear, like the steam from the locomotive in a
fine sunny day. Soon they were followed by larger films.
But still the general surface was not visibly affected; until
at last, as the process of dissolution continued, a sort of dim
translucency seemed to supervene, and the higher range of
objects and points, hitherto concealed, began to show themselves, much as if the flood was settling away rapidly, and
beginning to leave the trees and higher grounds uncovered.
The first object to be seen distinctly was the small group of
Scotch pines near the old parish church; the emergence of
which was speedily followed by that of the church itself; and
then the whole west bank of the dale came into sight; and
finally, and almost as if by a species of legerdemain, so rapid
and effectual was the process, the whole remaining cumulus
of white vapour was caught up, torn to shreds and films, and
completely dissipated.

But still, illusive and fleeting as the scene had been, it had
effectively served to aid the mind and the imagination in
forming and retaining the conception not only that water had
once filled what are now the main valley and its offshoots, the
dales, but that its part in fashioning and finishing the said
valley and its dales, as we now see them, had by no means
been an insignificant, even if in reality only a subsidiary one.
Every new section of the bank of the Esk itself, or of one of its
many feeders draining the dales as well as the moors above;
every cutting or other excavation carried through in railway
construction, or other considerable work; every drain sunk a
couple of feet or so lower than the average three feet; every
digging for a foundation, or sinking of a well,—all serve to
show, and often with a singular power of illustration, what
the agency of water has been, in the dawn of the hoariest eld,
in making and leaving our country what it is. "What do

you think of this dales country?" I said one day to the then
engineer of the North-Eastern Railway Company, who, as I
knew well, had been put to no ordinary trouble by the wanton
behaviour of the "batters" or slopes of the sides of the cuttings,
which had to be made below Danby End for our railway, then
in process of construction. The answer was emphatic, in force
as well as in form :—"It is a devil of a country." The said
batters had been laid at the usual angle ; and why not ? The
soil, as every one could see, was a fine, firm clay, and with no
apparent weak or watery places in it ; and the slopes when
finished were as neat-looking and seemingly as likely to be
stable as any in any district whatsoever. But the incidence
of a wet season soon altered all that. Before the wet time
had lasted a week, these fair-seeming batters had begun to
move, to give way, to slide down bodily in many places, and
in none had they stood firm. Large lumps had come away,
leaving ugly-looking cavities in the bank, and cumbering, perhaps filling up, the space destined to receive the sleepers ; or
else there were treacherous, lazy flowings of soft mud, spreading themselves, in places two feet deep, along the level bottom
of the cutting. "The batters were too steep" was the view
taken ; and accordingly, when the navvies were able to get
to work again, two or three yards, or more where the cuttings were deepest, were taken off the higher parts of the
slopes, and lessened out by degrees as the level of the intended permanent way was reached. It was a slow process ;
but at last all was made good, and the neat slopes—only
much less steep than before—were left in their naked regularity. But again the wet time came ; and again the unlucky
batters began to slip and slide, and discharge massive lumps,
and form great mud-puddles. And yet again had the weary
work of repairing damages and clearing away débris, of lower-
ing the inclination of the slopes, and digging great trenches
up and down the sides, filling them up with blocks of clean
broken freestone, to be gone through ; and, to mention but

one place in which the result of all this work may plainly be
seen, there is a longish slope, just below the Danby End
Station, the angle of which cannot be much more than twenty
or twenty-five degrees, having been originally, I suppose,
hardly less than forty-five.

The quantity of earth that was dug out and "run to spoil"
in the process of making good what had been damaged and
ruined by the untrustworthy nature of the soil of this "devil
of a country" was something enormous. I forget how many
hundreds, or even thousands, of truck-loads had to be removed,
but there was a huge mound of the useless material deposited
on a space between the beck and the line, some half-mile or
so on the Whitby side of the Danby Station. And besides
that, wherever a few loads could be vented nearer the place
it was taken from, in the way of filling up a hollow, or raising
the access to one of the new gateways which had to be formed
in divers places, giving passage across the line from one part
of a severed enclosure to another, or what not, there a suffi-
ciency was sure to be deposited. It so happened that I was
passing along one day by the beck-side over a hollow that had
been thus filled up, and with a gateway approach leading
across it; and there lay the material that had been removed,
under my feet and on either side, as I stopped to take note
of the fact. And, inasmuch as it was no long time since the
work had been completed, numbers of the symmetrical pieces
of clay raised by employment of the navvy's "hollow-tool"—
seven or eight inches in the blade by about six wide, and with
convex back and concave front—were lying almost as perfect
in shape as when newly freed from the tool which had dug
them. "Almost as perfect," but not quite. For I noticed a
sort of blur about the edges of several, which edges I knew
must have been cut quite sharp. These blurred edges, I also
noticed, were frequent, and not due to impact or forcible
action of any sort. Looking more closely at the objects in
question, I saw that the circumstance noted depended on

what almost might be called spontaneous exfoliation, or action peculiar to the shaped segments themselves. The edges were opening under the influence of natural causes. A few seconds of aroused attention and observation sufficed to demonstrate the fact that the structure of the clay was not homogeneous, but finely laminated, and that as the process of desiccation consequent on exposure to the air went on, the several laminæ of which the mass was composite began to separate, exactly as the leaves of a book that has become damp and is exposed to the influence of the sun or a fire always do. The thickness of each lamina was about that of ordinary stiff brown paper, and between each two of them was an almost imperceptible film of almost impalpable siliceous matter or sand. The explanation of the treacherous slippery nature of the apparently stable clay slopes, and of the tendency of the constituent parts to run into pools and streamlets of liquid mud, was given at once, and with a cheerful clearness. When the wet time came, water worked in through some of the countless fissures or cracks met with in all clay formations in times of drought, and finding its way along the sandy partings, induced motion of one lamina over another, motion led on to abrasion, and abrasion, in the case of such thin laminæ in a wet time, meant the abundant and still increasing formation of a totally disintegrated accumulation of semi-liquid clay with an inter-mixture of finely comminuted sand.[1]   No wonder the batters

---

[1] The thickness of the laminæ varied, as, on a moment's reflection, is seen to be inevitable. But the comparison with a block of sheets of thick brown paper, with the reservation that they shall not all be of one thick-ness, and that some of them may be thick enough to be of the very thickest material of that description, will be by no means misleading. In some of the pieces examined there was no difficulty in counting five-and-twenty or thirty "leaves," the thickness of each of the said pieces being well on towards four inches; and when the intercalation of the films of sand is remembered, a tolerable idea of the constitution of the clay as a mass is obtained. It may further be mentioned that a good many truck-loads of the material in question were employed as backing to the piers of two large girder-bridges thrown across the Esk, opposite

would not stand, and that the only effectual remedy lay in reducing the slope to such a degree that the superincumbent weight should be thrown as far back as possible, and in providing the readiest possible discharge for the water that must of necessity fall upon them or percolate through them from the adjoining strata.

But to avoid being tedious I relegate to the Appendix certain further observations on the nature of this deposit, and the deductions one has to make in connection with them. See Appendix B.

and a little below Danby Lodge, and to add to the height of the embankment at either end of the same, and that precisely the same difficulty ensued in these cases also : the packing and the added material simply melted away, and the work supposed to be done had to be done over again.

DESCRIPTIVE AND GEOLOGICAL (*continued*)

BUT before finally leaving that part of my subject which occupied the last chapter, it may be expedient to add a few words more, both as introductory to other like reminiscences and as illustrative of the significance, value, and importance of time as a factor, in any effort to estimate geological changes. And I do not think that the circumstances to be adduced are by any means the least interesting of those which have attracted my observation during my sojourn here.

There is a locality in the parish (indeed there are two) called by the name "Coums." The name has been variously spelt, and it is met with, similarly applied, in other dales besides Danby, Rosedale being one of them. But the sound is the same in either case, being that represented by the spelling *coombs*, the *b* being nearly silent as in *comb*. The name is probably coeval with the Celtic occupation of the district. The Coums I advert to is a roughly semicircular gap or hollow, with rather steeply-sloping sides, something like half a basin, scooped out of the side of the moor-bank. It is nearly half a mile wide from one end of the moor-brae semicircle to the other, and somewhere about the same from front to back, or from mid-diameter by the perpendicular radius to the circumference. On the western slope of this hollow or half-basin is a long narrow chasm, in all extending to about 150 yards in length. This in the six-inch Ordnance map is marked "gravel-pit," on the *lucus a non lucendo* principle clearly, for there is no gravel there nor anywhere near. But there chanced to be an uncouth-looking gap in the moor-side there, long and narrow, and so it had to be noticed and designated ; and the surveyor being, as it would seem, a man of imagination, it was named a gravel-pit. But the said surveyor's imagination was far from reaching forth to the fact that in that queer-shaped gully (which might have marked the site of a slip if only there had been a bank high enough for a slipping section to slide from) he had the key to the whole formation of the locality designated by the local name "Coums." For this magnified trench or gully is due to vertical subsidence, and it has been a part of my experience to note the process in full course. The high road into Fryup, past Danby Castle, lies directly across the lower part of the said trench or gully, and it chanced to me one day some seven or eight years since to observe, as I descended the hill-side above, two dark lines drawn (a little obliquely) across the roadway just where it traversed this strange gully—strange enough in the eyes of the country-folk to have led to the imposition by them of the name "Hell-kettle." On coming to the lines in question, it was apparent that they were due to slight fissures, vertical in direction, and apparently springing from some depth. When I returned some three or four hours later the lines were more marked, and it was already quite evident that there was a discernible difference of height in the two edges of the several rifts. The next day was Sunday, and as I drove over the place the jolt as the wheel crossed the first or higher edge to the lower level of the second was quite perceptible ; and a close examination made on the return journey showed a distinct settlement of three inches in the case of the higher split, and about two-thirds of that in the case of the other. Close and almost daily observation showed the process, whatever it was, to be in steady progress. It revealed also that the cracks or rifts were not confined to the roadway, but extended on either side of the road along the length of the gully, not at its bottom, but along its sides, and about two-thirds up their height. On the south the cracks could be traced to some distance beyond the termination of the gully itself; but on the other side of the road, after quitting the end of the gully proper, they descended into a sloping garth or garden enclosure, and one of the conical-shaped store-places for potatoes—"potato-pies," we call them—happening to overlie the course of one of them, was split, and its contents revealed to the eye. In the sequel it was observed that the total vertical subsidence of the part of the roadway between the two rifts had reached the measure of twenty inches, and that within the course of a few weeks; that depth being increased by four inches more before the movement totally ceased, or within about a year of its commencement. This was at the higher side of the segment affected. On the other side the sinking was not so great by seven or eight inches. Coincidently with this subsidence, and continued for months after its apparent termination, splits and rifts were seen—to mention two places only—in a grass field out of the line of the gully, but more in the hollow of the half-basin, and about two hundred yards distant; and again, at a point much more distant, and more in the circumference of the basin itself, where the moor-bank above is fairly steep. In these two places the rifts were wider, and the measure of the sinking considerably greater.

It may be necessary to make two remarks to accompany the statement here made. One is that the bottom of the basin or coomb is not at the lowest level of the adjacent district. On the contrary, the land slopes down gradually but distinctly for nearly a mile before the Esk is reached. And the other is that there is no water anywhere near, such in its quality or power as to occasion any local earth-waste of appreciable amount. Moreover, the phenomenon described is in no respect of the nature of a slip, or apparently due to the sliding of masses of earth along an immediately contiguous sloping and inferior stratum. The movement of the mass that settles is distinctly vertical, and there is no lateral motion whatever such as to reveal itself to even careful or scientific observation. Subsidence, in its unqualified sense, is the only word which can be applied to designate the movement in question.

In saying this, it is not intended to deny that there may be, or is, "lateral movement" eventually concerned in the subsidence, or that water may be closely connected with it; or even that a sloping inferior stratum may be implicated. For there is reason to believe that the two former are involved, if not in the immediate vicinity, yet within definite distance; and none to discredit the possible existence of a dipping bed of shale at a level below, perhaps far below, the present surface. As regards the water part of the question, one thing is noteworthy; namely, that while the gully itself lies fully two-thirds of the way down the hill descended by the road which crosses it, so that in wet times, and especially times of rapid thaws and violent thunder-showers, there is a very large amount of water running down the slope into the entire length of the gully, and especially down the channels on either side of the road itself—which water is diverted into pots or depressions on either side—still the said water never accumulates there, or remains above the surface for more than a very brief space. There is ready and effective drainage for it provided by some natural means. In other words, there is a very easy passage to the lower strata or beds for a large proportion of the very great amount of surface-drainage which finds its way into this remarkable gully or gaping earth-trough.

And then again, as regards the lateral movement: I may mention that I have had a good deal of experience as a fly-fisher in what used to be our troutful little stream of the Esk. If I were to say I have had a couple of thousand walks along its banks during the last forty years, sometimes with the fly-rod in my hand, at others with the gun, and at others again, neither few nor infrequent, armed with no more deadly weapon than a walking-stick, I should not exaggerate; and what I have seen during the whole of that period, and seen illustrated in divers manners, has been movement, essentially lateral movement, in the banks of the beck themselves, and in the fields lying, with more or less of a slope always, above, and at no great distance above them. I have seen, too, great changes in the bed of the stream itself, all more or less evidently connected with what I have spoken of as lateral motion. Thus, there is no perceptible extension of the width of the bed of the stream; the average distance from the brae of one bank to the brae of the other remains relatively the same. And yet, the waste of the steep earthy faces of these banks— many of them from seven to nine feet from the average level of the water to their uppermost edge—after times of long-continued drought, or other times of sharp and continued frost, suggests a total amount of abrasion which is not easily calculable, alike from its magnitude and from its indefinite factors. Say that a frost of from fifteen to twenty degrees lasts over three or four nights—and there are few winters in which that does not befall from half a dozen to half a score times—and that such frost affects or causes the exposed part of the bank to, so to speak, exfoliate to the depth of only an inch and a half; or that a drought of a third or a half the duration of that of the summer of 1889 pulverises the said surface to no more than the same extent; and that so, in either case, there is so much material, easy to be removed, placed at the disposal of the first "fresh" that ensues; of course the absolute linear space between bank-face and bank-face cannot escape being affected in the same proportion. Carry this process on over a year,—or much more, over a series of years,—and it is self-evident that the banks, considering only this absolute waste of either of them, must be receding from each other indefinitely; unless indeed there be some compensating energy at work. And that compensating energy is what I am intending by the phrase "lateral movement."

The action of this movement is seen, moreover, in other ways. Thus, for instance, there is not in all the extent of the beck with which we are concerned a "stream" or a "pool" remaining as it was, and exactly where it was, when I first threw a fly over its waters. Some of them have receded or otherwise altered from a hundred feet to a hundred yards in the positions occupied by them. In other words, there are now, and higher up in the river, beds of water-worn stones with a sharp run of the stream over them, where forty years ago there was only smoothly flowing water, with the bottom from a foot to two or three feet lower than it is now. Now these stones did not work their way up the stream, neither were they brought down from the rockier banks nearer the head-waters, for there are heavy mill-dams at Danby End and at Castleton; and as a matter of fact masses of rock or large blocks of stone are not driven over them. But these stones in the beck may be and are dug out by the stream itself from the banks which restrain it on either side. And these high banks, as I have described them, as pushed forward on either side by a slow progressive movement, would supply an adequate quantity of stony blocks and cobbles for the result alleged.

But this is by no means all. There is in the close vicinity of one of the "streams" referred to as having undergone great alteration, and also near a place where the southern bank of the stream shows very open tokens of slow but continued movement towards the water, a bed of yellow clay, of several feet in width, exposed to the continual action of a quickly running stream, and to all the attrition thereby involved, and which yet never seems to waste in the slightest degree. There it is still, within some eight or ten inches of the surface—that is, at what may be called the average level of the river—and there it has been these twelve or fifteen years, for I do not remember it during the earlier twenty-five years or so of my acquaintance with the beck-side, so far as ordinary observation can discern. And yet such a material, under such circumstances, must have undergone a process of degradation calculated to wear away many feet of its thickness. Of course then it must be rising towards the surface under an adequate amount of pressure. And that pressure can only be exerted by lateral superincumbent weight, alike local in character and in application. And yet in the close vicinity there are, as already noticed, more symptoms of relief of local pressure by the yielding of the bank in the immediate background than almost anywhere else. But whatever the bank may lose in this way— and the loss is evidently great—is fully compensated from behind, so that even after the lapse of forty years the said bank is practically unaffected and undiminished in volume, height, or general aspect and conditions. The inference seems plain : not only that what is worn away and lost in front is made good by what is supplied from behind, but that also there is a downward pressure somewhere in the rear, of great energy, and maintained in lasting vigour, the operation of which levers up the plastic clay-bed in the stream, and continually causes to be presented a renewed surface in compensation of that which is being continually abraded. And it is further, and thoughtfully, to be observed that, whatever is, as supposed, "made good from behind" is supplied, not by a series of slips perpetually falling forward and filling up the vacuities as they are created, but in some other way ; for in the first place, no such slips occur or have occurred, and in the second place, the slope from the foot of the Coums depression is so gradual and of such considerable linear width that mere slips within the higher area could in no way affect the condition of matters involved. But then there are these subsidences ; and the semicircular area over which they are in operation is a very considerable one, and the operation seems never to be subjected to either suspension or intermission.[1]

[1] Thus, at the foot of the moor-bank proper, about a quarter of a mile from the pseudo-gravel-pit, on the way to the Castle, is a wall of the

But if we are not merely permitted but compelled by
circumstances to assume that this is so, what follows? Surely
this: that, given the factor of time, there is presented a
forcible as well as intelligible explanation of the way in which
this remarkable-looking semicircular hollow or half-basin—
sufficiently marked to have been named "combe," or rather
"cwm," perhaps two thousand, perhaps three thousand, years
ago—first began to be and has gone on "being," and growing
and widening and deepening from the era of that said first
beginning in the far-away lost cycles of the infinite past down
to the fleeting times of the present measurable now. Yes,
only given the factor of time, this misnamed gravel-pit in our
well-named little local division of Coums supplies the clue to,
at least intimates the nature of, the explanation of the way in
which these sinking masses of material are disposed of in the
process of backing up the ever-worn but continually renewed
banks of that tireless little carrier, "the river of Esk."

ordinary mortarless description so common in this district, but well and
carefully built, and of a character to stand for a century with only casual
attention and repair. This wall has not been built twenty years yet,
and still it is perpetually in need, not of repairs merely, but of rebuilding,
in some part or other; sometimes even in two or three places at the same
time. It is seen to bulge and begin to overhang on the roadside, for
no apparent reason; and then, on some slight provocation of wind or
impact, over it comes for a rood together. Previously to the winter of 1888
three or four of these bulgings were patent to the most unobservant eye,
and it required no prophet to foretell the rebuilding which would become
necessary when once winter's winds and melting snows were past. And
the explanation is simply this: that the wall is built mainly along one
of the old lines of subsidence, and as the line of hard consolidated road
tends, in some degree, to influence the axis of subsidence by directing
it towards the more yielding material of the pasture-field on the slope
below, the support is gradually withdrawn from one part or another of
the foot of the wall, and naturally and necessarily it falls over on the
other side. Now the length of this wall is not less than the third of
a mile, and it terminates very nearly where the semicircular area called
Coums reaches, as to its highest part, its eastern limit. So wide and
extensive is the surface, over all of which some signs or other of vertical
displacement are perpetually to be traced.

MANNERS AND CUSTOMS

WEDDINGS—BURIALS—HALIKELDS AND THE
MELL-SUPPER—THE DOG-WHIPPER

DALES WEDDINGS AND THEIR ACCOMPANIMENTS

THE most typical Dales wedding I ever remember having witnessed was nearly forty years ago and on Martinmas day. But I should not have spoken of the event in the singular number; for there were, in point of fact, four weddings all to be solemnised coincidently. And, whether by arrangement or by chance, all four of the couples, with their attendants, came up to the church in one cavalcade. First, there were no less than seven horsemen, each with a pillion-borne female behind him. Three of these were brides; the others attendants. Of other attendants, male and female, there must have been at least as many more; and then came those who had gathered to see the weddings, and so forth. But besides, there were from a dozen to a score men, mostly young, who carried guns, and who, as the weddingers passed down the little slope leading to the churchyard gate, fired a salvo. As may be supposed, more than one or two of the horses, being neither sobered by age and hard work, nor yet trained to stand fire, were startled and began to plunge or rear. I fully expected a disaster. However, with the exception of one of the pillion ladies, who slid gently—though not without raising her voice—backwards down over the crupper of her steed, no casualty occurred. After the ceremony was over, great was the scramble among the small boys for the coppers, which it was and is customary for the newly married man, or his best man, to scatter the moment the chancel door is left. And then an adjournment to the field adjoining the churchyard was made, and there were a series of races, all on foot, to be run for the ribbons which were the gift of the several brides; and as some of them gave more than one, the races were multiplied accordingly.

Time was, and not so very long before the commencement of my incumbency here, when these races were ridden on horseback; and at an earlier period still, the race was a "steeple-chase" across country — the goal being the house whence the bride had come, and to which the wedding cavalcade was to return for the usual festivities. More than once, too, I have known, when the bride in some way incurred the suspicion of niggardliness, through not complying with the recognised usage of supplying one ribbon at least to be run for, the "stithy was fired upon her," *i.e.* a charge of powder was rammed into a hole in the anvil (much after the fashion of a "shot" in a mine) and fired in derision; well pronounced, if the loudness of the report counted for anything; as the wedding party passed on the journey home from the church. The direct converse of this, was the firing of guns as the party passed the residences of friends or well-wishers.

The almost invariable practice on the part of the newly married man has been, and still is, after the registration in the vestry has been duly attended to, and when the party are just on the point of leaving the church, to hand to the officiating minister, nominally in payment of the fees, a handful, sometimes a very large handful, of money, taken without the slightest pretence of counting it from his trousers pocket, from which the said minister is expected to take the usual fees for parson and clerk; and, that done, to hand over the surplus to the bride. Twice within my incumbency a deviation from this ritual—and a very pretty deviation—has occurred. The bridegroom, together with the ring, at the proper point in the service, has laid upon the book the aforesaid handful of money, so that, besides the direct pertinency

of the next following part of the service, viz. "With this ring
I thee wed," ensued a typification of the further sentence,
"With all my worldly goods I thee endow."[1]

The races still linger on, and only a week or two since
the bride gave two "ribbons to be run for"; and a few years
ago one young chap, fleet of foot, and with as much inclination
for "laiking" (playing) as for sticking to work—some folk said
more—was quoted as the fortunate winner of almost enough to
start an itinerant haberdasher in trade. But still, even so,
"what a falling off was there!" For nearly the whole, if not
the whole, of the usages under notice are, in the strictest sense,
survivals. To what an extent the original customs obtained in
the district may be as largely, as well as safely, inferred, perhaps,
from the memorials engraved on the tablets of the folk-speech,
as from any other source or authority. There are three terms,
of which it is almost incorrect to say that, however much
fallen into disuse, they are quite obsolete. These are, Bride-
ale, Bride-door, Bride-wain; and they are defined, the first, as
"the warmed, sweetened, and spiced ale yet presented in some
villages to a wedding party on its return from church"; the
second, as "the door of the house from which the bride proceeds to church, and at which the wedding festivities are to be
held afterwards: used in the phrase 'to run for the bride-
door'"; and the third, as "a waggon, loaded with household
goods, to be conveyed from the bride's father's house to the
bridegroom's." The late F. K. Robinson, the careful compiler
of the Whitby Glossary, and collector of unconsidered trifles
in the way of tradition, local legend, and the like, says, "To
'run for the bride-door' is to join in the race for the bride's
gift, run by divers of the young men of the neighbourhood,
who wait near the church-door till the marriage ceremony is
over. The prize is usually a ribbon, which is worn for the
day in the hat of the winner." That other great collector of
archaic words and phrases, usually quoted as Mr. Halliwell,
after giving a precisely similar statement, adds that "the race

[1] See Appendix K.

is run to the bride-door." But in Cumberland, according to
Brockett, it is customary for the bridegroom, "attended by
his friends on horseback, to proceed at a gallop to the house
of the bride's father. . . . After breakfast the whole party
ride to church together, and at the conclusion of the ceremony
they all proceed to some neighbouring alehouse, where many
a flowing bumper is drunk to the health of the happy pair.
Then they set off at full speed towards the future residence of
the bride, where a handkerchief is presented to the first who
arrives." In Craven, according to the same authority, after
the service is over, "a ribbon is offered as the winner's prize,
either in a foot or a horse race. Whoever first reaches the
bride's habitation is ushered into the bridal chamber, and after
having performed the ceremony of turning down the bedclothes,
he returns, carrying in his hands a tankard of warm ale, to
meet the bride, to whom he triumphantly offers the cup he
bears, and by whom he is presented with the ribbon as the
trophy of his victory." When making inquiries on the general
subject some twenty-five years ago, I found that much of
what is thus detailed was still carried on at St. Helen's,
Auckland, and other villages in the county of Durham; only
the handkerchief was supposed to be a delicate substitute for
the bride's garter, which used to be taken off as she knelt at
the altar; and, the practice being anticipated, the garter was
generally found to do credit to her taste and her skill in
needlework, and was made the chief prize in the ensuing sports.
In Cleveland, however, and the neighbouring district the hot
ale, duly sweetened and spiced, was presented by the friends of
the bridal party at some point or points of the return journey
from church. Mr. Robinson's testimony is to the effect that,
within the present half-century, the custom has been upheld
in full force at Robin Hood's Bay, as many as twelve hot-pots
having been brought forth and partaken of in the one-mile
distance between the church and the town.

Hardly more than half a century since these races

were hotly contested in Danby by mounted men, two or three of whom, together with their steeds, were well known for their exploits on such occasions of racing. One of these men, a member of an old and "yabble" (well-to-do) Danby family, was, if my memory serves me rightly, the retailer of a tradition, mentioned for my instruction, that in days gone by the race was always from the churchyard gate to the bride-door, and that the prize was not barely the bride's garter, but the added privilege of taking it himself from her leg as she crossed the threshold of her home. The hot-pots of the Cleveland dales, the liberal ale-drinking in Cumberland and Craven mentioned by Brockett, the rapid riding as well as the fact of the mounted cavalcade, all point to Northern customs, where the very word for a wedding—*brullaup*, or bride-rush or speed—is itself a standing testimony to what the marriage ride was in the old days; and as to that, let the following sentence bear its own witness: "The most ancient mode of wooing had at least the merit of simplicity; it consisted in carrying off the desired object by physical force. There are traces of the custom in a ceremony still occasionally practised on the marriage of a Welsh peasant. After the wedding the bride-groom mounts on horseback and takes his bride behind him. A certain amount of 'law' is given them, and then the guests mount and pursue them. It is a matter of course that they are not overtaken; but, whether overtaken or not, they return with their pursuers to the wedding feast." The old old usage in vogue when the matter in hand was the obtaining of a helpmeet amid the burdens and labours of life, which lives as a survival in the old classical myth of the Rape of the Sabines, — the usage which prescribed or compelled the securing of a spouse by an absolute abduction of her by force from another tribe or another district,—is more than faintly figured forth in the Welsh custom just named, while the horse-races of two or three generations back, explained by all we now know concerning the marriage customs of the

P

remote past, contain much more than an indication merely of what their real origin and meaning unquestionably must be. And, little as the fleet-footed young dalesmen think of it when "running for the ribbon," they are doing their little best to keep up the remembrance that, in the old days of their fore-elders' and predecessors' living experience, if a man wanted a wife, he had to go and seek her where it was known there was an eligible young lady, who might be won literally *vi et armis*, or by dint of the strong hand and fleet enduring horse.

As to the bride-wain the thing may be obsolete, but neither the feeling nor the practice connected with the name is so. The long lists of "wedding presents" we see paraded in the newspapers on occasion of some "high-up" bridal, and the array of less gorgeous but equally well-intended presents one may see in even our humble Dales habitations, alike testify to the survival of the idea which found its expression in the older days in the bride-wain and its accessories.

As to what the bride-wain really was. When I first came into residence here, there were few farmhouses in which there was not one of those fine old black oak cabinets or "wardrobes," with carved panels, folding-doors, and knobby feet, that have gladdened so many collectors' hearts; in not a few cases I have seen them in old cottages also. And not once or twice only, but many times I have heard the name "bride-wain" attributed to them. The word itself was sufficient to suggest if not to provoke inquiry. For the "wain" was a vehicle that went upon wheels, and upon two wheels rather than four; because the wain upon four wheels speedily became a waggon, and ceased to be a wain. But a press or wardrobe certainly is not a vehicle, however much it may be a repository.

But the wardrobe might be, and often was in the olden times, a constituent portion of the "wedding presents," which always partook of the homely and useful character, almost to the exclusion of the merely graceful or pretty, and much more the sentimental. And the closets above, with their carven doors, and the drawers below with their antique brass handles and lock-plates, so far from being empty, were uncomfortably full with articles of household garnishing or personal wear, made from home-grown, home-spun, home-woven, home-made material, linen or woollen. Much thereof might be the work of the bride's own deft, if toil-hardened fingers; but much, too, came of the many and heartily offered gifts of the neighbours and friends of the young couple. And it was once a thing of occasional occurrence rather than a custom that could be said to prevail, to place this wardrobe, so stored, on a wain—itself a gift like the rest, as well as the oxen which drew it—and convey it to the church at which the marriage ceremony was to be solemnised; making it a part of the wedding procession, in fact, and letting it stand by the church-door, or in the very porch, while the priest was fulfilling his function; and after the service to drag it thence to the future abode of the couple just made one. So by an easy transition of idea the wardrobe itself came to be called a bride-wain. "One such bride-wain," I have said in my Glossary, "which took its departure for the church from Danby Castle, was specially mentioned by my informant as having had no less than sixteen oxen yoked to it," many of the oxen so employed having actually been gifts (as noticed above), as well as the wardrobe itself, and no small part of its contents.

I see, too, that I have remarked at the place cited—what should hardly be passed over without note or comment—"that it was essential that the wain should travel along the ordinary or recognised 'church-road,' and not make short cuts or other deviations from the time- and tradition-hallowed as well as established route."

But all these things are altered now, and I am not altogether sure that all of them are altered for the better. I am no indiscriminate *laudator temporis acti*, but I cannot help seeing that more modern usages have shut out much that was simple, homely, and touching, without introducing any improvement upon the old downright, homespun code of manner and action.

I remember having an old man of nearly seventy pointed out to me in my father's Lincolnshire parish, who was said to own land and property to the value of a thousand pounds or so, and of whom it was told that, on coming away from the church on his wedding-day, he said to his newly-made wife, "I have the price of a pint still left in my pocket. Shall we go to the public-house and drink it, or shall we go and work?" And the lady was said to have answered, "Well, if it is left to me, I say, let us work," and work they did ; and they worked on from his twopence halfpenny to his thousand. I think there was the same downright and honest thrift and perseverance and industry throughout these dales in the old days ; and I think, too, it was better than the aping of the "wedding-tour" which is now getting the upper hand.

Not that there may not be some compensation. There is certainly less of the exuberant festivity on the occasion of a wedding than there used to be,—festivity which so continually degenerated into downright drunkenness and debauchery,—and the people generally have learnt to respect decency of expression and conduct. In the old days a spade was a spade, and there was no affectation of reticence about naming it.

BURIALS AND THEIR ACCOMPANIMENTS

I THINK I have had, first and last, within the last five-and-twenty years, either shown me or brought to me, something like a large wheelbarrow-load of fragments of pottery taken out of the earth thrown up in the process of digging the necessary graves in the Danby churchyard. It is mainly of one character—coarse, rough, and red; red, however, of different shades. Most of the vessels of which these sherds are fragments seem to have been of the jug or pitcher description, having handles, plain or lined or twisted, with mouths, not of large size in proportion to the other dimensions, flanging outwards a little, and glazed inside for some little depth, and with the glaze in some instances straying a little over the outside of the neck.

That these vessels are of mediæval date there can be no doubt. Precisely similar vessels—similar, that is, as to ware, colour, shape or average form, handles, glaze, etc.—may be seen in any collection of such pottery, notably in the York Museum.

I have, in some cases, seen portions of five or six different specimens taken out of the earth thrown up from one grave; and in very few instances indeed is a grave dug without the occurrence of some of these reminiscences of a past and forgotten usage.

But besides these old sherds, there is disclosed in almost every case more or less charcoal, sometimes in quantities such as to attract the trained eye at once, and always in particles the size of a small bean, or in small sections, admitting of easy identification when looked for. I have occasionally seen half a spade-graft of mould brought to the surface, nearly one-half or one-third of which was composed mainly of charcoal. In fact my sexton—who was trained to the watchful part of the barrow-work, so that he became one of my two best men —still lives in hope of finding such a mass of charcoal in connection with the pottery as to enable us to come to a satisfactory conclusion touching the presence of the substances throughout the churchyard.

For connection there must have been, and, as necessarily, an explanation dependent on that connection. And, for my own part, I think there is a connection between finds of this and finds of yet another sort, made in the same place and under the same circumstances, which deserves some attention. At least half a dozen small silver coins have been noticed among the mould thrown up in the course of grave-diggings, picked up and put into my hands. One may have been a coin of the time of Henry III ; the others were of the reigns of the Edwards. When one looks at these small objects, and considers their tenuity and their lustreless, tarnished, almost decomposed condition—one or two among them are as frail as chippings from the shell of a boiled egg—one cannot help thinking, " Well, for one that is seen and rescued, the chances must be that many others are never detected, and remain where they were placed—at least, 'beneath the sod '—never coming within the range of a speculative antiquary's eye, nor able to attract even passing observation." It was but the other day that, in the course of my casual reading, I met with the record of a silver coin being found still between the jaws of the skull of a man who had been buried three centuries or more ago, and it reminded me of what had happened at one of the churches in this neighbourhood not twenty years since, as far as my recollection serves me. On the disturbance and removal of the remains of a former interment, when the skull came to be moved something was heard to rattle in among the bones of it, which, on examination, proved to be a silver coin about the size of a Commonwealth half-crown (or rather florin, I suppose). And it was evident that its original place of deposit must have been between the teeth, or at least just inside the mouth.

While I was closely occupied over the final sheets of my Cleveland Glossary, a correspondent (Mr. Baring Gould) wrote to me as follows: "I heard some rustics talking about an odd old man who had been buried somewhere up your way a few years ago with a candle, a penny, and a bottle of port; and, as they explained it, the candle was to light the way to Jerusalem, the penny to pay the ferry, and the port to sustain him on the journey." And Professor George Stephens of Copenhagen about the same time gave me the following quotation: "Within the coffin, along with herself, she got a pair of new brogues, a penny candle, and a hammer, with an Irish sixpenny-piece to pay her passage at the gate."

And these old, old coins found in my churchyard, and, to my knowledge, in several others in the district as well, have the same story to tell to quickened ears as these two instances of so much later a date, and the multitudes of others that may be found by looking for them; and that story, I conceive, is not so very widely different in its essential characteristics from the story to be told by the pottery and the charcoal obtruding themselves on the notice of the observant in the old, but not as yet compulsorily disused, graveyards of our country churches.

One of my earliest recollections as a boy is of places—houses, always old and mostly old-fashioned, barns, lanes, the moated sites of old manor-houses, "four-want-ways" or the place of intersection of two cross-roads, churchyards, suicides' graves—which were spoken of, dreaded, avoided after nightfall, as being "haunted." There were two barns, one local "hall," one moated site of an old mansion, one road-side grave, all within half an hour's walk of one of my homes in the days of my boyhood, besides a long-disused old house of considerable size and pretension, a grove, and an old ruinous building, which once, I suppose, had been the parish pest-house, close to the place of my schooldays—to say nothing of a long, dark passage behind two of the dormitories at the school itself—all of which were "haunted." And there was a large section of an old moated mansion in another of my father's curacies, with a tapestried chamber in it, the subject illustrated thereon being the beheading of John the Baptist, with his bleeding head in the charger, wrought in right grisly fashion; as to which I heard a man, mainly employed in my father's garden, tell a right gruesome story of his own experiences there one night when storm-stayed.

I found no difficulty in entering into the feelings of the narrator, and understanding the impression produced upon him. And perhaps I was enabled to trace the mental process throughout; for the district he lived in was full of common-place, unimaginative superstition. But there is no need to give a catalogue of the apparitions, ghosts, spirits, which were said to beset the district, or to enter into exhaustive details. A sample or two will suffice. There was the lady who, at a certain hour on a certain night, depending on the moon's age, walked abroad in her bloodstained night-gear, but without her head. There was another of the same sex, and habited also in her white night-gown, who "walked" with her hands chained and her lower limbs fettered, sobbing and crying, and jangling her chains. There was the great dog *minus* his head, who ran to his destination—where he vanished suddenly—as well as if he had had his eyes in the usual place to guide him. There was the black wide-horned creature with great glaring saucer-eyes, at the old moat. There was the shape of the suicide, with his self-murdering knife, his gibbering features, trembling limbs, and pitiful moans,—all of these, and many more. And the story was, this man had cut his own throat, and by "crowner's-quest law" had been buried by the roadside with a stake driven through his body. I make no doubt all that was true to the letter. And then there had been a jumbling together of the old tradition and of older folklore ideas, which had got mixed in the process, and the issue of the process was the ghost.

There is no doubt that the self-murderer, or the doer of some atrocious deed of violence, murder, or lust, was buried by some lonely roadside, in a road-crossing, or by the wild woodside, and that the oak or, oftener, thorn stake was driven through his breast; but not because of any intended scorn, or horror, or abhorrence. These were the characters who—to use an expression common enough among us to this day, though perhaps we do not trouble to think of its origin or meaning—could not "rest in their graves." They *had* to wander, nay, often they were self-constrained to wander about the scenes of their crimes, or the places where their unhallowed carcases were deposited, unless, that is to say, they were prevented; and as they wanted the semblance, the *simulacrum*, the shadow-substance of their bodies for that purpose—otherwise there could have been no appearance—the body it was which was made secure by pinning it to the bottom of the grave by aid of the driven stake. Here is an explanation which has long been lost sight of, and replaced by notions involving the ideas of ignominy, abhorrence, execration, or what not; and it is just the explanation that was wanted. The corpse of the fearful malefactor, cast out of hallowed ground, as belonging to the devil and not to the saints, must be disabled, as well as the guilty spirit itself, for further mischief or ill-doing.

And there were other means adopted with the same end in view. The head was severed from the body and laid between the legs, or placed under the arm—between the arm and the side, that is. Or the feet and legs were bound together with a strong rope. Or the corpse might be cut up into some hollow vessel capable of containing the pieces, and carried away quite beyond the precincts of the village and deposited in some bog or morass, so as never to come within the precincts of the hallowed ground.

Now these things are not the creation of fancy. The records of such sentences and of their execution exist in the Dooms-books or other judicial records of this country and other lands in the north of Europe, and there is a sort of uncanny recognition in them of the apparitions of headless ladies and chain-rattling ghosts, ghastly bearers of cruel knives, and the like.

I remember when, some twenty-five years or more ago, I became acquainted with Hylten Cavallius's admirable book on the ethnology of a certain district in the south of Sweden, I was greatly struck with the passage of which the following is a translation : " For the purpose of preventing restless, unruly, sinful, and intensely worldly men from 'going again after death'"—the Cleveland idiom is "coming again"—"our Wärend folk have been in the habit from a very remote time of employing various characteristic measures. The very oldest among these takes its origin from the ancient fire-cult, and the still older sun-worship. It is to this that we must refer the presence, for the protection of the dwelling against ghosts (*gengångare*), of a red cock, the solar bird, on his perch over the house-entrance. To the same again must be referred the custom of consuming with fire the mattress on which a man has breathed his last ; of casting live coals (charcoal, notably) after a corpse on its removal from the dwelling, and of strewing ashes, salt, linseed, or the seed of the water-hemlock, around the homestead, or across the approach to the house, beyond which limit the ghost may not pass. On the same principle, subsequently to the time at which men became acquainted with the use of steel, the custom has been to drive in an axe or some other sharp-edged tool above the door of

the house-place. And at a later period still it became usual
to tie the feet of the corpse together, to stick pins into the
shroud in such wise that the points were opposed to the feet;
as also to place hooks and eyes in the coffin, or else a stake
wrenched out of the fence round the homestead. Moreover,
when a corpse is carried out of the house of death, it is invariably borne forth feet first, in order to prevent the dead
person from 'coming again.' Nay, even in the days of hoary
eld, it was a custom to whisper in the ear of the corpse that
he was not to 'come again'; while, finally, there was the old
practice of laying earth on the body, which was a heathen
practice long before it was adopted in the Christian grave-
service. And even yet the accustomed Wärend name for the
burial ceremony is to 'earth-fasten a corpse,' or to 'earth-
fasten the dead person.'"

Turning all this over in one's mind, and remembering
at the same time that the idea represented by the word
"haunted" is as yet by no means an extinct idea, there is no
great difficulty in suggesting an explanation of the presence of
charcoal in these old graves in the churchyards.

But it is possible to illustrate the living reality of this
superstition by a reference to what took place here not so
very long before my personal acquaintance with the place
commenced. An old woman who lived in Fryup, and whose
chief celebrity depended upon the allegation that she kept
the "Mark's e'en watch," and was able in consequence to fore-
show the deaths of the coming year, one St. Mark's day, when
she was questioned on the subject after her vigil, announced
her own death as among the foredoomed ones, and assigned
her reason for saying so. "And," she added, "when I dee, for
dee I s'all, mind ye carry me to my grave by t' church-road,
and not all the way round by t' au'd Castle and Ainthrop.
And mind ye, if ye de'ant, I'll come again."

Now the church-road lay straight past her house to the
foot of a very steep moor-bank, up which it went—and goes

yet—with two zigzags. It is a stiff climb at any time, even
when one has only himself and his coat to carry; but with a
burden such as a coffin, with the grisly occupant inside, it is
"hosses' wark, not men's." Well, the old lady died as she
had predicted, and she died in a snowy time. And the
difficulties of the church-road in a snowy time are almost intensely enhanced. I have gone both up and down the bank at
such seasons, and speak with feeling. But the bearers faced
the difficulties—perils, in a sense, they almost amounted to,—
and waist-deep sometimes; still they persevered, and eventually got through with their undertaking and their burden.
In plain words, they were ready to face anything; and many
among them must have had such a day of toil and effort and
fatigue as never before nor after fell to their lot; but they
could not, dared not, face the chance of the old woman's
"coming again."

My own idea, entertained now for a very long time past,
relatively to the presence of charcoal and broken pottery in
our graves, is that they were placed at the first in the original
graves in conjunction; that is to say, the charcoal, in the
form of live coals, was placed inside the earthen vessels.
And while it is possible that the purificatory energy of
fire may not have been lost sight of in the observance,
all the probabilities suggested by such collateral items of
evidence as those I have quoted go to show that the deposit
was of the nature of the casting of live embers after the
departing corpse, burning the straw mattress on which the
departed had given up the ghost, strewing ashes, salt, or what
not, or striking some sharp-edged instrument above the house-
door, with the avowed object of keeping ghosts, or *the* special
ghost, in abeyance. And at this point there is another fact
which it will be by no means irrelevant to advert to. And
that is, that in all the burial mounds I have myself opened or
seen opened, or the opening of which as described by competent
observers, taking special notes of all incidental and collateral

particulars I am acquainted with, I do not remember an instance in which the absence of charcoal is recorded. I do not mean that there were always such evidences of burning as are attested by the presence of charcoal in mass, or sensible quantities, but that the unvarying rule appears to be that charcoal occurs in all these mounds, scattered up and down throughout the greater part of the hill. Even in the small houes, fifteen to twenty feet across, and a foot and a half, or little more, in height (of which literally hundreds have existed on these moors, and many scores of which are still in being, and none of which ever covered a burnt body), there are small fragments of charcoal in every individual mound, varying in size from a bean to a nutmeg, far more than enough to convey the inevitable conclusion that it was not there accidentally.

The speculation, the corroborative considerations, and the conclusion as to the why and because of the occurrence of charcoal and potsherds in our Danby graves, are all, whether entertained or no, matters of no slight or merely local interest.

BURIALS AND THEIR ACCOMPANIMENTS

(*continued*)

I HARDLY cared to enter upon my recollections or experiences
in relation to the peculiarities which have characterised Danby
funerals—or, to use the older Cleveland word, "burials"—some
of which even yet are hardly things of the past, without
first adverting to the occurrence of both charcoal and broken
pottery, in marked quantity, in the oft-stirred earth thrown
up in the process of digging our modern graves. That occurrences of this kind are not exceptional, that they are not
confined to Danby alone, I am well aware. I have never
examined the earth thrown out of a new-made grave in any
one of the churchyards of the near district without finding
samples of the pottery; and I will specify the churchyards of
Great Ayton, Westerdale, and Sneaton as among those most
prominent in my recollections. I have also heard the same of
one or two other churchyards wherein I have had no opportunity of personal examination. One other remarkable case,
however, is almost worth special notice.

Many years ago I had undertaken a week-day service in
the schoolroom at Dunsley. In some way or other, after the
service, the subject of graveyard potsherds was referred to, and
the schoolmaster remarked that he had collected a number of
such fragments, which appeared to answer the description I
had been giving. He produced a quantity of them, and without exception they were similar to those with which I was so

familiar, except only that they were all portions of broken
pot- or pitcher-handles. But on inquiry, it proved that these
only had been preserved, because they were not mere sherds
from the broken sides of the vessels. I further learned that
all came from a place in the close vicinity of the school, namely,
the site of the ancient Dunsley chapel. I went with the master
to the place, and he showed me where the greater part had
been met with, and although he did not seem very hopeful that
renewed search would be successful, still certain small pieces
were found. I will only add that my informant made no doubt
about the sherds coming from the old graves; and old graves
they certainly were. Young's memorandum concerning the old
chapel is as follows : "It was older than the Hermitage of
Mulgrif, and it subsisted longer; for it continued until the
Dissolution;" and in a note he adds : "An imperfect inscription
shows that it had been used as a cemetery prior to the Reform-
ation. . . . The foundation of the north wall has been undermined by people digging up materials for repairing roads, and
the bones of the dead have been exposed to view."

This is a valuable testimony as bearing upon the dates to
which I have assigned the original deposits of pottery and
charcoal in our own churchyard.

But to come to more recent times and later "reminiscences."
It is a well-known circumstance that—to use the formal term
employed in the old county records—the "people called
Friends" were once both numerous and influential in these
dales, and nowhere more so than in Danby. I should be
more than justified if I extended the remark to a very much
wider North Riding area than this parish only, as a list of
North Riding places licensed for the Quakers' worship about
the time of the Toleration Act, which I compiled for publication in the North Riding Records Volume for the year 1889,
abundantly demonstrates. Indeed they were so numerous here
that no less than three of their burial-places exist on the west
side of Danby-dale only.

There were still five or six Quaker families in the Dale when I first came to it. Of course I knew them all, and had a great respect for more than one of them, as well as simple regard. Indeed, one of them—he died, turned of eighty years old, many years ago—was a man much looked up to beyond the limits of the Dale; and was often called upon to act as arbiter and peacemaker in cases which might otherwise have led on to litigation. He was a man of shrewd, sound sense and judgment; and it was with the feeling of having lost a personal friend and a helper in all efforts for the good of the parish and the district, that I heard of the death of old William Hartas.

The days of his lifetime were the days in which church rates were collected. Dear old William and his co-religionists never paid a penny of the "cess" they were liable for. But somehow or other, when the churchwardens went their collecting rounds, a sheaf or two of corn, of an approximate value to the sum set down against their names, stood handy to the said churchwardens' hands, and no inquiry was ever made as to the person who had "conveyed" the Quakers' corn.

There is a story told of old William which I have every reason to believe is a true one. It is, I suppose, well known that there is no grave-service in use among the Friends. The ceremony of depositing the body in the grave is a silent one, unless some one or more among the attendants on the funeral feels called on to address the bystanders. My friend William was often in the habit of speaking on more or less public occasions, both in the parish and out of it; and when he attended a funeral of a Friend it was by no means unusual for him to "speak a few words."

On one such occasion no one spoke after the coffin was lowered to its resting-place, but there seemed to be a sort of expectation that William would "say a few words" before the party separated. And so he did. After looking long and fixedly into the grave in still silence, he gave utterance at length to the following speech: "Our fri'nd seems vara comfortable. Thou mun hap him oop,"—these last words being addressed to the sexton.[1]

Many a time have I seen this worthy old man, and others of the sect, in attendance at the funeral of some old and respected parishioner. Sometimes I have seen them, as I went out in advance of the coffin into the graveyard, the first part of the burial service over, sitting in the church porch. But not once or twice only I have seen them come inside the church and sit the service through—hatted, as a matter of course; and I had more reasons than one for not being intolerant enough to insist on the removal of themselves, if so be their hats were unremovable. I was glad to see them among the throng of other parishioners who came to pay their last tribute of regard to the person who had long lived among them, a neighbour among neighbours and a friend among friends. And I was not going to take any step which might have the tendency to lessen good feeling, either general or particular.

Besides, I could not, with anything like consistency; for the rule was the country-side throughout, as it had been even in Scarborough up to less than ten years before I took up my abode there, for all the male relatives of the deceased person present among the mourners to sit close round the coffin during the reading of the burial-service psalm and lesson with their hats on. I had for divers reasons, and with the full concurrence of the patron and others concerned, resolved to let the practice wear out, instead of suppressing it with the high hand, as the Vicar of Scarborough had done; for I did think that people who had had the good example of the parson and his

---

[1] I should like to record one other characteristic saying of this good old man's, communicated by Sir Joseph Pease, which I had likewise heard from another member of the same family, but in the graphic dialect of the country: "If," said the old man, "if my horse falls with me *once*, I forgive him; it may have been more my fault than his. If it happens a *second* time, I part with him; as, if any accident occurred through his doing it a *third* time, I should blame myself."

brother the parish-clerk, to say nothing of the churchwardens, customarily wearing their hats in church, and never doffing them even on Sundays until they had got to their several places in the church, had a very fair claim to be treated with some sort of tolerance, and be shown the better way, instead of being driven into it at the cost of much heart-burning. And so I let the hats alone, and did not interfere with my good old friends the Quakers.

But truly the "burials" were rather a thorn in my side for long. It is almost "a tale that is told" now, but it is perhaps worth recalling and recording. As soon after the breath had left the body as was possible, the next day at the latest—often the same day, if the person had died early—the person whose professional name was "the bidder," went round from house to house among those who were to be "bidden to t' burial," to "warn" them that the burial was fixed for such and such a day, and to add, "and so and so"—naming the principal friend or friends of the deceased—"expect you at ten o'clock in the morning." The "minister" was always among the first to be bidden. Sometimes when the dead person had been long in the place, had borne parochial office, and had won the goodwill and respect of all the neighbours, or if he was a man with numerous relations and connections (a very common case), or for whom general sympathy had been aroused, these invitations might be numbered, not merely by the score, but by the hundred. I have myself counted more than three hundred seated in the church on at least four, if not five, different occasions. And the rule is, and, still more, was, that the preponderating majority of these "went to the burial" at the house where the corpse lay, beginning at ten o'clock and continuing to drop in, according to convenience or distance to be traversed, throughout the morning and afternoon till it became time to "lift the body" and make a start for the church.

And all these were fed—entertained, rather—at the house of mourning, if it chanced to be that of one of the principal inhabitants. All day long, in relays of from a dozen up to a score, according to the dimensions of the reception-room, the hungry host came streaming in, until all had been "served." Those who had been the first to enter went and sat about wherever they could find seats, whether in the house or outside, or in the farm premises, or at some neighbour's, smoking (not without the necessary "wet," it might be) and chatting, as on any other occasion when friends and acquaintances were wont to meet. The last part of the entertainment, at least in the later days of the old practice, was to hand round on salvers or trays glasses of wine and small round cakes of the crisp sponge description, of which most of the guests partook.

I do not know if these cakes are still in vogue,—"funeral biscuits," I have heard them called,—but I was greatly interested one day some twenty years ago or more, on going into a confectioner's shop in Whitby, to see some of these cakes in a dish, but not, as it were, exposed for sale. I forget how the talk began; but the shopkeeper—an old, gray-headed, tottering man, as I saw him a short time ago—had somehow come to tell me what they were, and for what funeral they had been ordered; and by the merest chance he gave me an, if not the, old name for them. He called them, not funeral biscuits, but, as it sounded from his lips, "averil breead," or, as it should be written, avril bread.

As will be readily conceived by any one who knows of my eighteen or twenty years of persevering "dialect-word" hunting, and, more especially, by any one who has ever occupied himself personally in that engaging (if not exciting) pursuit, I pricked up my ears on hearing this word; for I recognised it at once, and it was as good as half-a-dozen shots in the turnips, and never a miss among them. I had had years before many a struggle over the origin (rather than the derivation merely) of such words as *dozz* or *duzz, wossle* or *wursel*, and so forth; and it was not without trouble and difficulty that I had got these forms, rather than words, which, as it were, had been turned inside out like a stocking, turned back again to the right side outwards. *Dozz* or *duzz* was the country pronunciation of *dorse* or *dirze*, as *dorse* or *durze* was of *drose* (from an original Scandinavian *drösa*, cognate with our English *drizzle*), and *wossle* or *wursel* was the same sort of dissolving-view word from English *wrestle*, and so forth. On the same rule—that of the transposition of the letter *r* and its following vowel—*avril* was simply *arvil* or *arvel*, and that was neither more nor less than *arval*, or succession-ale, where *al* or *ale* has just the same weight and substance as in bridal, still current, and the leet-ales, scotales, church-ales, clerk-ales, bid-ales (all quoted by Skeat), and toll-ales, and another or two, all obsolete. And as to the word itself, entire, that is, arvel or arval, "At arvel—heir-ale—feasts," says Sir G. W. Dasent, "when heirs drank themselves into their fathers' land and goods, there was great mirth and jollity, and much eating and hard drinking of mead and fresh-brewed ale" (*Burnt Njal,* i. p. cxv.); this among the old Icelanders and their compatriots.

So much for the "arval bread" which, in the form of the cakes and biscuits aforesaid, was handed round with the wine by two young women who, from the discharge of this function, were—are yet—termed "servers," and whose place it is, as the funeral procession marshals itself at the churchyard gate, to walk immediately in front of the coffin.

As to the preparation made for supplying the bodily wants of such great concourses, I have again and again heard statements made as to the number of "stones of beef and ham" provided and consumed. Notably this was so in the case of one of the worthiest of the many worthy Dales yeomen—"freeholders," they call themselves—it has been my privilege as well as my pleasure to know, who was one of the church-wardens when I came here, and who died at the age of eighty-eight, never having paid a doctor's fee up to his death-illness, which was rather cessation of life than sickness. When he was buried, between two and three hundredweight of meat, mainly beef and bacon, was put on the tables; and when the keeper and owner of one of the inns at Castleton died—a man universally popular as well as known to all—the amount provided was said to have been even greater still.

These great assemblages and colossal providings are now mainly things of the past, although even within the past year I have twice seen upwards of one hundred and fifty to two hundred persons assembling or assembled in the church and churchyard to be present at a funeral.

Necessarily when there were such numbers of friends and relations to be fed, and such scant accommodation as cramped space in the kitchen, as well as at the board, entailed, there was great loss of time, and often exceeding unpunctuality in the starting, and, much more, the arrival at the churchyard of the funeral cortege. Once in my predecessor's time the arrival did not take place until after dark, and the service in the church —which is near no house at all save one, and that is a third of a mile distant—had to be read by the light of a tallow dip, procured after some delay, and the grave-side service by the wavering, flickering light of the same held in the sexton's hand.

Delay too would naturally in such a district as ours be caused by distance and bad roads; and other causes also led to unpunctuality. For in one case, when the funeral was fully two hours late, the procession had started in ample time, and the detention had arisen from a totally unforeseen and, in practice, unaccustomed cause. It was a long way that had to be traversed, undoubtedly—nearer twelve than ten miles, I should say—and much more than half of it over highways that crossed the moors. Yet there was a short cut that might have been taken, but was not taken, contrary to the intentions and expectations of the organiser of the journey. For on reaching the point of divergence from the accustomed way, or the "highway," the proposed deviation was at once demurred to, and in the issue a sort of parliament was held on the highroad, and the decision to proceed by the high-road was deliberately come to.

And why? Nobody doubted that to take the longer way round would add still more to the delay occasioned by the debate; but there was a graver consideration than that, and one with which the weightier part of the mourners could not and would not deal lightly. The person to be buried was no other than the man previously mentioned more than once in these pages, namely, our friend Jonathan, who had fought the witches so strenuously with the best weapons at his command. "Take Jonathan to his last home otherwise than by the 'church-road'! Why, it wasn't to be thought of! He would never rest in his grave. He would come again. Didn't every one know that such as were carried to the church otherwise than by the 'church-road' were provoked, and got the power to come again?"

We remember the old woman in Little Fryup, who threatened her friends with what she would do if they did not carry her to her burial by the church-road, and how the dread of her menace forced her bearers to that terrible snow-hindered march up the steep bank and across the moorland ridge. And here was another case of the same kind, accentuated in a somewhat different manner, but quite as strongly and decisively marked.

I have been interested in finding repeated references made in the old County Records it has been my lot to deal with during the last eight or nine years, to the "church-way" or the "church-road," in divers parts of the North Riding, and the observance evidently attached to it in every individual instance. How old the notion is, how long ago it came to be held that a way over which a body was borne to its burial became thereby a recognised high-road, and obtained a certain sacred sanction therefrom, there is probably no one to tell us, and there may be no means of finding out. Probably also it might prove very hard to decide whether, in the case of this

bit of folklore, the survival is in the idea of the consecration
of the way by the carrying of the dead over it, or in the idea
that any not carried along the dedicated way are sentenced to,
or become qualified for, a restless unconfined sojourn in the
grave. But at least we know that, among our Scandinavian
ancestors at least, the hell-way and the hell-shoes and the
difficult and perilous passage to be essayed by the dead were
as constantly thought of and provided for as the occurrence of
death itself. The matter is a curious and interesting one, and
well deserves careful investigation.

But there are yet other matters to be remarked, or our
notice of the observances at a Dales "burying" would be left
imperfect. Thus the coffin is never borne on the shoulders
of the bearers, as is most customary elsewhere. So far as it
is "carried by hand" at all—which, from the distance of the
church from all the constituents of the population, is very
little, usually only from a few yards outside the churchyard-
gate to the trestles set to support it in the western part of the
nave of the church—it is carried by the aid of towels knotted
together and passed under the coffin, the ends on either side
being held by the bearers, six in number (or three pairs).
And as regards the bearers, the usage was so consistent and
so steadfast that there would be no impropriety in speaking
of it as "the rule." Thus a single young woman was borne
by six single young women, a single young man by six of his
compeers, a married woman by married women, and so on
all through. Nay, it is no unusual sight even yet to see the
child carried by six children, varying according to the sex of
the dead child. In the case of the young unmarried woman,
moreover, some peculiarities of costume were always to be
observed about the bearers. Their dress was not all unre-
lieved black. White sashes or scarfs were customarily worn, and
white gloves always. Much of this remains still, but the observance in such matters is hardly so religious as it used to be.

Another usage struck me very forcibly, when I was as

yet a stranger in the district, and to its ways and customs. This was the practice of singing at divers places and times during the proceedings. The custom used to be to sing a hymn, or part of one of the old version of the psalms, when the body was brought forth from the death-room, and set on the chairs arranged for its reception in front of the house. Singing was continued or repeated on "lifting the body," and again once or oftener on the road to the church—that is, in the days preceding the acquisition and use of the hearse, which, I believe, was a sort of joint-stock property at first. There were, indeed, in some places regular stations at which the body was rested and a hymn or psalm sung. Invariably, too, in the old days, and even in some instances in later days, when the funeral procession began to move down the grassy slope by which the churchyard is approached, a hymn was raised, and the singing was continued until the churchyard gate was reached. In point of fact, in the days immediately preceding my incumbency, the practice was such that the rubric prescribing the meeting of the corpse by the priest and clerks at the churchyard entrance, and their singing or saying the prescribed sentences as they preceded the body into the church, was not only practically but completely ignored. The singing was persevered in to the very entrance of the church. The singers were supreme, and "the priest and clerks" nowhere. This I stopped by remaining steadfast in the entrance to the churchyard until the loudest and longest-winded of the singing men had sung themselves out. And yet again, within the church, the strains were upraised on the conclusion of the reading of the lesson by the officiating minister. And as the old clerk drawled the words to be sung out, two lines at a time, and the voices, though many and strong, were restrained neither by training nor any niceties of pronunciation, modulation, or time, the effect was not usually either harmonious or such as to conduce to solemn or sober feelings.

Before long I was requested to give the hymn out myself, and the men who sang were members of the church choir. Previously the Wesleyan hymn-book was freely used, and the man who acted as reader of the two lines at a time outside the churchyard, and leader of the band, seldom darkened the church doors save when officiating as chief songman at a burying.

Some of the singing scenes I was privileged to witness, when I was still a stranger more or less, were, considering the occasion, painfully ludicrous. But it is all past now.

HOLY-WELLS, MELL-SUPPER, HARVEST-HOME

So far as I am aware, we have no well or spring in Danby
of reputed old-world sanctity; no wishing-well, rag-well, or
pin-well. A later name—in one sense later, if not in another
—is hâlikeld, holy-well; and, perhaps, the latest of all, St.
John's well, St. Hilda's well, or some other prefix embodying
a saintly name. What I mean to imply by speaking of these
terms or names as the one of them later than the other, according to sequence of time, is that almost certainly such names
as pin-well or wishing-well are distinct indications that, in the
remote times of our remote antecessors, some sort of religious
cult, some offering of adoration more or less pronounced, of
vows, gifts, wishes, uttered or conceived, found its expression
and its ritual at that place; that a well-preserved survival of
both sentiment and practice or observance continued, in the
early days of a brighter faith, to attach the idea of sanctity
and severance from the merely natural to the springing
waters, and to the place from which they gushed; and that
next, in the sequence of such succession, the name of some
saint, some great one in the annals of the new faith, should
either arbitrarily or for some special reason of force in the
vicinity, be attached to the hallowed keld, spring, or well.

Probably few persons except such as are in the habit of
poring over not only the six-inch Ordnance sheets, but old
plans or maps of parishes, estates, and farms, old charters and
other like documents dealing with grants of land and the

boundaries involved,—and last, but not least, old legends, old
folk-notions and feelings, old folk-practices and sayings, or
what not,—have any idea of the number of pin-wells and wishing-wells, of what used to be rag-wells, of hâlikelds or holy-
wells, and saints' wells, there still are, whether with or without
their old prestige, reputed sanctity, or Pool-of-Siloam virtue,
still duly accredited to them, scattered up and down throughout our Cleveland district. And a further remark that may
be safely ventured is, that the neighbourhood of the church
is not at all infrequently a clue to the vicinity of some such
spring or well. Such instances as those of St. Hilda's well
in Hinderwell churchyard, St. John's well at Mount Grace—
to which large and fully-organised pilgrimages were wont to
be made, even after the Dissolution—of the hâlikeld just
through the churchyard at Liverton, of the holy-well at
Crathorne, just outside the churchyard, of course occur to any
one moderately acquainted with the legends and local ideology
of the district. But besides these there are divers less
obtrusive instances of the same kind. And that there must
have been one of these now unsuspected and undreamt-of
wishing-wells or hâlikelds in Danby one can doubt but little,
land of fountains, wells, and springing waters as it is; only
there is no local name, no sort of folk-saying even, to indicate
which or where it was.

It may be supposed by some that much of this is merely
fancy; that, admitting there may have been the practice of
well-worship, of the offering of vows or wishes, or gifts, to the
spirit of the springing water or the running water, in the old
days that are gone, still there can be no survival of what is
essentially paganism in the nineteenth century; that ignorance
and superstition cannot extend to such a length as that, even
in far-away or out-of-the-way places, in this enlightened day
of ours. But there is no doubt possible on the subject. I
have seen pins enough in some of these pin-wells—many of
them as bright as when just taken out of the paper, and not

so very many years ago—to have furnished the votive pin-
cushion presented at a baby's birth; and although many of
them now may be put in in the way of frolic, and by the
sportive members of pleasure parties—as may be seen to one's
discontent at such wells as that at Mount Grace—yet there
is no doubt as to the *bona fides* with which the greater portion
of these votive offerings are dropped within the circle of
the mystic well.   There is something very suggestive even
yet to the mind of one accustomed to look into the reason
of things in J. R. Green's notice of the struggle between
Christianity and heathenism in England, and the tenacious
survival of the latter in divers matters and various directions
even after the apparent victory of the former.   "But if the
old faith was beaten by the new," he says, "it was long in
being killed.   A hundred years after the conversion of Kent,
King Wihtred had still to forbid Kentishmen 'offering to
devils.'   At the very close of the eighth century synods in
Mercia and Northumbria were struggling against the heathen
practice of eating horse-flesh at the feast to Woden.   In spite
of this resistance, however, Wodenism was so completely
vanquished that even the coming of the Danes failed to revive
it.   But the far older nature-worship, the rude fetichism which
dated back to ages long before history, had tougher and deeper
roots.   The new religion could turn the nature-deities of this
primæval superstition into devils, its spells into magic, its spae-
wives into witches, but it could never banish them from the
imagination of men; it had in the end even to capitulate to
the nature-worship, to adopt its stones and its wells, to turn
its spells into exorcisms and benedictions, its charms into
prayers.   How persistent was the strength of the old belief
we see even at a later time than we have reached: 'We
earnestly forbid all heathendom,' says a canon of Cnut's time.
'Heathendom is that men worship idols; that is, that they
worship heathen gods, and the sun or the moon, fire or rivers,
water-wells or stones, or great trees of any kind; or that they

love witchcraft, or promote *morth-work* in any wise, or by *blot*, or by *fyrht*, or do anything of like illusions.'" But although the secular arm was stretched out to stop the continued practice of heathen usage, either backing or being backed by authority of spiritual men, so that a witch-wife—the first in the grisly host—was drowned at London Bridge in the course of the tenth century, still there were many heathen usages against which "even councils did not struggle. Easter fires, May-day fires, midsummer fires, with their numerous ceremonies, the rubbing the sacred flame, the running through the glowing embers, the throwing flowers on the fire, the baking in it and distributing large loaves and cakes, with the round dance about it, remained village customs. At Christmas the entry of the boar's head, decked with laurel and rosemary, recalled the sacrifice of the boar to Frigga at the midwinter feast of the old heathendom. The autumn feast lingered on unchallenged in the village harvest-home with the sheaf, in old times the symbol of the god, nodding gay with flowers and ribbons on the last waggon. As the ploughman took to his plough he still chanted the prayer that, though christened as it were by the new faith, remained in substance a cry to the Earth-goddess of the old,—'Earth, Earth, Earth, Mother Earth, grant thee the Almighty one, grant thee the Lord, acres waxing, and sprouts wantoning, . . . and the broad crops of barley, and the white wheat-crop, and all crops of earth.' So, as he drove the first furrow he sang again, 'Hail, Mother Earth, thou feeder of folk, be thou growing by goodness of God, filled with fodder, the folk to feed'" (*Conquest of England*, p. 11).

Mr. Green's references are to Kemble's *Saxons in England* and to *Saxon Leechdoms*, published in the Rolls Series, and the incantation to Mother Earth and on the occasion of driving the first furrow are from the Cottonian MSS., headed by the editor "A Charm for bewitched Land," and commencing, as translated literally from the original Anglo-Saxon, "Here is the remedy how thou mayest amend thine acres, if they will not wax well, or if therein anything uncanny have been done by sorcery or witchcraft," and of which it is safe to say that the ceremonies and observances prescribed and the incantations enjoined could not be outdone for sheer pagan superstition, reliance on occult nature-craft, and manufacture of spells, by half a dozen arch-impostors of the school of the noted " Wise Man o' Stowsley." And the mass-priest is to have his share—by no means an insignificant one, the very altar of the parish church being the scene of some part of the " ritual "—in the mummeries ordained ! And what is more to the point, some of the directions given are such that in them are involved the principles lying at the root of more than one of the very most superstitious of the many superstitious practices it has fallen to my lot to note in this district of old sayings, old usages, and unforgotten traditions.

Two or three pages before that on which the " charm " thus noted is found, but eighteen pages from the commencement of a series of like or analogous charms, as they are collectively termed, stands one which is not a little curious and no less interesting, by reason of its more than possible suggestiveness. It is again in Anglo-Saxon, and derived from the same source as the last, namely, the Cottonian MSS., and the translation is, "This is St. Columcille's (Columbkill) circle. Write this circle with the point of thy knife upon a meal-stone, and cut a stake in the midst of the enclosing hedge, and lay the stone upon the stake, so that it be all underground except the written - upon part." There is nothing to specify the particular purpose or object of the circle, a diagram of which is given, except certain inscribed words, from the character of which some surmise as to the intent of the charm may be risked. The saint's circle consists of two concentric circles, the inner one of which is divided into four equal sections by two lines passing through the centre at right angles with one another. In the upper left-hand segment are a series of Roman numerals arranged in five horizontal lines; in the lower segment on the same side, three rows of the same; in the upper right-hand section, "cont'. apes ut salvi sint, & in corda eorum .s'.a.h."; and in the remaining section simply the numeral xxx.   That it is a spell or charm to ensure the wellbeing of the bees belonging to the man making use of it seems then to be apparent; and one might venture the expansion which would afford the translation, "Compass the bees about, that they may be kept safe, and that human intelligence may possess their hearts."   But this is comparatively immaterial from the point of view from which I would fain regard it.   The peculiar use of the peculiar article mentioned, namely the meal-stone, is what arrests my attention.   The translator, than whom no more competent Anglo-Saxon scholar existed, gives the explanatory rather than alternative meaning of *quern* for *meal-stone.*   Admitting this rendering, the use of the meal-stone or quern in the manner indicated, or in the practice of rites which can only be spoken of as connected with pagan observances or acts of heathen worship, is certainly one to be noticed under any circumstances.   And it is not impossible that it may suggest an explanation where an explanation is admittedly very much wanted.

Let us recall Mr. Green's remark that the "autumn feast," characterised by him a few sentences before as a "heathen usage," "lingered on unchallenged in the village harvest-home with the sheaf, in old times a symbol of the god, nodding gay with flowers and ribbons on the last waggon."   But we cannot use the past tense even yet in speaking of this accompaniment of the harvest-home, albeit the "harvest-home," in the historian's sense, is no longer the village festival, but one that is celebrated on divers farms all comprised in the same parochial district. And that is true over very wide districts of our country. Here in our own Yorkshire, and especially in our own dales, notwithstanding the modern "harvest-home," which is essentially a resurrection rather than a survival only, of the

old "village festival," we know well what the "mell-sheaf,"
the "mell-supper," or "kern-supper," truly is; and scarcely a
generation back the sheaf and the festival so called were of
as regular occurrence as the harvest itself on many and many
a primitive farm-hold or hilly dale-side occupation throughout
our northern districts.

All the same, there long has been, and there still is, no
little uncertainty about the meaning and the origin of both
the names "kern-supper" and "mell-supper." In the Cleveland Glossary the definition of the former is, "A supper given
to the work-people by the farmer on the completion of
'shearing,' or severing the corn, on a farm;" of the latter,
"The harvest-supper, or supper given by the farmer to his
work-people on the conclusion of the harvest; that is, as
regards reaping or cutting the corn, not the leading or
carrying." The "kern-baby" is described as "an image, or
possibly only a sheaf of the newly-cut corn, gaily dressed up
and decorated with clothes, ribbons, and flowers, and borne
home rejoicingly after severing the last portions of the
harvest;" while "mell-sheaf" is called "the last sheaf of the
harvest, which used to be formed on finishing the reaping with
much observance and care." Perhaps the most characteristic, certainly the most suggestive, and it may be the most
instructive account of the matters under mention is that
which is given by Mr. Henderson in his *Folklore of North
England*, p. 7. What he says is as follows: "Our most
characteristic festive rejoicings accompany the harvest, namely
the mell-supper and the kern-baby. In the northern part of
Northumberland the festival takes place at the close of the
reaping, not the ingathering. When the sickle is laid down
and the last sheaf of corn set on end, it is said that they have
'got the kern'; the reapers announce the fact by loud shout-
ing, and an image crowned with wheat-ears and dressed in a
white frock and coloured ribbons is hoisted on a pole and
carried by the tallest and strongest man of the party. All

circle round this 'kern-baby' or harvest-queen, and proceed
to the barn, where they set the image up on high, and proceed
to do justice to the harvest-supper." This harvest-supper is
called the "kern-feast" a little farther on, and it is added
that "the mell-supper in the county of Durham is closely
akin to the Northumbrian kern-feast." It is more than
possible that a distinction may have been made at some
period and in some districts between the "kern-supper" and
the "mell-supper"; and indeed there is ample reason, alike
from what I have myself collected among my elder parishioners
in the old days and from what has been recorded by Eugene
Aram, as well as others less notorious, that in various parts of
North Yorkshire both the one and the other were celebrated,
but the one on the completion of the severing of the corn,
the other on finishing the ingathering. Originally, however,
there can have been but one festival of the nature indicated,
and the distinct probability is that the one name of the said
festival being from the beginning interchangeable with the
other, in order to suit the fact to the word, as has been done
in such multitudes of instances, two separate suppers have
been arbitrarily distinguished by these synonyms. This
seems to be the conclusion that is pointed to by every
consideration. And perhaps even the perplexity and uncertainty about the very form, as well as the origin and
meaning of either of these names, is neither the least nor the
least significant of these considerations.

The prefix in kern-supper, kern-feast, kern-baby, is variously
referred to "kern," our Yorkshire word for churn, and to the
word "corn"; while the "mell" in mell-supper, mell-sheaf,
etc., has been diversely attributed to French *meler*, to mingle,
and also *mêlée*, a contest; to Teutonic *mehl*, meal; to Old
Norse *melr*, wild corn; to *mell*, a mallet or wooden hammer;
to English *meal*, a service of food; and even to Norse *amilli*,
between, intermediate! Possibly nothing could show forth
more conspicuously the utter uncertainty as to the actual

source of the word in question than such a preposterous array of impossible and, many of them, nonsensical derivations. Indeed if one were not only too well acquainted with the extravagances of the amateur derivationists of place-names and personal names, he would be surprised at the fertility of folly displayed by such as have attempted to account for the words or names under comment. But just as it has begun to dawn on the minds of a few among the great host of derivers of place-names that the only safe method is the historic method, that the name or word under inquiry must be hunted out, as far as may be, to its original forms, and connected, if it be possible, with fact, to the passing-by of fancy, so it is a thought that should have presented itself to the minds of the imaginative people who have helped in supplying that plentiful crop of absurd connections for *mell* and for *kern*, and that must be entertained by any one bent on the same quest still, that historical considerations not only cannot be out of place, but must of necessity be entertained. It is not, however, certain, *a priori*, that such considerations will lead on to discovery at all, and much less to a complete elucidation of the doubts and difficulties which beset all such inquiries.

Now the first fact in this connection that presents itself for recognition is that which is stated so simply and plainly by Mr. Green, namely, that it is the autumn feast of the old paganism which lingers on in the village harvest-home, including the minor but most pregnant facts that the sheaf borne in rejoicing was in old times the symbol of the god, and that still, as the kern-baby or the mell-sheaf, it is borne nodding gay with flowers and ribbons on the last waggon. Surely what is thus faithfully preserved, alike in fact and in usage, may be reasonably expected to have retained, together with such marked attendant recollections, some survival, however faint and indistinct, of the old terminology connected with it. In other words, "the nodding sheaf the

symbol of the god," and the effigy—surely a more pronounced
symbol of the god—as they must have had distinctive names
in the time of their early survival, may be not unreasonably
questioned as to whether or no they have been utterly
divested of any or all trace of the names by which they used
to be called. It is strange if a sheaf which lives on to this
day, and is a special sheaf in such various parts of the country,
—here appearing as a mighty burden of corn, heavy and
large enough to task a strong man's strength in the bearing
of it ; there small but made with fastidious neatness, and
plaited about the parts below the ears with a remarkable and
most taking cunning,—the sheaf comprising the very last of
the severed crop, should have nothing at all in the names it is
known by to serve as a reminder, a reminiscence even, of what
it was wont to be called in the elder days of its survival.

Is it then altogether impossible that the *meala-stan* of the
old Anglo-Saxon charm or incantation, with its alternative
of "quern," as given by Mr. Cockayne, should furnish some
sort of a suggestive hint as to what may have been the early
expression of the early idea, crystallised alike in the fact and
in the name of the mell- or kern-sheaf or -feast ? The *meala-
stan* is that which grinds ; and, says Professor Skeat, under
Quern (A.-S. *cweorn, cwyrn*, Icel. *qvern*) "originally, that which
grinds." But this is not all. Under *Churn* the same great
authority says, speaking of the root-words he quotes as
connected, "All these words are closely related to E. *corn*,
with all its Teutonic cognates. The root of these latter is
GAR, to grind, pulverise. . . . From the same root, and from
the same notion of grinding, comes the remarkably similar
M. E. *quern*, a handmill, with its numerous Teutonic cognates,
including the Gothic *kwairnus*, a millstone."

Thus we have the fact that the meal-stone or quern was
actually employed in what we speak of as the superstitious
acts of the ritual of the old days ; the further fact that, in
attempting to account for the origin of the familiar old terms

mell-sheaf, kern-baby, mell- or kern-feast, etc., men have
fallen upon the words *churn*, *corn*, *meal*, etc., as furnishing
possible suggestions of derivation ; and the philological facts
that quern, corn, churn are all cognate, and that meal-stone
and quern are synonymous, even in the far past of the Gothic
day. Is it altogether too far-fetched a notion that the ideas
connected with meal, meal-stone, quern are intimately connected not only with the old pagan harvest festival, but with
the perplexing terms associated with the survival of the said
old, old autumn feast? Let us take an illustration of the
possibility accompanying this hypothesis from an authority
which will hardly be questioned even by the agnostic in such
a matter as this : "Speak unto the children of Israel, and
say unto them, When ye be come into the land which I give
unto you, and shall reap the harvest thereof, then ye shall
bring a sheaf of the first-fruits of your harvest unto the priest ;
and he shall wave the sheaf before the Lord, to be accepted
for you. . . . Also, in the day of the first-fruits, when ye
bring a new meat-offering unto the Lord, . . . ye shall have a
holy convocation," etc. And this "meat-offering," what of it?
This : "And when any will offer a meat-offering, his offering
shall be of fine flour." Flour, otherwise "meal," in some form,
or ears of corn, or corn out of the ears first and specially
gathered, this was the "meat-offering" ; and one whose attention has not previously been drawn to the circumstance might
well be a little surprised at the incessant mention in the
directions for ritual given in Leviticus and elsewhere in the
same part of the Old Testament, of the meat-offering and its
concomitant observances. The baking of great loaves and
cakes in the embers of the great fire lighted at one of the
great seasonal festivals of pagan times, and the distributing of
them after, is referred to by the historian, and it is surely idle to
suppose that there was no eating and drinking at the autumn
feast ; and what more natural than the supposition that at the
said autumn feast of the ingathering there should have been

not only the equivalent of the harvest-sheaf we have just been reminded of, or of the "meat-offering" in its most usual form, but also an imperative requirement that new corn should be forthcoming, fresh meal procured therefrom, kneaded into cakes or loaves, and baked and consumed, and that the meal-stone or quern should have had a sufficiently important part to play in the function to be made to bequeath its name and that of its produce alike to what even yet is admittedly the representative rather than the survival merely of the old autumn feast of our pagan ancestors?

THE DOG-WHIPPER

FORTY years ago the "Dog-whipper" was still an institution
in this dale. Auld Willy Richardson was then the hereditary
holder of the office, his father having been dog-whipper
before him; and when Willy himself died, the office, the
honour, and the insignia passed to his brother John.
For the office was by no means one without outward signs
and tokens of its existence. The office-holder held also
a whip, and whenever he was on duty the whip was *en
évidence.*

Poor old Willy, the first dog-whipper of my acquaintance,
was a little man of about five feet four, with legs that were
hardly a pair, and which it would have been slander to call
straight or well shapen; and, as was natural perhaps, he
shambled in his gait. His usual garb on the Sunday was an
ancient drab coat, cut—if a tailor had ever been concerned in
the making of it—after the fashion described as that of
Dominie Sampson's, with broad skirts falling quite below the
knee. There were side-pockets in it, opening just upon the
hip; capacious and with a sort of suggestiveness about them
that they were not simply meant to contain sundries, but were
put to such a use by wont and custom. On Sundays, and days
when a "burying" was to be—for Willy was sexton also, and
kept the depth of his graves religiously to under three feet—
the short handle of the whip he bore reposed in the right-
hand pocket, but the lainder and lash hung outside; the latter,

inasmuch as the bearer's stature was not great, trailing on the ground.

Willy was valorous in the execution of his duty, although he may sometimes have seen occasion for the exercise of a wise discretion. I knew of two such instances. In one the intrusive dog was made slowly to recede before the duly-armed official, who was fairly well able to command the whole interspace between the pews which runs the length of the church; but when it came to turning round the corner and backing towards the door, the dog did not see the expediency of the desired course quite so clearly as Willy did; and so, having more room in the crossing in which to attain the necessary impetus, he made a bolt for it, aiming at the archway presented by the dog-whipper's bow-legs. But the archway proved to be less than the dog had assumed it to be; and, in consequence, after riding backwards for a pace or two, poor old Willy came backwards to the pavement, and to grief besides. The dog on the other occasion was more resolute, or else less accommodating; for he met all Willy's advances with a steady refusal to budge an inch in a backward direction. Willy persevered; the dog growled. Willy showed his whip; the dog showed his teeth; and the teeth having a more persuasive look about them than the whip, the man gave way and the dog did not.

Willy Dog-whipper's successor, as I have said, both as to the office and its badge, was his brother John. Him I induced, by the addition of sixpence from the parson's magnificent burial-fee of eighteenpence, to his own pittance of one shilling and threepence for digging the grave, attendance at the funeral, and filling up the grave at the close, to dig the graves an extra foot in depth. But it was an innovation to which, despite the—by comparison—easily earned sixpence extra, he never completely grew reconciled. He thought a coffin with twenty or twenty-two inches of soil upon it was "weel eneugh happed oop for owght." John wore a ring, made out of the old coffin-tyre he met with in digging the graves in the well-worked churchyard the Danby "kirk-garth" was, until I got an additional half acre laid to it. This ring was good against "falling fits." His predecessor's particular wear had been earrings of the same material.

These two worthies held other offices, either by favour or by inheritance or descent. Willy was the "bidder to the burials," while John was in extensive request on occasions of pig-killing; and, having a considerable number of patrons and friends among the farmers, and others who had pigs to kill in the course of the winter, he had very many engagements of that kind. It was said that, in addition to his food and a small money fee on these occasions, he had the pigs' ears as his perquisite; and that he always kept count of how many pig executions he had attended in the course of the season, by aid of small reserved and preserved pieces of the said ears.

But there was a matter to be noted in connection with this family which may be more worth recording than any yet mentioned. Besides the aforesaid Willy and John, there was a sister, Nanny, who would assuredly have been credited with the character of a witch had she lived two or three generations earlier, and have met with the observance usual in such cases. In fact, there were some whose opinions on that subject were not quite settled, as it was. Not three months since I was asked, "Had she not had that reputation?" This woman, a good match in symmetry and size to her brother Willy, was, during the greater part of her life, after my acquaintance with her began, practically voiceless. She could not even so much as whisper audibly; and it did wear an uncanny look to see her, so to speak, trying to talk—lips, mouth, tongue in rapid motion, and with a sort of emphatic action—and yet not be able to hear a sound. Some even of my own children thought her alarming, and were shy of being accosted by her. But the noteworthy matter remaining to be chronicled in connection with her, and certainly one of her brothers, if not both, was that practically they lived by begging. But that expression must not be misunderstood. They were not professional mendicants; but they were the survivals, and the last survivals, of an outworn system. Thus Nanny, to the last day of her life and ability to go her accustomed rounds, had her dinner one day in the week at one particular farmhouse, and another dinner another day at another house; and besides this she had "a piece" here and "a piece" there given her, to carry away in her bag for home consumption. The system is, of course, utterly obsolete now, and in England generally it has been so for long. But it was an accredited system once; and I think accredited by at least unwritten law as well as custom. What I mean will appear from the following extract from the Orders made at Quarter Sessions held at Thirsk, 4th April 1654: "In regard the parishioners of Osmotherley withdraw their charitie, which formerly they gave at their doores to Alexander Swailes, a poor man, it is therefore Ordered that the parish officers there shall, for the future, pay the said poor man 12d. weekly." Our parishioners here did not "withdraw their charitie" from poor, voiceless old Nanny up to something more than twenty years ago. I buried her in 1867, and as long as she was able to walk about I used to meet her with her accustomed bag, and knew she had a place reserved for her once a week at Howe End.

HISTORICAL

HISTORICAL

THE history of the parish divides itself naturally into the prehistoric, the ancient, and the more recent.

As to the prehistoric, no one can walk over our moors without having his attention drawn to the numerous grave-mounds scattered over all the higher and drier portions of the wide expanse. Some of these are of large size, many of moderate dimensions, and a vast number so small as to be comparatively insignificant. Not a few too have been removed bodily, and only spaces of wiry grass with a few brackens, and surfaces bare of any growth of ling, remain to testify to their former sites. Of these larger or more conspicuous houes there may be (or have been) perhaps thirty to thirty-five within the limits of the manor; while of the smaller ones it is not easy to estimate how many there have been. They have been removed in great numbers simply for the sake of the stones which had been rudely piled together in the making of them. One man told me he had himself destroyed not less than thirty in the course of building one single enclosure wall.

That these smaller hills—they are from ten or twelve feet to sixteen or eighteen in diameter, and about two feet or less in height—are grave-mounds, rests rather upon assumption than proof. I have opened many of them with my own hands, and, save in one instance, I have met with no distinct trace of any interment, and Mr. Kendall of Pickering told me that his experience was of the same character as my own. In one I found a very fine scraper of red flint ; but in all without any exception I have found chippings of flint and fragments of charcoal—but only very rarely sherds of pottery—which are such invariable adjuncts to houe-burial and houe-building in general, that it is, I think, safe to infer from them alone the sepulchral character of these minor mounds also.

The contents of the larger houes are such as to leave no uncertainty on this point, or as to the approximate date of their construction. They belong unquestionably to what is now universally styled the Bronze Period, and to all appearance to the later division of the same. It is indeed remarkable how very few bronze articles, implements or weapons, have been found in Cleveland in all ; and the whole of these, without any exception, so far as my information extends, have been of the less archaic style of form and manufacture. My own individual findings have been limited to a few mouldering fragments of very thin plate, found with the unprotected bones of a cremated body, and not sufficient to fill a very small pill-box half an inch in diameter. And yet I have thoroughly examined no fewer than eighty to one hundred houes in Cleveland alone.

The last and most interesting, because most local, find of the sort that has come to my knowledge was a rather fine socketed celt which was found a few years ago near the stone quarry on Glaisdale side. This is now in Canon Greenwell's collection.

These grave-mounds or houes then serve the historical purpose of giving irrefragable testimony to the fact of the former existence in the district of a people who were not unacquainted with the use of metal, in the form of bronze, but who seem to have become so acquainted later on in the bronze epoch, and to have possessed but a very scanty supply of what must have been in those days, at all events in this district, a very costly material. But, it may be said, they are memorials which connect themselves only with the cessation of life among these early inhabitants, and not with their actual life. That is certainly true, but only in a limited sense.

We hear of Christian burial, and the decencies and privileges of it; we hear of cremation, and the recommendations and alleged advantages of it; we hear of funerals that cost hundreds or thousands of pounds, of others less costly but made historical by the numbers of mourners, relatives, friends, dependants, clients, connected with the deceased and brought together by a community of strong and powerful feeling. But all these things, however much they may have to do with the dead, have more still—much more, in the historical sense —to do with the living.

So too with the builders and makers of these lonely, exposed, and, in the older days, doubtless, gruesome receptacles of the dead. Cannot one see the toiling tribesmen, labouring for days and weeks, maybe, raising that mighty mound we call Robin Hood's Butt, ninety-five feet in diameter and seventeen or eighteen high, basketful by basketful, almost handful by handful, brought together with infinite pains and care, and strewed symmetrically with accurate adjustment? Or that lesser mound, near to the foot of the great Freeburgh Hill, with its enclosed cairn of whinstone blocks, each of them brought three or four miles over the trackless moor, and despite of swamp and morass, from the only source from which they could be quarried or obtained? And these instances, remarkable as they are for such a district as ours, are a mere nothing as compared with corresponding memorials in other districts with a fuller population and fewer physical obstacles.

One cannot but allow for the presence of very potent considerations and very strong and sustained feelings in the breasts of the people who acted thus. Whatever their belief or their superstition (if we are "sectarian" enough to allow for nothing better), yet they were capable of acting in concert, of a great respect for the dead, of a conviction that life was not yet totally at an end, even for their cremated or inhumed fore-elders, relatives, friends, leaders. There might be, there probably was, fear as well as respect or reverence mixed up with the funeral rites and observances. There might be, there probably was, a desire to restrain the " umbra," the "ghost" of the departed to his own department and interests. There might be, almost certainly there was, an idea of purification in the fire wherein the body was burned, without application of which, in some form, it is probable no body was consigned to the houe or the ringed-in grave ; and a dozen other analogous or co-ordinate suggestions might be made. But in every one of them a feature of the life of the men of the time strives for recognition, and we are not so much enabled as compelled to recognise the kinship in con-viction, emotion, purpose, and action, between the constructors of those impressive mounds and the throng who took part in the great military funeral of last year, or the consign-ment to her last resting-place of all that remained below of a beloved and respected Yorkshire lady but a day or two after.

No mean workmen either were these dwellers in the wilds of the old times. The more we think of them in the con-nections just noted, the less able are we to think of them as half-clothed or skin-clothed savages ; and as we watch them in a sort of mind-picture surrounding the funeral pyre, sedu-lously collecting the calcined remains, consigning them to the cinerary vase prepared for their reception, that very vase itself tells us of no mean advance in the fictile art. The modern potter himself, with all his appliances and all the aid of nicely constructed and adjusted machinery, is not quite secure from the risk of collapse of some weak place in the walls of the large-sized vessel he is fashioning ; while these people, without so much as a rough " wheel " to help them, made their sepulchral vases eighteen, twenty, twenty-five inches high, and ten, twelve, fifteen to eighteen in diameter, symmetrical, well, even gracefully, shaped, firm enough to bear the pressure of the decorator's simple tools, and of a consistency to bide the effects of moisture and the natural reagents of the soil for a period of twenty, twenty-five, or even perhaps thirty centuries. However imperfect or, in a sense, inartistic the ware on the whole, still this is an achievement, and a great one.

But there are other things which connect themselves with the doings of the life of these early dwellers in the Danby district; although of these there is no occasion to speak at length in this place, because they have already been discussed elsewhere : I mean the ancient earth and stone works, defensive in their nature, which are met with in so many places on our moors. Whatever their intention and *raison d'être*, there can be no question as to the testimony they bear to the existence among them of military skill and experience, as well as of social or tribal co-operation.

The question of date; the inquiry, "When did all this houe-piling and shaping, all this intrenching and walling, take place?" is one to which there are a hundred things to hinder if not to baffle, and scarcely one to suggest a reasonable answer. The "when" may have begun six, eight, ten centuries before the Christian era, may have lasted on, in part or degree, until after the Gospel era had been inaugurated. It is a fact as certain as that the houes themselves exist and are sepulchral in their origin and design, that many of them give the most explicit and unhesitating testimony to the lapse of considerable epochs of time between their earliest inception, or the piling of the mound over the original interment, and what are called "secondary" interments, of which sometimes as many as four or five took place successively.

It is equally true—and any conclusions arrived at as to comparative scantiness of the prehistoric population tend in the same direction—that the contents and interior fashion of not a few of the houes of the district are such as to suggest

s

wide intervals of time between the relative periods of their erection. But still, all that we arrive at, in the way even of inference, is of the vaguest, shadowiest description. Professor Rhys, while adverting to the questions archæology has not yet attempted to solve, perhaps even to formulate, admits that it undertakes, and in the main correctly, "to distinguish the burial-places of the Celts from those of the pre-Celtic peoples of Britain, the former having the round barrows assigned to them, and the latter the long ones; and that, may be, the archæologist has no data to help him to more exact results." But, proceeds the writer, "he should remember that his study of the tombs falls short of the historian's wish so long as he cannot tell the resting-place of a Brython from that of a Goidel" (that is, a Celt of the later or second invasion from a Gael or one of the former invasion), "and both from those of the neolithic native."[1] And then the Professor surmises that both the neolithic native and the first Celtic immigrant may, according to the latest archæological investigations, have buried—as the former of the two unquestionably did—in long barrows; while, as for the later or Brythonic branch, "there is no difficulty in supposing them to have continued in Christian times their use of the barrows."

But while the somewhat diffident suggestion or surmise just adverted to—namely, that the "Goidel" as well as the "neolithic native" may possibly both of them have buried their dead in long barrows—may be safely left as a problem for the archæologist to solve, there is no doubt that the later Celts, or "Brythons" (as Mr. Rhys calls them, in the wish to escape the confusion which results from the use of the more indefinite term Briton), used the fashion of round barrows for the inter-

---

[1] "The two last, the Goidel and the neolithic native, would seem to have buried in long barrows; but some of those barrows contain the dead placed with care to sit grimly in their subterranean houses, while others disclose only the huddled bones of men and beasts, as though they were the remains of cannibal feastings. Can they be ascribed to the same race? We doubt it." (*Celtic Britain*, p. 246.)

ment of their dead, and as little that our Cleveland barrows, or houes, without any exception, belong to that class, and that the class itself belongs to a period of very considerable, although indefinite, duration. And if we were able to speak with less uncertainty on this head, we might also be able to give some sort of an estimate of the age of the earthworks. For while from one point of view it might be possible to speak of them correctly as coeval with the epoch of the barrows, from another it would be safer to say that they were conterminous with it.

For, being both systematic and found to extend laterally over so wide a space, it is not possible to look upon these earthworks as thrown up with the view of repelling mere petty border aggressions. The attack which, if made, was intended to be warded off by their aid, was emphatically an attack from the south, and attacks from the south on the scale indicated— that is, with a front of at least seven to eight miles—by tribesmen or clansmen against their fellows can hardly be looked upon as probable. In other words, the struggle, whether actual or anticipated only, could scarcely have been a struggle between Brython and Brython. It must have been between Brython and a foe to the Brython. And if so, the earthworks in question must have been either of an aggressive or a defensive nature. If aggressive, they must have been designed to cover an advance from the north towards the south by the Brythons themselves ; if defensive, their object could only have been to impede, if possible to frustrate, an inroad made on the Brythons from the south ; and such inroad could, it is obvious, have been made by no Celtic people or tribal section. This subject is dealt with elsewhere,[1] and it is only referred to here as belonging to the ancient history of Danby, and showing why the defensive barriers across the ridges between Danby and Westerdale, across the Ainthorpe ridge, across the ridge between Fryup and Glaisdale, and that across the Glaisdale

[1] " Earthworks," p. 153 *et seq.*

End ridge, must be attributed rather to the beginning of the later Celtic occupation than to the approaching close of the same.

From the close of the houe-raising epoch, of whatever duration it may have been, and from whatever cause it came to an end, the history of Danby is a blank; and if we accept the conclusion that there is too little in the way of evidence to assure us that the Anglian colonist ever set his foot in the district, while it cannot be alleged that there are no reasons for thinking he did not, the blank in question becomes wider and vaguer than ever. We have to wait until well on into the ninth century before we can descry the approach of the settler, or listen to the strokes of his axe commencing the needful "riddings," and making way for his cumbrous plough and its unwieldy team. And even then our inquiry is not fully closed; for we have to ask the question, "In which direction are we to look with the view of descrying the approaching settler? From what quarter, or from what centre, does he come?"

The ready answer to this question as to many—not to say most—parts of England would be, "From the sea, and along the course of this or that river." But that answer is one that cannot be given offhand in the present case. The first non-Celtic settler or colonist in Danby did not come up the river from the sea, because for one thing it is an absolute certainty that two hundred years before Domesday, access to Danby along the course of the Esk was impossible by boat and impracticable along its banks. Our pre-Domesday survey of the Dales country, and its condition as to water and weed, assures us of that.[1] The immigrant must have come from the south or the west, for the north and the east were closed against him.

From the immediate west, with the forests and wild woods of Westerdale, Kildale, Greenhow to traverse, the access may not have proved too easy, although we must not overlook the Thorkell-sty to Broughton and Stokesley, or the wild, rough

[1] Appendix C.

way yet farther west, in which Norman William had to face the dour, merciless intensity of a northern moorland winter's storm. These may have been, probably were, tracks two centuries earlier. But besides these there was a grand route open from the south in the Roman Road from Malton through Goathland to Goldsburgh, which would be easily available as far as to Hazlehead.

And here let us recall the leading conditions of the Danish occupation of the north of England so far as they bear on the matter we are considering. A brief sketch of the history reads somewhat in this way. "While the Ostmen," says Mr. Green, "gathered in a fleet of 200 vessels under Olaf the Fair, and threw themselves on the Scot-kingdom across the Firth of Forth, a Danish host from Scandinavia itself, under Ivar the Boneless, landed in 866 on the shores of East Anglia, wherein they were enabled or permitted to winter; and it was only in the spring of 867 that they horsed themselves and rode for the north. Their aim was Northumbria; and as they struck over Mid-Britain for York they found the country torn by the wonted anarchy, and two rivals contending, as of old, for the throne. Though the claimants united in presence of the common danger, their union came too late. The Danes had seized York at their first arrival, and now fell back before the Northumbrian host to shelter within its defences, which seem still to have consisted of a wooden stockade crowning the mound raised by the last Roman burghers round their widened city. The flight and seeming panic of their foes roused the temper of the Northumbrians; they succeeded in breaking through the stockade, and pouring in with its flying defenders, were already masters of the bulk of the town when the Danes turned in a rally of despair. From that moment the day was lost. Not only were the two kings slain, but their men were hunted and cut down over all the country-side, till it seemed as if the whole host of Northumbria lay on the fatal field. So overwhelming was the blow that a general terror hindered all further resistance; those who survived the fight 'made peace with the pagans,' and Northumbria sank without further struggle into a tributary kingdom of the Dane." It was after, and consequent upon, this that " the doom which had long ago fallen on Jarrow and Wearmouth fell now on all the religious houses of the coast," and that among the rest "Streonshealh, the house of Hild and Caedmon, vanished so utterly that its very name disappeared, and the township which took its place in later days bore the Danish name of Whitby" (Green, p. 93).

Now Whitby would be reached by the sea, of course; but besides the difficulty of doing more than merely reconnoitre the country west of Whitby from Whitby itself, it must be borne in mind that the central point from which the Danish movements as a whole in the north of England were directed and carried out was and continued to be York. It was from York that the plundering raids upon divers parts of the district at large were organised. It was from York that the systematic attack upon Mercia was designed and executed. It was from York that the ravages in Lincolnshire were entered upon and effected, and other expeditions emanated as from a general centre.

With the struggle in Wessex and the conquest of Mercia we have nothing to do here, but we may remark that the general issue of these operations "gave the Danes a firmer base from which to complete their conquest of the island, both in north and south" (Green, p. 106); so that "in the spring of 875 Halfdene marched northward to the Tyne to complete the reduction of Bernicia." And one thing more is to be noted, that "although their victory at York had left the district occupied by the present Yorkshire in their hands as early as the spring of 868, they contented themselves for the next seven years with the exaction of tribute from an under king whom they had set over it" (*Ibid.* p. 117). "But in 875 Halfdene, with a portion of the Danish army at Repton, marched northward into Northumbria, and proceeded unopposed to the Tyne.

From his winter camp there 'he subdued the land, and oft-
times spoiled the Picts and the Strathclyde Wealhs.' With
the spring of 876, however, he fell back from Bernicia to the
south, and 'parted or dealt among his men the lands of Northumbria; so that thenceforth they went on ploughing and
tilling them.'" And then the historian adds, "The names of
the towns and villages of Deira show us in how systematic a
way southern Northumbria was parted amongst its conquerors.
The change seems to have been much the same as that which
followed the conquest of the Normans. The English population was not displaced, but the lordship of the soil was transferred to the conqueror. The settlers formed a new aristocracy,
while the older nobles fell to a lower position; for throughout
Deira the life of an English thegn was priced at but half the
value of a northern 'hold'" (Green, p. 116).

But while in a large proportion of the immediate Dales
district of which Danby forms part there is a presumption,
almost if not quite amounting to proof, that there was
no "English population" to be displaced,[1] there remain
the same features of approximate inaccessibility characterising the said portion of the country. Halfdene marches
from the north—the Tyne—to the south, but he could surely
come no farther to the east on such a march, with his whole
force, than the Conqueror on a like march two hundred years
after; and the "dealing" or parting of the country could only
have been carried into practical effect in detail, and by the hand
of men who were virtually, if not by express distinction, commissioners.

And then comes the allotment of what was eventually to
be Danby, and the settlement or actual colonisation, and the
naming of the name. Such names as Ormsby, Normanby,
Ugleberdesby, Thormodby, Thoraldby, Elwordeby, Bergelby,
Barnby, Asulfsby, and the host like them, give us no trouble,
for we are familiar with the names Orm, Norman, Ugleberd,

[1] See Appendix C.

Thormod, Thorald, Elward or Ailward, Bergulf, Asolf, as with "household words." But as surely as Norman was a personal name, so surely was Dane also, and the names Dane, Norman, Ugleberd, not to mention others, survive as the names of Domesday *tenentes* two hundred years later than the earliest period to which we can relegate the effectual settling of Danby. The place was allotted to a man called Dane, and of course almost certainly because he was a Dane, as Norman was a Norwegian—and there were two Normans wanted to stand as godfathers to places in Cleveland—and he, as was the practice with fully one-half of his co-allottees, named the allotment after his own name, and it still remains to hand down his designation, if not his memory, to future generations.

But while we thus unhesitatingly and unerringly indicate the force and application of the first element of the name, or *Dan*, what about the second, or *by*? Much too generally this question is answered in a half-flippant, careless, inexact way, with the explanation "a house, a dwelling." Canon Taylor himself writes, "The word originally meant a dwelling, or a single farm, and hence it afterwards came to denote a village," and he relegates to a note what is not merely the most significant part of the requisite explanation of the syllable in all such names, but the altogether essential idea that ought to be conveyed; for in that note he says that the *by* at the end of place-names "denotes Danish colonisation. In places visited only for purposes of trade or plunder no dwellings would be required." Just so; "it denotes Danish colonisation," and colonisation, in all cases of possession and occupation for cultural purposes, meant a good deal more than merely a dwelling to cover the head of the colonist himself against the assaults of the elements or the winter's cold. True, there must be the settler's "shanty," but there must be also shanties meaner than the master's for the men who came with him for the colonist's work in the forest and on the land ; there must be stables for the horses, byres for the cows, sheds for the oxen, refuges for the sheep, the swine, and the other live stock necessary to make the settlement efficient from all the requisite points of view. So that a *by* from the first, instead of being an isolated dwelling, was a farmstead in the old full sense, when the men who worked the land were all thought of and provided with adequate dwelling-places, however rough, as well as the live and dead stock of the agriculturist. It was in this way that, when the clearings and the cultivable area became enlarged, and the population increased and went on increasing accordingly, the *by* afterwards came to denote a village.

Well, Danby was simply a *by* first—simply a Danish colonist's settlement, and he called it after his own name—Daneby, a word of three syllables (the second being due to inflection, or marking the possessival case), which afterwards became shortened into two, just as Normanneby became shortened into Normanby, Witeby into Whitby, Asulfesby into Aislaby, and so forth, without stint. A little land was cleared, and then a little more, and so on, until by the time of King Edward the Confessor it had become a hamlet of some size ; and the original farm-settlement of Dane, with its grouped shanties and sheds, stables, byres, etc., had expanded into a vill [1] of thirty or forty cabins, with here and there a dwelling of slightly more pretension than the rest, and possibly an outlying station or two belonging to such as had thriven and expanded into something like the *bonder* of the old Danish fatherland. That there were serfs—slaves captured in foray or fray—tilling the lord's, the chief man's, holding or demesne, I do not doubt ; but that the men who had in all likelihood served under Dane in the wars preceding the parting or "dealing" of the country were mainly or exclusively free men is, I should suppose, a conclusion that will be gainsaid by none conversant with the

[1] See Appendix D.

general subject; least of all by such as have remarked the manorial and cognate peculiarities observable in what are now called the "Danish counties."

Time passes on, and the Conquest comes, and is ultimately the means by which we are made acquainted with the scanty scraps of information of which we have availed ourselves in the inquiry into the pre-Domesday condition of Danby and its sister districts,[1] and through which we are enabled to gather a few other scraps as to its condition in the Confessor's time, and as to the lord of the fee—if we may so express ourselves — in the years preceding the Conquest. For we learn that in 1086 not only was Hugh FitzBaldric lord of Crumbeclive, Lelum, and Danby, but that he had been preceded in that possession by Orm; and on looking over the other parts of his fee we see that Orm had been his predecessor in so large a part of it as at once to indicate that he had been by no means an unimportant personage.

Besides, there was a Gamel who was a predecessor of Hugh FitzBaldric in many of the manors which in 1086 were of his fee. Whether this Gamel were related to Orm, either as father or son, must be a matter of surmise only. For it would appear there was a Gamel son of Orm and an Orm son of Gamel; but there is no question that both Orm and Gamel had held parts of the fee which is entered as the fee of Hugh FitzBaldric. Young (*History of Whitby*, p. 744) says that "Orm before the Conquest was lord of Kirkdale, then called Chircheby or Kirkby, and had ample possessions in that neighbourhood, and in the vale of the Esk." He is wrong in identifying Kirkby with Kirkdale, the place meant by Chircheby being quite certainly Kirkby Moorside, but there can be little uncertainty attaching to the identification of the Orm named with Orm the son of Gamel, who was murdered by Earl Tostig in 1064, under circumstances of great treachery; and as little in assuming that he was the

[1] See Appendix C.

Orm son of Gamel who rebuilt the church at Kirkdale, and commemorated the fact by the celebrated Anglo-Saxon inscription on the stone over the south door.[1]

But this being so it is sufficiently evident that in the days preceding the Conquest Danby was a part of the possessions of a lord who was no mean man ; he ranked among those whom the historian of Whitby terms the nobles of Northumbria, and the historian of the Conquest terms thegns. And it would seem that, through whatever change of fortune or chance of personal or political preference the fee had ceased to be Orm's, on passing into other hands it passed into the possession of no mean man again. Hugh FitzBaldric was of sufficient importance to be Sheriff of Yorkshire, and so to sustain a dignity and a charge which amply bespoke the consideration he was held in by his clear-sighted and practical royal master. And possibly there may be more implied in saying this than we are ·

---

[1] This inscription is said to run thus, being translated : "Orm Gamalson bought S. Gregorius minster when it was all to-broken and to-fallen : he it let make new from the ground, to Christ and S. Gregorius in Edward's days the King and Tosti's days the Earl." And as Tostig was Earl from 1055 to 1065, we have the limits of date within which the church was rebuilt. This clearly brings to our minds the conviction that the Gamel who was murdered by Tostig and the Orm who rebuilt Kirkdale Church were the Gamel and Orm mentioned in the Domesday entry as to Hugh FitzBaldric's fee, as holding adjoining lands under the previous disposition of the said fee, were nearly connected ; and that, allowing for the historical connection, they were connected as father and son. And this justifies Young's assumption that Orm's father Gamel "ranked among the Northumbrian nobles." Dr. Freeman's notice is, "Two Thegns, Gamel the son of Orm and Ulf the son of Dolfin . . . had been treacherously slain by Tostig's order," and in a note he adds, " Dolfin and Orm both appear in Domesday, seemingly as holders under William of small parts of great estates held under Eadward," in other words, they had been great men in the Confessor's days. "Orm married Æthelthryth, a daughter of Earl Ealdred and sister-in-law of Earl Siward, though Gamel was not her son." It is apparent, then, that the Orm who had formerly held Danby—there being many reasons for identifying him with the Orm who held the Kirkby and Kirkdale lands, and none whatever against it—was originally, or in the pre-Norman times, a man of name and note.

prepared to recognise, unless we bear in mind the circumstances of the time. We have no definite information, it is true, as to how long Hugh FitzBaldric had been sheriff; but at least we do not hear of any other occupant of the place of responsibility he now held (for under all the circumstances the responsibility far outweighed both the honour and the profit) between William Malet and himself. And William Malet had been not simply an unlucky sheriff but an ill-judged one. He had told his master that he and his fellow-captains of the York garrison could hold out against the enemy from Daneland (who were known to be on the coast), and of course their allies from the country-side, for a year if necessary; with the result that all was lost at nearly the first assault. But this was not all. Among those who delivered the assault were two who had held high office under the king in this very Northumbrian province, one of them a previous sheriff, namely Mærleswegen, with Gospatrick, formerly earl, and Archill, one of the most potent thegns of the Northumbrians, all of whom had proved utterly faithless to William. And to William Malet the unlucky, who was next in order after Mærleswegen the traitor, Hugh FitzBaldric seems to have been the immediate successor. Nor is it only this that leads us on to the inference that he was greatly trusted by the royal Norman; for we find that when it was deemed expedient to bring the Ætheling Eadgar to William's court, it was Hugh the son of Baldric who was deputed to "meet him at Durham as he journeyed south from the Scottish court," and by whom he was "attended through the whole length of England, and across the sea into Normandy." But the most interesting mention that is made of him is in the pages of Simeon of Durham, who when detailing the circumstances connected with the foundation of the abbey of Selby states that the "cross on the founder's cell was seen by the sheriff of the shire, Hugh the son of Baldric, who was sailing along the river (Ouse), accompanied by a large body of soldiers, a way of travelling which was necessary in those times on account of the attacks to which all Frenchmen were liable at the hands of the revolted English. The sheriff has an interview with the hermit Benedict, he leaves him his own tent as a temporary dwelling-place, and directs the building of a chapel for his use" (Freeman's *Conquest*, vol. iv. p. 795). The historian, however, does not seem to be quite confident that Hugh FitzBaldric was certainly sheriff of Yorkshire, his words being, "Hugh appears in the Nottingham Domesday as Hugo filius Baldrici Vicecomes. He was therefore sheriff somewhere, and it is very possible that he may have been appointed sheriff of Yorkshire late in 1069, after the capture of William Malet." Still, in the previous reference the words employed are, "There he (Waltheof) was met by Hugh the son of Baldric, who had succeeded William Malet in the sheriffdom of Yorkshire;" so that I think we may assume with perfect safety that the Domesday owner of Danby was no one less than William's trusted sheriff of the district.

During the considerable interval between 1069 to 1071 and 1086 we are left to infer that there may have been no change in ownership affecting the Danby possessions, although it is impossible to affirm so much. All that is clear is that, whether by the death or forfeiture of Hugh FitzBaldric, or Hugh FitzBaldric's successor, at some date later than 1086, Danby, with Crumbeclive and Lealholm, was again in the hands of the king to bestow. And the man on whom he bestowed it was Robert de Brus, the Rotbertus de Bruis of the late entry in Domesday.[1]

The old story about this baron is that "he came in with the Conqueror." It is like a good many other old stories resting rather on a guess at what might have been, than on any reasonable consideration of the circumstances. No doubt he got a good grant when he did get one; but we are not even able to say that the grant was actually made by the Conqueror at all; and if made by him, it could not have been made before

[1] See Appendix E.

the year 1086-87. It is surely the very reverse of likely that a man who had served the king since 1066 with such zeal and fidelity as to have a claim upon him which could be acknowledged only by such a princely gift as the "feudum Rotberti de Bruis" proclaims, could have been overlooked so long. And if perchance the gift came not from the first, but from the second William, of course the old fable falls to the ground. Beyond all reasonable doubt Robert de Brus came late into the field of action; and when he did come, rendered such good and acceptable service as to call for rather than simply warrant such a munificent acknowledgment.

There seems to be little doubt that Brus lived to a great age. His death is believed to have taken place about the year 1145. But between thirty-five and forty years before that he had merited so well of the first Henry that he received from him further grants, so large and important as almost to outvie the greatness of the first royal gifts. And this led to important changes which affected Danby, and may therefore be fittingly mentioned here. For the grant in Henry's reign involved the ownership of Skelton, and the possession of Skelton involved the transference of the head of the lordship from Danby to Skelton. For there can be no doubt that during the first quarter of a century and onwards, for perhaps a decade or so longer—or until the great and strong pile which Skelton Castle unquestionably became had been erected— Danby Castle occupied the position of the head of the Brus barony. On no other ground can be explained the transference of the manorial seat from Crumbeclive to Danby, the building of the enormously strong castle at Danby, and the exceeding great regard and interest felt by the Brus family for the Castle and Manor of Danby.

The castle—the site of which is declared by the name "Castle Hill" at Castleton—occupied a very considerable area, much more considerable than is allowed for, in all probability, by nineteen out of twenty of those even who know or speculate as to the possible former existence of a castle there. As it is laid down in the six-inch Ordnance map, the measures over all from east to west are 110 yards, and from north to south 130 yards. But the former of these two measures is deficient, inasmuch as the surveyor was not aware of the fact that the moat on the west side had been dug through fully twenty-five yards farther in that direction than it was competent to him to allow for, dealing as he necessarily had to do with only the contours left by modern innovations. The existing road to the station is in reality cut through the castle precincts, and the mound on the castle side is actually in no small part due to the accumulations of soil accruing from the cutting and removed thither. The foundations of the adjacent Primitive Methodist Chapel were dug for through the puddled bottom and side of the original moat on that side.

But if we allow for 130 yards in the one direction and 135 to 140 in the other, it is at once seen that, for a very early Norman castle, the dimensions are such as to indicate that it was no mere insignificant fortalice; and if, besides, we take into account that the moats were more than ordinarily elaborate, inasmuch as while the one on the north was at a considerably lower level than that (or those) on the south-east and south, and that over and above the carefully arranged and constructed water-defences, the mason-work bulwarks were enormously strong—the walls on the east side and round the north-east angle having been eleven feet thick at the ground level—it is impossible to come to any other conclusion than that the founder had special reasons for holding it, and dealing with it as of importance and probably of personal as well as military moment. Certainly if Danby were not the head of the wide and valuable Cleveland lordship, comprising over forty vills, there was no such head in any other part of the district.[1]

[1] The list given at p. lxx of the *Yorkshire Facsimile* runs thus: Appleton, Hornby (not in Cleveland but in Allertonshire), Worsall, Yarm, Otrington, Harlsey, Welbury, Levington (both Church and Castle Leving-

Twenty-five or thirty years later it was a different thing, for Skelton was then in existence.

There is one historical matter connected with Danby Castle to which no adequate measure of justice has hitherto been done; and, in order to arrive at it in due sequence, it may be well to remark at once that there is no uncertainty now as to the Cleveland Brus's genealogy. In all probability, in order to obviate the difficulty created by making the first baron, the Rotbert de Bruis of the Domesday entry, "come in with the Conqueror" (a coming which would have made him, supposing him no more than twenty-five at Senlac, a mere youth of ninety-seven at the Battle of the Standard), another Robert de Brus was raised up unto him as a son! It need hardly be said that there is no historical authority whatever for such an assumption as this. There was but one Robert, and he died at a good but vigorous old age, as has been mentioned already. He was succeeded by his son Adam, his second son Robert having become enfeoffed in the county of Durham and in Scotland, and so becoming the progenitor of Scottish kings. To Adam the first succeeded Adam the second, and to him in succession came three Peters, the last of whom, or Peter the third (his only brother John having predeceased him), dying childless, the male line became extinct. But this again calls for a word or two of comment. Dugdale and others make a fourth Peter de Brus. But there is in reality no uncertainty about it; "Petrus de Brus tertius et ultimus" died in 1271, and his vast possessions were divided between his four sisters, married respectively to Walter de Fawconberg, Robert de Ros, Marmaduke de Thweng, and John de Bellew. Two other sisters, probably three, were nuns; and so ended the name of the great English Bruces.

ton), Morton, Bordelby, Arncliff, Ingleby, Busby, Crathorn, Foston, Hilton, Thornaby, Marton, Newham, Tolesby, Aclam, Faceby, Tanton, Goulton, Borrowby, Nunthorp, Morton, Newton, Upsal, Pinchingthorpe, Kildale, Ormsby, Lazenby, Guisborough, Stanghow, Moorsom, Crumbeclive, Danby, besides the two Hanktons and Lealholm.

But to return : Dugdale states that King Henry II "took the Castle of Danby, with the Lordship and Forest thereto appertaining, and gave him instead thereof the Grange of Micklethwait, with the whole fee of Collingham and Berdesey," from Adam de Brus, son of Robert, the founder of the family and of the priory of Guisborough. To the statement as made by Dugdale, Ord (*Hist. Cleveland*, p. 248) adds that Adam by "adhering faithfully to Stephen throughout his stormy and disastrous career, had incurred the displeasure of Henry II," who thereupon acted in the way just named. It would be interesting to know Mr. Ord's authority for this statement ; for the ordinary historian, under the impression that there was "no love lost" between Stephen and his successor, would be slow to discover the likelihood of the feeling attributed to the latter as so originating. The probability surely rather is that the motive for the deprivation was of a political nature. We cannot read the account that is given of the part played by Robert de Brus when the Battle of the Standard was imminent, or of the motives which animated him to take it, without becoming sensible of the strong feeling towards Scotland and her monarch which reigned in Brus's breast ; and as his second son, besides his patrimonial lands in the north, soon acquired wide domains in Scotland, it is not to be supposed that the feeling of the Brus barons would become less warm towards the Scottish kingdom and its wielder. And, perhaps, even the being suspected of such leaning might almost amount to a direct charge of disaffection in times of such critical relations between the two kingdoms as those were. It is at this point that it becomes of interest to remember the great strength of the Brus stronghold at Danby, and its importance from a military point of view, as commanding one route from Yarm and the north through Kirkby Moorside to York. And surely on such grounds as these we can most easily account for an exchange of his Danby Castle and manor for other and even more valuable lands in the Leeds district being forced

T

upon Adam de Brus, the then occupant and owner of the same.

For it is indisputable that the exchange was most reluctantly made, and was never acquiesced in peacefully by either of the barons who continued to be affected by it.

Nor indeed is that a matter to be wondered at. When we call to mind the long list of North Riding lands and lordships enumerated as forming part of the possessions of the great Brus family, there seems to be something more than merely invidious, something almost insultingly marked and pointed, in the deprivation enforced by the compulsory surrender of the seat of the barony and the residential castle alone out of all the rest.

In support and illustration of the foregoing, or some parts of it, I append the following translation of a document which I do not think has ever been much noticed before, and certainly at no great length by either of the former historians of Cleveland. It is from the *Rotuli de Oblatis*, p. 109, and under date 1200: "Peter de Brus has restored and quit-claimed to our Lord the King and his heirs for ever, the vills of Berdsey and Colingham and Rington, with all their appurtenances, as well in advowsons of churches, as in demesne lands, fees, homages, services, reliefs, and in all other matters to the said vills pertaining, without any reserve, in exchange for the vill of Daneby, with all its appurtenances, and the forest of Daneby, which the King has restored to the said Peter and his heirs, to be held of him and his royal heirs by the service of one knight, in lieu of the aforesaid vills which King Henry, the father of the now king, had formerly given to Adam de Brus, the father of the said Peter, in exchange for the said vill and forest of Daneby. And the said Peter is to deliver over to our lord the King the aforesaid vills free and quit from all those who have been enfeoffed in them by himself or his said father during the time they had been held by them or either of them. And in consideration of the eager desire entertained by the said Peter for the compassing of this exchange, and at his instant prayer for the same, he has induced our lord the King to receive from him one thousand pounds sterling, two hundred and fifty marks whereof is to be paid into the Treasury at Easter now instant, and thereafter two hundred and fifty from Treasury-term to term, until the whole shall have been paid up. As Pledges for the fulfilment hereof, William de Stuteville stands bound in 100 marks; Henry de Neville in 60 marks; Hugo Bard in 40 marks; Robert de Ros in 200 marks; Eustace de Vesci in 200 marks; Robert FitzRoger in 100 marks. And the said Peter's bond is delivered to William de Stuteville, who, together with Robert de Ros and Eustace de Vesci, undertakes that the said Peter, at the first ensuing Court of the County of York, shall find sufficient pledges for the remainder of his obligation, and such that our lord the King shall obtain full satisfaction for the same."

In the *Rotuli Chartarum* also there are two other documents, the one by the king formally restoring Danby to Brus, and the other from Brus as formally surrendering the West Riding manors, specified above, the former dated 7th February in the same year, and the other doubtless of the same date, so as to make the exchange in due form. The witnesses to either are the same, beginning with "R. Andeg. Episcopus," who is followed by Hugo Bard, Eustace de Vesci, Robert de Ros, William de Stuteville, Robert FitzRoger, William Briwerre, Robert de Turnham, Symon de Pateshulle, and the usual *cum multis aliis.*

But there is yet another historical incident affecting this same Peter de Brus, and through him the Castle and Lordship of Danby, which should not be passed over in entire silence. The contest of the baronage with King John, and its issue in the concession of Magna Charta, is a matter of such familiarity in our minds that there is no occasion to do more than advert to it in the briefest terms, merely bearing in mind that the revolt of the barons practically took form when they were called upon to follow the king over sea for the campaign which ended with the battle of Bouvines in July 1214; and it is in distinct relation to this that J. R. Green writes :[1] "From this point indeed the northern barons begin to play their part in our constitutional history. Lacies, Vescies, Percies, Stutevilles, Bruces, houses such as those of de Ros or de Vaux . . . had done service to the Crown in its strife with the older feudatories. But, loyal as was their tradition, they were English to the core; they had neither lands nor interest over sea, and they now declared themselves bound by no tenure to follow the king in foreign wars. Furious at this check to his plans, John marched in arms northwards to bring these barons to submission." Langton's intervention, when the king had already reached Northampton on his way to attack the nobles of the north, combined with political considerations, "induced the king, after a demonstration at Durham, to march to the south again. But the defeat of Bouvines gave strength to the king's opponents, and the open resistance of the northern barons nerved the rest of their order to action," and early in January of 1215 they appeared in arms to lay, as they had planned, their demands before the king; and Magna Charta was extorted as we know.

Here we pause for a moment to notice that Danby (castle, manor, and forest) had been grudgingly and of necessity, as is evident, restored after urgent and pressing insistency on the part of de Brus, and with the accompanying exaction of an unconscionable fine; that de Brus is one of the most powerful of the northern barons named by Green as taking a decisive part against the king as early as 1213; and that the king was proportionally enraged—"furious" is the historian's word; and next we go on to observe that the last thing that John either wished or intended was to abide by the terms of the Great Charter extorted from him in the time of his weakness. And in the issue, when he knew the mercenaries he

[1] *History*, vol. i. p. 287.

had hired were near enough to make such a procedure safe, he positively refused to abide by what he had bound himself by oath not to attempt to revoke. And then the briefest *résumé* of the subject that can be given is: "The mercenaries arrive in September (1215), and John immediately begins to ravage the barons' estates, and takes Rochester Castle; after which, accompanied by 'that detestable troop of foreigners' whose leader was Falkes de Breauté, and carried away by his fury, he began to lay waste the northern parts of England, to destroy the castles of the barons, or compel them to submit to his order, burning without mercy all their towns, and oppressing the inhabitants with tortures to extort money." That is the testimony of Matthew of Paris. Very early in 1216 John advances into Scotland ravaging the country, but soon turns southward, and thence and thus the following extracts from public documents become intelligible, and with a hitherto unnoticed connection. They are from the *Rotuli Litt. Pat.*, and I append the several dates:—6th February 1216, "Peter de Brus has Letters of safe-conduct from King John, to last from the Sunday next after the Purification of the B. Virgin for the eight following days, issued from Gyseburn (Guisborough)." On the 8th, 9th, and 10th the king was at Skelton Castle, Bruce's Cleveland stronghold. On the 15th, at Kirkham, the king engages to receive, under safe-conduct from himself, "Robert de Ros and Peter de Bruis, with all such as they should bring with them unarmed, to a conference, to treat with him about making their peace with him; and the said safe-conduct shall hold good for one month from St. Valentine's day. And for greater security our lord the King wills that . . . . , Archdeacon of Durham, Wydo de Fontibus, Frater Walter, Preceptor of the Templars in the district of Yorkshire, with one of Hugh de Bailloel's retinue, shall go with them in person to the Lord King, and escort them; and they have Letters Patent from the King to that effect; and the said letters are the same day handed to the aforesaid parties, Thomas, Canon of Gyseburn, being further added to their numbers." On the 26th of the same month, John, being then at Lincoln, issues the following mandate : "The King to Philip Marc' etc. We command you that you receive and see to the safe keeping of the prisoners whose names are underwritten, taken at Skelton Castle, who will be sent to you by Dame Nicholas de Haya—that is to say, Godfrey de Hoga, Berard de Fontibus, Anketil de Torenton (Thornton), Robert de Molteby, Stephen Guher, William de Lohereng, Robert de Normanby, Roger le Hoste, Robert de Gilling, John de Brethereswysel, Thomas Berard's-man, and Ralph de Hoga." With scarcely an exception, if indeed there be an exception, these are the names of men holding of Brus in different parts of Cleveland, and the fact that they had been captured at Skelton Castle, coupled with the fact of John's personal presence at Skelton for three days, leads on to a self-evident inference. The castle had fallen, whether taken by assault or surrendered because untenable in face of the king's force.[1]

But the castle at Skelton having fallen, in whatever way, what were the chances that the castle at Danby, in the matter of which a good deal of unpleasantness as between the baron and the king had already occurred, would be suffered to go scot-free ? There is no manner of doubt that at the date of the death of the last Peter de Brus, in the year 1271 (or some fifty-five years subsequently to the events now under notice), the castle and immediate precincts were in a state of ruinous decay ; for the first entry under the head of Daneby

---

[1] It may be noticed here that in connection with the prisoners taken at Skelton Castle on the 8th July the king commands Brian de Insula that he should arrange, as much to the king's advantage as possible, about the redemption or ransom of two knights taken at Skelton Castle, and then in his (Brian's) custody ; and, their ransom having been paid, let them go free. And then, 13th August, at Shrewsbury, a further order is given that all the *servientes* taken at Skelton Castle should be at once put to ransom.

in the " Partitio inter Hæredes Petri de Brus " is "Capitale
mesuagium, cum parvo parco, valet vis. viiid.," a valuation
so absurdly small when contrasted with those that immediately
follow, where the acre of arable or pasture land is set at a
shilling for either, that no conclusion save one as to the condition of castle and park is in the least degree admissible.
And the question then becomes, not as to the condition of
ruin and decay, but at what time and under what circumstances ruin befell the castle and its precincts.

And the question seems to be one of no material intricacy.
The castle was but a generation or so old when seized into the
king's hands in the time of Adam de Brus. The king might
of course have dismantled it during the half-century it
remained in the royal power ; although I can see no sufficient
reason for thinking it was so, and all tangible reasons lead to
the conclusion that he would be much more likely to preserve
it in its integrity, if on no other account than that it was important as a singularly strong border fortress, which, however
dangerous in the hand of an unfriendly or a suspected ally of
the more than possible Scottish foe, could not but add to the
defensive strength of the district it commanded. And that it
had remained in the king's hands during its alienation is
apparent from the terms of the documents of restoration.
There had been no enfeoffment of the castle and manor to
any one who needed to be dispossessed when once the
restitution was resolved upon.

There would seem then to be not only no reason for
supposing that the castle was rendered ruinous before its
restoration to de Brus at the outset of John's reign, but
good reason to conclude it had been carefully kept in its
pristine strength ; and if that is conceded, the only explanation that can be given of its pitiful condition in 1271 is that
it had been taken and dismantled, or rendered untenable, in
the progress of John's vengeful expedition against the northern
barons, which took place in the early part of the year 1216.

Only a few lines more to note the further progress of events connected with the relations of the lord of Skelton and Danby castles with his royal master. On the 12th April of the same year John issued from Reading the following mandate to John, Constable of Chester, Gerard de Furnivall, and Geoffrey de Neville: "We do you to wit that we do not so much wish to take money from the barons of England who have been on our contrary part, as we long for their good and faithful service. And we therefore charge you that if Robert de Ros, Eustace de Vesci, and Peter de Brus shall be willing to give full assurance in the matter of good and faithful service to be, for the time to come, rendered by them, forgoing on our part the exaction of any money from them, it is our good pleasure that they come to our presence, and that you bring them in all security and safety to the said presence. And if it happen that all of you be not able to conduct them as aforesaid, it shall suffice if they come with two of you, and if that cannot be, one shall suffice. And we send herewith our Letters Patent concerning the safe-conduct for the said Robert, Eustace, and Peter." And there is yet one further entry on the Rolls dealing with the same negotiation, which is unhappily imperfect (or rather illegible) in places, the part of it which can be made out being as follows: "The King, etc., to Robert de Ros, William de Mulbray, Eustace de Vescy, Peter de Brus, . . . Richard de Percy, . . . Roger de Merlay. . . Your messengers, bearers of your presents, have come to us at Dover on Wednesday next after the Feast of the Invention of the Holy Cross (11th May), who had been despatched to us on your behalf. . . . (Understanding) that it is your desire to be reconciled to us, we send back to you the same messengers, and with them Robert de Kerneford, our knight, that he our will and pleasure may . . ."

Here the legible part unfortunately ends, and we are unable to follow the record any further.[1] But perhaps for

---

[1] From other sources we know that the barons had offered the crown

our special object there is no necessity to proceed with the
history of the time, either local or general, beyond the point
we have reached. Assuming, as it would appear we safely
may, that the ruin of Danby Castle, in spite of its enormous
massiveness, was deliberate and intended, the old tradition
which was still freely current less than half a century ago,
namely, "that the castle had been destroyed by fire, and that
the stony materials had been employed in building the church,"
takes on such an aspect that, with the single substitution of
the word "rebuilding" for "building," it is seen to involve
much more than merely the elements of probability. It is a
fact that the materials of the ancient castle are not to be found
in the walls or houses of Castleton. In reality the village of
Castleton did not exist until almost down to the present
century, and walls were not wanted where there were neither
houses nor enclosures. But there were enormous stores of
wrought stones embedded in the construction of such a building as the castle unquestionably was, and the inquiry, "What
became of them?" is one that will suggest itself. It is equally

to Lewis, son of the King of France, about the end of March; that John,
on the approach of Lewis, is said to have withdrawn westward; that
Lewis sends aid to the barons, and lands himself at Sandwich 21st May;
that he takes Rochester, and receives the homage of the barons at London
on 2d June, that Lewis besieges Dover ineffectually, and loses his fleet,
captured by the English fleet. From the above document it would appear
that John was at Dover in person on 7th May, probably in order to put
the place in a good state of defence against the coming storm. Green
sums up the whole position at the time in the following graphic sentences :
"In the April of 1216 Lewis accepted the crown in spite of Innocent's ex-
communications, and landed some time after in Kent with a considerable
force. As the barons had foreseen, the French mercenaries who constituted John's host refused to fight against the French sovereign, and the
whole aspect of affairs was suddenly reversed. Deserted by the bulk of
his troops, the king was forced to fall rapidly back on the Welsh Marches,
while his rival entered London and received the submission of the larger
part of England. Only Dover held out obstinately against Lewis. By a
series of rapid marches John succeeded in distracting the plans of the
barons, and in relieving Lincoln; then, after a short stay at Lynn, he
crossed the Wash in a fresh movement to the north." The rest we know.

a fact that the oldest existing part of Danby Church when I first saw it, nearly forty-six years ago, was distinctly Early English, and not of late date in that period; while all the fragments of the church which was destroyed in 1789, to be replaced by the existing barnlike edifice, that I have been able either to note or to recover, agree in point of age. In other words, the tale they have to tell concerning the time at which they were made to replace the preceding Norman fabric is such as to connect itself with a period not much over a score of years later than the ruination of the castle by John or his emissaries. If we couple the singular scarcity of stones bearing the impress of the Norman axe and chisel at Castleton with the abundance of squared stone we know was employed in the old Danby Church with its nave, aisles, and chancel, it may serve to remind us that the old, old traditions of a place or district not infrequently embody an historical truth which may be disclosed by aid of patient analysis and inquiry.

But there is yet another consideration which must be taken into account, and such that we should do unwisely to ignore it altogether. It is true the patronage of the parish was in the hands of the Prior and Convent of Guisborough, and it may seem unlikely that the church would be destroyed as well as the castle by the troops of the king. But whether or no that be so, the fact remains that the church was practically (and I think *entirely*) rebuilt about the time assumed above, or *circa* 1240-45; and the materials of the castle were de Brus's to give. Under what influence or actuated by what considerations we are ignorant, but Peter de Brus, Eustace de Vesci, Hugh Wake, and other nobles, presumably northern, went to the Holy Land in 1241, from whence Brus never returned to England alive. At the least, it is not improbable that the influence of the same motives or considerations which sent him on that long crusading expatriation of his, may have also led him on to give such aid in rebuilding the church—

from whatever cause such rebuilding became either expedient or indispensable—as would be afforded by the supposed grant of material. That it was so may be a surmise merely, but, at the least, it is a surmise which is neither inconsistent with probability nor irreconcilable with the facts.

Peter de Brus the second, who has been the baron so frequently referred to in the preceding paragraphs, was *de facto* succeeded (although not actually, but only legally or morally dead) by his son, Peter the third, in 1240; at least the latter paid the accustomed relief, as on succession to his father in that year. He was, as already noted, one of a large family—eleven in all—one brother, John, who predeceased him, and nine sisters. Two if not three of these sisters were nuns, and four others were married and surviving when their brother died without issue in 1271. These four ladies were his heirs, and his great estates were divided among them. One of them, Lucia, had, at least thirty years before, married Marmaduke de Thweng, baron of Kilton, and owner of other possessions in Kirkleatham and the vicinity. Her share comprised Danby (castle, manor, and forest), besides Lealholm, Wolvedale, Brotton, Skinningrove, lands and tenements in Yarm, Great Moorsham, with other valuable matters in Cleveland, and some manors elsewhere. But Thweng's baronial seat was at Kilton, as has been said, and so the dilapidated condition of Danby Castle[1] would, it would seem, have made no material difference to him, and Kilton, as a matter of fact, would continue to be the baronial residence of the Thwengs after the intermarriage with so great a personage as a sister of the great Baron of Skelton. These are facts hardly to be extracted from the current local histories; but they are certainly facts, and attested as such by a *coram rege* plea dated in 1242, the gist of which is that Robert de Thweng, father of Marmaduke, affirms his gift to the latter of the manors of Kilton and Kirkleatham for the endowing of Lucia de Brus his wife; and as we proceed further with the document it

[1] See Appendix L.

becomes apparent that both Marmaduke and Lucia were under age, inasmuch as it is provided that the wardship of themselves and their lands should remain with Robert the father, together with that of the lands accruing in virtue of Lucia's marriage settlement, and that this arrangement should hold good until Marmaduke should attain his twentieth year.

The Thwengs, it is hardly necessary to say (for the name itself reveals the fact), were East Riding people; but it is not easy to say who the first that took the territorial name was, nor where he came from, nor at what exact date he lived. But certainly they held lands of value and importance besides Thweng (nowadays Thwing) itself. There may be suspicions, arising partly in their heraldic bearing (the three popinjays), and partly from the fact that they were subinfeudatories of the great Percy family, that in some way they were originally connected with Henry de Pudsey (Puteaco), himself a son of Bishop Pudsey by Alicia de Percy (one of the sisters and co-heiresses of the last male of the original family of Percy). The first of the family of whom I have any note is a Marmaduke, who in 1205 gave three marks to recover seisin of certain lands in the manor of Lund, of which Henry de Pudsey had possessed himself on the occasion of de Thweng's imprisonment—for homicide, if I remember. The next is Robert de Thweng, who, with his wife Matilda, is heard of in 1229 as defending a suit brought against them by the Prior of Guisborough *in re* the Advowson of Kirkleatham. And here naturally the question arises, "How could Thweng, an East Riding man, have any interest in, or anything to do with, a North Riding benefice?" and the attempt to answer the question brings in a rather pretty historical induction.

To revert, then, to Robert de Thweng and his wife Matilda. In the year 1221 Richard de Alta-ripa and his wife Matilda claim the advowson of the church just named against the Prior of the said convent, who asserts that the advowson belongs to the convent in virtue of the gift of the said Matilda's uncle,

William de Kilton (Matilda being his next heir). The rejoinder is that William de Kilton made the gift when he was not only on his deathbed, but *non compos sui*, or not competent to make a will or demise a grant. But it is clear that de Alta-ripa's right to appear at all depended on the fact that his wife was de Kilton's heir; and it is at least equally clear that de Thweng's like right could only depend on the same fact: his wife too at that date must have been the right heir of the last male de Kilton. Put that into other words, and what it amounts to is, that the widow of de Alta-ripa had remarried, Robert de Thweng being actually, in point of fact, her second husband.

But there is a yet further consequence depending upon this conclusion, and that is that the inferred marriage of de Thweng with the right heir of the last male de Kilton explains at once how Robert de Thweng became Thweng of Kilton and lord of Kirkleatham, Coatham (or rather of certain portions of either), and other possessions in the same vicinity.[1]

At whatever date Marmaduke succeeded his deceased father, we find that in 1257 he obtained a charter of free-warren in all the demesne lands of his manors of Thwenge, Kirkleatham, Kilton, Moorsom, and Kilton Thorp, besides weekly markets at his manors of Lund, Thweng, and Coatham, with fairs at either place as well.

Marmaduke and Lucia had issue (besides other children) an eldest son Robert, and a second son Marmaduke. Robert's marriage is assumed rather than declared by Dugdale. From other sources, however, we know that his wife was Matilda, daughter of Gilbert (son of John) Haunsard; but as to the date of his marriage nothing perfectly definite seems to have been ascertained. His daughter Lucia, however, was born at Kilton Castle in the year 1279, and baptized (two days after) on Palm Sunday, at the chapel of that vill. The said daughter appears to have been the only offspring of the union; for on

[1] See Appendix F.

Robert's death the headship of the family and the inheritance
of the family manors came to his brother Marmaduke, except-
ing, of course, such as had been settled on Robert himself, his
wife, and their heirs.

Our interest centres in Robert's daughter Lucia, and her
only as connected with Danby. For to her fell her grandmother's share and interest in the Brus inheritance, and as
married in 1296 (at the age of seventeen) to William le
Latimer the younger (for his father was still living), she
carried the same to her husband, and their heirs, should
there be any.

And there was such issue, namely, another William le
Latimer, who was returned at his father's death in 1327-28 as
being then of the age of twenty-six. Thus he would not be
born until some four or five years after the marriage of his
parents in 1296.

In Dugdale's *Baronage* there is an entry which, as at
least apparently connected with just this time, looks more than
ordinarily perplexing. The matter stands thus: William
le Latimer, Lucia de Thweng's father-in-law, is mentioned as
being in 1300-1 "in the garrison of Berwick," and as having
"obtained the king's charter" in the following year "for a
market and certain fairs" in divers manors of his in Kent,
Surrey, and Yorkshire; and intermediate between the statements of circumstances thus dated stands the following: "To
this William King Edward granted the manor of Danby in
Com. Ebor. for life, with free chase there, the remainder to
William his son and Lucia his wife, and to the right heirs of
Lucia." The difficulty at first sight is evidently perplexing,
and as such sure to lead to suspicion of misconception or mis-
construction of the charter in question, and to surmises as to
the motive of the grant, and even of the grantee, all of which,
when examined into, appear to be impossible or fallacious.
For instance, one such supposition is that " William le Latimer
senior, having his misgivings about the marriage of Lucia de

Thweng with his son, insisted on a life estate"! Rather late in the day, surely, for such insisting, the marriage having taken place some five years before; and besides that, upon whom was his insisting to become imperative? Scarcely upon the king himself. And yet there was no one else to be influenced in such a matter.

The real explanation will be found, I think, or at the least suggested, in certain entries in Kirkby's Inquest, the date of which we must remember was 1284-85. On p. 125 it is stated that a change in the secular status of the vills of Kilton, Brotton, Kirkleatham, Moorsom, and Danby—or the joint estate of Marmaduke de Thweng and Lucia de Brus—had been effected, now for ten years past, by the late Marmaduke de Thweng himself. The thing for us to note, however, is that Lucia de Brus's husband is dead before the inquest is taken,[1] or about 1284. The next entry for us to notice is that headed "Yarom," on p. 127, of the first (and pertinent) part of which the following is a translation: "The heir of Marmaduke de Thweng, who is in the wardship (*custodia*, as a minor, namely) of our lord the King, holds eight Knights' fees and a half; he holds also Danby as one fee of our lord the King *in capite*, and the vill of Yarm as a free burgh." But at this date (1284-85) the heir of Marmaduke de Thweng, an infant under age and in the custody of the king as the feudal lord, could be none other than Lucia de Thweng, born, as we remember, just before Easter 1279, and consequently at this period a little girl of about five years of age. Of course this is "another way of saying" that her father Robert is dead, which again throws light on the perplexing circumstance that so very little is heard of him in history,

---

[1] This does not tally with Dugdale's statements, nor consequently with the pedigrees given by Graves, Ord, and Co., which are founded upon Dugdale. Our Inquest entries, however, are such as to show beyond question that Dugdale was wrong. The fact is, that with both the de Thweng and the Latimer families Dugdale's mistakes and confusions are as numerous as they are perplexing.

either private or public. Married in 1279 or thereabouts, he was dead some years before his grandfather paid the debt of nature, and his little daughter, with her inheritance, was a ward of the king, and her lands and eventual marriage at his disposition.

And thus we arrive at a dispersion of the mystery hitherto attached to, and an explanation of, the true nature of the king's Danby grant to the elder William le Latimer. Under the circumstances named, it was competent to him, as to any or every other guardian of a young lady and her inheritance, to "give (or sell) her marriage," as it was termed, to any one he wished to favour or who offered a sufficiently high price, and the favoured recipient acted at his discretion in the matter. In the present case William le Latimer was the fortunate applicant, and it was no new thing in his career. For Dugdale tells us that in 1260-61 he " gave the king (Henry III) twelve hundred marks for the wardship and lands of the heirs of Hugh de Morewick, and benefit of their marriages ;" as also that in 1296-97 he " obtained a grant of the marriage of Isabell, the daughter and heir of Simon de Sherstede, to be a wife for John de Latimer his son and heir." And indeed, if ever a man deserved consideration at the hands of his sovereign, William le Latimer was such a man. As early as 1253 we find him in sufficient repute to be made Sheriff of Yorkshire, and Governor of the castles of York and of Pickering, and as late as 1302-3 "again in the wars of Scotland"; while the list of services with which the interval between those two dates is absolutely filled, is very greatly too long to be reproduced here. He served in Wales, in Gascony, in half a dozen campaigns in Scotland, went with Prince Edward to the Holy Land, was Sheriff of the county again, and Governor of other important castles as well as of those named before, and in fact died in the service of his king and his country, being summoned to Parliament the very year of his death.

With such claims on the royal consideration there is little wonder that he should have obtained "the wardship and marriage" of the heiress of Marmaduke de Thweng, and as little that he should have arranged the marriage of his second son with the young lady; and one wonders whether (hoping almost against hope that he did not) he lived long enough to see the disastrous issue of the said marriage. He died in 1304-5, and Lucia, his son's young wife, left her husband's mansion at Brunne (Kirkburn, not far from Driffield) to go and live in adultery with de Meinill, the Baron of Whorlton Castle, by whom she became the mother of an illegitimate son. After Nicholas de Meinill's death she married, first, Robert de Everingham, and next, Bartholomew de Fanacourt. There is no reason to think that, although after many delays she was divorced from William le Latimer in or about 1312, she was ever married to her seducer, de Meinill.

The lordship, castle, and manor of Danby passed of course to her son by her first husband, William le Latimer, the third of the name in succession. He was, as has been already noticed, twenty-six years of age when his father died in 1327-8, and had livery in due time of the manor of Danby and the other lands of his inheritance. He lived about ten years after, and by his wife Elizabeth, daughter of John de Botetourt, had a son, also named William, who was a child of six years old when his father died. This baron is said by Dugdale to have been resident at Danby, and to have been made Governor of the fortress of Becherel in Brittany in 1360, and the year after "Lieutenant and Captain-General to John Duke of Brittany"; and after this again he seems to have seen much and honourable service in the same province. But in his case also, "it is not all gold that glitters," and towards the close of the now weak and licentious king's reign grave charges of peculation, malversation, and even worse, were brought against him (Latimer) which were held to be proved, and the removal of the offenders was effected. The previous situation

U

is thus summed up by one annalist of England : "Much
discontent is occasioned by the extortionate and illegal
proceedings of the Lords Latimer and Neville, the king's
counsellors, and of Alice Perrers, his mistress ;" while Green,
in his *History of the English People*, expresses himself thus :
"Edward was now wholly swayed by Alice Perrers, and the
duke (of Lancaster, John of Gaunt) shared his power with
the royal mistress.   But if we gather its tenor from the
complaints of the succeeding Parliament, his administration
was as weak as it was corrupt.   The new lay ministers lent
themselves to gigantic frauds.   The chamberlain, Lord
Latimer, bought up the royal debts and embezzled the public
revenue.   With Richard Lyons, a merchant through whom
the king negotiated with the gild of the staple, he reaped
enormous profits by raising the price of imports and by
lending to the Crown at usurious rates of interest.   When the
empty treasury forced them to call a parliament, the ministers
tampered with the elections through the sheriffs.   But the
temper of the Parliament which met in 1376, and which
gained from after times the name of the Good Parliament,
shows that these precautions had utterly failed. . . . The
presentation of a hundred and sixty petitions of grievances
preluded a bold attack on the royal Council.   'Trusting in
God, and standing with his followers before the nobles whereof
the chief was John Duke of Lancaster, whose doings were ever
contrary,' their speaker, Sir Peter de la Mare, denounced the
mismanagement of the war, the oppressive taxation, and
demanded an account of the expenditure."   John of Gaunt
made a scornful retort, "but the movement was too strong
to be stayed.   Even the duke was silenced by the charges
brought against the ministers.   After a strict inquiry Latimer.
and Lyons were alike thrown into prison, Alice Perrers was
banished, and several of the royal servants were driven from
the Court."

It is true that this proceeding was reversed shortly after ;

but only through the imperious will of the duke.   For the
old king died, and the young king, a boy of thirteen years
old, was set upon the throne, and Gaunt was again master of
the situation—for a time at least—and we hear of Latimer's
employment and action in divers matters of some importance.
But his race was nearly run, and we read of his death in the

DANBY CASTLE BRIDGE.   BUILT *circa* 1386.

fourth year of the boy-king's reign.   Statesmen and warriors,
good men and true, a diligent judge learned in the law (the
last Peter de Brus), had been among the lords of Danby.   In
this William le Latimer we seem to have had a man of
a different stamp.

By his wife Elizabeth, daughter of the Earl of Arundel,
he had issue a daughter, also named Elizabeth, who was the

second wife of John, Lord Neville of Raby;[1] and by his will, dated 14th April 1381, he (William Latimer) directs that all the manors of his paternal inheritance should pass to the said "Seigneur de Nevill" and his heirs, who (the heirs) should thenceforward bear his (the Latimer) arms; and he was accordingly summoned to Parliament as Lord Latimer (in right of his wife). The issue of this marriage was a son, John, who died without offspring, and a daughter, Elizabeth, who married into the Willoughby family, and is erroneously spoken of by Ord (*Cleveland*, p. 330, "Pedigree of the Lords of Danby") as "sole heiress to her brother and the barony of Latimer." For many of the lands and lordships in question were affected by the dispositions of the last William le Latimer's will just named, and the "Seigneur de Nevill," to whom they were devised, had a son and heir by his first wife, Matilda, namely, Ralph Earl of Westmoreland. And this is Dugdale's account of what ensued : "Divers of these lordships whereof he (the John who died childless) died seized, being, for want of issue of his body, entailed on Ralph his elder brother (half-brother, more correctly), he, the said Ralph, settled them by feoffment upon George Nevill, one of his sons by his second [first, it ought to be] wife. Which George was thereupon summoned to Parliament as Lord Latimer the next ensuing year" (1431-32). The claim to the barony, how-

---

[1] The arms of this nobleman are conspicuous both on the Castle of Danby and the old bridge below the castle. And perhaps the fact is the more noteworthy because of the direction in Latimer's will that his heirs should bear the Latimer arms. In my *History of Cleveland* I have remarked upon the shield, or rather the escutcheon, on the south front of the castle that it is "peculiar"; for that "the Nevilles, Lords Latimer, whose arms they are, usually had two griffins, and not a griffin and a lion, as supporters ; and either a black roundel or a black annulet as the difference. Moreover the saltire does not reach the edge of the shield." It is possible that this so-called saltire—for it is an even-armed Latin cross set obliquely rather than a saltire—may be intended as a sort of acknowledgment of the matter of the father-in-law's injunction or permission (whichever it was intended to be) as to the eventual bearing of the Latimer arms.

ever, was not entirely uncontested; for in George Neville's grandson's time a counter-claim was urged by Willoughby, Lord Brooke (*Graves*, pp. 274, 275), the issue of which was in favour of Richard Neville, Lord Latimer, the grandson just named.

Richard was succeeded by his son John, Lord Latimer, who ought not to be passed by in entire silence, as one of the lords of Danby, seeing that he was the former husband of the lady who afterwards became Henry the Eighth's last queen;[1] and it was his son John who was the last lord, and who left four daughters, the eldest of whom, Elizabeth, as the wife of Sir John Danvers of Dauntsey, carried the manor, castle, and lands of Danby into another family.   The issue of this marriage, as far as we are concerned, were two sons and a daughter.   The elder of the two sons was Henry, described as "Lord Danvers of Daventree," and as created "Earl of Danby" in 1626; and as having grant in the following year "of the goods, chattels, and debts of all felons in the manor and forest of Danby."   The second was John Danvers who, on the death of his brother without heirs of his body, succeeded to the Danby property (among others), and was the person who alienated the said property to others under the circumstances detailed in another place.   [See next section, On the Contents of an old Oak Chest.]   The sister was Eleanor, who married Thomas Walmsley, and by him had a daughter

---

[1] This is the only grain of historical fact in the legend which tells of a personal visit of Henry VIII to Danby.   The legend is to the effect that Henry riding from York (necessarily over the moors) to visit Lady Latimer at Danby Castle, was caught in a storm and forced to take refuge in the farmhouse in Danby Dale, which still bears the name of Stormy Hall.   As a matter of fact Henry's fifth queen was, when he was at York, still living, and he never came north of York, either then or later.   The name of the farm is in reality due to the fact that the land had been held from the thirteenth century by members of the family (well known in Cleveland) of Esturmi or Sturmy.   And in the first written occurrence of the name of the farm with which I am acquainted it stands as Sturmy Hall.

Anne, who became the wife of Sir Edward Osborne of Kiveton, the father of the well-known Sir Thomas Osborne, High Treasurer of England in 1673 ; created Baron of Kiveton and Viscount Latimer by Charles I. ; soon after made Earl of Danby, and, in the issue, Duke of Leeds.

AN OLD OAK CHEST AND SOME OF ITS DISCLOSURES

THE oak chest stands in "the Jury room," and the Jury room is an oak-panelled room in the castle, with a grandly moulded late mediæval fireplace in it—only hidden away from view by modern "Gothic" innovation. The chest itself is about three feet and a half long, by twenty inches high and twenty-four in width. The oak of the sides and ends is more than an inch thick, and it is barred and cross-barred with iron bands, so that the parallelograms of oak left uncovered are not of imposing size. And the documents it contains have been in it for nearly two centuries and a half, and the chest was not new, but was probably venerable, when they were first entrusted to its keeping; for it has a till in it, and a secret compartment below the till; its present purpose being to hold secure the counter-parts of a long series of conveyances affecting the division and distribution of an estate that comprised, in one form or another, nearly twenty-three thousand acres of land.

I have been engaged for more than eight years in the most careful and prosaic examination of the written Records of the Quarter Sessions' proceedings in the North Riding. In this process I have either copied out myself, or most heedfully per-used the copies made by another of, the lists of the men serving on the Grand Juries from 1604 to 1680. The rule for these lists is that with one, two, or three—rarely more—"gentle-men" at the head of the catalogue, the rest of the names, to

the average number of three or four and twenty, were those of
men described as "yomen." The total number of names thus
recorded in the space of time indicated is certainly not under
five thousand. And the men whose names are found in this
lengthy roll-call come, as they are summoned, from every nook
and corner of the whole Riding. At least, that was as the
matter appeared to the writer for many months after his work
had become as systematic as it was possible to make it. One
day, however, he happened to notice that his own parish was
an exception to the general rule. No jurymen were supplied
by that parish, save it were an occasional "gentleman"; and
this happened so very seldom that it could with difficulty be
tortured into the proverbial "exception." And even at last,
when it was actually noticed, it was rather with a vague sort
of surprise than with any thought of seeking an explanation.
Still, there was the fact. Small places not one-fifth the size
of this parish, and of much less mark in other particulars, sent
their half-dozen or half-score representatives of the yeoman
class; but this great and, by its connections, important parish
did not supply a single one. The writer might speculate, and
he did speculate; but the speculation was as unprofitable as
speculations very often are; and it was not until years of the
examination of minutes and orders had run their course that
explanation of the mystery suggested itself. But one day a
bit of the popular history of the parish flashed across his recollection, and it solved the whole difficulty. For he recollected
that up to the time of Charles I., though not for long after,
the entire parish was still in the hands of one sole and single
owner. There could therefore be no room for yeomen, in the
sense of freeholders, under such conditions. And on this fact
depends a series of transactions, which are not without their
interest from the "local history" point of view, and all the
more so from the fact that the whole series of circumstances has
hitherto been misconceived and misdescribed alike by the local
historians, such as Graves and Ord, in their several histories

of Cleveland, and, as a matter of course, by the whole corps of copyists at large. In the latter class the most astounding muddle is found in Murray's *Handbook for Yorkshire*. There we are told that a " certain branch of the Nevilles," owners of the estate in question, " ended in females, the eldest of whom retaining the estate was wife of Sir John Danvers. Their son was Charles I.'s Earl of Danby—a title which died with him. . . . Sir John Danvers, father of the earl, sold the greater part of the estate to five Danby freeholders ; and the residue, about 2500 acres, with the manor and its rights, was sold to Mr.—afterwards Sir John—Dawnay." It is difficult to characterise this statement otherwise than as I have just now designated it—an astounding muddle. The father of the earl did not sell the estate ; on the contrary, the earl, who died in 1643, died possessed of it. He was succeeded in the possession of the said estate by his brother John, Sir John Danvers of Chelsea, his grandfather having been Sir John Danvers of Dauntsey. In the year 1647 Sir John Danvers of Chelsea, being involved in very serious pecuniary difficulties, was compelled to make arrangements to meet at least a part of them. These difficulties, as it seems to me, may best be described in the words of the old document itself, dated 1st May 1647, from which the information given is derived. It recites that " Sir Thomas Sawley, Bart., now deceased, in his lifetime, at the request of Sir John Danvers, and together with him as his surety, and for his only and proper debt, became bound in the following obligations, viz. to Isaac Jones, Esq., in an obligation of £3000, dated Feb. 12, 1641, conditioned for the payment of £1500, principal debt and interest : to Sir Gerwas Ellwes and Jeremy Ellwes, in an obligation of £800, dated Oct. 22, 1640, conditioned for the payment of £500 : to Anne Rewes, widow, of £800, dated Oct. 25, 1640, for £500 : to Angelo Grey, in £6000, dated April 16, 1638, for £3000 : to Sir William Acton, Knt. and Bart., in two several obligations, one of £2000, dated Nov. 30, 1645, for £1000, and the other of

£1000, dated April 25, 1646, for £600 : And that Sir Peter Osborne, Knt., became bound with the said Sir John Danvers, as his surety, to Thomas Crompton, Gentleman, in an obligation of £2000, dated Dec. 18, 1639, for £1000 : And that John Mountford, D.D., became bound with Sir John Danvers to Francis Lucye, Esq., in £2000, dated May 24, 1638, for £1000 : And that the said Sir John Danvers became bound to divers other persons in divers other great summes of money, for all or the greatest parte whereof some other of his ffreindes, or some of his serwants, stand ingaged with him as his suertyes in severall other obligations : And that the said Sir John Danvers, out of his greate care to have all such debtes as are his owne proper and just debtes, and not any other, for which he stands bound or ingaged as suerty with or for any other person or persons, to bee paid, and to have his ffriendes, servants, and suerties, and their estates, kept harmelesse and without any damage or losse by reason of any of their ingagementes for him, for which, if the times had not bene soe troublesome, and his losses by reason of those troubles soe greate as they have of late byn, hee intended to have done before this tyme. But finding those his owne debtes to bee since these troubles soe much encreased by the greatnes of his losses, as that for the present hee hath noe other meanes to satisfie them, hee is now desirous and resolved to make some provision for raysing of moneys for that purpose by the leasinge and selling either absolutely or by way of mortgage of some of his landes of inheritance. And conceavinge his property hereafter mentioned in the County of Yorke, in respect of their remoteness from the rest of his landes, which, for the most partes, lye in the County of Wiltes, may be fittest for that purpose : and that the same is intailed, and that he hath issue heritable to that estate-entail, and at present he only designs to pay Sir Tho. Sawley, Sir Peter Osborne, and Dr. Mountford," he therefore covenants with Rowland Jewkes senior to levy a fine at Westminster, before the end of Trinity term next, of the Manor and Castle of Danby, and the Forest and Chase of Danby, and the Rectory of Danby, and all tithes in Danby, Leleholmes, and Glacedale, together with Bennington and Flixton in the same county, and all Lectes, Lawdayes, Viewes of Frank pledge, etc.; and the fine is to enure to the uses declared in the deed to the parties of the third part, viz. Thomas Yates of Chelsey, Clerk, Nathaniel Bostock of Heston, Clerk, Edward Thorne of Twickenham, Gentleman, and Rowland Jewkes, the younger of London, Gentleman, upon trust to sell, etc., and pay his debts.

The covenanted fine was accordingly levied before Justices Peter Phesant and John Cobbold on the 28th of May following; and there the matter seems, in the absence of any evidence to the contrary, to have hung fire for a period of seven years. Whether or no the " times soe troublesome " had anything to do with this delay, is a matter of speculation only; but at least such a supposition is by no means inconsistent with the history of the times and what we infer (if we do not absolutely know) of Sir John Danvers himself, and the almost certain explanation of the fact of his difficulties and their origin.

For we remember that Sir Henry Danvers of Dauntsey, brother to Sir John of Chelsea—our Sir John that is—had been created Lord Danvers of Daventry by James I., and was afterwards created Earl of Danby by Charles I. in the first year of his reign (5th February 1626); [1] and in June of the following year he had grant from the same monarch of the goods, chattels, and debts of all felons in the manor and forest of Danby. There is enough in these facts to indicate

---

[1] I am aware this is not as the story is customarily told. Ord, for instance (*Hist. of Cleveland*, p. 330) writes, "Henry, created Earl of Danby, James I.," and quotes Defoe in support of the allegation as follows: "Henry Danvers, created baron of this place (Danby) by James I., though by Charles I. made Earl of Danby. He had distinguished himself in Queen Elizabeth's Irish wars, was good as he was great, and died with glory," in 1643. From which it is clear that Ord has blundered his authority.

that Sir Henry Danvers stood well with James I., and certainly
not less well with King Charles. And it would be anything
but a random supposition if we assumed that there were good
reasons, such as attachment and devotion to the House of
Stuart and its interests, for the circumstance so ascertained.
Assuming, then, the existence in the breasts of the Earl of
Danby and his brother Sir John Danvers of such a feeling, is
it a mere coincidence that the period at which these money
obligations are seen in their inchoative and most urgent stages
corresponds with the period at and through which " a voluntary
war-tax was levied in every county for the purpose of equip-
ping forces " to fight for the king, and when " gifts of money
and plate " for the king's service became the order of the day
among the royalist adherents, whether public bodies or private
gentlemen and nobles? The year 1638 was the year of the
said "voluntary tax," and 1643 that of the "gifts of plate
and money"; and it was in the year 1638 that Sir John
Danvers incurred the obligations of £6000 to one party and
£2000 to another, adding £3500 more the following year,
and increasing the burden still further in 1641. But whether
or no the contemporaneousness of the incipient and augment-
ing indebtedness of Sir John Danvers and the necessities of
Charles I. be taken to afford a very strong presumption that
Sir John was one of the goodly band of noble and faithful
gentlemen who impoverished themselves and risked all they
held most dear in the effort to support a doubtful cause,
certain it is that all practical difficulties appear to have been
cleared out of the way of the proposed alienation of Danvers's
Yorkshire property, for the purpose of liquidating at least
some of his liabilities, by the earlier part of the year 1655.
For it was on 21st February of that year Sir John Danvers,
Tho. Coppin, Esq., Tho. Gunter, Gent., with Nath. Bostocke
and Will. Baxter, Clerks, with the consent and approbation of
Rich. Sallwey, Tho. Estcourt, Rob. Atkins, Rowland Jewkes
sen., Will. Yorke, Esquires, and Tho. Yates, Clerk, engage

and agree "that the Mannor and Lordshippe of Danby with
the demeasne lands, messuages, farmes, tenements, Royaltyes,
priviledges, and hereditaments thereunto belonginge, late
the landes and possessions of the Rt. Honble. Henry, late
Earle of Danbye, together with the Rectorye and tythes of
Danby, shall be sold and conveyed unto Samuell Levingstoune,
Clerk, and John Agarr, yeoman, or to such other persons as
they shall appointe, uppon this special Trust and Confidence :
That all and every the tenanntes and farmors within the said
Mannor and Lordshippe shall have full freedome and power
to purchase all and singuler their severall and respective
farmes and landes as are now held by them respectively, att
such reasonable rates and values as they are now agreed to be
sold att, the purchase and value of the said Manor and Lordship, together with all necessary charges and expences about
purchaseinge and dividinge the same duely considered :
Provided always that the said Sam. Levingstoune and John
Agar, and all and singuler the said tenants and farmors,
shall pay and satisfye unto us, the aforesaid Coppin, Gunter,
Bostocke, and Baxter, for the purchase of the said Manor, etc.,
the full sum of £17000, in three instalments, to be severally
due and payable on the 24th June next after date, the 28th
November next following, and 28th May next after that :
with a proviso, however, that all rents, etc., due on the said
lands be all paid up by or before the Feast of Penticoste next
ensueinge the date of the deed to the four persons already
specified."

And after this date affairs were not suffered to drag their
slow length along as in the years after 1647. No doubt there
were reasons quite sufficiently forcible to account for the delay
in the one case and for the promptitude in the other, and
which suggest themselves the moment we recall the contemporary history of the country. In 1647 everything was
in confusion or worse than confusion. In matters political,
ecclesiastical, civil, nothing was assured, nothing save the

present certain.   The king had newly fallen into the hands of
the Parliament, the army and the Parliament were not at one,
an accommodation between the army and the king seemed
possible, was negotiated for ; a second civil war was imminent,
nay, speedily ensued ; and it was but an unpropitious time for
such dealings as that under notice, or indeed for any dealings
at all that would possibly admit of postponement.   In 1654-55,
on the contrary, whatever view we take of the Protector's
action, peace had been ensured, a strong government existed,
the prosperity of the country was returning with rapid strides,
and there were no threatening clouds looming up from abroad.
Men might prudently and safely and wisely invest their money
now, and find every necessary facility as well as encouragement
to do so.   And thus, tripartite indentures of agreement or of
conveyance, bearing the several dates of 7th July 1655, 11th
July immediately following, and 25th June of the following
year, are drawn up and duly executed, each of them being of
interest in its own way.

It will be remembered that in the deed of which the substance was given a little above, two trustees only were nomi-
nated (Samuel Levingstoune, the non-episcopal "minister" of
the day, and John Agar, a yeoman of the place, occupying
a farm then and now called Didderhow), but with the alternative proviso, " or to such other persons as they shall
appoint, upon this special Trust and Confidence " always ; and
accordingly, as will be seen from what immediately follows,
these two trustees had effected the addition of three others to
the original number of two.   For in the "Indenture Tripartite," dated 7th July 1655, Tho. Yates of Chelsey, Clerk, Nath.
Bostock of Heston, Clerk, Edward Thorne of Twickenham,
Gentn., and Rowland Jewkes junr. of London, Gentn., of the
first part, with the consent and approbation of Sir Francis
Lawley of Spoonehill, Shropshire, Richard Salway of Short-
hampton, Oxon., Tho. Estcourt and Rob. Atkins, both of
Lincolns Inn, with Rowland Jewkes senr. and Will. Yorke,

of the Inner Temple, all designated Esquires, of the second part, agree and covenant to convey to Sam. Levingstoune, Clerk, John Agar, Rob. Prodam, Geo. Harrison, and Tho. Watson, yeomen, of the third part, in consideration of £6200 already paid, and £11,114 further to be paid to the first party, "the Mannor and Castle of Danby, with the Forest and Chace of the same, the Rectory of Danby, with all tythes, etc., and all the rights and appurtenances whatsoever." And herein we notice that, besides the addition of three others, yeomen, to the original two trustees, we have the four gentlemen who are named as of the third part in the deed of 1st May 1647, now as the parties actually covenanting to convey the aforesaid manor, lordship, etc., of Danby to the said trustees, but as in co-operation with two gentlemen (one of them directly concerned in the matter as bondsman for and with Sir John Danvers to a heavy amount), and four other gentlemen, all learned in the law, who may be regarded as engaged on behalf of the baronet aforesaid, and the other creditors whose names have been above specified.

Quite possibly, it will have been noticed that although in the instrument of 1st May 1647 Sir John Danvers covenants to convey to Yates, Bostock, Thorne, and the younger Jewkes, and again in that of 21st February 1654-55 the same Sir John personally, with four other gentlemen named, engages and agrees that the said manor, castle, and so forth, shall be conveyed, in trust, to Levingstoune and Agar, still in this last deed of 7th July in the same year the name of Danvers does not appear at all. The explanation is that Sir John Danvers had deceased in the interim, and the receipts for the payment of the first instalment of the purchase money are signed by Tho. Badcocke *pro* Thomas Coppin and others, trustees for Sir John Danvers, Knight, deceased. The earliest of these is dated 13th June 1655.

The deed that follows next in sequence in connection with this transaction may safely be described as one of singular local interest; for it is entitled "Articles of Agreement Tripartite concluded and agreed upon by and between" the five trustees of the first part, John Dawnay of Cowicke, Esq., Rich. Etherington of York, Esq., and Rich. Alline of Danby, Gentn., of the second part, and 168 intending and covenanting purchasers (of either sex) of "such their severall and respective farmes and lands as are now held and enjoyed by them respectively." There are in all seven different clauses in the said agreement, placing the whole transaction on the most carefully considered business footing, and drawn up with a legal knowledge, skill, and precision such as to elicit high commendation from the conveyancing practitioner of the present day; while to the whole is prefixed "A Schedule of the severall purchasours of the Mannor, Castle, Lordshippe, Royaltyes, Lands and Tythes in Danby, Leleholmes, and Glacedale in the Countye of Yorke, with the severall valewes thereof, freed and discharged of all mannor of Tythes and Fee-farme rentes."

Of this schedule it is quite safe to say that it abounds with varied interest. There is matter in it for the student of local history, both personal and topographical; for the student who confines himself to the observation of manners rather than men; and for the student who pursues the intricate subject of the decadence of the old Common-field system, and the building up upon its ruins of a system of land-management of a singularly different nature.

But there is one revelation in especial made by it, which is of a nature such as alike to discredit popular tradition and to confute the most trusted deliverances of the accepted historian, and still more his unquestioning copyists. The mistakes made in Murray's *Handbook* have already been noticed. Ord's account is more than equally incorrect, both as to person and circumstance. And even the sober and diligent Graves can give no better account of so important a transaction than the following: "Sir Henry Danvers, Earl of Danby, having in

his lifetime sold this lordship to five freeholders, inhabitants
of the place; of whom the castle, manor, and greatest part of
the estate were purchased by Sir John Dawney, of Cowick,
knight." The popular notion or tradition, however, does not
go quite so far astray as either of the authorities last named;
for, instead of making Mr. (not Sir John) Dawnay purchaser
of the whole estate, manor, etc., as Ord does, or of the greater
part, as Graves does, it attributes to the gentleman named
quite another share in the bargain; and the view that is thus
represented is, that whatever the freeholders at large did not
buy of the five was bought by Mr. Dawnay, as well as the
manor, castle, lordship, etc.—in other words, that he was a
sort of residuary purchaser.

As has been seen already, all these representations are
essentially erroneous, and this in several particulars; and
the schedule we are noticing sets all the mistakes about Mr.
Dawnay and his share in the transaction in a painfully clear
light. It will have been noticed that in the agreement by
the five freeholders of the first part to the 168 intending
purchasers of the third part, the names of three gentlemen
are mentioned as of the second part; and they were the
Mr. Dawnay in question, Mr. Etherington of York, and Mr.
Richard Alline of Danby, described as "gentleman," the other
two being esquires. From this alone we see that Mr. Dawnay
was much more than a residuary purchaser, or even the most
considerable purchaser—which, indeed, he by no means was,
except in comparison with individual purchasers. And on
coming to look into the details of the schedule we find
him named among the intending and, indeed, covenanting
purchasers in connection with four out of the 158 lots into
which the estate was parcelled out. And these four lots were
as follows: In the first, Mr. Dawnay, with four others named,
agrees to give £258 for the west end of Oakley side; in the
second, he covenants to buy three-fourths of a certain enclosure, a water-mill, and twenty-three several farms, giving

x

£3050 : 18 : 8 for the lot ; · in the third, he engages to give
£148 : 16 : 6 for several intakes, certain free rents, and also
free rents and tithes issuing out of certain freehold lands ;
and in the fourth the covenanted purchase is of the castle and
its farm, the park, a tenement in Whitby, with the manor
and manorial privileges thereto appertaining, the sum to be
given being £550, the total purchase money amounting to
about £4000, out of a grand total of between £18,000 and
£19,000 to be paid by the collective purchasers.

But it is when we come to study the conveyances which
made the aforesaid agreement effective that the mines of
information, local, economical, customary, archaic, illustrative
of divers matters of interest, begin to be developed ; and they
are of such a nature that it is impossible to do more than
glance at the fact of their existence here. But what ought
not to be omitted is the fact, or the series of facts, that there
is much variation between the list of actual or eventual
purchasers, as compiled from the conveyances themselves,
and that given in the schedule ; that the total number of
conveyances—strictly speaking, they are the counterparts of
the original conveyances—contained in the chest is but 138,
as against more than 150 specified in the schedule ; that
three out of the four conveyances made to Mr. Dawnay do
not appear, only the conveyance of the castle and manor
lot being present ; that more than one of the conveyances
extant deal not with single holdings, but with a group of
farms (six or seven, or even nine in one case), and without
precise details of any kind connected with them, except
as regards the names of the persons who were in present
occupation ; and, lastly, that the whole series of transactions connected with the sale, purchase, conveyance, and
delivery of all these several allotments, comprising the entire
extent of the parish and manor of Danby (Glaisdale, as of
necessity, included), was carried through and completed within
the course of the year 1656. Not one of all the 138 convey-

ances referred to is dated otherwise than in that year. And this prompt execution and completion of the business is covenanted and provided for in the second and third of the seven articles which the agreement comprises. The latter of these two articles specially provides that there shall be no further addition at any time to the existing number of freehold farms, each with its own especial common right—a rule which is most strictly insisted and acted upon down to the present day.

All of these articles contain some curious reading, and their preciseness in a variety of particulars is of a nature to arouse general local interest. But of all, perhaps the fourth is the most marked in this particular; for it defines alike the rights and privileges accruing in virtue of his purchase to the lord of the manor and his successors, and also his (and their) obligations and duties as towards the rest of the purchasers, or, in other words, the resulting body of freeholders.

As a case in point it not only authorises, but requires him, in case of any encroachment on the peculiar rights of the freeholders, such as the removal of turf, ling, brackens, etc., by non-freeholders, or such as do not possess a common right, to take proceedings against the offender. And this has actually been done within the past year. A man living in the parish, but not the holder of a common right, cut and carried away a certain amount of brackens, and, when fined by the jury for the encroachment, made difficulties about the payment of the fine, and eventually altogether declined to pay it, and strove, under bad advice, to resist the infliction of it. The case was referred to the proper court, and then, under better advice, the defaulter gave in and paid the fine.

There is, indeed, far too much calling for notice in this mass of documents to be dealt with at the close of one of these sections, or indeed, it may be, in such a book as this.

MISCELLANEOUS

NOTES ON NATURAL HISTORY: CHIEFLY
ORNITHOLOGY

ONE of my old parishioners, for whom I entertained lively
feelings of regard and attachment—a stalwart-looking mason,
who died, however, of consumption some twelve or fifteen
years ago—told me one day, while detailing certain facts
which he had verified touching the moats which had originally
encompassed the original Castrum de Daneby, from which
the hamlet of Castleton derives its name, that one portion
of the system of moats had been dug through by himself
when excavating for the foundation of a chapel, the construction of which had been entrusted to him; and that he had
helped to fill up another portion situate in a field in his own
occupation. These details were of great interest to me for
many reasons, and I listened with great attention. I was
myself tolerably well acquainted with the said system of
moat-defences, part of which is still extant, and part has been
filled in to help find space for a garden, since I have been
here; and what he told me cleared up a great difficulty in the
way of a satisfactory conception of what the water defences of
this castle had been. I had seen the basement of the walls
on the northern side laid bare by this same man and his workmen, and had found the width of them in excess of eleven
feet; and it had seemed that there might have been some
reason for this enormous strength in the fact that from the
position of the castle the moat could not be carried round it

on that side, because the ground fell away abruptly from almost the very foot of the wall as I saw it had been built. Still my friend's positive and matter-of-fact, as well as detailed, statement left me in no doubt that this considerable, and certainly important, early Norman fortress had had water-defences also on the north side; although, and of necessity, at a lower level than on the eastern and southern sides and, most likely, on the western side as well.

But this is not going to be an antiquarian chapter, and I only mention these details to lead on to another statement made by my poor friend Frank when he told me he had done so much in the way of filling in the moat on the north side. He described the condition of the place filled. It had been a place for the habitation and breeding of toads as long as he could remember, and much ill-usage the poor toads had experienced at the hands of the Castleton boys; and "a vast of filling in" it had taken. But he and the mason he had been apprenticed to had "a great vast of masons' rubbish" which they were glad to be able "to vent" anywhere, and it had gone to fill up this place, and make a good firm road into the field, a purpose it serves still.

Well, one day when I was talking to Frank about many things, one of us adverted to some notice or other which had recently been going the round of the papers about a toad found enclosed in the boll of an old tree, which was being split up (or cut up) for firewood, or something of that sort; and Frank asked me what my opinion was as to the rights in that much-vexed question. I expressed my unqualified incredulity, both as to the alleged fact itself and as to the authenticity of the statements in regard to it. But Frank did not take my view, that was clear. He did not see why it could not be. "Why, pricky-back otchins (urchins, hedgehogs) slept all the winter thruff (through), and he himself had offens seen the backbearaways (bats) hinging up in the church-tower, and au'd garrets i' different spots, and a few weeks more or less of winter seemed to make no differ to thae; and besides folks did say that swallows had been fished up out of the bottoms of ponds and such like, all hinging together like bees iv a swarm, and all as wick (alive) as gam'-some kitlins (frolicsome kittens)." But I saw there was more in my companion's mind than even these natural history recollections, and after a little trouble I got him to tell me what it was. He believed toads could live, and did live, "a weight of years even," if they happened to be covered up, ay, and blocked up so they couldn't stir and much more get out. "Why, he had heared thae teeads (toads) that had been covered up years and years ago, with loads on loads of broken stone, rubble, earth, old mortar—all sike-like minglements as came in mason-work, from pulling down old buildings and putting up new—five foot deep in some places; and yet he had heared them croaking, not once or twice only, but scores of times; and that showed they could live in such spots." And nothing could shake this good man's faith that the toads he had heard were the toads whose dwelling-place he had helped to fill up so many years before.

I do not for a moment doubt that my poor friend had heard the croakings in question, nor even that they had come from the place he affirmed them to have come from. I no more disbelieved his statement than I disbelieved the evidence of my own eyes one day when, amid a little scene of excitement among my fellow-workers, I saw a living viper disclosed from a pile of stonework in the heart of a barrow on the moor, which stonework lay below a superincumbent covering of earth at least two feet in thickness. But then I could account for the presence of the toads where Frank said he had heard them just in the same way as I could account for the presence of the hagworm three or four feet below the surface of the houe. Some means of entrance and access to the interstices between the piled stones existed in either case, although it escaped notice, and even suspicion, in the case of all the observers, myself only excepted. It is the habit of the toad, equally with the viper, to "choose for its winter retreat some retired and sheltered hole, a hollow tree, or a space amongst large stones, or some such place," as Mr. Bell writes, and so the old habitat below the castle would still be occupied during the winter, and when the spring came again, and the toads awaked from their long slumber, they would be likely to croak as naturally as a man yawns under the like circumstance every morning.

I do not like to misuse the words fancy and imagination. The latter is a grand thing, and the other a pleasant thing. And so I do not care to say, "What a lot of imagination or what an amount of fancy is expended upon very everyday topics connected with natural history!" but I would rather say, "What an awful lot of unthinking, unstable supposings or assumings, based upon no real or genuine observation, is continually put forward in almost every vehicle of natural history 'Notes and Queries'!" and my dearly-beloved starlings are among the sufferers thereby.

A few years ago there was a craze among some fancy ornithologists to make the cock starling a bigamist. Positively the theory was started that he customarily had a couple of hens attached to him, and that this accounted for the groups of three one perpetually saw in the breeding time! For one thing, although I have been on very intimate terms with starlings for some sixty years, I did not even know that "groups of three" were to be recognised at all. Certainly I have often seen three together, but the same observation holds good of most other species of birds, I think; but as to a male starling mating with two female starlings at one and the same time, the idea is simply absurd to any one who has the opportunity, continued for dozens of years, of watching all the domestic proceedings of some ten or twelve pairs of the bird in question during the entire breeding season; five to seven of their nests, moreover, being placed within three yards of his seat by his own dining-room window.

Starlings "pair," literally and simply; and if I were asked to give the impressions produced in my own mind by what I have observed in connection with my own private colony here especially, I should say that I am by no means sure they do not remain paired all the year round—at least in some cases. Thus, they always come back to their haunts in the ivy surrounding their nesting-boxes, and they always come in even numbers. To avoid begging the question, I say—not that there are three pairs, but—six birds here now, and for the last six weeks there have been always either two or four or six. I have seen two of these roosting for the night in a large sweeping thorn-tree night after night, two in a spruce fir near, and two in the ivy. The last two weeks, or since the weather became very cold, they have quartered themselves for the night mainly in the ivy. They sit on the chimneys or the pinnacles of the house for half an hour or more before bedtime, and converse, cheerfully and musically always, and sometimes mocking-bird-like. But that is the more usual practice of the springtime of the year. But they are always separable into twos, only greatly more then than now.

Another craze of the fancy ornithologist, with the starling for its object, is occupying some pages of the *Naturalist* at the time of writing, the question being, "Is the starling double-brooded?" or, in other words, "Does the starling bring off two broods in the same season?" The question, on the face of it, is nonsensical; for it does not appear that any one of those who write on the affirmative side is willing to display so much of a crack, rather than a craze merely, as to advance that the rule with the starling is to produce two broods annually unless exceptionally prevented : and as certainly no one of those writing on the negative side disputes the fact that in divers instances they have been known to multiply to that extent.

To be sure, one gentleman on the affirmative side writes, "My reply to the question, Are starlings double-brooded? must be distinctly in the affirmative." But there is the most artless innocence of any attempt to produce evidence to support, and much more establish the soundness of, the verdict given. The "united experience of himself, the members of his family, and the school-children"—it is absolutely so written—"is that, with hardly any exception, these birds"—the occupants of nine nests within a radius (*sic*) of little over one hundred yards—"reared two broods every season." As the good gentleman winds up by making "Turdidæ" of the nine pairs of starlings in question, besides adducing such a mass of well-digested facts in evidence, it may perhaps be assumed that the affirmative side might have been none the weaker had his remarkable contribution been withheld.

Of course the starling, like other birds, is double-brooded on occasion. And I suspect that qualifying "on occasion" goes to the root of the matter. Thus, I am aware that the much larger proportion among my own home favourites were double-brooded during the breeding season of the year 1889, and that for a special cause. Owing to unusually mild and indeed warm weather in the early part of the year, the starlings—one pair of them at least, and I think another—and some other birds, including a pair of blackbirds and a pair of chaffinches, began nesting operations at a most unusually early period, and I had reason to be assured that the starlings had eggs as early as the first week in March. Then came three nights during which severally my thermometer registered 18°, 21°, and 22° of frost, after which for a week there was, as a rule, more or less snow falling; and it was not till the end of that week that I heard or saw the first pewit of the hundreds that annually breed about our fields. During all this time—nine days in all—the starlings had disappeared; and when they returned, the nesting work, which had so far prospered before, had to be done over again. It was two days after the pewits came that the starlings resumed their operations; but only two, or at most three, pairs of them.

Now for a parallel case. Some thirty years ago, or nearly, Whitmonday here signalised itself not only by the blowing of a great wind (which levelled the section that was left of my haystack), but by the falling of about three inches of snow, and two nights—those preceding and succeeding it—of very hard frost. One of the consequences was the bursting, under the tender mercies of the frosty temperature, of hosts of the grouse eggs on Westerdale moors and the equally exposed parts of our Danby high moors. The birds, however (in the majority, as I was led to think), nested again; and the consequence was that the proportion of "cheepers" upon the moor was so great, that the practical effect was the postponing of "The Twelfth" for a fortnight or three weeks. My impression was that perhaps one-third, or nearly so, of the broods on our high moors that year were hatched from a second laying of eggs. Yet surely no one would think, from any number of such instances of this—and they are by no means few—of styling the grouse, in the language of the *Naturalist*, double-brooded.

But even under more ordinary circumstances I could adduce similar instances from observation of the "ways and the tricks" of the partridge, the ringdove, the waterhen, the dabchick, and divers other birds. Rob them, by whatever means, of their first laying of eggs sufficiently early, or let them get off their first brood unusually soon, and they are likely to lay again and hatch the second cletch of eggs. And with the blackbird, the thrush, the robin, the chaffinch, and a score or two more of our most familiar birds, this happens in numberless instances almost every year; actually every year, I do not doubt. As to the robin, I positively knew one case in which the same pair of birds built three nests in contact with each other—like three tenements under one roof

—and brought off three broods, one from each nest, in quick succession.

Here is another statement made by one of the writers of notes in these *Naturalist* papers which reads very strangely to me : " It may interest readers of the *Naturalist* to know that in dry times the starlings will leave the meadows to make descents upon strawberry beds, and that when they do this they take all before them, whether they be green or ripe." Now on this point my experience is not small. I should say my average annual crop of young starlings for the last five-and-twenty years has been somewhere about five-and-thirty. I have had as many as twelve broods, averaging four each, brought off in one year. The year 1868, in young starling time, was so dry that I had not a green blade left on my fairly large grass-plots. This past summer (1889) was something the same, only the fields were not quite so parched, although the grass in many fields about was half hay before it was cut. And the year 1887 in strawberry time was like. Now I grow a good breadth of strawberries. During the past summer we gathered an average of fifteen pounds a day for thirty-five to forty days. And for the last forty years the average yield has not been less than that ; indeed, more rather than less. During these said forty years the blackbirds, ring-ousels, thrushes, and, occasionally only, the missel-thrushes have fairly worried me as well as the garden. I have shot scores on scores year after year. I remember once being in the lower part of the garden, under cover from the adjoining field where my men were then cutting the wheat in a field that had only come into my possession two or three years before, and which I had cultivated with a view to laying it down in grass. " Why, here's a black ussel," I heard one say to another. " And here's a moor blackbird," cries a second ; and a minute after, " Why, here's another and another. Wheea, t' land 's wholly mannered (manured) wiv blackbirds ! " One day actually one of my lads, getting his younger brothers and sisters to "drive the garden" for him, shot fifteen of these depredators from one stance, having three different drives.

But all these years, and with such potential array of bad example before their eyes, I have never once seen a starling on the strawberry beds, or been led to imagine, and much more suspect, that they had even tasted so much as one. Let the fact stand. *Valeat quantum.*

All the same, the starlings are not entirely blameless as visitors in the flower - garden. One day, years upon years ago, I was visiting an old man, living in one of the old-fashioned houses that are hardly believed in as having ever been in use as human dwellings, and I was talking to his wife, a woman still young enough to take an interest in her garden—younger than her old husband by thirty years, I should say; and she was speaking of the starlings' misconduct in her limited little bit of flower space. I asked, "Was she sure it was the starlings?" She had no doubt about it; and, as luck would have it, a couple of the alleged criminals flew down into the little plot just under the window of the room we were sitting in, and began deliberately to pluck off the crocus flowers under our very eyes. And the flowers did not come easily; they took a good deal of tugging, and mending the bird's hold, and tugging again, before the decapitation was fully effected. I had not another word to say for my clients. Their ostentatious indulgence in the crime imputed to them shut me up for good.

And in this garden they take great liberties of the same sort with our early primroses, polyanthuses, and so forth. Not often with the crocuses; though, with the many thousands blooming within a score or two of yards of the nesting and roosting place, the temptation cannot be said to be wanting. But my experience is that one peacock will do more mischief in the ways alleged in one short spring morning than all my colony of starlings in the year.

I mentioned the missel-thrushes as occasional plunderers. One year, why or wherefore I never could understand, they were very troublesome. They came in a flock of thirty and upwards, and always settled among the raspberry canes. If I shot at them—though I hardly succeeded in stopping more than about two in all, they were so very wary—they were back again in half an hour, and circling once or twice high up in the air, as if to see whether the coast were clear, down they swooped upon the unlucky raspberries. This was the only instance of their coming in a flight. Odd birds, or two or three at a time, I see not infrequently.

But the moor blackbird or ring-ousel is the bird of all birds to " walk into " your fruit of the berry sort. I do not know for certain that birds do blush, or else I should say he is the most unblushing, the most unabashed of all possible delinquents in the fruit-stealing and wasting line. His effrontery exceeds that of the Irish member of fiction, of caricature even. The blackbird flies away when caught in the act with a startled cackle ; the thrush retires with an apologetic cheep. But the moor blackbird—always a past master in birds' Billingsgate—swears at you, calls you all the choicest names in his repertory, blackguards you for inter- fering with his meal, and if forced to make himself scarce, does so with the assurance emphatically delivered and repeated that " you are no gentleman." I have sometimes ventured to represent to them that I thought I had a little right in my own garden, even if it was only to see what sort of a feed they were getting. They flatly and insultingly declined to see it. I suppose it must have been the rankling of their contumelious treatment of me which always made me gloat with a fine sense of compensation obtained, whenever one of them fell a victim to my avenging gun.

Some years large numbers of these birds are produced on our moors. Sometimes I have seen them, when out with my gun, well on into September, in flocks of some hundreds together. This would be of course at the commencing stage of their making ready to "flit" at the accustomed "term." If it so happens that there is a plentiful harvest of bilberries, it is very seldom we see them in the gardens very early. Nay, even our common blackbirds go up on to the moors to share in the feast, when it so befalls. During this past autumn I have seen the plainest evidences that foraging parties of blackbirds had gone from the very centre of the dale, and had not come away empty. If any one suggests that there is no reason why blackbirds, and thrushes too, should not have an occasional picnic on the moors as well as what the Suffolk people used to call "humans," I have nothing to say against it, except that I think they must picnic every day of the week, for ten or fifteen days together.

When the bilberries are exhausted, then down come the moor blackbirds; and if they are let alone, they show that bilberries are better appetisers than sherry-bitters, or even than the boasted solan. I have literally seen them fifty at a time in this garden, on occasions when they had been left undisturbed for two or three days. It is then that they resent so bitterly and so abusively your intrusion upon their refresh-ment-room. After the somewhat precarious time in the gardens is over, and that much-grudged supply is exhausted, they fall back upon the berries of the mountain-ash or rowan-tree, and as these trees are fairly abundant throughout the district, there is usually a fair board spread for their enjoy-ment during the greater part of the period they have yet to spend in the haunts of their callow-hood. And after that comes departure.

Certainly I should be quite willing to have my mountain-ash berries spared, and it is a little trial to me to see their beauty destroyed in the shamelessly wasteful, extravagant manner in which these marauders deal with them. They begin before they are quite red-ripe, and for one they eat out of the gorgeous clusters, they seem to squander three, and drop

Y

them recklessly to cumber the paths and beds beneath. But that is the character of all the plundering perpetrated by these members of the Thrush family. They run their bill through the ripened or ripening side of a big strawberry—big enough to furnish such a bird a full meal for the time—and then pass on and do the same by another and another, wasting at least twice as many as they consume. It is only among the smaller varieties of the strawberry that I ever find a hull from which all the berry has been cleanly cleared away. It is the same with the currants, the gooseberries, the raspberries. Your red currants and your black currants spot the ground beneath the bushes with brilliantly translucent coral and lustrous beads of jet; but they are beads that will never be strung or gladden a creature's eye. The poor gooseberries too, their skins hang half empty on the bushes and rot; and the raspberries droop in raggedly granulated halves, or stick in dismembered grains on the leaves or ground below.

And yet it is not so with them in respect of other matters of food. I have seen the thrush who had caught a big earthworm incautiously looking out of its bore upon the morning, tug, tug, tug at its prey, leaning back with its effort till its tail touches the ground, and you think if the worm was spiteful enough or wide-awake enough to break, or otherwise give way, what a head-over-heels tumble there would be, and a tail all rumpled and broken. It would be so easy for the bird to secure a good big bite of the worm, and end at once the meal and the struggle too. But no; he sticks to his capture, tugs and tugs on, gains a little bit, almost imperceptibly, or loses a hairbreadth or two by reason of the slipperiness of the victim. And then you see him mend his hold with a lightning-like dart; and the struggle rarely ends without success attending the thrush, usually in the form of the whole worm; if not, always with the bigger half of it. It is the same in the winter time, when the blackbirds come and eat of the crumbs which fall from the parson's breakfast-room window. They get hold of a big piece, a corner of half-softened crust, a shred of the tougher part from the side of the loaf, and away they go to the covert of the shrubs and worry every fragment of the edible morsel.   Nay, more; even at this time of the year they are plunderers.   The robin or the shufflewings—I like that name; it is as descriptive as a mediæval nickname—the sparrow or the chaffinch, get a bit too large to be disposed of easily, and make for the bushes with it.   But they very seldom enjoy their "gettings" themselves; they are not "havings" to them, poor little weaklings.   There is a black-bird under each of the most frequented little bird haunts among the shrubs, and the pelf passes to the strongest pilferer. It is a lesson after the morning's meal, and when there has been a fall of fresh snow, retaining every impress of foot and claw, to see whose footmarks betray the actual eaters, and how the robins and sparrows and cuddies (hedge-sparrows) have been forced to act as the blackbirds' providers.

The poor rooks certainly do the same, but in a very small degree, and with a sadly abashed and apologetic demeanour. In a long hard time they come and sit on one of the larches or spruces growing a score or two of yards from the house; but it is rarely indeed they venture to come to the terrace below the window, where the crumbs and so forth are scattered, and act as if they knew they were invited guests.   I have, however, sometimes induced even these distressful vagrants— I can hardly call them mendicants—to look about as if thinking food might be found that had actually been laid for them. Pieces of boiled potato spared from the yesterday's dinner, or a lump of parsnip, or a tenacious bit of dumpling, would always serve the purpose when once the poor starving "crows," as our Clevelanders call them, had got into the way of taking a flight of inspection,—a sort of "circular tour" about the precincts of the lawn.

But the birds that have distressed me most by their con-tinued endurance of any amount of privation, rather than come

to our window soon enough to save themselves from absolute
death by starvation, have been the fieldfares. I remember
once, nine or ten years ago, one morning when I was on my
way to Fryup Church in a bitter frost, by then of many
days' duration, and with some inches of snow all over,
seeing eight or nine of these birds in the last extremity of
privation struggling to make a scanty meal off a few
scattering[1] holly berries growing on a stunted holly-tree
which used to stand in front of the bar window of the Hare
and Hounds "public" at Ainthorpe, and even although this
took them almost into contact with the window itself. I am
afraid every individual in the scattered flocks there were in
this district—caught by a sudden storm of snow and frost—that
year perished miserably. And I know nothing sadder than the
sight of a wild wary bird, always on the alert and careful to
give a wide berth to everything and everybody capable of
looking suspicious, so dazed and benumbed and demoralised
by hunger and cold as to become dulled, muffled, unvigilant,
uncaring, and even tottering wisps of feathers.[2] I had gone
down the beck with my gun one day, three or four winters
ago, and I found myself in a field with some three or four score
of these birds hopping slowly, desultorily about, and so numbed
in all their perceptions that they let me come within a few
yards of them. One poor bird was so weak and so hopeless
that its wings drooped from its back as if injured, and it
permitted me to come within the length of my gun of it.
And even then it only faintly fluttered a few yards away. I

---

[1] This is good Yorkshire if not good English. I once asked one of our
farmers if he had a fair crop of apples. "Ay," said he, "there's a canny
scattering few." He meant that, although the boughs were nowhere laden
with fruit, still few or none of them were without a sprinkling. The
idiom for "very few" would have been "amaist nane," while for a more
abundant crop than the "canny scattering few," the expression might
have been "a good few," and for an abundant, or very abundant produce,
"a vast," or "a strange vast."

[2] Compare the Winter's Tale in W. Warde Fowler's *Tales of the Birds*.

looked back over sixty years and remembered myself a schoolboy gunner, and what a triumph it had been when I had
managed to stalk an actual fieldfare, and carry home the
game to my admiring sisters and mother.

But perhaps the most pitiful case was that of one of
the two or three whose faltering pinions have borne them
to my window. It was on a Sunday. Our early dinner
was over, and I was giving the poor bird-pensioners their
midday dole, when I noticed a stranger feather-ball amongst
the expectant lot, sitting below the window at the very
foot of the wall. It scarcely troubled to stir on the opening of the window—always a welcome sound to half a score
robins, cuddies, and house-sparrows, who flew down at once with
ready expectancy. But this poor fluff of fieldfare feathers only
moved a yard or two, and when it saw the other birds pecking
away for dear life, it seemed too stupefied to understand that
they were finding food, and that there was food for it too, if
it would. Presently it came to its old place under the window,
and I dropped food upon its very head and back; but all in
vain. It was growing time for me to make ready for afternoon church, and the snow-enforced struggle to get to it on
foot; but I found time to go and take the bird up and bring
it into the warm room and try and get a little food down its
throat. But it was all in vain; and though I left it in charge
of a sympathetic member of my household, it was as good as
dead when I got back again.

The strangest bird visitants that ever presented themselves
at this dining-room window were a couple of snipes, which came
regularly, twice always, and sometimes three times a day, to
the meal provided for distressed birds; and for their especial
benefit bread soaked in milk, enough to soften it, was put out.
This went on, if I remember, for eight or nine days continuously. Once a grayback crow came, and the same winter with
the snipes a single water-hen; and regularly, moreover.

But the queerest bird visitors—the queerest, I mean, in their ways and gestures—I ever had on this bird-trodden terrace were a pair of landrails or corncrakes, which came into my garden as their place of temporary residence, while they took a look round to see where they might advisedly—not exactly pitch their tent, because that is not their habit—but "squat" or settle for the season. I had a patch of lucerne growing in the north side of my garden ground then; and it afforded the landrails beautiful shelter and abundant food. But they made divers excursions from the place of their shelter, and invariably on foot. More than once or twice their vagrant humour led them on to the lawn, and from the lawn to the foot of the terrace, and twice on to the terrace itself.

One memorable morning, breakfast was just over, and I had risen from my chair and as usual drawn nigh to the window. The corncrakes were just coming under the hedge of rhododendrons which skirted the lucerne and cut it off from the lawn. I called my wife and two or three elder children to come very cautiously and quietly to watch these quaint-looking, quaintly-moving fowl. The birds drew on, approached the slope of the terrace, mounted it, advanced, came right up to and under the window, to within half a dozen feet of the four or five pairs of watchful eyes which were eagerly surveying every movement, every feather of their bodies almost. All at once they seemed to become conscious that they were not so much in private as they had assumed. They stopped suddenly from their somewhat gliding manner of advance and fixed their view intently upon us. We hardly breathed. The boys had enough of their father in them to be as quiet and as motionless as the birds themselves. The gaze from without continued for many seconds, the gazers continuing to draw themselves up in the most surprising way till they stood more like small posts driven into the ground than anything else. This continued for nearly two minutes, and then in a flash they were gone! And they ran; they never stirred a wing—a feather, I was going to say; but the incredible rapidity with which they disappeared has always rested in my mind as about the most marvellous bird-achievement in all my sixty-five years of observation.

A pair of quails once came into the same part of the garden, but they never offered themselves to view. I hoped they were going to nest somewhere near, as they stayed for four or five days in the fields a little east, and later a little north-west of the house. I saw them one day in the field last named, after much trying ; but I never saw nor heard them again.

ORNITHOLOGY (*continued*)

IT is hard when on with my birds, which in some way or other have been the objects of great interest to me for more than threescore out of man's allotted threescore and ten years, and in many individual cases my pets and my friends too, to turn away for any other attraction whatever; and I daresay if what I am writing in these reminiscences is ever read by any one out of my own family, I shall be held excused for one little gentle canter farther on one of my stud of especial hobbies.

One thing, however, which I do not propose to do is to give a formal catalogue of the "birds I have known" in Danby, although there have been some interesting occurrences among my experiences. Thus, one Sunday afternoon I had a White's thrush on the grass under my study window for perhaps ten to fifteen minutes, examining him at my leisure with the aid of a pair of excellent field-glasses, so that every feather and feature was as clear and well defined to me as if I had held him in my hand. My eldest son was with me at the time, and drew my attention to him as being different from any bird he had before seen. I was getting things ready to go to church, and did not want to be bothered. However, the lad's urgency constrained me to give it a look, and then I wished it had not been almost church-time. My boy wished it had not been Sunday, that he might have taken his gun. I think I was glad, in that connection, that it was

Sunday, for I hate the slaughterous propensities of collecting, and still more, of only curious, ornithologists.

Not so very many years ago three kingfishers were seen in the beck; and positively one afternoon I saw five fellows with guns, all bent on the destruction of these poor harmless, but unluckily gorgeously plumaged birds. Another day I heard the note of the great spotted woodpecker. The day after he obligingly flew across the road in front of me, and settled in a stunted oak-tree within a score or so of yards, and as I walked quietly on he let me come within five or six paces. I thought to myself, "You are much too tame," and it was but a day or two after I heard he had been shot by one of those wretched gunners who persecuted and slaughtered the kingfishers. One of these same beautiful birds—I mean the spotted woodpecker—made his appearance in the parish just about the year I came into residence, and was shot by the gamekeeper, who showed his prize with great pride to "my lord." But he got such a wigging from "my lord" for the slaughter that I do not think he showed his next "rare bird" victim.[1]

Woodpeckers were anything but uncommon here till lately, but what with cutting the wood down and what with shooting the occasional visitors, the visits of these harmless, interesting, beautiful birds are strangely like those of angels. I wish our bird-murderers had as much sense as Balaam's ass, and could recognise the angel of kindness to living creatures when she steps in between them and their intended victim.

The raven has been extirpated within my time. The barn owl—they used to breed in the church-tower—had gone

---

[1] The gamekeeper mentioned here was my old friend Robert Raw. Although a gamekeeper, he was still in many particulars a bird-lover, and he is mentioned later on in these notes as being such. I was, however, unable to convert him to my view touching the harmlessness (in the game connection) of the kestrel. It was a "hawk," and the name was as fatal to the poor birds that bore it as the proverbial "bad name" to a dog.

a few years before. The brown owl, wood owl, or screech owl, if it exists still, is represented by one pair only; and I used to know of two nests in the Park [1] alone, and there were other two or three pairs about the woods near the lodge, and again others in the Crag Wood; and any still evening one could hear their note in two or three different directions. But now it is seldom indeed that I hear the—to me, as well as to Gilbert White—musical hoot of the owl of the woods.

The beautiful merlins, too, are comparatively little seen, and their place almost knoweth them no more. For they had a place since I have been here. There was a moorland point no great way from the so-called British village on Danby Low Moors where they bred regularly—at least, nested; for their eggs seldom escaped the gamekeeper or his watchers. Indeed, there were often two pairs on that part of the moors; and in days yet older they were not infrequently found haunting the high moors. And I have not seen a harrier or a buzzard these thirty years. Last year a sparrowhawk dashed into a spreading thorn-tree which shelters part of my lawn, sweeping very near me as he did so; and he took his sparrow from a chattering, squabbling group, who, if they had not been so loud and spiteful in their mutual recriminations, might not have attracted the hawk, or been so unluckily blind to his proximity. But the hawk of all others I miss the most is that bird of graceful flight, and almost gracefuller poising and balancing, the kestrel or windhover. The "little red

---

[1] The Park is the name of one of the two bits of old woodland till recently left in the parish ; but the wood in it now is no longer old wood. All the old trees have been cut down within the last twenty-five years, and the ground replanted with spruce, larch, and Scotch pine. The imposing-looking name is due to the circumstance that it was a part of the " park and warren " granted by the king to the old Brus barons. It was of great extent ; for, beginning at a point westward of the site of the Brus stronghold, it extended to below Lealholm Bridge, as is abundantly testified (if need were) by the many local names along its length still embodying the element " park," as Park-end, Park-nook, Park-house, Underpark, etc.

hawk," they used to call him here, as they called the merlin the "little blue hawk." But alas for the poor kestrel! Among the most useful and quite the least harmful of predaceous birds, the beings whose "eyes have not been opened" either by angels or otherwise, have given him a bad name, and plundered and shot him and his too nearly to the verge of extermination.

One of the watchers here told me one day, in the manner of one who had accomplished a feat, that he had been helping in a raid on the little red hawks in Crunkley Gill, that they had killed—little and big—seventeen, and that there were still another or two left, which they meant to have yet. I am afraid I made some uncomplimentary reply; at all events I put my friend William on his mettle. "Dee nae ho't amang t' gam', saidst 'ee?" he began; "Ah aims Ah kens better 'an that!" And then he thought to cover my face with confusion as well as shut me up; for he told me he had shot a kestrel going into its nest (containing young ones) with the hind quarters of a young moor-bird in its claws. Perhaps it was wrong of me to smile, and not to look confounded and abashed; but I did not, and I asked William if he had seen many birds, game birds or other, which had been struck down by hawks, and furnished the aggressors with a meal. "Ay, he had, a good few. They were gey and good to tell." So I thought, I said, when they were big enough not to be made one mouthful of, so to speak. "But what had that to do with the hover-hawk not doing any hurt among the game?" Well, I said, when you have found, say a partridge or a young moor-bird that has been killed and eaten by a hawk, which part has the hawk eaten? "Wheea, breeast and wings, for seear." Yes, said I, and how much, and what part was left? "Wheea, back and hind legs, in coorse." Exactly, I rejoined, and yet you make the poor hover-hawk just leave the breast behind him, and bring the back and hind legs to feed his young with. What a precious fool a hover-hawk must be!

I think William smelt a sarcasm, and felt a little conscious that " parson might not be altogether in the wrong," or the kestrel the only wiseacre. But I went on to ask him about the hover-hawk, and his balancing over a pasture-field, or a fallow, it might be, as free of herbage fit to cover a game-bird or even a lark, as his own fustian jacket; and by continuing the catechism I got him to admit that " mice and such small deer " must form a great part of the kestrel's ordinary captures. All the same the kestrels are ridded out of the country; and so are the weasels, as well as the owls. And what is the consequence, or one of the consequences?

An inordinate increase of field mice, long tails and short tails, and all sorts of tails together. It is a fact that my gardener killed down the mice in and about this garden last year to such an extent that he thought there was not another left anywhere near. It is a further fact that, our first snow falling on 27th November, the official just named saw that he must set his traps, and sunken pankins of water, and other mouse-catching enginery at work, and within the eighteen days which have passed since then he has caught thirty-five mice—mostly long tails—in the garden. And only yesterday our principal farmer said to me, " The mole-catcher keeps down the moudiewarps all right; but we shall have to have some-body to look after thae mice. They're getting to be over bad for owght with the holes they mak's in the fields, and the heaps of earth they brings out." And this was *apropos* to my complaint that they had got into the church—not a house near it anywhere—and had injured our valuable American organ to such an extent that it would cost several pounds to make the damage good. They have actually eaten some of the wooden stop-couplers quite through.

But to return to our birds. I have twice seen the great gray shrike; once a fine mandarin drake has appeared in the beck—an escaped bird from some aviary, of course. Once during a walk by the beck-side I saw a goosander—either a

hen or a young bird of the year; for it was in the so-called
"dundiver" plumage—and an interchange of attention passed
between us. It came up from a fishing-dive close to the bank
on which I was walking—so close to me that barely four feet
of space intervened between me and it. Luckily I saw it
before it saw me; and there might be a reason for that; for
it had something else to attract, and, indeed, occupy its
attention. I said it had come up from a fishing-dive, and it
had the prey it had captured all alive and kicking between its
serrated mandibles, and as the said prey—a nice little trout
of about six inches long—lay crosswise of the bill, the
wagglings and quiverings of the fish affected the bird in some
degree. But whether the fact that I saw the bird before the
bird saw me might thus be accounted for or not, the result
was that I had time to pull up short and stiffen myself as
rigidly as I could. And there we remained for, I should say,
a hundred seconds, the bird watching me and I watching the
bird. I knew it would dive like a flash if I moved a finger,
and I constrained myself to be still. At the end of the said
seconds the diving-duck brought his trout adroitly and
quickly round—too quickly for me to see how it was done—
so that its head was in the gape and the tail outside ready to
follow. And follow it did. In a moment where there had
been a trout there was a straight vacuum, and the next
instant the dundiver was in flight.

On similar walks I have seen a golden-eye, not in full
plumage; and a good specimen of the tufted duck; and my
eldest boy one day got an immature red-necked grebe. This
was a rare bird indeed; and Graham, the bird-stuffer at York,
told me it was but the fourth he had seen in forty years'
experience.

Once, and only once, I have seen a little grebe or dabchick
in our stream; but two or three times I have come upon the
water-rail. One I shot as it ran along the nearly dry bottom
of a deep ditch with sufficiently steep banks, thinking it

was a rat; for the movements of this bird, as well as of its congener the landrail, are of an even, non-undulating, gliding character, not what we usually understand by the word "running." See the awkward, grotesque action of the Cochin-China fowl, with its long ungainly legs, or of a full-grown turkey, and compare them with the rapid, even running of the partridge or grouse, and you have the very sublimity of absurdly awkward action and movement suggested and illustrated. But even the partridge, as compared with the rails, runs much as the old cow does as contrasted with the graceful tripping of the milkmaid the poet's eye is able to behold.

Another day I was sitting on the bank of the beck at a point where the current widens out into a good sheet, after having come rollicking down a series of sharp streams, and as if pausing to take breath before going a header over a sharper descent still, with a narrower course, and a bottom rockily uneven enough to insist upon a good deal of acrobatic motion on the part of the stream. As I sat, perfectly still, with a high bank opposite to me sloping up to the grass field above, and more or less overgrown with whins (many of which, however, had been burnt and stubbed not so long before), all at once a water-rail came in view, perfectly at home and entirely unconcerned, and gave me a glimpse of the ways and manners and tricks of the bird in its private life. It glided in and out among the coarse and somewhat sparse herbage, never pecking, as other birds do, on or about the ground, but evidently on the look-out for its own peculiar class of "grub," and finding it where such classes of food are to be found, viz. sticking to the stems of grasses or other coarse vegetation capable of supporting the weight of a small snail shell with its occupant inside. It flirted its tail now and then, when it made a rather longer glide or twist than usual, much after the fashion of the water-hen; and it was curious indeed to note how it steered itself among the intricacies and obstacles besetting its path. I was able to observe all its actions, gestures, movements, captures (as it appeared), for a space of ten to fifteen minutes, when something or other disturbed it, and in a moment it was gone.

Indeed, the ease and rapidity with which these birds—both the landrail and the water-rail—move amid the obstacles apparently presented by the thick growth of herbage, whether in a corn-field, or in a clover-field or meadow, is a matter I have seen adverted to in many different notices of the habits or peculiarities of the genus by divers writers on natural history topics. Yarrell, I think it is, who suggests that the bird is specially framed for such a purpose, having what he calls "a compressed form of body." It is perfectly true; and equally true that both birds trust, and with good reason, to the expedient of flight on foot in preference to that of flight on the wing. It is almost impossible to flush a rail a second time, even if the dog be put on the track almost immediately after the bird has reached the covert.

Another habit characteristic of both birds—which, however, I have only seen illustrated in the case of the water-rail, but find described at some length by Jesse, whose account is quoted at length by Mr. Yarrell—is that the bird, as school-boys express it, "shams dead" in the presence of inevitable danger. The account is amusing, and in brief is as follows. A gentleman's dog catches a landrail and brings it to his master, unhurt of course, as is the well-trained dog's way, but to all appearance perfectly dead. The dog lays the bird down at his master's feet, and he turns it over with his toe. It simply moves as it is moved, all its limbs limp. Continuing to regard it, however, the man sees an eye opened, and he takes it up. The "artful dodger" is quite dead again in a moment, head hanging and dangling, limbs loose, and no sign of life anywhere. It is put in its captor's pocket, and not liking the confinement, begins to struggle. When taken out it is just as lifeless as before; but being put down upon the ground and left undisturbed—the gentleman having stepped to one side, but continuing to watch—it lifts its head in a minute or two, and seeing all apparently serene, it starts up on a sudden and "cuts its lucky" with singular speed.

In the case of the water-rail which came under my own observation, it was picked up on a snowy day by the most intimate of the friends of my youth and early manhood. He assumed that it was dazed with cold and perhaps what we Yorkshire folks call "hungered" as well. So he brought it home with him, and laid it on a footstool in front of the dining-room fire. Five minutes passed, ten were gone, and still the lifeless bird lay as it was put down, dead to all seeming; only not stiff, as it ought to have been if dead of cold as well as hunger. A few minutes later my friend, who was very still, but yet with an eye to the bird, saw it—not lift its head, like the landrail, and take a view, but—start off in a moment with no previous intimation of its purpose, and begin to career about the room with incredible rapidity. It never attempted to fly. Any other captive bird in its position would have made for the window at once, and beaten itself half to pieces against the glass. Not so the rail. With it, in its helter-skelter and most erratic course, it was anywhere rather than the window or the fire. Round the room, across the room, under the sofa, under the table, from corner to corner and from side to side, steering itself perfectly notwithstanding legs of chairs, legs of tables, the sofa-feet, footstools, or what not, on and on it careered; and it was not without some patience and many attempts that it was eventually secured. Within an hour or two of its capture, moreover, it took quite kindly to some raw beef cut in thin long strips, and did not appear to find captivity too irksome. It was frequently let out for a run in after-days, and always started on the same random course, never once taking wing or making for the window. It was not very difficult to catch it at the close of one of these excursions after the first day or two, and it soon became tame enough to go and take food out of its master's hand.

It was but three or four years ago that a young pewit, which I had been told by its parents was somewhere very near me, and which, after two or three minutes spent in the search, I succeeded in detecting, and had taken up from its skulking-place, had the consummate " cheek " to try the same dodge upon me. It struggled hard for some seconds after its capture, and I had to be very careful to hold it securely, and yet so as not to injure it. Finding struggling did not pay, it tried the other plan and grew limp. I knew it was not hurt, and I did not believe it was all exhaustion. I opened my hand and let it lie on my palm. It lay quite still, and equally limp. I put it down on the ground, and except that I could see it heard its parents and quite understood what they meant—for there were little tremors or jerkings not due to the action of the heart when they came very close and gave us both (there was no doubt about that) a bit of their mind—there it remained quite quiescent. It was no use for it, poor pinionless birdie, with its as yet ramshackle, lanky apparatus of legs, to jump up and cut off—the slang is so expressive, and must be forgiven—like the full-grown, well-practised, fleet-of-foot water-rail ; so it was more cautious. It looked up, got up, tottered a step or two, but stopped in a second if I moved to recapture it. When the old birds saw it on the ground, they receded to a greater distance. If I took it up again they were at once "as before." I did not wish to prolong their anxiety, and after putting it down again I let it totter along in its half imbecile way for ten or a dozen yards. Something made me take my eye off it for a few seconds, and when I looked again it was lost. I think I spent ten minutes looking for it in the close vicinity of where I had seen it last; but I saw no more of it. It had skulked out of my sight altogether and effectually.

A young snipe was caught one day by two of my boys, who must needs bring it home to show it to me, a mile and a half away from the place of its capture. It was already two-thirds the weight of its mother or father, with a bill however

z

not longer than the pewit's, and with such a preposterous set of what it would have called legs, I suppose, if it could have spoken our vernacular; if not, shanks would have been the word. Those loose-jointed toys which are made to execute certain antics called dancing by the pulling of a string between their legs, would supply almost as good a pair of understandings as our young snipe's; and for proportion of body to legs see the pictorial representations of "Ally Sloper." The poor little bird was taken back to the place whence he came, and when set down on the ground again tottered feebly away.

When I looked into Yarrell's account of the rails just now, and noted his remarks on the subject of the imitation of the landrail's note, and the way in which it was effected, I was reminded of two or three other circumstances of the same kind. I have been able myself to produce a very good imitation of the method described by Yarrell, as also a very fairly success-ful one of the call of the partridge. At least it sounded very good to me and another who knew the call in question and its intonations as well as I did myself. But how it sounded in the ears of the partridge, distant by the space of a field or two, might be, and no doubt was, quite a different thing. All the same, I used to be well aware that such calls were made and were used not unsuccessfully. The materials were a glover's thimble, a piece of parchment or vellum, and a longish round and strong horsehair. I had no difficulty either in imi-tating the cry of the little grebe or dabchick.

But besides these empirical attempts on my own part, I have known one man or more who could call the hare by imi-tation of the note or cry used in the breeding season; and one man in particular, who had retired from the honourable and lucrative profession of poacher as it used to be carried on in this moorland district—which he did on becoming tenant of a cottage belonging to the lord of the manor, and with the fullest understanding, couched in no kid-glove terms, that if ever he was caught indulging in the old tricks, however little, out he would go, custom and term alike notwithstanding—he it was who told me that he had often shot from four or five to six or seven grouse at one standing, having called them thither by his own vocal imitation of their note or call. That his story was true I had no doubt. I once had a reclaimed poacher in my stated service, and my formal engagement—or his with me—was in these few and pithy words, "Now, John, if ever I know you either poach or drink, your engagement with me terminates thereby and therewith." John neither drank nor poached, and a capital man he proved himself. It was his cleverness and adaptability when working for me at some deep drains I was putting in, in very difficult ground, that first attracted my attention to him. I had known for long enough that it took no fool to make a good all-round poacher, and I wanted a man who was not a fool; for in taking the glebe lands (which I was draining) into my own hands, I was aware I was doing rather a venturesome thing. And so I engaged John. After a while we became very good friends; and John, besides doing his various work as groom, gardener, hind, increasingly well, was quite willing to be communicative as to what I may call "trade secrets." As to making a wire and setting it, and two or three other matters of the same kind, I was already a pretty fair proficient; but there were niceties about both I had never dreamed of. I did not know till he told me that even partridges could be wired, and how it was possible to get from three to half a dozen hares—of course where hares were numerous, as in the days when I have seen five at once in my own garden, discussing the flavour of my winter greens by moonlight—from one selected standing only. From him, too, I learnt other (and corroborative) matters touching the calling of grouse and other birds, either by the voice only, or by the voice assisted by art (as in some of the Canadian hunter's experiences), or by artificial means only.

One day, some twenty or twenty-five years ago, I had arranged with one of the principal yeomen here to go with

him to Glaisdale Swangs — a wet, morassy division of the
Danby and Glaisdale high moors—our object being to get, if
we could, a few couples of golden plover. I had for long practised the imitation of the cry uttered by the golden plover,
especially when they are on the ground ; and I flattered myself I could do it rather well—as, indeed, I think I could.
Our plan was to walk towards and over the likely haunts, and
get a shot or two before the birds became restless, as they do
when disturbed by intrusion into the haunts which are usually,
after the height of the grouse-shooting, but little interfered
with either by shepherd or dog. The moor thereabouts is too
wet to be so much affected by the moor-sheep as other parts
are. We got two or three shots in this way, and then we
separated to take our own private chances of a passing flight
or a few stray birds still about the ground, and either stalking
or calling any of whose comparative vicinity we might become
aware. I do not think either of us was remarkably successful
for a full hour after we had separated, and I was beginning to
think our bag would be light. Suddenly I heard the call of a
plover, and under what seemed to be the most favourable circumstances   The moor rose from where I was standing with
a gradual slope, but little broken for the third part of a mile or
more, and the call came from the upper part of the ridge, but
quite evidently from some little distance on the other side of
it. I replied to the call, and to my delight there was an almost
immediate answer. A minute or so elapsed, during which I
was cautiously approaching the point from over which the cry
seemed to come, and I called again. Another response, and
evidently the bird had been drawing nearer to me as I had
been drawing nearer to it. The same interchange of call and
reply continued at the intervals of a half-minute or so, and for
a sufficiently long space to allow me to have got to within
forty or fifty yards of the ridge. I was crouching as low as
possible all the latter part of the ascent, and I made sure that,
on rising from my stooping attitude and making a quick rush

to the ridge, I should have a shot within very easy distance. The call from the other side came just then, and my reply was the best spurt I could make with my gun at the ready. I had not covered two yards when I saw my companion's hat, and a second later his gun, at the ready also. He had been answering my calls as regularly as I addressed them to the supposed plover. I hardly need say that the only explosion which took place was a united one of rather shamefaced but very hearty laughter at our mutual discomfiture.

To pass to a different subject. Every lover, nay, every friend and acquaintance, of birds knows that there are difficulties, and very serious difficulties, in the way of identification of eggs, occurring from time to time. I have had eggs sent to me by young folks who happened to have fallen in with my book on *British Birds' Eggs and Nests*, asking me to identify such and such eggs which had puzzled them; and my correspondents have hailed from all points of the compass and all parts of the kingdom. In many instances, not having the nest to refer to, and no adequate description of it, all attempts at assurance were defeated. But I have met with instances in my own experience which were such that, unless all the circumstances were known, no satisfactory decision could have been arrived at by any one save the finder, and by him only if he were both accurate and observant. Thus, I took an egg one day from a nest I assumed to be a chaffinch's. I was quite certain as to the identity of the nest, and had no doubt that the bird I had seen leave the nest was actually a chaffinch. But the egg was of such a character that I went to the nest on two successive days on purpose to ascertain the absolute identity of the bird, and further, that my egg was not exceptional as compared with the other eggs in the laying, as well as co-ordinated with the average chaffinch's egg. "Pale purplish buff, sparingly streaked and spotted with dark reddish brown," is Mr. Yarrell's description; and Hewitson, giving the average egg—and a very good representation, moreover—adds, "They rarely differ much from the type given," although he has "taken some of a light blue, blotched with reddish colouring, and much like those of the bullfinch." But the eggs in my nest had no "pale purple," or, as I have elsewhere called it, "a vinous tinge," no "streaks or spots of dark reddish brown," only the buff, but more than pale, and just the slightest suspicion of a tinge as if it had been "shot" with a woof of correspondingly pale "vinous." Delicately beautiful they were; but, besides the general shape and make of them, there was nothing about them to remind one of the chaffinch. But the bird I saw on the nest, as well as leave it three several times, was just an ordinary, everyday chaffinch.

Another day, in my garden and within twenty-five yards of my study window, in some ivy growing thickly on the wall running along the road-side of the garden, I found a nest; and I never saw a nest with all the characters of the thrush's nest if that were not one. But the egg already laid in it was a blackbird's egg. Mistake or doubt about either the egg or the nest was impossible; nay, inadmissible. The next day another blackbird's egg was deposited in what was to all intents and purposes, according to unvarying experience, the nest of a thrush. Then I made it my business to see the mother bird, and saw it; and it was as veritable a blackbird as ever flew. The next day, however, the mystery—for mystery there was—began to be solved; for coincidently with the laying of the fourth egg the lining of the nest, after the fashion of the blackbird, had been commenced, and before the close of the following day had been completed. There was now as perfect a blackbird's nest as had ever been looked into by my well-accustomed eyes, and with five as typical blackbird's eggs in it as could be desired.

But what a grand opportunity for a paragraph on a wonderful instance in which a blackbird had been discovered laying in a song thrush's nest was lost by the habit—

uncomfortable to so many in such circumstances—of "looking before you leaped" to a conclusion in the matter.

Another day, not very far removed from the date of the incident just recorded, I was coming up from the beck with my fishing-rod in my hand, when I noticed a bird, which I never thought of doubting was a hen blackbird, fly out of a bush in the hedge overhanging the ditch I was walking beside. It being the time of year, I looked for a nest and saw it directly. There were two eggs in it, and they were not blackbird's eggs, but thrush's! I took them out and looked at them closely, scrutinisingly. There they were—blue eggs, and spotted, but with none of the streaking and spotting and speckling which are characteristic in the colouring of the blackbird's egg. Yarrell does say they are "occasionally found of a uniform blue, without any spots whatever"; but these were spotted, and the only difference between the spots on them and those on the average thrush's egg was that the spots were quite as decided about the smaller end as, with the latter, about the larger end. Of course I watched that nest, and saw the whole complement of eggs laid, and the hen bird well on with her task of sitting, before I discontinued my visits of observation. I may add, however, that they were duly hatched, and produced blackbirds.

Thirty or forty years ago I could see three or four pairs of the dipper any day I walked by the beck-side, or rambled up the course of one of our brattling moor streams on their downward run to help the volume of what we call, by way of distinction, "the big beck." But now, where I used to see six or eight or perhaps ten pairs, I barely see one. I wish I had a fairy godmother, and that fairy godmothers were as potent as in Cinderella times! The favour I would try my most ingratiating ways to obtain should be—nothing truculent or bloodthirsty, although I do not love the reckless shooters of rock-birds, rare birds, swallows for practice, pigeons at blackguard pot-shop matches, *et hoc genus omne*—

but that every gun-carrying lout who wantonly shot a poor harmless bird of any kind whatever without a cause, should be sentenced—not to judicial or other blindness, but—to inability to hit his mark again for ever and a day. What earthly good or satisfaction there can be in shooting a dipper I cannot conceive; and yet they have been thinned in the way I have mentioned. In the loneliest walk they are always companions, and always cheerful besides. To see him come out of the water as if on purpose to say, "Good morning to you! Isn't it a nice cheery morning? Oh, it's so jolly," and then to hear him sing his cheery little song, standing on a stone just awash in the bed of the stream; and then to see him, with something very like a nod and a wink with his bright eye, just trip into the water and go tumbling and toddling along the bottom for half a score yards—why, it is as good as killing a couple of snipe, right and left, to an embryo sportsman.

I have come across their nests now and again in the district around. One of the small tributary becks running down this dale proceeds by way of Ainthorpe, passing through a spacious garden by aid of a capacious culvert; then comes into the open air again in a wild little griff; then is culverted over again; and when it emerges it is just bursting into the road to the Station, but after a leap of a yard or so, is caught in the open mouth of another culvert, down which it slips abashed right underneath the roadway. Just within the rude arch of this culvert a pair of dippers bred for some years. But one unlucky day some of the boys from the school, intent on getting their feet wet, or some like piece of schoolboy self-indulgence, found it; and the haunt once known, there was no future peace for the poor dippers. Another nest I knew was in a hole in one of the piers of a bridge guiltless of arches, lying on the road from Danby End to Castleton. A couple of young fellows then living in my house were fishing one day close to this bridge, when a very heavy thunder shower

came on; and for shelter, their feet and legs being already
wet with wading, they resorted to the landward arch-space
(as it should have been), and so were in a position to see the
ingress of a dark bird which flew straight to a put-log hole;
just above their reach as they stood, but which they managed
to explore nevertheless; finding therein a dipper's nest, and
in it well on to half a dozen white eggs. Another I knew of
just under the slightly overhanging brae of a ditch or drain
which served to convey a stream of water on its way to the
larger stream just below. Also among some old masonry that
had once served as a pier to an old forgotten bridge, and
so on.

But I am warned by the number at the head of the page
that I shall do well to bring these bird reminiscences to an
end. Yet, at the risk of being a little prolix, I should like to
add a few lines more, and on a matter that has from time to
time interested me greatly. I was coming through the upper
part of our Crag Wood one evening several years ago, after a
day's shooting in Fryup, when, seeing a wild pigeon flying
over my head and rather high up, I fired, in the belief that it
was within range. It fell to the shot, evidently killed on the
instant. Falling from a considerable height, which was added
to by the fact that it fell some little way below me on the
very steep hill-side I was standing on, it dropped with great
velocity, and the force with which it struck the ground—for
the wood-pigeon is a weighty bird—was very considerable. I
have written "struck the ground"; but in reality it struck
a bare rock-fragment, and to my surprise I saw a sort of
springing jet of brilliant scarlet objects sparkling upwards
from the place of its fall. It lasted but a moment, of course;
but it was striking enough for that moment. On going to
pick the bird up, I found more than half a pint of holly-berries
strewed all round it. The fact was, it had been getting its
evening meal from among the many and large holly-trees
which abound in the wood in question, and having filled its

crop to repletion—you may see these birds' crops actually protrude from fulness as they fly past or over you on their way to their night's roosting-place—naturally it burst when the bird fell with such force against the hard rock.

Another evening, on a similar occasion, I was passing through the higher part of a considerable plantation of larches growing on the upper part of the slope of one of our steep moor-banks, and a small flight of wild pigeons happening to cross within easy shot, I fired both barrels, getting a bird with each shot. On picking them up I was a little interested, as well as surprised, at finding my first bird was a wood-pigeon or ring-dove, and my second a stock-dove. But the difference of species was not all. They were flying in to roost in company, but the places in which they had been feeding were as different as the constituents of their repast. The ring-dove's crop protruded (as noticed in the last paragraph), and was quite turgid. It felt like a thick bag of marbles tightly tied, for the hard objects contained were separable as well as hard. The stock-dove's crop, on the other hand, was quite flaccid, and apparently not more than half full, and its contents moved when manipulated with a sort of liquid motion, just as small shot loosely held in a bag might. On opening the two birds, so as to ascertain what the contents of the craw of each might be, I found a large double handful of acorns in the one, and about two tablespoonfuls of "runch" seed (that being our name for that pestilent weed on carelessly farmed holdings, the field-mustard or charlock) in the other. I knew very well where the runch seed had come from, for I had seen the gamekeeper fire the two barrels of his gun only a week or two before into a great flock, principally consisting of greenfinches, and pick up some thirty-five of the slain—to be used for ferret-meat, as he said. And as I helped him pick up the victims I saw the seed lying on the ground in such quantities that it might have been taken up in spoonfuls. That was on the farm of our witch-fending

friend previously named. But I never heard that he
"faulted" the witches for the luxuriant growth of the runch.

The interest, or even surprise, I felt at noting the two
varieties of wild pigeon I had shot in the way mentioned
originated thus. The old gamekeeper—or rather the gamekeeper of those old days—had (as I daresay has already been
remarked) some sort of interest in the birds of the district.
In fact, when he died he left quite a nice little collection of
birds a little out of the common way, which he had shot and
had stuffed. He was not slow in finding out my interest also,
and that I was not altogether an ignoramus in the matter of
ornithology. Perhaps I had been here a year or thereabouts,
when he came into the house I was then living in, bringing
with him a bird which he had newly shot, and as to which he
was in utter perplexity and doubt. He knew it was "a doo,"
and that was all. Could I tell what it was? "He had nivver
seen owght lahk't afore." On taking it from him I saw at
once he had got a stock-dove. The interest to me was, and is,
that in and about the year 1846-47 the stock-dove was rather a
"rare bird" in Danby. My good old friend Robert never
willingly shot another, as he wished they might increase and
multiply about the manor. And so they have ; and I know
that as many as half a dozen or half a score pairs now breed
annually. And, to mention only one fact more, I have this
year twice found one of the pair which has nested for many,
many years past in Little Fryup Head, feeding among the
moor blackbirds on the bilberry beds growing on the moor
brae overlooking Little Fryup Dale.

One other bird Robert tried hard—and under the strict
orders of his master, moreover—to "preserve," if possible ;
and that was the black grouse. There was a brood of nine on
the low moor in the year 1846, including the two old birds.
But although no one was killed on this moor, and single ones
were seen on the adjacent moors, yet after a year or two no
more was seen or heard of them.

WINTER IN A MOORLAND PARISH

YES, I have seen some winter weather in this out-of-the-way place. I have seen the snow gathered in drifts of fifteen, eighteen, twenty feet in thickness; I have seen it gathering, piling itself up in fantastic wreaths, sometimes busy only in accumulating substance and solidity, like a yeoman of the elder days, and gathering at the rate of six feet or seven feet in thickness in from twelve hours to twenty-four. And once I saw it gathering—and gathering a foot deep in the hour, moreover—before ever a flake of new snow had fallen, and when the old snow was caked over with a crisp crust, the result of diurnal or sun-thaws and nocturnal freezings again. And the manner of it was on this wise.

It had been a fine day till past twelve o'clock, and it seemed good for walking. There was a young farmer in the parish, at the very eastern boundary of it, distant four miles and a half of good walking the way I had to take, whom I wanted to see. Besides being the son of one of the oldest and stanchest friends I had in the parish—the old gamekeeper, in point of fact—he was in great trouble. He had been engaged to a young woman, also belonging to the parish, for a number of years; the banns had been asked out, and the wedding-day was fixed. On that very day I had to bury her. She had been seized with illness while ordering some of the wedding gear, and died in two or three hours. And I wanted to go and see him, and talk to him a little. My walk to his place was accomplished without difficulty; pleasantly indeed, as far as roads and weather were concerned. But I had noticed before I had reached my limit in that direction that the day, and the weather most likely, were going to change; and so I was not surprised on setting my face southwards, instead of westwards and homewards, to find that the wind was rising, and rising sharply, not to say fiercely. But I wanted to see another parishioner, the widow of another old and stanch parochial friend, who had been ailing lately, and so I persevered with the extension of my walk. This led me into Fryup Head, the house I sought being well on to three miles from the house I left. It was still perfectly fair overhead, the sun shining brightly at times; and the snow—no great thickness of it anywhere; perhaps two to three inches where it was thickest—was crusted over, as I said. But the wind grew colder and colder as it increased momentarily in force; and long before I got to my widowed parishioner's house the crusted snow had begun to be broken up by the force of the wind, and to drive along in most incisive fragments. There were already, when I got to within a field or two of the house, drifts formed in parts of the road approaching it such that the wheels of a recently-passing vehicle had cut through some of them to the depth of eighteen inches. Almost my first remark on entering the house was to the daughter, of whom I asked if the wheel-tracks I had noted were made by any trap driven by a member of the family, hoping that, if so, he would not be long away, or else he "would be matched to get home again; for it was safe there was going to be a 'hap.'" I did not prolong my visit, for things were looking badly for my walk home—a more than four miles' walk the nearest way I could go, and that way from corner to corner of fields, over the loose stone-walls; and real rough walking.

It was quite time I was afoot. Some idea may be formed of the fury of the wind from the fact that, as I paused at the corner of the second field, up which the drift of the

snow - crust had pursued me with cutting sharpness — the
pause being due to the strong necessity of making my way
safely over a broken wall with a deep drop on the other side
—the sharp-edged particles driven with the full force of the
wind against the nape of my neck and the more exposed ear
and cheek, inflicted such acute pain that it required some
nerve to bear it and keep busy with getting over the nasty,
dangerous place.   Once over, the worst was also over.   There
were still two more walls to surmount, but then downhill,
across a sloping field, and into the road again.   My way lay,
for the most part, for a mile under the lee of a five-foot wall,
and I got along well.   But when I came to the gateways
through the wall there were snow-banks across the road and
a thick stifling drift of sharp snow-powder to work through,
as well as the loose snow about my feet and legs.   I met one
of our farmers on horseback, who could scarcely speak so as
to be heard for the blast and the powdery snow.   But I
managed to hear part of his greeting as we met and passed.
"It's a savage day, mister," was all I heard, and I echoed his
sentiment.   On reaching the castle the direction of my march
altered, and I had the wind behind me.   But there was a difficulty at the first gate across the road I came to.   There was
a drift just through it, nearly four feet thick, and it reached
several yards along the road.   And I have known things
easier of doing than plunging through three or four feet of
utterly loose snow.

All this time not a flake of fresh or soft snow had fallen.
It was perfectly fair overhead, though thickening up from
half-hour to half-hour with a prophetic intimation of what
was yet to come.   And come it did, though not for two or
three hours after I reached home, and had at last got the
snow out of my hair and beard.

All that night it snowed, and the next day.   I wanted
to go to the station and the post on the first of the two days,
and the roads were known to be so full, and the drift was so

very bad, that my people would not let me go alone; so my gardener and eldest lad at home—the latter for the fun of it —went with me. Within a quarter of a mile of the parsonage I found snow in the road over seven feet thick in one place; and, for scores of yards together, my track lay along a snow-covered fence—above it, not by the side of it. The next day the seven feet of snow in the road had become fourteen, and there was not a place in the entire road for the distance of six or seven hundred yards where the snow lay less deep than five feet, and in places it was from eight to ten. To get along at all, we broke the fences and plunged along the fields parallel with the line of road.

These accumulations in the roads, however, are all in the way of business, and we are used to them. But the pranks played by the snow at times would be amusing, even interesting, if they were not so baffling and tiresome. A great wind, with snow dry enough to drift, either already on the ground or still falling, or, as likely as not, both together, catches hold of the snow as it sweeps over these lofty moorland ridges and drives it irresistibly before it until it loses its grip; and that is when the force of gravity becomes greater than the force of propulsion; and this happens on the lee side of a wall, and *a fortiori*, on the lee side of one of these mountainous moorland ridges. But the snow has this curious circumstance attending it, that it does not fall perpendicularly on reaching the sheltered part; on the contrary, it seems to become slightly cohesive, and begins to form a projecting ledge from the edge of the sheltering object. I have watched the process on the sheltered side of a seven-foot wall, the top of which was almost level with the face of the land on the other side of it. First the level was attained by the lodgment of snow above the wall. Then the ledge began to form, slightly curvilinear in section; the ledge itself being, so to speak, undercut like a volute in sculpture. Below, on the sheltered side, there is always a sort of gentle undercurrent of air, the action of which

is to keep the foot of the wall—if it be a wall we are watching
—free from any accumulation of snow for a foot or two away
from it, according to height; but also to blow the falling
particles upwards against the under side of the growing ledge,
which is thus thickened both from above and below, as well
as helped to grow in the direction of its projection.   One
Sunday morning as I was going to my service at Fryup I
noted all this going on at one particular place, almost devised
on purpose to permit observation of the process, and I took my
notes with some nicety.   I returned the same way something
under two hours later, and found that the ledge had advanced
about six inches, and grown in proportional thickness as well ;
as, perhaps, goes without saying.

   This was on the road-side of a stone wall nearly seven
feet high.   As I stood face to face with it and watched it, on
my left, sloping upwards from my very feet, for upwards of
one hundred and twenty yards of actual altitude—and the
last twenty yards very steeply—was the flank of one of our
moory ridges, and I have once and again seen the ledge
of snow I have been trying to describe project from the edge
or brae of the ridge from sixteen or twenty feet to sixteen
or twenty yards.   Once, in going to my afternoon service
on foot—I could not have gone half a mile either on wheels
or horseback, as the roads were all full—on reaching the brae
at the point where my ordinary track begins to descend, I
found a snow precipice of sixteen feet deep, apparently cutting off all further progress.   But there was a projecting
ledge of snow about a foot in width some ten feet below the
upper edge, and I thought I could let myself drop or slide
down to that, and bring myself up there.   The plan was
successful.   But on considering my landmarks on reaching
the foot of this wall of snow, I found the edge I had dropped
from was at least eighteen to twenty yards in advance of the
edge of the brae.

   There were thirteen of my Fryup parishioners gathered for

the service at the foot of the slope, watching my proceedings.
The greater part of these inclined to think I would not
attempt the descent. Those who had known me longest
said, "T' priest wadn't be bett." And the event justified
their confidence. But the service over, there arose the
question of how I was to get back again; and when I said,
"The same way as I came," one oldish man besought me not
to attempt it; "it was over parlous for owght." Nay, he
was so urgent that he actually shed tears over my foolhardi-
ness, as he considered it. However I was not to be dissuaded, and though it was a "parlous" thing in a way, it was
safely accomplished. One of my boys, a lad of about sixteen,
was with me, and one of us had a strong stick and the other
an equally strong umbrella. These I stuck firmly into the
snow wall, the one a foot higher than the other, and then
working holes in with my feet until I succeeded in getting
foothold, I was able to move one of my two handholds
a foot higher, and to get a higher foothold; and so on alter-
nately, until at last, after great labour and much delay, I succeeded in reaching the top. But had it not been for the sort
of channel worked into the snow by our downward slide I
do not think it could have been done.

But the most laborious, and perhaps the most venturesome,
snow walk I ever had was from Easington to Danby. I had
exchanged duties with my oldest clerical friend and neighbour,
George Morehead, Rector of Easington, with the understanding that, while he returned to Easington, the three duties
done, I, after my three at Easington and Liverton, should
stay all night at the rectory, and have my trap sent over for
me in the morning. There had been a slight shower of snow
while the Liverton service was going on, but hardly enough
to do more than whiten the ground; and when I had finished
the evening duty at Easington, it was a beautiful starlight
night, and no one had thought of, much less expected, a fall of
snow. But on looking out at eight in the morning, to my

2 A

intense surprise, there was a dense covering of white over all. It soon became apparent from the reports brought in that the passage of wheels along the level would be intensely difficult, and over such hills and moor-roads as lay between Easington and Danby simply impossible. I was most anxious to get home for different reasons; and, resisting the more than urgent entreaties of my dear old friend and his wife, I determined to set forth on foot. For the first three to four miles the walking, though very fatiguing—for there was not an inch of the way with less than a foot deep of the yielding snow, which permitted no firm foothold among it—was practicable enough. As I passed Sir Charles (then Mr.) Palmer's lodge-gates at Grinkle I ascertained that, there being somewhat urgent need to send a carriage to Danby Station, the road had been explored to see if by dint of sending on the snow-plough a passage could be effected; but the attempt had been given up as hopeless. However, I determined to persevere, and reached the purely moor part of the trudge at Waupley. Here the difficulties began in good earnest. Though there had been no drifting in the sheltered road, yet on reaching the open moor it proved to be very different; for every few yards drifts of from two to four feet deep intervened, and continued to intervene. However, I struggled on until I reached the highest level I had to cross over, and it was a dreary scene before me indeed!

I had already been a little impressed with the utter isolation of my walk. All life, even bird life, seemed to have disappeared. I knew the moors had hundreds of grouse on them. I never saw one nor heard one. I had seen two blackbirds when making my way along a part of the road which was also for two or three score yards the course of a small stream; and, strange to say, I had seen a goldfinch—the only one I have ever seen in this district—just after reaching the moor at Waupley. Besides these "feathered fowl" I saw only two or three moor pipits, usually numerous enough on the

moors at all times of the year. I hardly wondered at this
scarcity of bird life, for it was a cruel day. The intensity of
the cold may be estimated by this—that as I walked and
labouringly perspired (I was in fact so wet that I literally had
not a "dry thread" about me)—the perspiration settled and
froze on my eyebrows and hair, and freezing into little balls
tinkled against the steel of my spectacles more musically than
pleasantly; and naturally the birds and all other creatures
dwelling on or about the moors would be seeking such shelter
as could be found or made available. I did not even see or
hear a single moor sheep.

On reaching a given point on the level aforesaid, where
a cross-track deflected from the course of the high road
in such a way as to cut off an angle and save a distance of
nearly half a mile, feeling the temptation to try and save so
much of the trying fag I was experiencing, I attempted to take
the said short cut. The snow looked level enough, but I had
not allowed for the unevennesses and hollows of the moor
concealed beneath the fair-seeming surface, and before I had
waded five-and-twenty yards from the line of the road I found
myself struggling to get out of a dish-like hollow in which the
snow was deep enough to reach above my waist, and deepening every foot I advanced. Clearly the "short cut" would
be no saving, and I struggled back as well as I could to regain
the line of the road. I had almost begun to despair of getting
through with my walk, when I saw a moving object coming
over the top of the ridge next to that on which my path lay;
and I presently saw that it was a cart with two horses in it,
and two men in attendance on them. This gave me renewed
hope, not to say confidence, for they were coming the very
way I had to go, and of course they must have tracked the
road for me. At the rate of our relative progress it took a
long time to cross the intervening space, but at last we met.
They were Liverton men who had been under the extremest
necessity for want of fuel, and they had been literally forced

to make the effort to get to Danby Station for a load of coal. The snow was now drifting freely, and the travelling was momentarily becoming worse ; but even when they had started they had provided against the emergencies they foresaw by putting two horses to their cart, doubling also the ordinary force of men—two instead of one only—and providing themselves with shovels to clear their way if necessary, or dig their "draught" out, if need arose. All the load they had ventured to lay on with all their appliances had been six hundredweight, and only yesterday (4th December 1889) I met a man who had travelled the same road with a load of coal in a waggon drawn by three horses, who had then, as he told me, well on to two tons weight, easily drawn by his team. And the two men I met that day had to walk, partly because their horses were barely able to drag the cart with its light load without their weight added, and partly because the foremost had to guide the leader over the trackless white waste (with only a bit of ling growing on the braes on either side of the moor road to show here and there where it actually was), as well as help it in its plunging efforts to get through the deeper places ; and the other with the shaft horse to keep it steady to its work. They both of them knew me, and were simply astounded to see me there on foot alone, and under such circumstances and surroundings.

For the first half-mile after meeting them I found the track they had made of the greatest service to me ; although every step I took was through snow that reached above my knees ; and, even before I reached the top of the ridge on which I had first caught sight of them, the said track was being rapidly obscured by the drifting in upon it of fresh snow. On the other side of the ridge the track was gone in places ; but it was practically downhill now, the most part of the way, and my worst difficulties things of the past ; and I reached home safe, wretchedly wet, and more exhausted than I knew, or had allowed for.

The snow came on again before long, and before the week was out enough had fallen to make an even covering all over the face of the country of about twenty-seven inches thick. The Sunday following was without any further fall, and it was possible to get to my more distant chapel; but the man who drove me, and who had driven me, as he expressed it, thousands of miles—he was the Daniel of my houe-digging experiences —declared (and still declares) he had never had such a journey before. It was indeed, from the difficulties of the roadway alone, an awful drive. I think the fatigue in another way was as bad as that of the plunging, struggling tramp from Easington to Danby. And the next day I was in bed, very seriously ill. My medical attendant shook his head over me, and said he must see me again the next day—he had ten miles to ride to get here—and when he came shook his head more gravely still. "He would come again as early the following day as he could!" But he did not come. Another fall of snow made the journey from Guisborough here impracticable alike by road and by rail; and for six days I lay hovering between life and death, and the doctor not able to get near me!

That is one of my reminiscences of a moorland parish in the winter-time. I think it was the worst winter I have known here. The cross-road which runs east and west past the school, about a quarter of a mile north of the parsonage, was so full up with hardened, beaten-down snow, that one of my sons as he walked along it was able to pluck twigs off the road-side trees, which were high enough to admit of the passage beneath them of the mighty loads of corn or hay as they are piled up in order to be taken out of the fields into the stack-garth.

The earliest reminiscence I have of what the snows of winter might be in north-east Yorkshire refers to the winter preceding the May which saw my arrival here as a resident. I was living at Scarborough at the time, and saw the snow five to six feet deep in St. Nicholas Street, before that from the house-tops began to be thrown down into the streets. At this time I was taking one duty per Sunday at Hackness Church, riding the intermediate distance of five or six miles. The first Sunday after the fall of snow specified, the journey was utterly impossible. On the Sunday after, having ascertained that "the roads had been cut," I took my journey as usual, and on coming to Suffield Heights I found a somewhat narrow gangway cut, but wide enough to let a mounted man pass. In the deepest part of the cutting the depth of the snow-wall on either side, allowing for the addition made by what had been thrown up by the digging, was such that as I rode through with a tall hat on, the top of my hat and the tops of the snow-banks were as nearly as possible on a level.

Probably it will be anticipated by those who have read the preceding pages that on our wide, wild, shelterless moors here, even the Suffield Heights accumulation might be, or would be, outdone. And indeed it was. A little below the top of Gerrick Bank, on the highroad from Whitby to Guisborough, and on the side nearer to the last-named place, the snow was deep enough and compact enough to admit of being tunnelled through, so as to admit of the passage of the coach working between the two places; and the tunnel stood for more than a week.

On our Danby moors, at a place about two miles distant from the point named as Gerrick Bank-top, there is a narrow gully or rift, with steeply sloping sides, ling-covered, ascending to a height of about a hundred feet perpendicularly above the level of the trickling moor-stream running through the gully below. This was filled from bottom to top, so that there was an even slope from the slightly higher brae on the west to the lower one on the other side. And the old gamekeeper, who was the first to tell me of the incident, added that a very dry spring and early summer succeeded, and the moors became so dry that the moor-birds had to travel considerable distances to get to water, and that he had seen them come in scores to drink of the water which trickled from the melting snow as late as Midsummer day.

But the most extraordinary feat I have ever known as achieved in the way of the making of snowdrifts by our moorland blasts, took place during the winter of 1886-87, and the account of it was given me by the "gaffer" of the small band of road-minders and menders employed by the township. The wind had blown from the north and east when the snow began to be drivable, and he had had some difficulty in keeping the door of his own dwelling, a house on the very edge of the moor, three-quarters of a mile from the site of my own, clear, and one night he had taken the precaution to carry his shovel indoors, with the almost certainty that he would have to dig his way out in the morning; inasmuch as the passage he had cut and kept clear from day to day was filling fast at the darkening, and there was every appearance of a terrible night of snow and drifting. Armed with his well-brightened tool— for he had been snow-cutting for days whenever there seemed a chance of doing it to any effect—he opened his door in the early light, and strange, incredible as it seemed, there was no big wreath of snow there—no wreath at all worth thinking of. But at the other end of the house there was a gigantic accumulation piled up, and reaching almost to the gable point of the roof. The wind had shifted during the night and had transported the results of its action during the previous days from the one end to the other! And exactly the same thing had happened at the farmhouse some 200 yards more to the north, and similarly situated. My friend, the road-surveyor, was not the only one among us who went to bed with a shovel —not exactly under his pillow, but—laid quite handy for use the first thing in the morning; and who had to use it too. At the public-house on the hill opposite my house, and about half a mile distant, the oldish man who lived there and, in a sort, served the landlady, told me his first work in the morning for more than a week, after making on the fire and so forth, was to dig a way out, and both in front of the house and in its rear; and that "mostlings it teuk a lot o' deeing."

Late in the winter of the year before last there were five Sundays in succession during which access to the parish church was like matrimony—not to be "lightly enterprised or taken in hand." The first of these Sundays I had with some difficulty made my advance about half-way to the church when I met the parish-clerk, who had come forward to tell me there was but one lad at the church, and he thought it a chance if any one else either would or could come. It was a wild day indeed, the snow stouring in blinding clouds; and I thought Peter might be right, and so I turned back, meeting the wind now. It seems absurd to say so, but it was all I could do to keep myself straight with the aid of the low hedges on either side. But for the hedges I was only too well aware I must have gone hopelessly wrong in the third of a mile between the place where Peter met me and my home.

As it happened, two men turned up at the church after Peter met me. On the next Sunday the same two men and the boy were there to meet me. On the third Sunday the same trio and a young woman. One of the men had chivalrously essayed to carry the girl over the worst of the snowdrifts, and the treacherous crust had given way beneath the united weights, and a comforting and edifying roll in the snow had been the result. I saw the parties "laughing consumedly" as they came round the corner of the chancel, and I am afraid I laughed myself when I was told, in answer to my query, what had taken place. The fourth and fifth Sundays saw my two male friends already named, the boy, and two other men, present at the service. But all this time I could not get to my distant church in Fryup.

It seems absurd, as I said just now, to talk of being so easily lost, and within so limited a distance. It seemed infinitely so indeed to me until I had made personal and ludicrous acquaintance with it as a fact. Many years ago now, I had been at church on one of these bitterly stormy days which occur from time to time; and I had already been told of a funeral fixed for just after the service. The congregation had barely numbered half a dozen persons all told; and the snow and sleet were driving about on the wings of a fierce wind, so as to make even breathing difficult when one was forced to face it. One of my sons had gone to church with me, a stalwart lad of seventeen or eighteen, and on the conclusion of the service, seeing no signs of the funeral near, he decided not to wait for me but to go home at once. I waited half an hour, and still no signs of the approach of the procession. Another quarter of an hour, and the storm still growing worse every minute. Once and again both I and the clerk had gone out to see, as well as we could, if there was any sign, but without result. At last I began to think something must have interfered with the arrangements, and that we were waiting to no purpose, and I went out to look, for what was to be the last time. It was almost impossible to look out steadily in the direction the funeral was to come, by reason of the stouring snow which blew directly into one's face and eyes; but still I had satisfied myself that there was nothing in sight; and I had but just decided with the clerk that it was unnecessary to wait any longer. While I was still speaking the chancel (or priest's) door was opened and the figures of two or three men appeared. But they were men in white garments, men of snow in reality. I never saw such figures before. All of them, as usual at a funeral, in black clothes, and yet nothing that was not white with snow about them. They must have been within a hundred yards or so of the churchyard when I had gone for my last look, and yet, from their whitened covering, and the difficulty of looking steadfastly forth against such a storm, I had not been able to descry them. And their story was that they had left Castleton in good time, with the little girl's coffin in the hearse; that the difficulty of getting along the road had been considerable almost from the outset; that after the first half-mile it increased with every step, and at last when they had made their way to within three fields of the church, further progress had become impossible for horse or hearse, and they had taken the coffin out to bear it by hand. Then six able-bodied men had taken it—the body was that of a girl under thirteen years of age— and had left the road, and began to struggle across the fields. Before they had made much progress they were of necessity relieved, and other six strong men took up the burden; and alternating in this way, they had at length, and with extreme difficulty and the greatest exertion, achieved the passage of the three fields, or the total distance of less than half a mile.

The service at the grave was a continued physically pain- ful experience. I was compelled to stand with my back to the blast, or it would have been alike impossible to see or to read in such a fierce, savage stour; and the sharp, hard sleet and roughened snow were driven against the unprotected parts of my neck and face with such vehemence and impinged with such force upon the parts already aching with the bitter cold, that no flogging I ever got was in the least to be compared with the smarting experience of those ten minutes.

But at last all was duly done and I started on my home- ward way, having the stormy wind and drift directly in my teeth. I could not see ten yards ahead of me distinctly, but it was only a small field of half a dozen acres I had to cross diagonally, to get into the road. But before I had got half the distance, as I reckoned, I saw the boughs of a tree on my left hand which I recognised as growing in the left-hand fence of the field, whereas my road lay along the right-hand fence; and at the same moment a voice hailed me with the words, "You've getten wrang, Mr. Atki'son." I laughed over my error and tried again, making for the corner of the field at the end of the right-hand fence. But instead of reaching it, I was brought up by the fence running transversely from that on the left to that on the right—which I followed to the place where I would be. I had thus gone astray twice within an area of less than 300 yards square.

Smiling with myself at the absurdity of the misadventure, still I was preparing myself for the laughter which, I was sure, would greet the recital of my erring and straying when I got home. Somewhat to my surprise, no one laughed; my wife even looked grave. But the explanation soon came. My strong, stout son, unbothered with spectacles as I was—and they *are* a bother in a thick mist or a roke; and worse still, in heavily driving snow—he too had gone astray on his walk home; and even worse than I had, and from the same cause. The snow lay very deep upon the road which runs along the hedge of the fifth field from the church, and he had gone a little way off the road on to the land, with the purpose of finding easier walking, and the intention of walking parallel with the said road; which indeed he had no idea he was not doing until he found himself face to face with the angle formed by the meeting of two fences. The truth was he had insensibly, under the influence of the pitiless storm and drift, borne to the left as I had done in the much smaller field by the church; and it had not been without difficulty, owing to the impediments offered by the accumulated drifts, and the manner or disposition of them, that he had succeeded in recovering his right road. After this, I never needed any explanation how easy it was for storm-caught travellers over unenclosed spaces to lose themselves, and with the issue of having to be found by others. One poor fellow lost his way thus some eight or ten years ago, and lay fifty-nine days under the snow before his body was found. And the actual place at which it was found proved that he had been so baffled and dazed as to be unaware that he was going in exactly the opposite direction to that which would have led him home.

Such are some of the amenities of a moorland parish in the winter-time.

MOORLAND SCENERY IN WINTER

IT would be easy enough to multiply experiences as to the difficulty, and at times the absolute impracticability, of any locomotion, either by parson or people, in respect of going to or from church, during what are in the vernacular called " ho'ding storms." I will but give an illustration or two, and then pass on to another topic. This house is, I suppose, some 1600 yards distant from the church—not quite a mile, but approaching to it. Two winters ago, and as late as the month of March, the drifting of the snow, under the violence of a wind blowing more from the east than from the north, had been so great that, of the said distance of nearly a mile, there were about fifty yards just near my garden, and fifty yards about half-way between this house and the church, not so snow-blocked as to forbid me to walk along the road. All the rest—say 1500 yards and more—was covered with snow to the depth of three or four feet and upwards—in most parts, six feet—and for the whole width of one field from eight up to twelve feet. Fifty yards away from my garden gate I had to break through the fence on my right hand, and make my way parallel with the road along the strips of the fields which had been swept more or less bare by the wind. To accomplish this I had to make my way through two fences running at right angles to the direction of the road, then over two loose stone walls, then through (or over) another quickset hedge, the line of which I could barely distinguish for the snow piled on and over it; and so into the field adjoining the churchyard. For three weeks there was no traffic along the road. The farmers "up the dale," who were forced to obtain access (on account of their live stock) to Danby End, the mill there, and so forth, made a track for themselves along the land in the fields alongside the road, making gaps in the stone walls named above, and some sort of a difficult passage into and along the lane past my house. All this traffic was done on horseback. Sacks of grain to be ground, sacks of meal to be carried home, were all conveyed on horseback.

Another time, I remember, more than twenty years ago, I had myself made my way to the church by dint of breaking the fences and eschewing the roadway, and when I got to the church I had not the "legal congregation." I waited till ten minutes past church-time, and seeing no prospect of any addition to "Dearly Beloved" the parish-clerk and another official, I set off homewards. Half-way between the church and the parsonage I saw some one leaning against the stone wall by the side of one part of the lane or road. Coming nearer, I saw it was the schoolmaster, a tall, strong, stout man in the prime of his age and strength. I stopped to speak to him, and added it would be no use his going on ; there was no congregation, and I was on my way home. Mr. G——, in a voice that was not cheerful, said it made but little difference ; he was spent, and could neither go forward nor get back home again. And indeed he did look exhausted—as well he might. For he had toiled through and through the deep snow cumbering the road for more than half a mile. I had tried it, and after the experience of the first hundred yards, had given it up as hopeless, and had broken the fence as above described. This expedient had not occurred to Mr. G——, and indeed it was the first time I had adopted it so fully myself ; but when I mentioned it to him, he cheered up greatly, and readily followed my lead in clambering over the wall I had found him leaning against, and after a struggle with the deep snow for a few yards we found ourselves getting along without very heavy toil.

As may be assumed without previous searching inquiry, when a big stalwart master and a well-hardened and fairly resolute parson encountered such difficulties in the way of getting to and from church, it was fairly certain that children due at school might not find it very easy to get there. One week, when the snow covered the road to the church as above described, the attendances at the school (excluding the master's two sons) ranged thus: the first day of the week, two boys out of the average eighty; the second day, three; the third day, two; the fourth day, three; and the fifth day, four. It was almost amusing to look in, as I did every day, and see the master and his select scholars hugging the school stove in such an affectionate manner. But another time, about six years ago, one incident of this sort almost verged on the comic. I was making my way down, not without effort or difficulty, to the station and post. Between the school and the first dwelling on the road in question lay a section of highway quite sure to be filled up speedily, given adequate snow to be driven, and a wind from the north equal to doing the driving. Neither of these elements was wanting on the day in question, and within threescore yards of the school it became necessary to take to the fields, and through the stackyard of the house aforesaid. It was a fearful day, and drifting so fast that newly-made tracks were obliterated with strange speed in places. And there were such tracks before me. Passing the stacks just named, the road was less encumbered, and when I had nearly got to the viaduct over the railway by the station, I saw a figure before me struggling through a drift six feet thick on one side of the road, and about three on the other. Through this shallower part a horse had been made to force its way, and it was in the sort of squandering, sputtering track thereby made that I saw the little object in front of me. I came up with it just before the passage was accomplished, and found it was a small boy of about eight or nine years old. "What are you doing here, such a day as this?" I asked him. "Please, Ah's gannan yam." "Why, where do you live?" said I. "Please, sir, anenst t' blacksmith's."—"Well, but what are you out here for?"—"Please, sir, Ah've been te scheeal."—"Been to school!" I rejoined, "why, there'd be no one there!"—"Please, sir, yes, sir, there was me and t' tweea teachers." The sturdy little chap had got through all his difficulties, and was within a hundred yards or so of his parents' house; so I gave him what coppers I had in my pocket and sent him home wishing for another and like snowy day's adventure.

But it is by no means only in such ways as the foregoing that winter signalises itself in our moorland district. Some of the optical effects produced in times of copious snow, while it is as yet unsullied, and alike unaffected by wind or sun, are of almost incredible beauty. Almost forty years ago, at such a time, a great electrical disturbance took place in the atmosphere. I avoid the use of the term thunderstorm, because it might be misleading. The thunder was very loud, and repeated in long bellowing rolls, and the lightning was, I think, as startlingly brilliant as I have ever seen it—two occasions only excepted. But there was no downfall: neither snow nor hail nor sleet accompanied the disturbance. My children were then very young, and there was some trouble among them by reason of the alarming loudness of the thunder, and my wife was with them. I was a little startled at hearing her cry to me from the nursery door to come quickly upstairs; but the explanation was that she wished me to see the lightning and note the marvellous beauty of the scene, as flash after flash lit the whole snow-covered dale before us, and its steep retaining moorbanks on either side, with an effulgence that defies description. But the dazzling, almost intolerable brightness of the lightning-lit snow—white indeed, and with a whiteness such as "no fuller on earth can whiten"—that forced exclaiming rapture rather than quiet admiration; while it was the most marvellous succession of most marvellous tints and tones of colour which dwelt on the retina many seconds after the flash ceased its splendid being, that dwelt in the mind and imagination. The total duration of this after-vision could not have been less than sixty seconds ; and as the heavenly whiteness faded it began to be replaced by the most delicate tinge of rose, deepening by distinct gradations through darker tones into steel-blue, which in its turn gave place to the customary showing of snow by night, the night being unlit by a moon.

I have witnessed this wonderful display of nature's lights and colouring three several times now, but in no case have I seen the unimaginable glory of the first display outshone. And the remembrance of it I think is indelible.

But this strangely beautiful succession of delicate rose tints and steel-blue tones of deepening intensity has been witnessed by me once and again since the night of that marvellous display ; only with this difference, that the succession of shades and colours was not a succession of time, or sequence in order of progression, but simply of distance and altitude. Or to put it another way : At your feet and in the foreground your eye rested on the unsullied snow ; in the mid-distance, or on the steep slopes of the ascending moor-banks, you saw the tinges and tints of the rose ; and in the far distance, or above the braes of the walls of the dales, you gazed out upon the matchless blues. The colours might be fainter than as they glowed forth after the magic operation of the lightning's blaze, but they were all there ; and waited there to be gazed on with a sort of reverent admiration, until the sun had sunk too low behind the western moor-bank for it to be called day any longer. The first time I saw this exhibition of nature's colouring was on Christmas eve in the year when my walk home from a fruitless visit to the church, in company with the schoolmaster, took place. It was freezing with intense sharpness, and the night was one more intensely cold than usually befalls, even high up among the moors. As it was, at this sunset my beard and moustache were frozen into one icy mass while I stood and gazed on the gorgeous panorama ; and it has only been on similar occasions of very sharp frosts, with a perfectly quiescent atmosphere, that I have ever witnessed any repetition of it.

There is still, however, one phase of winter scenery which has engraved itself as deeply as any other on my recollection, and it is one I have observed under various aspects, and on divers different occasions. What I refer to are the singularly lovely creations of a rime or white frost, on the occasions on which there is so large an amount of moisture in the atmosphere as to lead to a heavy deposit.

I remember one occasion on which the deposit was so heavy that ordinary rushes became rods of more than half an inch in diameter, the merest dry bents—windlestraws, or winn'lstraes as we call them here—the thickness of a big cedar pencil, and every small twig in the hedges a bar of glittering jewellery. It was a glorious winter's day, with some three to four inches of snow on the level in the fields, and with a temperature so frosty in the morning that the moisture of my breath congealed with every expiration on the hair about my mouth and chin. On looking at any of the objects I have named with a little attention it was seen that the incrustation depended on what may—for the purposes of illustration—be described as a coating of fur, every constituent filament in which was as compound as the upper shoot and branches of a fir-tree. There was the spire on an infinitesimal scale, with the whorl of radiating spurs at its foot, and the same repeated at the foot of the second shoot of the leader, and so on. Anything more strangely, mysteriously, ethereally beautiful I never beheld. Each twig, each grassy seed-stem, each blade of grass, and especially each longer and thicker shoot or rush, was a miracle of symmetry, beauty, perfection, composite of myriads of marvels on a lessened and lessening scale.

2 B

But these wonderful creations by nature's jeweller were not limited only to the vesture of such objects as those I have named. When I went forth on my afternoon's expedition to Fryup Church—for it was on a Sunday that this fairy world of ornamentation greeted my eyes—and had made my way into a large smooth field, on pausing to look back towards the north-west and north sides of the snow-scape, having the brightly shining sun on my side as I did so, my eye was caught by the myriads of glittering points that gemmed the whole surface of the snow. The whole area for hundreds and hundreds of square yards was lit up in this way; and there was not a hue or a lustre displayed by the diamond that was not repeated by thousands of resplendent facets bestrewing the field. There were simply acres of lustrous diamonds!

Naturally I turned to a closer examination of the circumstances and conditions leading on to the marvellous scene which gladdened my eyes; it was indeed the "joy" of a "thing of beauty." And I then observed, what my somewhat impaired sight had not suggested to me before, that the entire surface of the snow was covered with—to use the word once already applied in the same connection—a thick fur of sprays of frost-work like that on the twigs and grass, only three-quarters of an inch in the pile. Every step I had taken had crushed and destroyed myriads of frost-gems, all symmetrically perfect and beautiful, and set as no jeweller on earth could set them. Still, though these glimmered with a sort of pearly lustre in the sunbeams, the sources of the flashing, lustrously-hued diamond rays were not in them; but set among them in infinite numbers were facets of such reflecting and refracting power as only Nature herself can produce, and set at every conceivable angle, as well as endlessly diversified in size. I no longer wondered that the brightness and the splendour were so dazzlingly glorious to behold, when I came to regard the enginery from which they resulted.

One other instance of filigree work of a like nature may

also be mentioned. I have seen it only during two winters, in the course of which we had not only much snow on the ground, and very heavy drifts of the same, but also after the drifting wind had subsided a series of intense frosts—the thermometer down to zero, and one or two nights three to five degrees below. If any one can imagine the filaments of a spider's web encrusted as I have tried to describe the twigs and grass as being, and can further try and realise them, not as in the radiations and concentric circumferences of the great field-spider's geometrical work, but erring and straying in all sorts of graceful and unstudied confusion from one fold of the wreathed snow to another, some of them six or seven inches long, and many less than half that, and all being more or less vertical, he will have a faint idea of the decorative energies of hoar-frost where there would seem to be no substratum of fibres for it to work upon. This kind of work, however, was always on the wall-like drifts on the north side of the roads, or where the sun during the short period of his winter's warmth had been exercising such softening influences as were permitted to him under such circumstances.

Once or twice also I have seen the snow in such places and with such aspect look as if, so to speak, honeycombed, but in the most delicate fashion, by the agency of the sun's rays; and then the aggregate group of tiny borings and indentations all furred at the edge and in the cavities with a cognate garniture of minute crystallisations,—again one of the most beautiful vagaries of the frost-artist.

Again, the sun may "come forth as a bridegroom out of his chamber, and rejoice as a giant to run his course," but, of a surety, this Dales country of ours with its mighty moor-banks, when draped and veiled in the marvellous garments of pure, undriven snow, may be the image of the bride ready to respond to his first smiles in the coming morning.

But similes apart, the dales are so deep, and the moor-banks are so up-sweeping when mantled with fresh and deep snow, and the snow itself is so white, that while the accustomed eye revels in the return of unforgotten beauty, and recalls with gratified recognition this or that well-known feature, the unaccustomed eye is fairly bewildered with the strange, pale beauty of the snow-scape, and for a time at least seems to be incapable of fixing on any idea save that of an immensity of whiteness. The recognition of beauty and grandeur comes later.

But, indeed, it is not only in the winter time, or when the hills are snow-draped and the dales snow-clad, that the marvels of beautiful colouring are displayed for the delight of the watching eye. A hundred times, and again a hundred, I have seen in the early autumn evenings, when the sun was sinking behind the western banks, all the moorland heights towards the east and north, as they rose in their receding order, take on the most lovely and delicate hues of violet and purple, glorified with the bloom of the plum and the sheen of infinite velvet.

Once, too, in the late autumn, in the afternoon of a rayless day, I was coming from Westerdale over the end of the ridge traversed by the road from thence to Castleton, when the most amazing, unimaginable study in colour was spread out before my astonished gaze. For I had seen the moor-scape a thousand times before, and enjoyed its varied beauty, here rough and rugged and there softened and swelling with graceful undulations; but I had never dreamed of the glory it might wear when gorgeously apparelled in array of Nature's own garnishing. At my feet and in the near foreground was what, on ordinary days, we looked upon as the ling dulled and browned by lapse and wear of the past season; in the middle distance, and rising just beyond it, were the valleys of the youthful Esk and the Baysdale beck, still green and fringed with green, and backed by the strong slopes of the Crown End and other moorland banks, all swept and charactered by broad fields and patches of russet bracken; and in the remoter distance, just bank behind bank rising in dim solemnity, and all clad in the dulled uniform brown of the ling of autumn. But to-day, although the contours remained, and with them the material features of the scenery throughout, all else was changed. All that was everyday, commonplace, dull, was refined, all that was worn and faded was renewed and glorified; and not a thing left to remind us of the old, the worn, the faded, or the unbeautiful. At my feet and before me was, as it were, a carpet, hundred-piled, of the richest brown, such shades as I had never seen nor imagined; the greens of the valleys were become the greens—and only there seen—of the sky in a gorgeous sunset; the fields and sheets of bracken were spaces of "old gold" and burnished gold, and all the great space behind was in vast expanses of richest purple gorgeous with heaven's own perfect bloom.

If one were to characterise the district as "a District of Surprises," I think it would not be very difficult to justify the description. To any one who may have studied the country in what may be termed the physical geography way, but little in the way of justification would be required. I remember a visit from one of the most accomplished men I ever knew. He covered my dining-room table with the six-inch Ordnance maps of this part of the country. He spent the greater part of two mornings in the diligent study of them, mastering all the details. And at the end of the second morning he remarked, "I have got it all in my head now. To-morrow I shall go here and here and here"—indicating three or four high points from which, it was clear from the maps, he could get a very wide out-look—"and survey the whole fashioning and contour of all, and bring away a complete impression of the whole as a mind-picture."

I knew well enough what his thought and feeling and idea were, for I had gone through the same process myself, only with worlds less of geological knowledge; and, besides that, the mind-picture or plan of this immediate portion of the district which he had thus worked out for himself was but a part of the mind-picture or plan which I had once on a time been aided to form with respect to the entire district of Cleveland. For I had seen, and been able to give some amount of attention to, a most carefully and accurately constructed model of the whole area named, planned and carried out on the scale and according to the lines of the Ordnance Survey. All was in proportion, the lengths and the breadths, the depths of the depressions, the elevations of the heights, the windings of the becks, the broader but hardly less tortuous wanderings of the rivers, every physical feature of the district lay there before me—on a small scale, it is true, but such and so true as to enable me easily to piece together such portions as I had been enabled to mark, study, and learn, according to the scale of Nature's own works.

And this helped me to realise how truly the district is one of surprises, and not only from the geographical point of view. To illustrate this.   You toil up from the depths and gullies of Danby Head, and you find yourself with a wide sweep of moor in front, mounting still, on the whole.   You trudge or toil, as the case may be, according as the ling is short or knee-deep and the walking easy or beset with damp and not wholly untreacherous places, and almost before you know or think about it, you find an enormous area for your eye to wander over.   It is a clear day, and you see miles upon miles over the widening, lengthening prospect.   You are ready to rub your eyes, and think they are playing you tricks.   But it is York Minster you see, separated from you by only the small linear space of thirty-three miles or so.   Wondering, you look on, and realise that the great pile lies there before you, like a huge ship at anchor on the surface, but not the extreme limit of the surface, of a great, smooth, still ocean.   It is central on the sea, and not on the horizon.   And the interpretation of that is, that you are looking over and beyond York and far into the more southerly distance.

Or you are a pilgrim and have been visiting the unsatisfactory shrine of the reputed British village, and have
approached it from the Waupley side; and now you are
breasting the ling-covered ascent between you and the
Beacon—stopping for a moment, maybe, to note the stone
which tells in simple words that there a man, lost and
bewildered in a snowstorm, had been found dead, and
shuddering a little perhaps at the thought of finding yourself
in such case amid such a scene. And you climb up the last
and steepest part of the hill, and mounting to the summit of
the Beacon Hill—which has shut everything else out from
your sight for the last twenty or twenty-five minutes—you
pause and look round. And what a panorama it is that greets
your eyes! Bold mountain ridge and coy shrinking dale from
left to right as you face the south, and spreading round so as
to overlap on the right side; and then turning seaward, the
sea from Redcar Sands to almost Whitby, and right away out
to the north the coast of Durham, beyond Sunderland and
northward still, with an outline that seems to lose itself in the
dim distance beyond. And a moment since you saw but a
barren ling-covered moor-bank!

But to meet with surprises of the same class, it may be,
but on a more limited and more appreciable, inasmuch as
more familiar, scale, one should prowl about on the rough
braes of the broken moor-banks, and within the romantic
fastnesses of the Dales Heads. Every twenty yards almost, as
you wind in and out, climb up or climb down, some new
feature, some new object, some new scene, something you
would give much to be able to photograph on the instant, and
carry away with you indelible for ever, simply comes to be
looked at; and, as you turn aside, or press farther on in your
course, gives way to another, equally beautiful and equally
desirable in its beauty. In one word, our moorland scenery
needs to be lived among.

LOST ON THE MOOR

"Lost on the moor!" It has an unpleasant sound at any time, and under any circumstances. But lost on the moor with a dense wet fog—what the Dales folks call a "roke"— when you cannot see the grouse that spring into flight almost at your very feet; when your companion (if you have one), if he goes ten feet away from you, is a dim object looming in a mysterious way at an indeterminate distance,—that is a more uninviting experience still; but to be lost on the moor, with deep snow on the ground, snow still falling in fitful squalls, and an oppressive fog over and round and all about you, —that is of all others the worst way of being lost on the moor! And this was the experience it once fell to my lot actually to realise.

The incident was thus. It was the end of the season, and I wanted a few brace of grouse, which, if not shot that day, could be shot on no day at all. Certainly the moor was covered with snow; and getting near the birds under such circumstances was a matter of difficulty, and only to be thought of by one who did not mind walking in deep snow, and walking far and fast,—one well acquainted, moreover, not only with the moor itself, but with the haunts of the grouse at such times and under such circumstances. Well, I knew every inch of the moor, and I did not mind walking it in snow; nor did I know what it was to get tired with even a long day's shooting. Besides, I had one of the under-keepers with me, who knew as well as I did the haunts of the birds, and all the bearings of the moor, and the different beats which might be taken with the especial object of circumventing the game [1] and getting a few shots from time to time within reasonable distance. Certainly the birds not only saw us as soon as we ascended to the moor-level, but flew off with more decisive promptitude than under ordinary circumstances at that time of year. But then we had this advantage too, that we could see them half a mile off, and even more than that when the packs were considerable; and we could see too whether there was any chance of a successful stalk of any of the packs within range of our eyesight. Suffice it to say that, sometimes by coming down upon them from above, and sometimes by surprising them from below, I got several shots, and very nearly the same number of grouse.

We had followed a lot which had sped their way from the higher part of the moor to a rather narrow tongue of moorland which stretched itself downwards in the direction of the part of the dale in which my house stands; and after another successful shot, we were about turning our steps in the direction of the higher moor, when all at once, for we seemed to have had no previous warning, we found ourselves in the midst of one of the thickest snowstorms I had ever experienced, even in these northern parts of the kingdom. Luckily it was not a "hoddin' (holding or lasting) storm," for the snow ceased in less than half an hour; but it was succeeded, and as suddenly as it had burst upon us, by a fog so dense that we could not see ten yards in any direction—at times not ten feet. After a pause of a few minutes to see if the fog would lift in the same unforeseen and unaccountable way as the snow had come, had ceased, and been succeeded by the fog, I said to my companion, "Well, William, I think we shall do no more

[1] This was many years before the modern system of driving had been so much as heard of. There is no difficulty now in getting birds if wanted; but thirty or forty years ago the case was very different.

good to-day ;" his reply being, "Neea, Ah aims it's overed for to-day." And so we determined to set our faces homewards.

When this decision was taken we were on the eastern verge of a lofty but narrow ridge of moorland, the utmost transverse width of which at the point we stood on did not greatly exceed half a mile. Our object and intention was simply to cross it from east to west, and then to descend slopingly, so as to reach my home by the readiest way. Even if we had not been practised moorsmen, both of us, with a personal knowledge of every inch of the moor for miles away, we should have had no misgiving about the result. We had but to set our faces with our backs to the brae we stood upon, and keep on straight ahead, and fifteen minutes would take us to the point we meant to reach.

But we walked thirty minutes, and still no sign of the moor-edge we wanted to get to! At last the fog seemed to lift a little ; and in a minute or two we saw it was because we were near the western edge of the ridge. But instead of being where we had intended to be, we were at least a mile farther up the ridge, and a good mile and a half from my house, instead of only three or four fields above it.

Laughing a little at our discomfiture, we proceeded to retrace our steps, having to go more out on to the moor in order to obtain a better trackway ; for we thought that, where we were, it would be easy to skirt the moor-edge ; and we had no idea but that we were skirting it as we continued our trudge. But when we next came to a point at which it was possible to recognise our landmarks, we found we had been traversing the ridge in a north-easterly direction, and had reached its verge a little above the hollow we call Coums !

Yet once more we addressed ourselves to what was proving to be rather a difficult task ; and this time, when we came to the brae again, it was at a place not more than half a mile south of the intended point, and about less than a mile distant from the parsonage.

Now in the course of our vagaries we had crossed the Church-way twice, and another moor-road called the Mill-way four times, both of them tracks which had been worn down by weather and traffic to the depth of from a foot and a half to nearly three feet (in places) below the level of the moor, and along the side of each of which are set divers tall posts of unhewn stone to act as indications of the line of the said ways ; but we had crossed them without knowing we were crossing, although, of course, we had to plunge through the snow with which they were filled ; and as to the guide-stones, unless we had almost run against them we could not have seen them for the fog. So that to all intents and purposes we experienced all the sensations of being lost, short only of the anxiety and the sense of peril from absolute ignorance alike of which way we ought to go and of the path we ought to select ; and the experience was by no means a pleasant one.

Another case of "Lost on the Moor," very much more real and actual than this, took place in the instance of two lads very well known to me. They were boys of twelve or thirteen years of age, and, as the custom was, and more then than now, they had gone out "St. Thomasing," that is, visiting the farmhouses on St. Thomas's Day (20th December) and asking "Thomas's gifts." These were usually pieces of "pepper-cake" (or the customary thick Christmas ginger-bread), with perhaps a modicum of cheese, or a bite of cake, or maybe a few halfpence. The day was dull and raw, but not bitterly cold. They had reached the farm called Stormy Hall, and then, finding the afternoon growing dark, and more thickness setting in, they made up their minds to give up for the day, and to turn their steps homewards the "soonest way" they could go ; and this was to leave the fringe of farmhouses that lie all along the dale just about the level of the highest enclosure, and the rough road that gives the means of going from one to the other all along, and making up the hill slopingly in order to reach the main road running along the top of the ridge from Kirkby Moorside to Castleton, where their parents lived. All this, however, was not made out until the next day, for the poor boys had never reached home. The anxiety of the parents—the boys were cousins—need not be dwelt upon.

It so happened the next morning that I had to take an early walk into the outlying part of the parish which Fryup is, and it was near mid-day when I returned to the Parsonage. Just before entering the garden from the Fryup side I heard a number of voices in the lane, and presently saw the speakers coming down the lane from the school. This was so unusual at the time named, for twelve o'clock is invariably called "dinner-time," that I knew there must be some greatly exciting cause to account for this neglect of the mid-day meal; and instead of going into the house I went into the road to meet the men I had seen. Nearly the first person I met was a stalwart mason, then and always a great friend of mine, who told me that the two boys I have mentioned had never reached home, and to judge by the answers to inquiries made along the line they had taken the previous afternoon, they must have spent the night totally unsheltered on the open moor. My friend Frank's voice shook as he told me this. He was no ways related to the missing lads, but he was himself the father of lads of about the same age, and there was no lack of natural feeling about him. In fact he was a good fellow all round.

We organised our plan of search at once, and passing in loose order along the fields on the west side of the dale, we made towards the moor above Stormy Hall as directly as we could. We had not proceeded far before a shout came down the dale, and was passed on to us in the rear with a speed that seemed almost marvellous, to the effect that "one of the lads had been found, and though very stiff and lame from the exposure, still not materially the worse."

We soon met with further and fuller intelligence; and it

appeared that the boys, bewildered by the fog, which they
had found very dense as they ascended the moor-bank from
the farm, and indeed increasing in thickness the higher they
reached, had almost immediately, and in a way which they
could not explain, gone astray from the right direction ; and
the deviation once made, although in the clear light it might
seem to have been an unimportant one, yet, as always in a
thick fog, it had the inevitable consequence of leading step by
step to bewilderment.   Our poor luckless little lads soon found
they were out of the track, and effort after effort to recover
it only ended in disappointment and hopeless discomfiture.
And then the darkness of coming night began to intensify
the heavy gloom of the fog.   But the brave, hardy little chaps
did not give up or lose either heart or head in their trouble.
They were lost, and they must spend the night on the open
moor.   Well then, they must make the best of it, and do what
they could towards making the inevitable as bearable as they
could.   And so they looked out a hollow way worn by the
feet of the sheep, and dry, and sheltered by a growth of tall
ling ; and then they pulled some more ling to hap themselves
withal, and munching some of the gifts of food they had got
at the different farms they had visited, they prepared to spend
the night as comfortably as wet boots and stockings and damp
clothes would permit.

When the morning broke at last—and the nights are long
indeed towards the end of December, and even sometimes to
those who have more luxurious appointments than a down-
pressing canopy of dull grayish-white fog, with damp ling for
coverlet, and moist shoes and stockings, and clothes in general
far from dry, for sheet and blanket—only one of the two was
capable of movement, and he stiffly and with difficulty.   But
with an effort he " got hissel' scratted oop," and began to
think what was best to be done.   As he sat and thought as
well as he could, poor little chap, he fancied he heard the
tinkle of a bell, and if so, it would mean deliverance !   It was

no sheep-bell that, if a bell at all; but it would be the bell of the leading horse of a "draught" (team), and it would lead him to the high road, if only he had strength and feet to struggle so far.

A minute or two, and he is assured it is a bell; and then he hears the driver speaking to his horses. Away he goes, hobbling as well as he can; but the passage of the draught along the beaten road is faster than his with his numbed feet over the hindering ling, and the sounds of the rescue that might be are getting a little ahead of him. With a choking sense of something nearer like despair than any yet, he musters all his strength for a last yell, and luckily he is heard. It was time; for his strength was spent, brave little fellow that he was! The driver, who was making his early way to the Rosedale Head coal-pits, stopped his draught, shouted in response, and presently had the poor, chilled, foot-numb, aching little waif safe in his arms, hoisted him into the waggon, covered him with the hay the horses were to have eaten while taking in the intended load of coal, weighing it, paying for it, and so forth, turned away straight back for Castleton, and dropped the rescued youngster at his father's door.

But the boy had not forgotten his fellow in the night's bivouac, who, moreover, as being less hardy than himself, was really and sadly disabled, but had given such an account of his own position when he first heard the sound of the bell, and of the way he had taken in trying to intercept the draught, that there was no difficulty for William Robinson, the rescuer, to give minute directions to such as he fell in with on the road how to look for the lost and helpless sojourner still left in his comfortless night's lodgings. And thus, before the party I had joined had had more than time to spread themselves out in a long line, each individual within hailing-distance, if not sight, of his right- and left-hand neighbours, and to begin the systematic search of every yard of the moor before us, the news came up from behind that the boy had been found, had been taken down to Stormy Hall, and was there quite "safe," though by no means "sound."

In half an hour's time the poor boy had more visitors than ever before or since in his life. We found him near a cheery farmhouse fire, were told he had enjoyed some warm milk, and, except that he had for the time lost the use of his legs and feet, did not seem to be materially the worse. The doctor too had seen him; for he had come riding up to join the army of seekers, and was on the spot almost as soon as wanted; and had said that he must stay where he was for a day or two, and then might be taken home without hurt; and that after a few days he would be as well again as ever.

But, thick as the fog was, there was more mist than could be accounted for on that ground in the eyes of more than one or two of the hardy rugged men who had joined in that search, when we realised what exposure on a North Yorkshire moorland in a December night must be, and did not as yet even fancy to ourselves that these strayed boys might have had coolness enough, and bravery besides, to try, hopeless as their case seemed, to do the best they could for themselves.

The brother of one of these boys paid me a visit only a few months ago. He had come home from one of the most distant of the English colonies to see the old place again, and he came to see his old friend the parson, and our talk fell on this episode among his early recollections; and we both of us seemed, at even such a long time after "all had ended so well," to feel what a "parlous" chance it was that his brother had passed through that night he was "lost on the moor."

APPENDICES

APPENDIX A

INCLOSURE WITHOUT ACT OF INCLOSURE

CERTAIN pages are elsewhere devoted to an effort to identify the
site of the ancient vill of Danby.[1] I am myself satisfied that the
identification is incontestable. But wherever the ancient vill of
Danby was situate, there is no shadow of doubt that, at the demise
of the last Brus Baron, the said vill was still extant ; and there
is like testimony in later Inquisitiones p. m., and correlated documents dealing with different parts of the Brus inheritance, that the
vill of Danby sustained no immediate or material alteration as to
site or otherwise. In short, I think there is presumptive evidence
that the vill of Danby remained much as it had been, and where
it had been, all through the fourteenth century, and most likely
some way on into the fifteenth. And then came a great and final
change. And in strict connection with this I ask attention to the
following extracts from a very valuable book, namely, Scrutton's
Commons and Common Fields : "The evils of enclosures were first
brought to the attention of Parliament early in the reign of Henry
VII, or about 1485. . . . In the year 1487 the Parliament passed
two Acts, the one local, the other general. The local Act refers
to the fact that 'many towns and villages have been let down and
the fields ditched and made pastures for cattle.' . . . The general
Act—'an Act against the pulling down of towns' (and the word
'town' is used here in the sense of 'village' or 'township')—an
Act sometimes referred to as the Statute of Enclosures, is directed
against the pulling down of houses and 'the laying to pasture lands
which customably have been used in tilth,' and it provides that all

---

[1] See Appendix D.

houses let within three years past with twenty acres of land for
tillage are to be maintained. This Act is confirmed and extended
by two Acts in 1514 and 1515. Both Acts complain of the pulling down of towns, . . . and they require the towns decayed to be
re-edified within a year."

But it will be observed that previously to the first date mentioned, or 1485, "many towns and villages had been let down";
yet it is not in every place we are enabled to see how such a state
of the case not so much was led on to as actually became an
accomplished fact. In Danby I think we can. But possibly the
best way for obtaining a clear view of the group of circumstances
involved may be by taking into consideration the historical conditions embodied in the further extract from Mr. Scrutton's book,
which I proceed now to give :—

"The causes which led in the sixteenth century to the inclosures which with the resulting discontent and rebellion play so
large a part in the history and literature of the time, have their
origin in the great plagues of the middle of the fourteenth century,
the Black Death, in which nearly half the population perished.
Prior to that date the progress of agriculture had been in the conversion of waste and wood into arable land. The lord had no
difficulty in cultivating his demesne lands, at first by the services
due from his customary tenants, and when those services gradually
became commuted for money payments, by labourers hired with
his customary revenue thus accruing. But the great scarcity of
labourers caused by the ravages of the Black Death, and the consequent rise in wages, averaging fifty per cent in all employments,
made this method of cultivation both difficult and expensive, and
the lords endeavoured to revert to the old customary services of
their tenants, now far more valuable than their money commutation.
This attempt to set aside the customary payments led to great discontent, and was one of the chief causes of the Peasant Revolt of
1381. The Statute of Labourers, intended to compel the labourers
to work at the old rates, also proved unsuccessful, and the lords
were compelled to abandon the old lines of agriculture. After a
transition in which a system of leases somewhat similar to the
metayer tenure of the south of France was in vogue, the lord finding stock as well as land, and the tenant returning the stock at the

expiration of his lease, a new departure was taken. The lords ceased to cultivate the great bulk of their demesne lands, and let them out to small cultivators, at first for short terms and in small plots, afterwards frequently by leases for three lives, or for twenty-one years. By the middle of the fifteenth century the bulk of the demesne lands both of lay owners and ecclesiastical corporations were under this system of tenure."

The author then goes on to say that "after the Wars of the Roses a new element entered into English agriculture. . . . A spirit of trade breathed through England ; the merchants of the towns turned their attention to farming, and especially to the growth and export of wool. But sheep could not be reared with advantage either on the open commons or on the small and scattered plots in which a tenant's or a lord's land then lay, and the desire to carry out sheep-farming as a commercial success led to the consolidation of holdings, the conversion of arable land into pasture, and, wherever it was possible by law or by violence, to the enclosure of commons. With the demand for land and the almost universal rise in prices came a great rise of rents ; the small freeholders and they that lived by the plough found it harder and harder to gain a living ; the poor men who had relied on the common for the grazing of their one cow saw it surcharged by the sheep of wealthy graziers, enclosed by rich nobles for their sheep-farms, or converted into a park for their deer."

All this may have been, no doubt it was, true, for many if not most other parts of England ; but it is eminently without foundation for that district of England of which Danby forms a part. The "common" was not "enclosed," is not now. The "small freeholders and those who lived by the plough" did not "find it harder and harder to gain a living" ; on the contrary, they made and saved money to such an extent that when the land on which they had lived came into the market in the first half of the seventeenth century, more than one hundred and twenty of them covenanted to buy the plots they had farmed. And the great lord did not "convert the common into a park for his deer," and for the best of all possible reasons—he had his wide, far-spreading park and warren already, and was as strongly desirous to convert the available portions of it into small or medium-sized farms as the would-be tenants themselves could be. And indeed I am very doubtful about the conclusive applicability of much of the former quotation—exclusive of the historical data—to the individual case of Danby. For instance, I feel no assurance that there was any lord's demesne at Danby at all, and if there were none, then there could be no endeavour to "revert to the old customary services of the tenants." It is quite true there were in the last quarter of the thirteenth century fifty-six bovates of land held in villenage in the township. But if we may trust the document from which this information is obtained (the "Partitio inter hæredes Petri de Brus"),[1] the commuted value of each to the lord was 5s. And there were also no less than twenty-two *liberi tenentes* or freeholders, such as freeholders were at that date; for it is expressly said of them, "Omnes isti liberi præscripti tenent per cartam." But there is no mention made of demesne land;[2] and naturally, for the *Capitale Mesuagium* itself was a ruin, and the residence of the baron was, and had been for almost a century and a half, at Skelton.

But the incongruities between the Danby facts and the writer's theory and assumptions are alike interesting and instructive. Granted that the lord did not here "cease to cultivate the great bulk of his demesne lands," nor "let them out to small cultivators," for the good and sufficient reason that there were none (or next to none) to let in that way, still the fact remains that a large proportion of the land in the township was, if not exactly "let for short terms or by lease" for any specified number of years, yet held of the lord *per cartam*, or in virtue of a written grant or charter.

---

[1] The document is injured by time, if not wear, and there are many blanks in it; and I am inclined to think that in some, if not several cases, the blanks are large enough to suggest the supposition that divers names are lost. Still, there are twenty-two yet legible.

[2] In writing thus I wish to limit the meaning of the terms "in demesne" simply to what is implied in Mr. Scrutton's words quoted above, namely, "The lord found no difficulty in cultivating his demesne lands," qualified as that is by the subsequent sentence, "on the small and scattered plots in which a tenant's or a lord's lands then lay." Of course I am aware that at the date referred to mainly, or 1271, among the fees of the late Peter de Brus, in the *Inquisitio* thereanent taken, Danby, viewed as the equivalent of "one fee," is returned as held *in dominico*. But the meaning there is one thing, and that of "held in demesne," as in Mr. Scrutton's words, is another.

And it is worth noting that while the acknowledgments rendered
—not the rents paid—by these *liberi* varied in the most extraordinary manner, or from 4s. for one carucate, 4s. 2d. for another
carucate, 3s., 4s., or 5s. for a bovate, to 30s. for twenty-five acres,
23s. for thirty acres, or a bovate or half a score acres for two barbed
arrow-heads (or, it might be, up to half a dozen), still the total
amount so held was already, taking all into consideration, very
considerable.[1] For, taking the carucate as roughly representing the
area of 100 acres, the record quoted from, imperfect as it is, yet
gives a total of 625 acres as in the hands of the *liberi*, a fact to be
collated with the further fact that there were fifty-six bovates in
villenage ; for it means that, while all the old carucatage, and indeed
distinctly more than that, remains, nearly as much more has been
added to the arable total, every acre of which has been added as
the result of essarting or clearing, inclosing and cultivating, what
had previously been forest, thwaite, or waste.

I do not think that, allowing only for the considerations, historic
and other, which have so far been adduced, this is an arbitrary or
unauthorised deduction. On the contrary, I hold it to be inevitable rather than only simply warranted. But there are other
considerations yet which tend to exactly the same conclusion.

There were in all, as elsewhere stated, certainly not less than
165 several farmholds, messuages, or tenements in the general
parish of Danby (inclusive, that is, of Lealholm and Glaisdale)
when the estate was sold out in allotments in 1656 ; indeed, I
am quite certain there were many more than the number stated,
for there are many counterparts of conveyances which are, the
moment attention is given to the inquiry, conspicuous only by their
absence. Why or how is a matter of speculation, perhaps of sus-

---

[1] The circumstance here noted is one that ought not to be passed by totally
unnoted. In the earlier part of the document it is stated that there are fifty-
six bovates held in villenage, or, in other words, seven carucates. Over and
above this area of cultivated land we have to reckon nearly or quite six
carucates more as held by the free men, making a total of thirteen carucates
at the least. This is a result to be collated with the Domesday Record, which
gives six carucates as the total amount of cultivable land in the township of
Danby in and for some indefinite time after the year 1087. The progress of
reclamation and improvement which had been made in the two centuries
between 1087 and 1271 had indeed been a marked as well as a real one.

picion, but it is unquestionably a fact. And from my local knowledge and examination I should be inclined to say that, allowing
for cottages with their garths, and small holdings such as would be
called cow-keepings now, the total number of messuages or tenements would certainly fall very little (if at all) short of two hundred,
of which at least three-fifths would be in Danby proper.

But while the greater part of these conveyances show the traces
of general, as well as of internal or divisional inclosure, and much
of the latter as more or less recent, several of them attest the fact
that some specified act of inclosure was not as yet complete ; that,
in fact, it was still proceeding, and proceeding, moreover, not in
the way of an underhand or illicit act, still less as an encroachment,
but as an overt and publicly recognised act. And one of them fortunately preserves for us a delineation of the process and means
employed, for it not only directs the "fencing in" of a certain close
called the "Moore Close," but adds that the said "fencing in" is
to be done "as it was formerly sett forth by the Bailiffe and Officers
for Sir John Danvers, late lord of Danby aforesaid."

This is a singularly significant clause. As long ago as 1886 I
drew attention to the facts that inclosures from the waste were
familiar things in quite the early part of the seventeenth century
in the parish of Egton, and that such inclosures or "encroachments" were made by and with the consent of the lord (*North
Riding Records*, vol. i. pp. 154, 155), but through the action of
what machinery, or how the assent and consent of the lord were
given, I did not know, and only surmised. "As it was sett forth
by the Bailiffe and Officers for the lord" revealed the whole procedure, for the bailiff and the officers exist to this day, and their
functions are as real and living as in the seventeenth century.
Encroachments on the common and settings forth by the bailiff and
officers for the lord have been made and done twice within the last
quarter of a century, in the case of the North Yorkshire and Cleveland Railway, and of its projected "extension." In both cases
strips of the waste were required for the construction of the lines
named, and in both cases the bailiff and the officers for the lord
marked out or set forth the portion to be taken.

For there is no reason to doubt that the "bailiff and the jury"
of the present day are the surviving representatives of the "bailiff

and the officers" of two centuries and a half ago, or that the last-
named body were the descendants and successors of a like body,
dating not only from the reconstitution of the manor under de
Brus, but in all probability from an earlier date still, ante-dating
even the *manerium* or predial domicile, with its appurtenances,
which preceded the day of Edward the Confessor.

But if we set ourselves to look steadily through the vista thus
opened up to us, what we look upon is a series of grants, each
protected *per cartam*, or—if not rather, and—of concessions, each
formally set forth and approved by the bailiff and the officers for
and on behalf of the lord, and each eventuating in—not delimitation merely, but—actual fencing or inclosing; and "dry-stone walls"
had become the means of definition and protection long before the
year of grace 1656 ; nay, some of the tenements of these *liberi
homines* of 1271 not simply remain—for they all doubtless do that—
to this day, but admit of recognition and identification.   Such, for
instance, is eminently the case with the carucate held by the "heir
of Robert Stormy," while Matthew of Glaphoue's carucate and
Robert Forester's "xxv. acres" admit at least of shrewd guesses
as to their locality.

But admitting and correlating the facts that up to 1271 fifty-
six bovates continued to be held in villenage ; that besides some
six hundred acres were held *per cartam* by some five-and-twenty
free men, all the result of grant and concession by the lord ; that
the process of grant and concession, beyond all possibility of question, continued to prevail, and in the systematised and regulated
form in which we recognise it nearly three hundred years ago ;
that the vill of Danby did cease to be, and so long ago and so
effectually that no scrap of tradition even remains, or has remained
for many generations, tending to so much as suggest that there had
ever been a former vill of Danby ; that a scanty fringing line of
houses, all detached and all farmhouses (in some sense and as to
their original intention), sprang up all round the sides of our dales,
just at or just below the line of inclosure, or where the farm-lands
cease and the moor-bank begins ; that these, up to the commencement of the present century, have been the exclusive abodes of the
population of Danby, there having been up to that date neither
" villa " nor hamlet properly so called in the parish,—reviewing all

these considerations, and collating them the one with the other, it is not too much to conclude that it is a very safe procedure to connect the "letting down" of the vill of Danby (or the "pulling down" of the "town" so called) with the allotment of these daleside farms and the construction of new homesteads upon them; and to localise— nay, rather, to identify—some of the sites of those old-world homesteads with the sites of these quaint old wrecks and ruinous skeletons which still maintain a precarious being; if not, indeed, to claim some of the most venerable of them as tottering survivals of human habitations four, or maybe nearer five, centuries old.

APPENDIX B

GEOLOGICAL CONSIDERATIONS

FROM whatever point of view considered, the bed of laminated clay, with intercalated seamlets of very fine sand, is a most remarkable feature in the general aspect of the district.[1] It is, moreover, of considerable thickness. The principal cutting in one place could not be less than thirty to thirty-five feet in vertical depth on its northern side, and a very considerable proportion of the whole gave up this kind of clay to the digger's spade. But what a revelation this involves of the manner and the duration of the act of its deposit! In the first place, the sediment which, by its falling from the water holding it in suspension, had formed those enormous deposits must have fallen from water which was practically quite undisturbed over a wide area, and for considerable periods of time together; succeeded, however, in every instance by other periods,

[1] A very little reflection or a small amount of observation is sufficient to convince the inquirer that these alternate laminations of fine sand and impalpable clay must have been deposited, so to speak, in pairs. First the sand would be dropped, inasmuch as, however fine its particles, they were still larger than the impalpable argillaceous matters on which the clayey part of the deposit depended. In the next place, the lapse of a certain amount of time must be postulated before the commencement of another pair of laminæ; because otherwise—that is, if the last thin layer of clay had not had time to become definitely consolidated—it would have been liable to disturbance destructive of its regularity, if not of its being, by the irruption of another volume of water like to that to which it owed its own being. As a matter of fact, we seem to be required to assume the existence of a large body of water, and of considerable depth, free from disturbance by currents or streams for considerable periods together, but liable to periodical invasions of very large volumes of water holding in suspension proportionably large amounts of argillaceous and arenaceous matters.

whether more or fewer, more or less frequent or infrequent, during which fresh matter for like suspension was worn fine by attrition, and gathered up by water in turbulent motion, ready to be deposited at the first ensuing and convenient season. And when that convenient season, a season of stagnancy, came, the sand would fall first, and then, more leisurely, the clayey particles. And as such consecutive deposits must have alternated in thousands of successions, with intervals of quietness, the mind is led on to the contemplation of a period of time which baffles calculation, during which the state of things I saw in that mimic valley-and-dale-filling flood must have been the standing rule. And this is a conclusion which provokes rather than suggests the inquiry, Was there or was there not a great collection of water, a fresh-water lake, of several miles in length but only narrow in width—a couple of miles or so, or not much more—filling the vale which is now the valley of the Esk, and the outlying dales and gills and slacks on either side of it ; and if so, how far down did the lake in question extend ?

Now it is not a little noteworthy that the Esk in leaving what might have been just such a lake-bed five or six miles in length, does so by breaking through a very narrow and rugged ravine, cleft out between closely approximating heights on either side at least 175 feet above the level of its bed. Taking the contours of the six-inch Ordnance Survey as our authority, the river-bed at this point is between 300 and 315 feet above the sea-level. The heights on either side, and scarcely more than two hundred yards apart, are 500. The inference is almost inevitable. Time was when these closely adjacent heights were united, forming an adequate dam for the support of the great body of still water required for the depositing of all that vast mass of finely laminated clay that is met with some three or four miles higher up the valley in deep beds, and that shows itself from time to time, where not swept away by subsequent degradation, at many intermediate points.

But the pursuit of this inquiry, interesting as it is, should by no means make the inquirer oblivious of yet another—" How came about this marked configuration of the district, these narrow ridges of lofty moorland and constricted depressions of deep [1] dales for

[1] Some idea of the comparative depth of the dales may be collected from the old nomenclature of certain portions or divisions of more than

the water to collect and remain in with lengthened periods of freedom from disturbance?" Certainly a giant's hand with a sufficient number of abnormal fingers might impress itself on the soft paste of a big bread-cake in its state of preparation for the oven; and a sufficiently big and misshapen giant-hand might be squeezed into a mountain mass of plastic clay. But the material indicated in our inquiry was not plastic clay. It contained or consisted of materials too intractable to submit to pressure, even if applied with Titanic force: such materials as freestone rock in beds of forty, fifty, sixty feet in depth, jet-shale rock as thick or thicker still, bands of ironstone, seams of dogger, besides many a series of thinner strata of sandstone, indurated earth, and such like. No amount of pressure would have sufficed in such a case, and Titanic fingers, pointed with nails of the diamond-borer description, would have wanted renewing an inconvenient number of times before their wearer could have grubbed out even one of the shorter dales, to say nothing of all of them, and the big central valley to boot. But still, there must have been some grubbing or eroding agency at work; and there are certain conclusions as to its nature which are not far to seek or hard to arrive at. For the indications of glacial action are sufficiently plentiful in this district. It is one thing, however, to speak of glacial action, and quite another to show how it may be made to account for the facts before our attention. Now there are the evidences of the presence of ice and

one of them. Thus, in Ingleby Greenhow there is a local division or sub-district called Greenhow Botton, of which Graves in his *History of Cleveland* says: "It is significantly called Greenhowe Bottom, it being a narrow secluded vale, so deeply intrenched with mountains that (like some parts of Borrowdale in Cumberland) in the depth of winter the sun never shines." Graves writes "Bottom"; but the word really is "Botton," and has been written with the *n* (not *m*) from a very early period, there being two or three documents in the Cartularium of Gysburne Priory, dating early in the thirteenth century, preserving the form *Bothine*. For there is a Botton in Danby also, named in the charters just referred to; and in this case, while the beck runs along fields 500 to 525 feet above the sea, the moor-bank on the west rises to 1200 feet, and that on the other side to nearly 1300. The original word is Icelandic *botn*, and it is applied to the head of a bay, lake, dale, or the like, the compound word *dals-botn* being a word of actual occurrence. Moreover, Vigfussen remarks that "Botn" is a local name still in Iceland.

the action of ice in powerful moving masses, in many a place throughout the district, and just out of it—to deal only with one set of evidences at present—on the broad unfurrowed surface of the moors ; unfurrowed, I mean, by such plough-marks as these valleys and dales of ours in reality constitute. The big ice-borne blocks or boulders—there are some of Shapfell granite even on the Fylingdales moors not far from the Peak, to say nothing of multitudes of others of a different nature, and much less travelled—these big ice-borne rocks testify with forcible evidence to the presence and the carrying power of the ice, but also, by their mere presence where they are, to the fact that the ice passed over their present sites without grubbing everything up in its passage. Why, then, should it have grubbed and eroded or dug out just where it did, and there only—I mean, in our dales and valleys ? I take it that the answer is the same in the case of that slow-moving stream, the ice-stream or glacier, as in the more quickly moving one of running water, whether it be the trickling of a gentle brook or the furious rushing of a mighty torrent ; namely, that it moves along in a track already marked out for it, if not actually prepared, by previous processes, natural or other. And here let the modern scientific geologist step in to help us with the solution of our inquiry. "The initial origin of these valleys," he says, "seems to be referable to lines of fracture produced by the elevating force [1]

[1] It may be better to make what is here quoted a little plainer by reproducing what had been previously advanced : "The liassic strata in Cleveland have a general dip south-east at a low angle. . . . This dip becomes changed, south of the Guisborough Hills, by the influence of the master anticlinal that stretches in an easterly direction by Botton Head in Ingleby Greenhow, Blakey Topping, etc., along which the liassic rocks attain their greatest elevation, and which form the watershed between the Humber and the Tees. Parallel to this on the north and south are synclinal axes—the northern one allowing the liassic rocks to appear on the coast, and the southern, more remote, forming the basin of the vale of Pickering—the one drained by the Esk, the other by the Derwent. Along the western escarpment the Lias has also a slight dip to the east, and in the south this is lost, and the beds have a north-westerly dip. They would thus form half a basin were it not for the above-mentioned anticlinal. This is also crossed by another at right angles to it, and of less consequence, as it scarcely affects the northern synclinal, and has its axis in Danby Ridge. The bases of the dales thus form a 'saddle.' These dales form a very interesting feature in the geology of

along the anticlinal axis. . . . The denudation has taken place along the lines of fracture. The heads of many of the dales are but lines of fracture still, notably that of Baysdale, as also of Bransdale and Bilsdale East; farther down their course the general denudation has widened them; but in some cases, as they encounter the oolite again, they are narrowed into gorges, as in Glaisdale, East Arncliff, Baysdale, Bransdale, and Rosedale. With regard to the epoch of their excavation, we must remark that the boulder-clay scarcely reaches higher than 350 feet in the North Riding, and thus that those dales which do not descend so low are free from it. At the bases of them, however, are great mounds of sandy clay, with various-sized rather water-worn stones of local origin, as at Ainthorpe, Fryup End, and Glaisdale End, which, from their unstratified appearance, seem best accounted for by glacial action. And as we descend lower in the same Esk valley the blocks become larger, and we reach, near Grosmont, true boulder-clay with foreign blocks. It would seem, then, that these valleys were excavated before the glacial epoch, but that they were scoured out during it by the ice, which left its accumulations in mounds at the ends."

Yes, no doubt one must conclude that there must have been a period, or periods, of upheaval, lasting perhaps through æon after æon, accompanied and followed by great tumults of waters. That seems to be what our imagination has to make effort to picture in conceiving the origin of our dales; the upheaval forming long ridges and blunt mountain-tops here, rupturing the struggling crust there with rendings and fissures and cracks; and the startled waters fleeing before the rising hills, and forcing their way of escape along the chasms which afforded them the readiest passage; and the process was renewed from period to period, as the throes

Yorkshire. They are true liassic inliers of the general form of an elongated ellipse, with the axis nearly N.N.E. in the northern, and N.N.W. in the southern. They have picturesque precipitous sides formed by the massive oolites which cap the Lias. None of them are connected by liassic surface rocks, except Glaisdale and Eskdale. The streams that drain them · have, of course, a greater fall than the dip of the rocks from the anticlinal at the head of the dales; but both in the southern and northern series the fall becomes afterwards less than the dip, and they flow over the edges of higher rocks" (*The Yorkshire Lias*, by Tate and Blake).

of the great movement were renewed ; and, in the intervals the slower but not less sure workings of what we speak of as the drainage, the natural drainage, of a district. Only time is demanded, and the power of water to erode, to eat away by slow degrees—why, it is a proverb in many languages. And of time in the cycles of the past Infinite there was no lack.

Then again, other epochs or æons, or fractions of the same mysterious Infinite, and another flood is upon the oppressed surface, the great ice-flood of the Glacial Period ; and its slow streams leisurely drifting down the chasms already fashioned by the water-floods complete the excavating process, and leave the rough model of our dales system to be worked into final finish by the finer finger-work of time and the elements, vegetation and decay, until, in the end, we see the romantic acclivities, the beautiful contours, the strangely harmonising hues, that go to make the great charm of the scenery of the " Dales District."

APPENDIX C

GLANCES AT A MOORLAND PARISH (AS PART OF A DISTRICT) FROM A PRE-DOMESDAY POINT OF VIEW

In the absence of any historical writing earlier than Domesday dealing ever so slightly with the parish in question, such a heading as this may seem at first sight rather fanciful ; and yet it may prove possible to elicit from the very brief and apparently inexplicit Domesday statements touching the parish, and the district it belongs to, some gleams of light and information as to its earlier condition.   And these faint indications may possibly admit of weighty corroboration from a certain series of facts and observations which may be alleged in support of them.

I have styled the Domesday entry as "brief and inexplicit"; perhaps "meagre" might have been a better, because a more descriptive, term.   And this is true, although there are in point of fact two entries.   The first of them, which is met with in its proper place, appears to have been blundered in the making, and is therefore repeated at the close of the special section it belongs to, and so is out of its proper place.   I give the first exactly so far as it is obviously correct, and then I append the second.   They are both found in that part of the book which deals with "Terra Hugonis filii Baldrici," on ff. lix.-lxi. of the *Yorkshire Facsimile* :—

"MANERIUM.   In Crumbeclive habuit Orm v carucatas terræ ad geldum : terra ad duas carucas.   Ibi habet Hugo [filius Baldrici] nunc i villanum et v bordarios cum i caruca.   Berewicæ hæ pertinent ad hoc Manerium :—Danebi, Lelun. . . . Silva pastilis iii leugas longa, et iii leugas lata.   Totum Manerium vii leugas

longum, et iii leugas et iv quarantenas latum. T. R. E. valebat
lx solidos : modo iii solidos."

"MANERIUM & BEREWICÆ. In Crumbeclive & Lelun &
Danebi habuit Orm xii carucatas terræ ad geldum. Terra est ad
iv carucas. Hugo habet, et wasta est. Silva pastilis iii leugas
longa, et iii lata. Totum Manerium vii leugas longum, et iii
latum."

There is, as we perceive, no essential difference between the two
entries as regards the material statement made. Crumbeclive (now
Crunkley) was the *manerium*, and Danby and Lelun (now Lealholm)
held the subordinate position of berewics to the same. Orm had
held it previously to the Conquest, but it was now in the tenure of
Hugh FitzBaldric.[1] In the entire territory, including the two
dependencies as well as the capital manor, there were twelve carucates of land liable to geld ; of these, five were at Crumbeclive, six
at Danby, and one at Lealholm, these figures being obtained from
the close of the entry touching the fee of Robert de Brus. But it
is specially to be remarked that, although the land liable to geld
amounts to five carucates at Crumbeclive, it is such, or in such a
condition, as to furnish work for but two full plough-teams, and
that is for twice eight animals, mainly oxen, if not exclusively so.

It is true the whole manor, with its appendages, is described as
"waste"; but still there must be something more than that implied
in the statement of fact just noted. Under ordinary circumstances
arable land, the crops upon which have been wasted, still remains

[1] "Hugh the son of Baldric succeeded William Malet in the sheriffdom of
Yorkshire, and his name figures in the legend of the foundation of Selby
Abbey" (see Freeman's *Norman Conquest*, vol. iv. p. 571). It does not seem
to be absolutely certain that he was Vicecomes of Yorkshire, but "inasmuch
as he is mentioned in the Lincolnshire Domesday as 'Hugo filius Baldrici
Vicecomes,' he was certainly sheriff somewhere, and it is very possible that
he may have been appointed Sheriff of Yorkshire late in 1069, after the
capture of William Malet" (*ibid.* p. 787). That he was a man of importance
as well as of large possessions is amply apparent. His Yorkshire fee is a
considerable one, and he seems to have had one hardly less in Lincolnshire ; besides which, he held lands in Hampshire, Berkshire, Wiltshire, and
Nottinghamshire. His son-in-law Wido is mentioned in the details given
touching the Lincolnshire fee, but nothing seems to be known of the circumstances under which his fees reverted to the king, as it is evident they did in
Yorkshire, probably by death without male heir.

in such state that the plough may be reinserted from the moment the cultivator finds himself in the position to resume agricultural operations. It was otherwise here. There were five carucates, or, in other words, tillage-land adequate in quantity to occupy five plough-teams in its cultivation ; but, as things were, there was but work for two-fifths of that number of beasts of draught. Whatever the explanation, which, however, is not, I think, far to seek, three out of the five carucates were practically no longer "arable"; they did not submit to the insertion of the plough. The land had been wasted seventeen or eighteen years before, and Nature had reasserted her sway ; thorns and whins, bushes and briers, were now growing, and growing rankly, in places where, previously to the wasting, the toils of the husbandman had met with no undue resistance and no ungrateful return.

But this circumstance comes out in still darker relief when we direct our attention to the corresponding figures regarding the whole extent of geldable land comprised within the specified limits. There were twelve carucates in all, and only work for four full plough-teams. Two of these, as we have seen, were at the head manor ; the other two must be spread over the area involving the other seven carucates—one in Lealholm, six in Danby.

Still, it is brought to our notice that, at Crumbeclive at least, there was not a totally desolate and depopulated district. Hugh, the lord, had there one villan and five bordars, who between them owned a plough-team. But for them, the labours of the husband-man had ceased out of the land.

But this, although a sufficiently noteworthy circumstance in itself, is not the circumstance on account of which the preceding extracts from Domesday were brought forward. There are two others yet to be noticed, and, as matters involving certain contemporary statis-tics, to be collated with certain other statistics of the same nature, only belonging to the present time. What I mean is the alleged extent of the *sylva pastilis* or *pasturalis*, and its relative amount in comparison with the total alleged area of the *totum manerium*, or entire manorial domain. The former is stated to have been three *leugœ* long by as many broad, while the latter is described as seven *leugœ* in length by three (or three and a half, in the other entry) in breadth.

It is certainly requisite in the outset to try and obtain as clear an understanding as possible of the significance attaching to the terms employed in the quotation under notice ; and this is eminently the case with the terms *sylva pastilis* and *leuga*.

As to the former, there can be little, if any, doubt, even if the conditions implied by the very words employed had not continued to exist down to the very close of the last century, and in a much less modified form than might have been supposed inevitable. Thus, while a fine between John, Prior of Guisborough, and Peter de Brus (probably the third of the name [1]), made in Easter term 1242, testifies to the fact that there was then *silva pasturalis* in "the Park beneath the Castle of Danby"—that is, the original Brus stronghold at Castleton—and in four launds or lawns in the Forest of Danby besides, the fact of the inclosure and partition of these launds, effected mainly during the last century, and not very early in it, remains to prove the enormous proportion of the area of the said launds,[2] and the enduringness of the *silva pasturalis* condition.

As to the second term noted, or *leuga*, it is difficult to conceive a measure admitting of such an extremely vague and uncertain value ; perhaps, indeed, it would be more correct to say embodying such a very indefinite estimate ; because in these Cleveland entries it is obvious not only that the assumed dimensions of a manor— the *totum manerium*—depended on an estimate, but that that

---

[1] It has not been positively ascertained when Peter de Brus the second actually died. There seems to be little doubt, however, that he went to the Holy Land in 1241, and none, I believe, that his son Peter the third paid relief on succeeding to his father's lands in 1240. The probable explanation of this fact is that, in view of his projected expatriation, arrangements were made in virtue of which Peter the third became *de facto* regnant baron, notwithstanding his father's actual continued existence. Indeed, simply as embracing a religious life, Peter the second would have placed his son in precisely the same position. It is probable, therefore, on this wise, that it was the third and last Peter de Brus who made the fine quoted in the text.

[2] The continued existence of such local names as Danby Lawns, Lealholm Lawns, Glaisdale Lawns, Lawns Gate, Lawns House, over and above the Low Wood, is sufficient to attest the importance and the extent alike of the lawns element in the former Forest of Danby. The Low Wood alone, inclosed and partitioned barely a century ago, contained nearly three hundred acres.

estimate depended, in too many instances, on the merest, most informationless guess. To illustrate this point, I take the entry touching the manor adjoining Danby on the east side—that of Egton, namely. It is as follows : "In Egetune ad geldum iii carucatæ, et tot carucæ possunt esse. Ibi habuit Suuen i manerium. Nunc habet Nigellus de Comite (Moretoniensi). Silva pastilis iii leugas longa et ii lata. Totum manerium iiii leugas longum et ii latum. T.R.E. valebat xx solidos : modo wastum est."

For purposes of my own—publication, in fact, in the *History of Cleveland* which I was then preparing—I made the most careful and accurate estimate I possibly could of the superficial area of the various parishes in the district, availing myself in the process of the careful measurements and delineations given in the six-inch Ordnance Survey ; and in the case of Egton I wrote : "From north to south—the shape of the parish being something that of an irregular four-sided figure—the medium length is about six miles, with an average breadth exceeding three miles and a half." Now, if we assume the *leuga* to represent a measure of a mile and a half, the estimate thus given coincides with the Domesday estimate with rather a singular correspondence. The four *leugæ* of length are exactly six miles, and the two of breadth three miles. But then, as regards the Danby district, my like estimate made on the same occasion, and with the same punctilious effort for approximate accuracy, was stated as follows : "The shape of this large tract is that of an irregular five-sided trapezoid, having the least side for its southern boundary. The greatest length from north to south is not less than seven miles, while the medium breadth can scarcely be stated as very much less than six, the diagonals from north-west to south-east and north-east to south-west being respectively eight miles and a half and seven and a half."

But taking the Domesday figures, seven *leugæ* long by three in width, and assuming the same dimensions of the *leuga* as at Egton—that is, a mile and a half—the result we arrive at is ten miles and a half long by four and a half wide ; the discrepancy between which and the reality is only too striking. Nor does the discrepancy become less when we ignore the striking difference between the shape of the district as presented in the Domesday estimate and as marked out in my description. In the former it is almost twice as long as it is broad ; in the other, five-sided and not much greater in length than in breadth.

Moreover, if we proceed to test the accuracy of the two estimates in the most practical way possible, namely, by ascertaining the exact number of square miles contained, as shown by the ascertained acreage, the discrepancy noted becomes more noteworthy still. The actual acreage as given in the Ordnance maps is 22,853 acres ; which represents a total of thirty-five square miles and seven-tenths within a very small fraction. This shows my estimate, or seven miles by about five and a half, giving a total of thirty-eight square miles and a half, to be excessive to the extent of nearly three square miles, while the Domesday estimate, or forty-seven square miles and a quarter, is excessive by no less than nearly twelve.

So that, even if the length of the measure called the *leuga* or *leuca* admitted of actual delimitation, still the vagueness with which it is applied in this part of Domesday would deprive it of any statistical value. But then it seems not to admit of any hard-and-fast delimitation, as will be seen from the following extract from Bawdwen's Domesday Glossary (which might be otherwise supplemented) : " *Leuga* or *leuca* is a measure of land consisting of 1500 paces. Ingulphus tells us it is 2000 paces. In the *Monasticon* it is 480 perches, which is a mile. . . . *Leuca autem Anglica* 12 *quarantenis conficitur,* according to Spelman." Skeat notices the word as follows : " Latin *leuca* (sometimes *leuga*), a Gallic mile of 1500 Roman paces : a word of Celtic derivation." The Roman pace, however, was about, or perhaps precisely, five feet, which gives us 7500 feet or 2500 yards as the linear measure of a *leuga* ; and in connection with the assumed mile and half as the estimated length of a *leuga,* taken above as admitting of tentative use, it is to be remarked that, the number of yards in a mile and half being precisely 2640, the specific difference between it and the 2500 yards just named is but inconsiderable. And in all probability this is, approximately, as near the Domesday measure intended to be indicated by the word *leuga* as we shall be likely to attain.

There is yet another term employed in all these Domesday returns, as touching geldable extent, which calls for at least passing

attention ; and that is " carucate." This term is universally taken
as signifying the quantity of land which could be adequately tilled
—in the usual agricultural year, of course—by the labour of a full
team of draught beasts—oxen mainly, or oxen and horses, eight in
number.

But any one the least conversant with the most elementary
agricultural details at once recognises the fact that, if this is a
trustworthy definition, it involves elements of almost endless
variation. An acre of land of one particular description—that is,
light or free-working land, sandy in its composition rather than
clayey—may be ploughed with two horses much more easily than
an acre of land, the soil of which is "stiff" or "heavy," which has
much clay in its composition, can with three horses. And the
fact is even so. The carucate varies in different districts, and even
in different parts of the same district, to the extent of a ratio of
two to three.[1]

For the carucate in all this district is made up, without any
exception, of eight oxgangs or *bovatæ*. And the extent of a bovate
in Cleveland varies between a minimum of eight acres and a maximum of twenty. The following notes, illustrative of the area of
the bovate in three adjoining townships, are from the Black Book
of Hexham : In Little Broughton the extent in some instances
was eight acres, in others nine ; in Ingleby Greenhow the bovate
contained fifteen acres ; in Great Broughton the number rose as
high as eighteen.

Now, in Danby, while I have one note of eight acres to a
bovate, I have others of twelve ; and I have reason to conclude
that that number is almost certainly the approximate average value
of the area embraced by the oxgang or bovate. And if so, the
total number of acres comprised in the carucate will be under

---

[1] In a long Roll, dating in 1299, in which are given the details of the
various landed properties of the Priory of Guisborough, so far as not retained
in the farming occupation of the Convent itself, we have a variety of very
valuable information of various kinds ; and in one place, dealing with the not
very large estate held by the Priory in the not very large township of
Ingleby Loringe, there is a very singular illustration of the statement thus
made. In one part of the estate the bovate contained twelve acres, in the
other eighteen, the variation depending, as I have ascertained, on the character of the land.

rather than in excess of one hundred. And this conclusion leads to a consideration of rather noteworthy bearing and importance. It is this: within the manor of Danby there were about 600 acres liable to geld, or, in other words, susceptible of systematic cultivation—"under the plough," as we say. Within the manor of Crumbeclive there were five hundred more, and in the berewic of Lealholm a yet further hundred; or 1200 acres in all, out of the great total of 22,853—not much more than one-twentieth part of the entire territory!

Such a deduction must surely be tested before we fully and finally admit it. And it may be tested in this way. There are in all 11,597 acres of moorland in the district under notice, which amount to eighteen square miles and a very small fraction. The land under the plough amounted in 1087 to less than two square miles more; and the *sylva pastilis*, estimated at three *leugæ* square, came to twenty square miles and a quarter, or forty and a quarter altogether. Now, we observed that the Domesday estimate on the whole, on the ratio of a mile and a half to the *leuga*, was excessive to the extent of nearly twelve square miles. Allow for the like excess in the estimate of the *sylva pasturalis*—that is, deduct three-sevenths of the said xcess—and the result obtained is as nearly as possible the precise thirty-five and a quarter square miles of actual measurement.

On the whole, then, there is no way of declining the conclusion that, according to the Domesday returns, out of the (in round numbers) 23,000 acres comprised within the parish of Danby (inclusive, be it remembered, of Glaisdale), barely 1200 were in any sense brought under cultivation. All the rest was bare moor to the extent of more than one-half; or else what the great Return terms "pasturable woods"—in other words, forest, marsh, swamp, or morass, with rough pasturage places interspersed. These two relative areas may be clearly brought before the mind by taking an ordinary half-sheet of notepaper, seven inches long by four and a half wide, and cutting out of it a piece of the exact size of one postage stamp and a half. The part removed would represent the cultivable land of eight hundred years ago; the great surface of the whole remaining half-sheet, the non-cultivable.

When one tries to realise what this amounts to, it is not simply that we find it easier to put the full meaning into Leland's descriptive *Danbeium nemus,* or into the sixteenth and seventeenth century name for the place, that is, "Danby on the Forest"; but we begin to admit a livelier and more vivid conception not simply of what life in such a district must have been, but of what attempted passage .through it must have meant. "In our own country," I read the other day, "the wealds of Kent, Surrey, and Sussex are remnants of the great forest of Anderida, which once clothed the whole of the south-eastern portion of the island. Westward it seems to have stretched till it joined another forest that extended from Hampshire to Devon. In the reign of Henry II the citizens of London still hunted the wild bull and the boar in the forest of Hampstead. Even under the later Plantagenets the royal forests were sixty-eight in number. In the forest of Arden it was said that down to modern times a squirrel might leap from tree to tree for nearly the whole length of Warwickshire" (*Golden Bough,* vol. i. p. 57). But this last statement is precisely that which I heard myself one day about thirty years ago from the lips of an old Danby man, who had received it from the lips of his uncle: "Ah heared my au'd uncle offens say 'at he kenned t' tahm when a cat-swirrel could gan a' t' way [all the way] down fra Commondale End to Beggar's Bridge wivoot yance tooching t' grund." And there is an old plan (rather than map) of the manor still extant, bearing date in 1751 — it belongs to the Viscount Downe, lord of the manor—which is such as to show most conclusively that the legend was absolutely and literally true. True, moreover, for both sides of the Esk, with very small allowance, possibly, on one side. "Laund" and "thwaite" succeed one another from above Castleton Bridge down to the very limits of the manor on the east; and in place after place they diverge from the line of the stream to the north or to the south for wide distances.

I think that perhaps of the two phrases employed just now, "What life in such a country must have been," and "What attempted passage through it must have meant," the latter may be the more suggestive.

Any one who has seen the Esk in flood, and even the modern raised approaches to the bridges under water for two or three score yards on either side; or who from the moorland heights on either side of the main valley has seen the sheets of water along its whole length, expanding here, contracting there, according to the nearer or more distant approach of the slopes of the higher ground ; or who from some higher vantage-post has noticed the contributory floods, supplied by the lesser becks running through each dale, often thrown back upon themselves by some obstacle, such as a bridge with too scanty passage-way for the sweeping waters, or an accumulation of branches of trees, dead rubbish, rails, sometimes masses of hay or sheaves of corn, all the *débris* a great volume of careering water can carry on its surface or propel before it ; and who remembers that all this takes place notwithstanding all the facilities afforded in these modern days for the escape of the flood-waters, all the care and pains expended on the effort to keep them to their proper course, to afford sufficient water-way under the bridges, to clear away potential obstructions, will not have much difficulty in picturing to himself what the condition of the Esk valley must have been in the old, old days when the hand of Nature was the only hand dealing with the drainage, superficial or other, of the whole of Esk-dale, from its actual commencement all the way down to Whitby.

For it is not simply the difficulties which clogged the transit of the flood waters, considerable, almost insurmountable in a sense, as they must have been, which have to be taken into account ; other considerations and of a significant nature must needs be added. Nowadays, owing to the prevalence of drainage, with its hundreds of miles of underground water-way, and with its scores of miles of superficial channels of greater or less calibre besides, the waters of even the heaviest downfall, or of the most rapid thaw of the masses of snow which get piled together on these wide, wind-swept moors, experience no great obstruction or delay in finding their way to the main water-carriers of the district. But then that volume of waters which now leads to a great flood, widespreading for six-and-thirty hours or a couple of days, and a "bank-full" state of the river for two or three or four more, was still only collecting when now nearly all has run off ; was justifying the nomenclature of a much later day wherein the field name "holm" occurs perhaps twenty to twenty-five times as descriptive of the character of the field named ; was leading to a perpetuity of swamp, "mires," or treacherous marsh-ground, thickets of " saughs " or sallows, willows, alders, and other water-loving· saplings, shrubs, and trees, as well as, in other and minor ways, tending to make passage through or across the country more and more difficult, often impossible for all but the *feræ sylvestres*, the natural denizens of such a wild and water-beset surface.

It is but a short time since that I succeeded in identifying the Karlethwaite mentioned in a document dating in the year 1242, and referred to above as a fine made between the Prior of Guisborough and the *de facto* Baron of Skelton. The latter reserves to himself the tithes of the hay from the park below the Castle of Daneby, and in four " launds " in the forest of Daneby— that is to say, in the launds of Souresby, Eskebriggethwoyte, Karlethwoyte, and that below Threllkelde. The name Carlewaite was still extant in 1751, and the old plan or map of the manor of that date shows that the " laund " in question had Little Fryup Beck on the west, Great Fryup Beck on the east, the Esk on the north, and the height clothed by the Crag Wood on the south. The area enclosed is nearly a mile long by an average of one-third of a mile in width, or somewhere about 200 acres, more rather than less. But the character of the greater part of this area is sufficiently marked. Nearly half of it is to this day " good snipe ground," and that not the part which is nearest to the river. Another part of it, higher up the slope still, is " black land," [1] full of the blackened *débris* of ancient wood-growth, and drained within recent times ; while yet a third part of it, lying within the inclosure of the Crag Wood, is soft, boggy, and treacherous, not- withstanding the drainage of the inclosures below, and the open dikes or trenches cut to let off the water contained in the spongy, miry soil of the surface. But if we come to the line of the Little Fryup Beck, and strike up south from its junction with the Esk, the still-existing testimony of the same kind is even more striking. We come to the closes called Pundermires, and on every hand one sees that the name Pundermires was not lightly given—that there was a miry spot there indeed—and in what is really the most elevated part of the extensive inclosures so named I have been more than once (and in spite of much " circumspection " as to my

[1] See Appendix G.

"walk"), when looking for a woodcock or two, in considerable danger of getting myself "bogged."

But on all sides evidence of the same general bearing and character is in reality inexhaustible. And perhaps, while dealing with this special vicinity or the old thwaite called Karlethwoyte in 1242 and Carlewaite in 1751, we might as well notice the character of the lands opening out into it on either hand ; the lands, in other words, constituting no small portion of the lower parts or "ends" of Great and Little Fryup. On the west side of Little Fryup Beck, beginning from its mouth, we have the lands that were called Butterwaites, the character of which in 1656 was that of all the other "thwaits" which lay in all directions in the old parish of Danby ; that is to say, lands with sparse timber-growth upon them, but with abounding thickets of thorn, hazel, alder, holly, bramble, and brier, with glades of pasturage-ground in between, here and there expanding into wider spaces, and possessing such an approximately level surface as to admit of being apportioned and applied as meadow-land, and used for haymaking purposes in the summer season.[1]

[1] I may as well adduce here what I have written elsewhere as touching the "thwaite." "The thwaites in the parish of Danby are Armethwaite or Armetthwaite ; Butter-thwait, -twait, or -whate; Mill-waite or -thwaite ; Stubbe-thwaite or Stubble-wait ; Thwaite or Thwaites-bank ; Thwaites or Whates ; Thwate-bank or Wheat-bank ; Thwait- or Waith-dike ; Upper or High Waiths or Whaits ; Nether, Lower, or Low Whaiths ; besides Carlethwait and Eske-briggethwayte. The two names last quoted are in a document dated in 1242, and it is rather worthy of remark that we should find what is usually held to be a Norse word employed in a name derived from a mediæval structure," —for that Eskebrigge assuredly was. "But not to dwell on this, let us direct our attention to Buttertwait or Butterthwaite. The place—it is a farmstead —used to be called by almost every one Butterwicks ; by the few exceptions, Butterwits. Naturally, perhaps, the latter was regarded as simply a folks-corruption of the former ; for why should not the name range with the two places named Butterwick in Yorkshire, and with the other two in Lincoln-shire ? Besides, when Canon Taylor writes, 'We find the (Icelandic or ancient Norse) name of Buthar in Buttermere, Butterhill, and Buttergill,' why should we not fancy we could trace another of the same name in our own Danby Butterwicks ? But unfortunately for such a theory the Butter-thwaits are mentioned in no less than four of the conveyances, all dating in 1656, preserved in the Freeholders' Chest, and in such a way as to prove that recent inclosures had been made there for agricultural purposes, and that

Proceeding up the dale in a southerly direction, on the Butter-wait side, we have a succession of black-land fields, only matched by those on the other side of the beck as regards the unmistakable testimony they bear to their own origin and the continued influence of the circumstances which had given them their being. Their very soil, for some feet in depth, is clear evidence of the wood-growth which had prevailed there from time immemorial. Perhaps a mile and a half to the south of Pundermires the black-land area contracts itself, and only a narrow slip of it remains on the western verge of the beck. This whole space, with the space occupied by Pundermires itself, must in Domesday times have presented an impassable swamp in any and every direction. Only systematic drainage could have effected the changes evidenced by its present superficial and subsoil condition.

And if we turn to the other or eastern end of the ancient Karlethwoyte or modern Carlewaite, or the part into which the extensive dale of Great Fryup debouches, the case is still the same. The two farmsteads, Furnace, on the border of the Great Fryup Beck, and Wheat Bank (which is but the corruption of the 1656 name, Waite Bank, Thwaite Bank, Thwaites Bank), have each of them their testimony to give. The cinder-hill or piled mass of

these inclosures had been apportioned between farms severally called Arme-thwaite, Lower Armethwaite, and Crossley-side House ; while, as to what thwaites, whates, or whaithes meant, such extracts as the following—one of a dozen or so—sufficiently show : 'A parcell of meadow-ground called by the name of "an acre" in the Low Whaites in Glasedale Lawnes, and also four averish gates throughout the Lower Whates and the Upper Whaites, in Glasedale Lawnes aforesaid, as it is now devided.' There were meadow-lands then in the thwaites, apportioned in acres (if not in strips, as it would seem from other entries), over which, after the hay had been severed and carried, there were also apportioned so many 'averish, average, or fog-gates,' or right of stray and pasturage for such and such a number of animals of the ox-kind, and these thwaits were in lawnes, launds, or spaces within the woodlands, open enough to admit of meadow-lands in places, summer-pasturage over perhaps wider spaces (the *sylva pasturalis* or *pastilis* of Domesday), but yet still woodland enough—as appears in manifold places—to allow of numerous rights of taking 'garsell, garthsel, hedge-boot or hedg-ing' (all these synonymous terms being employed in the various documents), for use by the privileged on their own lands as occasion arose." And thus we have explained the presence of so many "thwaits" in the one parochial area concerned.

mediæval iron-slag at the former rather impressively enforces attention upon the consumption of charcoal which had taken place there between the years 1200 and 1500, according to extant written evidence ; and the consumption of such huge quantities of charcoal postulates adjacent forest-growth, springing, waxing, and cut down times and again. The other name announces that down to the date given the "thwaite" character was still the character of that part of Great Fryup. And while on the Furnace or western side of Fryup Beck rough and jaggy surfaced black lands scarcely affect to conceal the dusky *débris* of the old, old wood-growth which had prevailed there from time immemorial, on the other or eastern side the present names, Finkle House and Finkle Bottoms (which are but corruptions of the 1656 Fringall, Frinkall, Frinkell House and Bottom, as Frinkell or Frinkeld is but a corruption of the old 1242 Threllkelde), do but remind us of the *launda* there extant, in which the last of the Brus barons reserved the tithes of hay, as well as of that growing on the launds of Sowerby, Eskebriggethwoyte and Karlethwoyte. If we leave the neighbourhood of the Frinkell House lands, proceeding southwards or what is called "up the dale," the conveyances of 1656 make it known that from the limit just named, or the Frinkell inclosures, up past the Beanley farm and the lower Wood Head, and back by Hawks Carr, and so to the southern and eastern foot of the isolated eminence called "The Heads," there was a great tract of pasture lands, known then by the name of Fryupp or Fryupp Agistment ; and what a great tract of pasture then meant we know by co-ordinating it with the launds and the thwaits we have just been taking note of.

Nor is this all. There is the tale-telling black earth in the whole area or portion of the lower part of the dale marked out by the boundaries of this great pasture-ground so described. Scores upon scores, nay, hundreds upon hundreds of acres are seen, on even passing inspection, by one who has eyes to see and experience or intelligence to comprehend, to have alternated in the older centuries between the condition of sturdy forest-growth with plentiful under-wood of many sorts, and that of swamp, marsh, and bog, each to be renewed or relieved by the other, once and again, as the slow-moving ages rolled on. Wherever the valleys which we speak of as " our dales " widen out sufficiently, and at an elevation a little above the alluvium at their bottoms, through which the several becks gnaw their way, there the water and the woodland-growth struggled for the mastery, sometimes the one prevailing and sometimes the other ; while the slopes ending in the steeper banks were unresistingly occupied by the forest with its lordly sylvan monarchs, its thickets, launds, and glades, dense and untracked as jungle, and equally with the jungle, the dwelling-place of the ordinary sylvan fauna, the wolf and the boar and the stag living on in great numbers until late in the period we speak of as "The Middle Ages."

And the becks themselves tell the same story. No longer ago than the day on which this is written I have been walking along one of these dale becks, and at a place scarcely a couple of hundred yards from the spot where an old parishioner of mine told me he had cut through three forests in digging a deep drain to relieve a waterlogged bit of his freehold, I saw a new section exposed, cut by the action of the beck during the somewhat heavy floods we had had since the late autumn. This section was about six feet in perpendicular height, and is worked through the beds of alluvium deposited by the beck itself in the past ages. Above is the soil of the fields on either side ; beneath it succeed beds of gravelly matter, mixed layers of rounded sandstone, from the size of marbles to that of a good-sized apple or a cricket-ball, strata of sand ; other strata of mixed material coloured dark with ferruginous matter ; a bed in which lay boughs and small trunks of trees, of the colour and consistency of bogwood ; another bed of iron-coloured rough gravel and sand ; and then below all, and washed by the running stream, a bed of peaty matter, of which I could see six inches in thickness above the level of the stream. And yet the place at which I noted all this is but a mile and three-quarters below the rift in the moor down which the baby Danby Beck wears its way, of dimensions such that an old man can without difficulty jump across. Within that short course mainly, it and its still smaller tributaries on either side have found the materials for all those beds enumerated above, and each of those beds, but especially the peat and the bogwood, has its own story to tell ; and the story that is told is of woodland growth alternating with the action of water, in motion and at rest; in either case such as to make transit through or along inconceivably difficult, if not altogether impracticable.

Now this I conceive to have been the character of the whole of this Danby district of the Dales country, as it was eight hundred years ago, when the carefully, strictly conducted and enforced requirements of the Conqueror led to the Return that, out of a total of 23,000 acres of land in the capital manor of Crumbeclive, and its two berewics of Danby and Lelum, at the very utmost 1200 acres were susceptible of the processes of agriculture; and of them barely one-half could have been actually subjected to the plough and the harrow.

This conclusion and the considerations which have led on to it may most likely help in supplying some illustration of what we have noticed as the vague and unsatisfactory nature of the Domesday measurements. They were spoken of above as "estimates" merely, and estimates that did not seem to have been very accurately or even carefully made. But as we have seen, under the actual circumstances of the district, this could not have been otherwise. An actual survey and anything approaching to local measurement were alike impossible. One might traverse the moor, and from such points as the Beacon Hill on the north side of the district, or the heights above Danby Head and Fryup Head on the south, contemplate the greater portion of the home dales with their verdurous fillings-in; but as to any actual survey, in the modern sense of the word, there was no scope for it. And there were, on the other hand, insuperable obstacles to hinder the simple passage, on foot or otherwise, through the entire district of the would-be surveyor.

But suppose the validity of the Domesday statements touching the then condition of Danby from the cultivable-area point of view, with all the corroborative considerations which have been alleged in the foregoing pages, be admitted—and I see no loophole open affording any probability of their being evaded—are there not other conclusions, and possibly of an unforeseen and unexpected nature, which are forced upon us by the very admission itself? For we are asked to believe that no impression whatever had been made upon nearly eleven-twelfths of the cultivable area by the possessors or the occupiers of the area in question during the generations which had preceded the Norman Conquest. The current theory is that the Angles, at least a colony supplied from that source, had possessed themselves of this among other portions or sub-districts of the Cleveland division of the North Riding, in the sixth century or thereabouts ; and that in due time they had been dispossessed and ousted by the Danish irruption in the ninth century ; and yet the united efforts of Angle and Dane, spread over a period of five centuries or more, had not proved equal to the reclamation of more than the very small proportion just specified of the available soil of the bit of country in question.

I confess that this is a conclusion which, stated in this crude, hard, unqualified way, I find it very hard to admit, and, much more, to reconcile myself to. I cannot but accept the Domesday statistics ; but this outcome from them seems to me alike irreconcilable with probability and with ascertained historical facts. I cannot bring myself to believe that a colony of Angles, with well on to three centuries to work in, could have succeeded in doing such a strangely small proportion of the work which lay before them in improving the sparse bits of open land, and clearing and cultivating the least densely clothed among the woodlands, as it must be assumed they did, if we assume too that a Danish colony, much more energetic in the way of felling the trees and taking and tilling the grounds so recovered than the Angles were, were only able, in more than a century and a half, to bring the total of reclaimed land up to the proportion disclosed to us by the Domesday returns. Nay, it is hard to conceive that the tree-felling Northman, with all his resolute energy, backed as it was by generations of like struggling with the arduous experiences of reclaiming the rugged spaces amid the Scandinavian forests, could have effected so little, could have been content with effecting so little, in so long a time, of what was so vitally important to him. On every hand it is evident there must be some explanation for facts that seem so altogether anomalous.

But if we cease to look upon Danby as a substantive whole, and begin to regard it as rather a sectional unit in a much larger area, I think the necessity of such explanation will be but the more apparent. Reference was made above to the township adjoining

2 E

on Danby to the east, and to the Domesday estimate regarding its
dimensions, but no attention was drawn to the revelations afforded
as to its physical condition and circumstances.[1] Briefly, the statement stands thus : there were three carucates to be taxed, and
there might be as many ploughs ; but it was then all waste. The
entire manorial district was four *leugæ* long by two broad, and of
that space pasturable wood occupied a full three-quarters ; in other
words, out of a total area of 15,600 acres, 300 acres or thereabouts
admitted of cultivation—the rest was moor, forest, laund, thwaite,
and swampy expanse. Or to recur to the sheet of notepaper illustration—remove a section, of the size of half a postage stamp, from
the half-sheet for the cultivable land, and take the balance to
represent the unreclaimed land! This may well seem an almost
inconceivable state of things, at least to such of us as know Egton
chiefly by a passing view from road or rail of the fields and
meadows and pastures of the modern township. Of course any
one conversant with the wide extent of moorland on the north
side of the main valley, and with the wider sweep of the same on
the southern side, will be aware of the extensive prevalence of
moorland country still. But for all that, it is very hard to realise
that eight hundred years ago there was probably not a single inch
of reclaimed land within the township of Egton south of the Esk,
while to the north, in the near vicinity of the poor, desecrated old
church, only the extent of about three of the modest moorland
farms, as they used to be a few years ago, was in such condition
as to submit to the imperfect appliances of the contemporary
farmer.

But suppose now we put the two imaginary half-sheets of
notepaper together, so as to make a connected whole, and then
make a blot something less than a florin just above the medial

---

[1] It is obviously unnecessary for the purposes of the argument to subject
the Domesday return as to Egton to minute analysis or criticism. I have
made such analysis and comparative examination, and find the general result
to be that the Domesday area falls short of the reality by six square miles and
a half, in contrast with Danby, where the same area is in excess by no less
than well on to twelve square miles. And further, that whereas the *leuga*
in the estimate regarding the latter place is found on calculation to be less
than a mile and a third, in the Egton estimate it must measure very nearly
a mile and three-quarters.

line of the left-hand leaf, another a little less than a halfpenny about the middle of the line made by the folding, a third not nearly so big as a threepenny piece higher up and a little to the left, on the same part of the sheet ; and yet a fourth higher up still, and more to the right, nearer a threepence than a sixpence in size,—those four attenuated blots would give us the relative sizes and position of the comparatively tiny patches whereupon the farmer of the day, since the era of the settlement of the district, had succeeded in making his effectual mark.

I do not think that this representation of the country or district embracing Danby, Glaisdale, and Egton—a district implying an area, in round numbers, of 38,600 acres—is in the slightest degree overdrawn. Perhaps even the sin, if sin there be, is in the contrary direction. The only source of error exists in relation to the estimated contents of the carucate ; and my impression, derived, as I have said, from a large number of notes specifying the extent of the bovate or oxgang in the district concerned, backed by personal knowledge of the lands in question, is that 100 acres to the carucate is in reality distinctly above the average. But assuming that measurement to hold good, the sum of six carucates at Danby, five at Crumbeclive, one at Lealholm, and three at Egton, amounts to just fifteen ; the estimated number of cultivable acres to a maximum of 1500 ; and the balance of moor and woodland of some sort or other, with swamp and morass liberally interspersed, to no less than 37,000 acres.

For reasons that are obvious we have confined ourselves in the preceding notice to the district of Danby (inclusive, of course, of Lealholm and Glaisdale) and the contiguous township (or parish) of Egton. But it would be wrong to assume that this large area was, as compared with the great stretch of eastern Cleveland skirting it alike on the east and west, altogether exceptional in its character and condition. On the contrary, so far as we can judge from the somewhat meagre information given in the brief Domesday notices of the minor or sub-manors north and east of Egton, the physical and superficial characteristics of the country in that direction seem to have been to a great degree analogous to those of Danby and Egton. Thus, Lythe, with a *totum manerium* of one *leuga* and a half long by half a *leuga* broad, had *sylva pasturalis* to the extent of a *leuga* long by two quarentens broad, with but two carucates of cultivable land. At Hutton Mulgrave the measures were four *leugæ* by one, and three carucates of arable land, three-quarters of the whole area being forest, swamp, and pasture. At Aislaby the proportions were a *leuga* and a half long, by one *leuga*, with a *leuga* square of wood pasture. At Seaton, all but about 300 acres would seem to have been under wood. In Goldsborough, Ellerby, and Mickleby, embracing a space three *leugæ* long by two and a half broad, there was a limited extent of wood pasture and a proportionably large one of bare moor, for the whole contained but twelve carucates of land capable of the plough. In Skelton, again, there was a very large area in wood pasture, besides a great space indeed of moor and swamp; and Kildale was nearly all covered with forest-growth and its adjuncts. Lofthouse, Liverton, Boulby, and Easington are not recorded as having been in the same category, except that a terribly wide acreage is left, after the cultivable portion is withdrawn, for barren waste, inhospitable moor and fen.

Kildale has just been mentioned as being nearly all "covered with forest." The relative proportions given are : the entire manor two *leugæ* long by one broad, and the *sylva pasturalis* of the same length by two quarentens broad, there being about 600 acres cultivable. But it is remarkable that no mention whatever is made of Westerdale, although the explanation of this omission may not be very far to seek.

The earliest mention of the place with which I am acquainted is in a charter of grant by Bernard de Baliol to Rievaulx Abbey, dating several years before the close of the twelfth century, and the terms employed in the said grant are so remarkable that excuse may readily be found for their reproduction here. After naming certain important gifts in Teesdale, the donor proceeds thus: "Moreover, I bestow two bovates of land, with all appendages, in my vill of Westerdale, and common pasture in the said vill, with all liberties and easements appertaining to the said bovates. I also give them [the monks] common pasture for six score beasts, throughout my territory and the whole forest of Westerdale, except the cornfields and meadows, in which also, however, after the severance of the crops, they shall have the same rights of eatage as the men of the said vill. . . . They shall also have pasture for twelve cows and two bulls, with their young, towards the support of their shepherds, the calves to be removed when two years old. They shall also have liberty to make enclosures, sheds, stables, etc., at Wolfdalebeck, below Howthwait, as well as a dwelling for the brother in charge and his assistants at Esklits ; and especially of setting traps for wolves," on condition that everything caught therein was to be Baliol's, with the sole exception of any cattle of their own ; besides which, their shepherds were to have full license "to carry horns, because of the wild beasts (of prey necessarily) and bandits."

Thus, then, a place which is unmentioned in Domesday, and which, as unnoticed by the Domesday Commissioners, could only, one must conclude, have been so passed by because there was literally no *terra ad geldum* within its limits, a hundred years later was still in such a condition that while very large and important rights of pasturage were conceded to a growing religious house [1] (there being, besides the six score *animalia*, the twelve cows—each with an average of two calves—and two bulls, an unspecified number of horses at pasture), the grant of arable land only amounted to two oxgangs. And if we also take account of the provision as to the setting of traps for the wolves, and the significant concession *in re* prowling wild beasts and marauding outlaws, as these *latrones* must have been, we shall have before our mind's eye a fair idea, not only of what Westerdale must have been about 1185, but also of what it actually was in 1086, before any enterprising and fearless colonist or settler had ventured to penetrate its wilds and take up a precarious existence there.

[1] There was another grant made, it is believed, by the same noble donor to the Templars, as to which the same terms as those employed in the text would necessarily have to be applied. No doubt before the Templars were suppressed the state of things indicated by the nature of these grants had passed away, and a large breadth of land had been cleared and improved, and, for the times, a thriving agricultural condition superinduced, as is most abundantly proved by the "extent" and inventories made by royal mandate on occasion of the suppression of the Order. But it must be remembered that the brethren of the Temple had been in possession for upwards of two hundred years, and consequently had had time to work the most radical change in the condition of the lands bestowed upon them.

But, to try and obtain a more comprehensive view of East Cleveland and its condition relatively to the facts of clearances made and the possibilities of agriculture eight centuries ago, I would observe that, beginning with Whitby Strand (exclusive of Hackness), and following the coast as far as Saltburn, striking southward thence by the borders of Skelton, so as to include Kildale and all that lies to the east, up to the southern hill-line limits of the district named, we enclose an area of nearly 121,000 acres of land. Within this area, eight hundred years ago, as we follow the details given by the Survey Commissioners closely and carefully, there were not quite 170 carucates *ad geldum*. Assume that they embraced a total of 17,000 acres, still 104,000 acres remained entirely unreclaimed ; and if we increase the estimate of acres to the carucate, and assume that there may have been 20,000 acres cultivable, still the balance of land as yet utterly wild and in nature's condition as to wood, water, marsh, and moor, reaches the great sum of 101,000 acres ; or five acres and upwards of waste land for every acre that had been made to submit, however imperfectly, to the forces within the reach of the cultivator.

Nor is this quite all ; for we are bound to remember that this geldable land, while lying patchwise even in the places where the industry of man had done most in the way of thrusting back the limits of nature's hitherto undisputed sway, did but represent a few small blotches on an otherwise clean sheet of paper. Kildale, Westerdale, Danby, Glaisdale, Egton, a very large proportion of Lythe and by no means a small one of Whitby, were all forest, thicket, or moor, swamp, marsh or mire — practically a trackless wilderness for miles and miles together as to the moor, and a pathless and all but impervious jungle as to the wilder and thicker woodlands. Nay, Glaisdale had no name in the Domesday Surveyors' note-book, and I think we have seen the reason why. Westerdale had no name either, and again we have seen the reason why. And yet a third place, which a century later, as in the cases of Glaisdale and Westerdale, had newly acquired a name for itself, namely Greenhow, had no name in Domesday, and whatever evidence remains goes to show that it was for just the same reason as with its two other nameless consorts.

For myself, after years of thought and consideration, I am

unable to accommodate to this series of facts and conclusions any theory save one—namely, that the forces of nature, supplemented by its almost more forceful *vis inertiœ*, were too great for the forces of human will and muscle brought to bear upon them. I am totally unable to reconcile myself to the theory that a considerable body of colonising Angles, displaced rather than succeeded by an equally strong body of colonising Danes, could have been, during a period of three or four centuries, not simply dwelling as settlers in this or any like district, but actually dependent for their subsistence on what they could force from the soil (untrained rather than unwilling), and yet have made no more impression upon the material source of such subsistence than is betrayed by the facts and figures we have been led into contemplating. And as the facts and figures, and the inevitable inferences dependent upon them, cannot be gainsaid, nor, as I think, materially modified, the conclusion which seems to be forced upon us is that the "body of colonising occupants" or "settlers" cannot have been so considerable or so strong—whatever the cause or explanation of the default may have been—as is usually assumed.

Now, I find myself writing, nearly twenty years ago, "We may adopt the conclusion that, very possibly, the Anglian population of Cleveland in the times of the Danish appropriations may not have been a very dense one ; may not even have been located in nearly the same number of home-centres as were to be found after a few decades of Danish occupation ; although we certainly cannot suppose that there were no Anglian occupants, or next to none, in the times of greatest throng of incoming Danish colonists, and still less that the said thronging immigrants utterly extirpated the occupants of Teutonic origin whom they found in possession, whether such possession were more or less partial. . . . The opinion that the country was not fully settled or thickly peopled antecedently to the times of the most active Danish irruptions seems to be one which may not only be reasonably entertained and even resolutely defended, but which commends itself to our sense of probability. But still, . . . it is impossible not to recognise some, and presuppose other, and certainly important, Anglian colonies." Had I, with the knowledge now at my command, to rewrite those sentences, I should, I think, use much more definite and decided terms. I should not certainly deny or dispute the fact of "the various and important Anglian colonies," but instead of writing that "very possibly the Anglian population in the days of the Danish inroads may not have been a very dense one or localised in so many home-centres" as a few score years later, or that we could not assume that there might actually be no Anglian settlements here and there to be seized upon by Danish intruders, I should most certainly affirm my conviction that, in many cases, what are now large parochial districts had never been apportioned among Anglian settlers, perhaps even trodden by Anglian feet, except possibly the feet had been those of an Anglian outlaw or runagate. And the reasons which have led to the building up of that conviction are not only based upon the extreme improbability of the supposition that occupation by a band of Anglians, succeeded by a band of Danes, and spreading over nearly five centuries, could have issued in nothing better or more marked than, *e.g.* the clearing and culti-vation of barely 1500 acres out of a total area of well on to 40,000 (as in the case of Egton and Danby united), but on other considerations also, of a nature altogether different.

Among the several and "important Anglian colonies" in Cleve-land which may most unhesitatingly be "recognised" is the town and district of Stokesley. The name is Anglian in both its elements, and is as English as the pre-Domesday church at Seaton and holy Hilda's well close by; or Easington with a like church and pre-Christian burials, which were neither British nor Danish; or Crathorn with its corresponding church and easily recognised name. Every one who knows Stokesley well, and condescends to matters of such small note as field-names, or casts his eye over the six-inch Ordnance map of the district embracing the town and the fields to the north of it, will notice a set of parallel fields with a very commonplace name attached to them. Before mentioning that name I will give an extract from what I printed in *The Antiquary* two or three years ago: "Everybody remembers the episode of our Lord's going through the cornfields, and His disciples plucking the ripe ears of corn as they followed Him. St. Matthew's expression, as given in the Anglo-Saxon Gospels, is—'He for ofyr æceras;' St. Mark's, 'He thurh æceras eode;' and St. Luke's, 'He færde thurh da æceras;' that is, He yode (went) or fared through the acres." And then I quote from Mr. Seebohm: "Obviously the English translator's notion of the cornfields round a village was that of the open fields of his own country. They were divided into 'acres,' and he who walked across them walked across the 'acres.'" The field-name in the map just a little north of Stokesley is "The Acres." Let us collate the name with the word in the three extracts from the Synoptic Gospels given above, only bearing in mind that the English of to-day is but the English of the days when the Anglo-Saxon Gospels were penned, with the wear and tear of a great many centuries upon it, and many subsequent accretions.

But if we go to what were the first "acres" known in Danby (and some other places in Cleveland like circumstanced nine or ten centuries ago), we find a series of fields, greater in area perhaps than "The Acres" at Stokesley, and the name we find applied there is one which may not be found in any English dictionary, although it may be in that or those of a Scandinavian tongue. The name in question is Wandales. And the meaning given to *vång* in Rietz's *Swedish Dialect Dictionary* is, "the enclosed lands of a township or hamlet as contrasted with the common or hill-sides." As to the final syllable of the word, it simply denotes the allotted share or division, or "deal," "dole," or "part dealt." For the "wandales," like the "acres," were simply divided or dealt out in parallel slips of an approximate acre or half-acre.

Nor is the word "botton," applied as a divisional name, a whit less exclusively or less significantly Scandinavian than "wandale." As it exists in writings six centuries old under the forms *bothine*, *bottne*, we need not pay much heed to the modern corruption which has sought to replace it by the by no means really equivalent "bottom." The Icelandic application of the term to the deepest part of a dale, or *dalsbotn*, is the precise application in our Danby case. And the men who cleared the plateau north of the church sufficiently for the purposes of habitation and tillage, as they gazed southward from its brow and looked on the deep gulf of forest filling the hollow between the high banks on either side, might well be prompted to use the word of their fatherland, and dub it the "botn."

But while manifold illustration of the same character is continually presenting itself in local names, names of conspicuous objects, and the like, it is on the name Wandales that the greatest interest and most pregnant suggestion is seen to depend. Even if it were a solitary Scandinavian term surviving among a company of Anglian ones, it would have its own testimony to deliver, its own statement to make ; for it would show that, while the Danish allottee had seen good to impress his own name on the place, his followers or dependants had been Danish enough and influential enough to discard the older and alien name for the *ager communis*, and affix their own northern name, unintelligible to all save themselves, in its place. But standing, as it does, one of a company of others all as national and as northern as itself—the Botton, the Howe, Clither-beck (Icelandic, *àr-kliðr* ; English, the clatter or murmuring sound of a stream), and the like—it does distinctly convey the information that such names were not usurpers displacing older synonyms, but in reality the original distinctive appellations applied to the several features in question.

And thus, while we seem constrained by the Domesday revelations touching the very limited proportion of the district in any sense actually brought under cultivation previously to the Conquest, to be doubtful about both the duration of the period during which reclamation had been proceeding and the actual amount of human energy applied, we find also considerations of a totally different character, forcibly impelling us to the very same conclusions. Practically, while there is no evidence to show that, over very extensive areas in East Cleveland, Anglian colonists had ever plied the axe or swept the soil of its encumbering wild growth, almost every detail arrived at through historical inquiry or inference tends to enforce the conclusion that, within these specified limits at least, the Danish occupants were not only the actual pioneers of cultivation, but the only people who had had the right to " call the lands after their own names."

Danby, then, I look upon as exclusively Danish throughout. And the " How and the Why," the manner and the mode in which this had come to pass, may perhaps be alike explained and illustrated by the following passages from Green's wonderfully suggestive as well as instructive *Conquest of England* : " It was not till the middle of the eighth century that dim news of heathen nations across the Baltic came from English missionaries who were toiling among the Saxons of the Elbe ; and an English poet, it may be an English mission-priest in the older home of his race, wove fragments of northern sagas into his Christianised version of the song of Beowulf. But to the bulk of Englishmen, as to the rest of Christendom, these peoples remained almost unknown. Their life had indeed till now been necessarily a home life ; for instead of fighting and mingling with the world about them, they had had to battle for sheer existence with the stern winter, the barren soil, the stormy seas of the north. While Britain was passing through the ages of her conquest, her settlement, her religious and political reorganisation, the Swede was hewing his way into the dense pine-forests that stretched like a sea of woodland between the bleak moorlands and wide lakes of his fatherland ; the Dane was finding a home in the reaches of beechwood and birchwood that covered the flat isles of the Baltic, and the Norwegian was winning field and farm from the steep slopes of his narrow fiords." Or this again : " In all the northern lands society was as yet but a thin fringe of life edging closely the sea-brim. In Sweden or the Danish isles rough forest-edge or dark moor-slope pressed the village fields closely to the water's edge. In Norway the bulk of the country was a vast and desolate upland of barren moor, broken only by narrow dales that widened as they neared the coasts into inlets of sea ; and it was in these inlets, in the dale at the fiord's head, or by the fiord's side, where the cliff-wall now softened into slopes to which his cattle clung, now drew back to make room for thin slips of meadow-land and corn-land, that the Norwegian found his home. Inland, where the bare mountain flats then rose like islands out of a sea of wood, the country was strange to them." In Danby, too, we had " dark moor-slopes pressing the village fields," " vast and desolate uplands of barren moor, broken only by narrow dales," and " bare mountain flats rising like islands out of a sea of wood." Here, too, men might " set themselves down, turn to, and clear the woods, burn, and settle " ; be told of, like Olaf of Sweden, " that they were clearing the forest," and, like him again, get called the " tree-fellers " ; for here, too, was a " great forest-land, with great uninhabited forests in it such that it was a journey of days to cross them," and that " pains and cost might be spent in clearing the woods and tilling the cleared land," besides "making trackways over morasses and mountains." [1] And to this actual district came, and settled there, the strenuous Dane and Norwegian, and did as they had done at home.

[1] See *Conquest of England*, pp. 53 and note, 56, etc.

APPENDIX D

THE SITE OF THE ANCIENT VILL OF DANBY

I HAVE been asked times without number, by friends and other visitors not resident in the neighbourhood, "But where is Danby —the village of Danby, I mean?" and the question is a very reasonable one. No one ever asks, and for the best of all possible reasons, "Where is Easington or Lofthouse, or Kildale, Harlsey, Staithes, Hinderwell, Lythe or Runswick?" For there are the villages so named to put the questioner to silence.

But it is different with Danby. There is *no* "village of Danby." And as far as any one can tell, after even careful searching and inquiry of the ordinary sort, there never has been such a village.

And yet that is such an anomaly that one scarcely feels disposed to admit it as a fact without some previous inquiry of some kind. That a man called Dane—and after precisely the same rule and for precisely the same reason that hundreds of people are nowadays, and have been for generations, called Scott, English, French, Welsh, Norman, and so forth—had the possession now called Danby allotted to him—say, one thousand years ago ; and proceeded in due course to construct his *by*, make his clearings—*riddings*, he would call them—begin farming operations ; and that thus the wooden dwelling, with stables, beast-house and cow-byre, lathes, bake-house and brew-house, and all necessary shanties for his free-men and serfs (all of the same material), would grow up with more or less rapidity, forming the sort of circumscribed hamlet the *by* actually was, is a matter which admits of no dispute. The simple existence of the place-name Danby is amply sufficient to prove it.

But this conclusion in reality only accentuates the question,

"Where is, or rather, where was, the vill or hamlet originally distinguished by that name?"

There are groups of houses nowadays at Castleton, Ainthorpe, Danby End (or, as it is more correctly called, Dale End), all in the parish of Danby. But both Castleton and Dale End have grown up to what they are within the present century; and Ainthorpe is more modern still. I know that the number of habitations at Castleton a hundred years ago was not more than six; while at Dale End there were but two. So that we cannot look for the original Danby at either of those places.

Now, here let me remark that another question to which I have had to reply times without number, has been, "But where is your church?" Once the question was put to me after the close of a Confirmation held in the chapel of ease at Castleton, and by archiepiscopal lips: "But where," said his Grace, "where is the parish church?" And I pointed it out, as well as I could, distant a mile and a half from the chapel near which we were standing; and I daresay I added, "And there are not forty souls living within the limit of a mile from it."

But one of the things that I have never learned in the course of my manifold inquiries has been that churches and chapels were built, any more in the old days than now, far away from the dwellings of those by whom they were designed to be attended. If Egton old church and Danby parish church—to advert to no others here—be far away from the mass of the presumptive worshippers, we are not at liberty to assume that it was planned so from the first; but rather that, for reasons good in the economy of things, the worshippers generally have shifted the site of their habitations from the vicinity of the ancient church. There can be no hesitation about accepting that as an axiom.

It will easily be understood, then, that when I have been asked for the village of Danby or its site, I have usually answered in the somewhat general form, "Probably somewhere in the fields to the north, but not far to the north, of the church."

Now my study of all available sources of information touching the parish—of the Domesday record, the Ordnance maps, the local names occurring in it, their meaning and general bearing, aided not a little by what could be learned from those multitudinous old conveyances in the Freeholders' Chest—has led me on to a conclusion which goes far towards an exacter localisation still.

No one the least cognisant of the contents of old documents dealing with local matters, and even so low down in point of time as 1550 to 1580—and indeed later yet—can but be aware that, at and through the period so connoted, wherever there was a dwelling—castellated mansions and so forth excepted—there was also a "toft" for it to stand in. *Toftum œdificatum* and *toftum non-œdificatum*, or, in the English of the Armada period, "builded fronts" and "unbuilded fronts," are the phrases which denote the site, or the possible or intended site, of an ordinary dwelling-house.

Now, with this maxim, that the "toft" implies the dwelling-house, let us couple the fact that one field to the north of the church lies a group of fields, six or eight in number, which are to this day distinguished by the general name of "Tofts." They are not all in one farm, but they are all in one compact group ; and, besides that, of adequate area or extent. Because it is not a very limited area that is required ; for in the year 1272 there were fifty-six oxgangs or bovates in villenage in the township of Danby ; and striking the fairest average we can for the number of villans among whom they were held, we cannot allow for less than thirty-five. Or, in other words, we want sites for at least thirty-five dwellings—probably more—in these tofts, each of which dwellings must have had its own proper and peculiar toft or inclosed yard, of from a quarter of an acre in extent up to a whole acre, to stand in.

Here, then, in this particular area marked out for observation by its significant name, deducing what are seen to be perfectly safe and warrantable inferences from perfectly well-ascertained premises, we probably find the site of the original vill of Danby. And in such vicinity and correlation with this site as strongly to confirm the inference so drawn, are the series of fields known by the very marked name "The Wandales." There are the traces, it is likely, of a somewhat later system of husbandry in the series of separate inclosures (as they are now) called the Long-lands, the Mill-thwaits, and so forth, which lie near hand ; but the name "The Wandales" belongs to a much earlier period of agricultural procedure than any indicated by such names as those last mentioned. For

Wandales, like Danby itself, like Clitherbeck, like Botton, like Howe as the name of two marked conical but natural hills in the parish, goes back to the time that Dane and his family of dependants, or their immediate successors, made their mark on the physical aspects of the country, and left their abiding impress on its habits, language, and local nomenclature. And it is a term such as to preclude the possibility of mistaking either its origin or its application. As noted above, the explanation of the primary element in the name Wandale was made on purpose to suit and illustrate the connection I have sought to trace between the original vill of Danby, its church, its site as marked by its tofts, and the closely adjacent Wandales : " the enclosed lands of a *by* or hamlet, in contradistinction to the common or waste belonging to it." And our Wandales are separated from our tofts now simply by the lane called Wandales Lane, exactly as the tofts themselves are divided into two parts by a lane parallel to the former, which ran through the centre of the old settlement, as its street runs through a modern village.

What revelations Danby Church may have had to make in the past bearing on this topic, or what disclosures it may have to make in the future, it is idle to speculate about. The Kildale Church of twenty years ago, with the weaponed skeletons of its old Danish lords—the trenchant swords and the scarcely less terrible battle-axe —had facts to detail that were read with avid interest in Sweden as well as in Denmark. Worsaae, Stephens, and others wrote to me for further and fuller details, and the acknowledgments of the writer first named—whose visit to North England and researches and inquiries there, touching on the same and correlated matters, were then comparatively recent—were very pleasant to read. That poor old Danby Church once had similar records entrusted to her, possibly keeps them still, there can be little or no doubt. The mediæval pottery found in hundreds of instances in the graves throughout the churchyard, with the accompanying charcoal—almost certainly committed to the ground in the form of live embers—has its own tale to tell ; but I, for one, should be very sorry to say that all the pottery I have seen taken from the graves there was no earlier than mediæval ; or that the old consecrated churchyard comprised all the ground originally devoted to sepulchral purposes.

That pagan Danes were laid to their rest there I make no doubt ; and that they were the fore-elders of a Christianised generation or series of generations is equally certain. And while the great men among these might well be buried, as at Kildale, within the precincts of the (since) sacred building, or, at least, so close to it as to be included within it at the rebuilding of a future day, the meaner dwellers in the *by* itself, as it expanded and grew to be a more populous place, would find their earthy beds to the south and east of the dedicated building. And the journey thither from the homes they had dwelt in would be, if our deductions are right, neither a distant nor a difficult one, and preceded by just such gatherings of friends and neighbours as are very far indeed, even yet, from being merely things of the past.

2 F

APPENDIX E

ATTEMPT TO CLEAR UP THE DIFFICULTIES IN THE DOMESDAY ENTRIES TOUCHING DANBY

UNDER the heading "XXIIII. TERRA HUGONIS FILII BALD-RICI" are the two following entries, the first on f. lx.*a* and the other on f. lxi.*b*.

"M. In Crumbeclive habuit Orm v. car. terræ ad geldum. Terra ad ii carucas. Ibi habet Hugo (F. B.) nunc i uillanum & v bordarios, cum i caruca.

"B. hæ pertinent ad hoc M. Danebi, Lelun, Bro ... Camise-dale. In his sunt ad geldum xi car. terræ. Terra ad v carucas. Silva pastilis iii leug. long. and iii leug. lat. Totum M. vii leug. long. & iii leug. & iiii quar. lat. T.R.E. valebat lx sol. modo iii sol.

"M. & B. In Crumbeclive & Lelun & Danebi habuit Orm xii car. terræ ad geldum. Terra est ad iii carucas. Hugo habet et wasta est. Silva past. iii leug. long. & iii lat. Totum M. vii leug. long. & iii lat.

"M. In Camisedale habuit Orm i car. terræ ad geld. Terra est ad dim. carucam. Hugo habet ibi i uillanum cum i caruca."

This second entry is placed at the end of the notice of Hugh FitzBaldric's *terra*, saving only the following :—

"M. In Hevvarde habuit Orm iii car. terræ ad geld. Terra ad i carucam. Hugo habet ibi i hominem cum i caruca. T.R.E. valebat x sol. modo v sol."

Over these three entries stands the heading "NORT REDING."

In several particulars, indeed in almost all, these two entries tally so precisely that, as regards those particulars, the one may be spoken of as the duplicate of the other. Crumbeclive is the *manerium,* Danebi and Lelun the *berewicæ.* The extent of *silva pasturalis* mentioned in either case is the same, and so is the extent of the *totum manerium.* The total number of carucates involved in the first entry is sixteen, and that, again, is the number involved in the second.

The occurrence of a second entry, involving so much of what is contained in a former entry, is in itself not only totally anomalous, but such as at once to suggest that an explanation is wanted, and also that it would be well to look for it and, if possible, supply it.

One explanation which, in a sense, suggests itself, is that the earlier entry might possibly involve a mistake made by the scribe, and detected either when just made or, it might be, on revision, and that the second entry was made as containing the rectification of the mistake ; and for myself, I am inclined to believe that this explanation will be found to cover all the difficulties involved.

But I would further remark that there is yet a difficulty involved, diverse in kind from any glanced at so far ; and that is, that the reading in the first entry, or rather at a certain part of it, is by no means ascertained, and I even think, by no means ascertainable. The word which begins Broc—I think it is safe to assume so much as ascertained—is not easily continued. In the *Yorkshire Facsimile* the doubtfulness is so great that I wrote to Sir Henry James on the subject, and the following reply was most courteously given by him : " The entry on page lx. of the Yorkshire Domesday Book is, I think, BROCTUN Camisedale ; but there is a blotch of scattered ink over the writing *Broc . . . Cami,* which makes the reading a little doubtful ; and so with the words *t'ra ad* in the next line. But this is undoubtedly *t'ra ad.* I cannot find where Broctun is ; it is probably near Denby, Barnsley."

We need not pause over the manifestly erroneous character of this surmise ; our business is rather with the fact of the blotched word. Is it quite certain that the said blotch was made inadvertently ? In the Recapitulation, Camisedale and Broctun come in immediate sequence the one to the other. It is surely not impossible that a slip of the pen should have, through the local facts involving this circumstance, been facilitated, and on being detected have been thus marked purposely. For it is manifestly a slip of the pen. Hugh FitzBaldric had no *terra*, and could have had no *terra*, in either of the Broctuns—Parva Broctun, that is, Magna or Alia Broctun (Little Broughton and Great Broughton), or Broctun near Skelton (now Brotton). There is no uncertainty as to the holders of lands in either or all of those places, and Hugh FitzBaldric is not one of them.

It was otherwise, however, at Heworth; for on f. i., where the locality dealt with is York and the immediate vicinity (much of what is now the suburbs of York), Hugh FitzBaldric is not only mentioned as holding four mansions—those, namely, of Aldulf, Hedned, Turchil, and Gospatric, with twenty-nine small dwellings and St. Andrew's Church (acquired by purchase)—but also as holding largely in Heworth. The entry is as follows: "In Heuuarde habuit Orm i manerium de vi carucatis terræ quas iii carucæ possunt arare. Modo habet Hugo Filius Baldri i hominem & i carucam. T.R.E. valebat x sol., modo v solidos." In immediate sequence to this is the further entry, "In eadem villa habuit Waltef i manerium de iii car. terræ. Modo habet Ricardus de Comite de Moritonio. T.R.E. valebat x sol., modo x sol. & viii den. Hæc villa i leug. long. & dim. latum."

Now, there is a degree of inconsistency between the statement touching Heworth in the Recapitulation and the several entries in the body of the record, there being another short one on f. lxv. as follows: "TERRA GOSPATRIC. M. In Hevvorde i car. terræ ad geld. Terra ad dim. carucam," and the notice of Heworth in the Recapitulation, which is, "In Heuuorde iii car.: Ibid. iii car.," the latter specified as holden by Earl Alan, and the former (at least presumably) by the Archbishop; which is such in its nature and extent as to arrest attention and claim some measure of investigation.

It does not follow necessarily that because in the first entry Orm is mentioned as having held six carucates in Heworth and Waltef three, these tenancies were synchronous, and that the united total, or nine carucates, is to be held the measure of the actual area of Heworth. Nor can it possibly be assumed that because Orm had held six carucates, therefore Hugh FitzBaldric held the same, for what he is represented as holding directly militates against any such assumption. What he is stated to have had there was "i homo & i caruca," his predecessor having had "iii carucas." It is evident on the face of it that there had been displacement and rearrangement.

Waltef, otherwise Earl Waltheof, had been arrested in the year 1175, the second half of it, and he had been tried at the mid-winter following, and beheaded 31st May ensuing. Gospatric also had been under the Conqueror's displeasure, and consequent forfeiture, and had fled for the second time near the end of 1072. The duration of his absence from England seems to be uncertain, but it must have lasted some little time, and it was not until its expiry that he received what Dr. Freeman speaks of as "the partial restoration of his lands." Here we have elements of displacement and rearrangement provided ready to our hand, and it is quite possible that between the giving in of the returns forming the bulk of the Domesday Book, and the labour of summarising which found its issue in the Recapitulation at the end of the book, the said process of rearrangement had been proceeding, and most likely received its completion.

It is more than possible that the entry in the Summary or Recapitulation gives us the total carucatal area of the township, viz. two *maneria* (or, at least, fees) of three carucates each; and besides that represents the final settlement of the tenures. And with this agrees the precise statement in Kirkby's Inquest to the effect that "in Heworth sunt vi car. terræ, quarum iii sunt de feodo Briani filii Alani, . . . et iii car. sunt de feodo Abbatis et Conventus B. Mariæ Ebor."[1] The former of these two fees is

[1] There are certain details given after the mention of Brian FitzAlan's fee which are inconsistent with the primary statement unless they are understood as a somewhat muddled account of the subdivision of the said fee. The editor, in a final note, remarks that "this account of the wapentake of Bulmer is very incomplete," and refers the reader to certain documents printed in the Appendix, from one of which we learn that Brian FitzAlan's fee was actually so divided, and that one division thereof, consisting of one carucate, was held by Andrew de Bolingbroke and Hamo de Grusey jointly. And this subdivision tallies with what we are led to infer from other sources, viz. the one carucate of the Gospatric fee, and the one-third of the entire fee of six carucates apparently held by Hugh FitzBaldric, according to the earliest entry of all (f. i.) And this, again, tallies with the three carucates of his tenure in Heworth as specified in the amended or corrected entry on lxi.*b*.

probably that held for a time only by Hugh FitzBaldric, and eventually by Earl Alan of Richmond.

There are yet other considerations to be adduced in connection with this suggested explanation of the duplicated and connected entry of f. lx., which, moreover, may be found more or less corroborative of the said suggestion. And one of these is, that no *berewica* in Camisedale either did or could appertain to the *manerium* of Crumbeclive. In the amended entry the *berewicœ* of Danby and Lelum are, and correctly, described as so appertaining, but Camisedale was in another district and another connection altogether. Besides the one carucate there in Hugh FitzBaldric's fee, the king still retained five carucates, and the Earl of Mortain three, and its local position is indicated as being both more in the Stokesley direction, and in near juxtaposition with Ingleby Greenhow and Little Broughton. But excluding the Camisedale carucate and the three carucates in Heworth, which, we have had suggested, were in the mind of the scribe when he began the blundered name of Broc . . ., we have the exact number of carucates required for Crumbeclive, Danby, and Lelum, and that is twelve—five in Crumbeclive, and (as we shall see later) six in Danby, and one in Lelum.

And here I would call special attention to the fact that it is Crumbeclive that takes the rank of *manerium*, Danby and Lelum both being merely *berewicœ* to it. Both the fact and the remark will probably be found in the sequel to be not without their importance.

For we have yet another entry bearing upon the three places thus mentioned and their relative connection. And that entry is found in the document which is headed, " Hic est feudum Rotberti de Bruis quod fuit datum postquam Liber de Wintonia scriptum fuit," the very last passage in it being, " Et in Eschedala xii car. & ii bov. : scilicet in Danebia vi car., et in Crumbecliva iii car., & in duabus Hanechetonis ii car., et in Laclum x bovatæ."

It will be at once observed that, save only the additional two bovates (or a quarter of a carucate) the area mentioned is precisely what it had been more than twenty years previously, or twelve carucates. The additional two bovates most likely represent some small accretion (whether by a correcter estimate or a process of assarting, cannot be alleged) made at Lelum, or near. But the relative connection and importance, and even distribution in a degree, have been altered. Crumbeclive is no longer the manorial head or superior ; and, besides that, it has been dismembered. Its original five carucates have been divided, and while but three remain as the dwindled portion now known as Crumbeclive, the other two are divided again between the " two Hanktons."

I am quite aware that this entry has never been read, or rather interpreted, in this way hitherto. Young reads "and *in duabus Hanechetonis*, the two Egtons, probably Egton and Egton Bridge," with " perhaps duabus *ham* Echetonis, the two hamlets, the Egtons," appended as a note. But anything more hopelessly astray than either of these solutions it is difficult to conceive. Egton was not only not in the fee of Brus, it was already in the fee of the Earl of Mortain, and Nigel Fossard was his sub-feudatory there ; and there were not two Egtons, or even two hamlets, Egton Bridge, so called, being a growth of much later date. Indeed it is a matter of question whether the name Egton Bridge had begun to be applied as early as the year 1500.

And again in my own incomplete *History of Cleveland*, although I advert to "the difficulty which besets the record," and offer a suggestion towards its solution, still the suggestion is insufficient, and the difficulty remains as clearly evident as before.

Of course, however plausible it may appear to assume that the original Crumbeclive *manerium* of five carucates may have been divided into the Crumbeclive three carucates of the Brus feudum, and the two carucate lot comprising the two Hanktons, something more than a mere surmise that it may have been so is required before such surmise becomes of any value except to its originator ; and I would suggest that what is advanced below may supply at least a part of the something more required.

In the first place, the name Hankton is a surviving place-name, and in the exact locality required. And, besides that, there is to this day a marked—nay, even a twofold—natural division between the Crumbeclive part and the Hanktons part. For the Crumbe-clive part is simply but indisputably marked by the vicinity of the old Crumbeclive itself. The name has been shortened into Crunkley, where the *kley* represents the ancient *clive* (or cliff), just as in the

Guisborough place-name Kemplah there is the survival of the older form Kempclive, the element *cliff* itself being retained in the name Cliff Wood, the alternative of Kemplah Wood. And between Crumbeclive and the part indicated by the still extant name Hankton there intervenes, besides a portion of common (along the length of which runs the roadway called Lealholm Lane), the stream now called Buskey Beck, the bed of the latter being more than 125 feet lower than the site of the existing farmstead and probable *mansio* of Domesday date. And, beyond even this, it is to be observed that close to Hankton Hill or Farm or House (for all three names are applied) is a farm now called—and for the last three centuries also—Wind Hill, the lands of which mainly face north, while those of Hankton face south. These two tenements then may well supply the *duæ Hanechetonæ*.

But besides this there would appear to be evidence still available adequate to show that the five carucates in question must of necessity be found in the localities indicated, for the good and sufficient reason that, if we admit the identity of Crunkley with Crumbeclive, there was no space for them elsewhere. Because the lands in question were in reality environed on all sides save the north—where there is the precipitous cliff, of over 200 feet in height—by lands that were not only uncultivated then, but remained as undivided, rough woody pasture down to less than a century and a half since. These rough woody pastures were severally called the Low Wood and Glaisdale Lawns.

I think then that the case for the assumed subdivision of the original Crumbeclive *manerium* into the later Crumbeclive section and the two Hanktons section is a fairly strong one ; especially as it is an ascertained fact that Hankton is a name of very old standing. It was extant, and as the established name, in 1656 ; and how much earlier we may not venture to guess except by referring to the old Hanechton of 1087-88.

But there is another matter to which a brief reference may be here made. I mean the transference of the manorial dignity or status from Crumbeclive to Danby.

It is to be observed that there is, in respect of the notice touching the Brus fee at the end of the Yorkshire Domesday, an indefiniteness as to the date thereof in reference as to all but the past. The fee had not been given when the Book of Winchester was written. It is, however, generally assumed that it was given by the Conqueror : an assumption which is perhaps probable, although it seems to be open to question whether it can be absolutely maintained. If it could be, the date of the grant would of course be ascertained within a few months, inasmuch as William's death in 1088 decides the question.

But still the date of the writing under mention would not be settled even then and so ; and there are reasons, palæographic and other, for assuming that the writing is sensibly later in date than that of the writing in the actual *Liber de Wintonia* itself. And for my own part I am inclined to think that, in the matter specially under notice, or the transference of the manorial status from Crumbeclive to Danby, there may be found internal evidence that the date in question is distinctly later than the date of the grant. Because not only is Robert de Brus spoken of as *de facto tenens* in the case of the lands and lordships mentioned, but it is self-evident that some little time must have elapsed before such changes in our Danby manorial lands could have been effectually brought about. Less than this indeed, on any adequate consideration of the circumstances involved, could scarcely be conceded by even a grudging questioner.

For there is no question that Robert de Brus placed the then head of his Cleveland barony at Danby. The castle and manor there might be overshadowed some twenty or twenty-five years later by the superior importance of the castle and manor of Skelton ; but the importance of Danby in the first Bruce's eyes is attested by the strong as well as massive [1] castle he built there ; and the estimate formed by his successors in the barony of its value and importance may be realised by aid of the recollection that when it had been forcibly abstracted—although with the substitution of more valuable lands and manors elsewhere—by the king,

---

[1] The walls on the north side of it were fully eleven feet thick, and water-defences outside the strong mason-work bulwarks thus supplied were of a singularly elaborate nature. Strong as the site was by nature—it occupied the end of a ridge with a decisive slope to the north and east, on which sides also there were moats as well as on the landward side—it was elaborately defended on the other sides also.

and doubtless under the strong influence of political motives and considerations, still the succeeding barons never rested until they succeeded in re-acquiring both castle and manor, and that too notwithstanding the enormous amount of the fine levied by the monarch in consideration of such concession on his part.

But as still tending towards the same general conclusion as touching the superior claims of Danby and the transference to it of the previous manorial importance of Crumbeclive, there are other considerations yet remaining to claim a measure of our attention.

Brus, as a man of war from his youth, must have been fully competent to the selection of the fittest site for the strong fortress he intended to erect, whether at once or after some inevitable delay. A moment's thought about the relative fitness of the site supplied at Danby and that available at Crumbeclive for such a purpose cannot but suggest to us that, while one of these sites was absolutely worthless from a strategical point of view, the other was characterised by the presence of singular advantages. Danby commanded the route from Tees Mouth to Kirkby Moorside, and beyond doubt controlled all similar passage along the line of the Esk on its eastern flank. Crumbeclive had no such command or control. In fact a stronghold like Danby made its occupant the arbiter of all ingress or egress from the north and west as regards the whole Dales district, and was a position to be valued accordingly.

No wonder then Crumbeclive had to yield the precedence, and to become subsidiary where once she had been paramount.

Perhaps even it might be possible to enhance some of the considerations involved in what has been last advanced, and especially as regards the control to be exercised over any traffic across the valley of the Esk for several miles to the east of the then Danby Castle. There are reasons for thinking the whole of the Esk valley from some point not a great way below Castleton, at one time formed the bed of what was a long narrow sheet of water with such a current through it as might be supplied by the volume and force of the Esk as it was then. And there is, if not equal, at least sufficient, reason for assuming that in the earlier days preceding Domesday, and quite down to the period of Domesday itself, a great proportion of the lower part of that which had once been the bottom of the said long sheet of water, consisted mainly of swamp, thicket, scroggy brush, and sparse timber-growth ; that, in fact, it was a district such as was not calculated either to invite or to facilitate transit. And yet, the simple facts that the quasi-table-land between Danby Beck on the west and the Ainthorpe ridge on the east, starting from the line of the Howe to Ainthorpe as the northern boundary, and going no farther south than the church—on which plateau the ancient vill of Danby unquestionably was placed—actually furnishes very much more than the carucatal area specified by Domesday, and that the swampy overgrown bottoms just referred to remained wild pasture-grounds, and nothing better, down to the end of the sixteenth century, are quite sufficient to establish all that is advanced above.

It would seem then, on the whole, that there are adequate reasons for considering the displacement of Crumbeclive by Danby explained, and for thinking that the former was thereupon dismembered, and for considering the *duæ Hanechetonæ* fairly accounted for as one of the results of such dismemberment.

One other remark touching this assumed displacement of Crumbeclive by Danby may be ventured here. With the old or original Castle of Danby, situated where it was, to accentuate the said displacement, one necessary inference is that the earliest solid bridge thrown across the Esk would be built on a site equally dominated and protected by the fortress. And it is thoroughly worth more than passing notice that the ancient bridge, locally known as Castleton Bow Bridge, not only occupied just such a site, but was such in its architectural features and details as to postulate a date not later than the last quarter of the 12th century. The bridge in question, of which a faithful representation is given in the frontis-piece, was as needlessly as unhappily destroyed only a few years ago. I am glad to be able to preserve this memento of it.

APPENDIX F

TOUCHING ROBERT DE THWENG

As connected with this personage there is note of a mandate from the king to the sheriff, dated in 1244, which by no means explains itself. The injunction given is to "make an extent of all lands belonging to Robert de Thweng within his jurisdiction, and to cause a valuation of all his chattels (all of which are in the king's hands) to be made." But de Thweng is not spoken of as deceased, although it is more than probable that he was, because at that date his son Marmaduke was almost certainly still a minor. For, if we recall the circumstances, Matilda de Kilton was still the wife of de Alta-ripa in 1221. Eight years later, it is true, she had become Robert de Thweng's wife ; but some portion of that interval of eight years must be allowed for Alta-ripa's demise and Matilda's widowhood, and if we suppose Robert and Matilda married as early as 1225, it is perhaps all that can reasonably be assumed. But if this is conceded, the 1242 deed of endowment of the young bride of Marmaduke de Thweng receives a remarkable illustration. Supposing his parents married in or about 1225, and himself born a year later, we have him a lad of sixteen at the utmost in the latter part of 1241 or early in 1242, and so wanting four years of his stipulated majority ; and it is very possible that he may have been younger still. But what makes the first surmise even more reasonable is, that in certain deeds preserved in the Harleian MSS., and assigned by Mr. Longstaffe to *circa* 1245, we find Marmaduke making grants of lands at Kilton Thorpe, or, in other words, acting as having attained his legal majority, and, in any wise, having succeeded to his father's lordships.

APPENDIX G

BLACK LAND

I ASKED one of our farmers the other day if he could give me any sort of an estimate of what the amount of "black land" in the parish might possibly sum up to. "Black land," said he musingly ; " why, there's a vast. So-and-so has two fields, all black land ; So-and-so else has three ; why, I have three myself, and—there's amaist nane but has some, more or less."

But I could not get any estimate of the total amount, all through the parish, out of him. He had not been accustomed to consider the matter in that way.

Let me try and give an idea of what "black land" really is, and how it comes to be black land.

Near upon forty years ago, soon after I came into the occupation of this house, at the request of the patron of the living I bought seven or eight acres of land, some of which lay close up to the immediate precincts of the house itself, and might chance, in the hands of an unfriend, to become a very sore nuisance to the inmate or inmates of the house, and, that is, to any parson of the parish and his family. I had a good deal of trouble over the bargain, and had to pay a heavy price for the land, as regarded only from the "agricultural value" point of view.

When the bargain was an accomplished fact, and the land turned over to the patron, I became the tenant of it ; and one of the first things to be done was to drain it. This was, for the most part, a straight-on-end piece of work ; but when we got to the far side of the farther field matters did not arrange themselves quite so readily. For there was about an acre there that never had been ploughed, and did not promise to yield too readily to the processes of the ordinary drainer. For if you walked over it the whole surface quaked under the impulses of your moving weight. Indeed, in seasons of long-continued wet the very cattle seemed to be chary of trusting themselves too confidingly to its undulating level. But I had led my main drain as near to the superficially-covered quagmire as I dared, and then the process adopted had been to drive outside—or skirting—drains in either direction, as close as it was possible to go to the treacherous swamp. In this way a considerable amount of water was permitted to ooze and "sipe" out and away. At last we thought it was safe, as it had certainly become necessary, to carry the work into the morass itself; and we approached as warily as we could, carrying drains as far as was possible wherever there seemed to be most promise of solidity. In this way we found it feasible, with the adoption of the ordinary precautions available to careful drainers, to carry the work continuously forward and to approach its completion.

One day as I was with the men, and talking to the one who was charged with the nicer or more critical part of the work, and who at that moment was engaged in taking out the third "graft" below the surface, and was congratulating himself on the freedom from disaster which might quite possibly have befallen, all at once, without a moment's warning, he sank down bodily to a depth of at least three feet below that at which he had been working a moment before. As he sank a quantity of thick, black, puddly liquid gushed up all round him, with the effect of giving him a most uninviting-looking bath far above his hips. The dismayed look of the man, and the utter mystery of the mishap which had befallen him, and the uncertainty as to how far it might proceed even yet, presented a mixture of the ludicrous with the startling which may be imagined but can hardly be described. It was a relief, however, to find that the man—Ditchburn was his name—after the first rapid subsidence, sank no lower. But he could do little or nothing towards extricating himself without assistance. From his feet to half-way up his thigh he was confined in a narrow cylinder; while above that was the narrow trench of the commenced drain, about two feet six inches deep, and presenting nothing at all in the way of what Archimedes modestly asked for, by availing himself of which he could, as his fellow-worker phrased it, " mak' hissel' a lahtle help." However, we soon extricated him, each of us giving him a hand ; but giving him also at the same time as wide a berth as we very well could ; for up to his armpits nearly, he was as black and as capable of blacking any person or thing he came into contact with as if he had been carefully and liberally painted down with the dregs of a few score blacking bottles.

The explanation of his sudden descent, and of the foully-besmirched plight in which he revisited the surface, was that a large tree-stump, still standing where the tree had originally grown, had been situate immediately beneath his feet at the instant he began to sink, and that more than two feet of its original roofing having been removed by the previous processes of the drain-cutting, the thin stratum left above the hollow stump had proved unequal to supporting the weight of the man, augmented as it was by the vigorous impulses of his digging exertions, and so had given way, and quietly let him through into the equally unexpected and undesirable bath of the black blood of the morass it stood in.

For this morass was the site of what once had been a section of primæval forest ; the tree, whose stump remained there firmly rooted five or six feet below the present surface, was one of many such trees. The piece of land on which my men were at work was the southernmost and lowest or last section of a considerable area of land of the same quality and consistency with itself—the skirting piece, indeed, to and through which all the semi-stagnant drainage of the whole area naturally worked its sluggish way, and the whole of it was, and is, full of the *débris* of former forest growth. The deeper the men drove their tools the more obtrusively evident all this became—hazel-nuts, the leaves of divers kinds of trees and shrubs, as easily identifiable as on the day they finally sank to the stagnant depths of what was then a vast pool (but not long before had been one of Nature's loveliest play-places) ; twigs, sprays, branches, limbs, trunks, all lay strewed about there in the veriest profusion. " As the tree falls, so must it lie " is true in a fuller sense than perhaps the writer of that pathetic hymn actually realised. The trees here had fallen, but not as uprooted by the irresistible hurricane, or as yielding to the slower but equally irresistible influence of natural decay, but they had fallen under the insidious action of stagnant water. One season in the far-away ages of the past had seen these monarchs of the woodland standing in all their pride and beauty side by side with clumps of hazel, thorn, holly, brier, bramble, and what not (all attested by the remains left at our feet); and the next, by reason of the formation by natural means—and who shall say how or by what agencies employed?—of a natural dam sufficient to head back the waters which threaded their way through the glades and along the natural slope, had beheld a sheet of water, of some thirty or five-and-thirty acres in extent, laving the trunks of the trees for some three or four feet of their height, and, while drowning all the lower growths, holding the bases of all the higher clumps in its watery embrace. And the death of all the sturdy timber-trees, tangled thicket, upthrusting sapling, branching bracken, frondy male-fern and shield-fern, had resulted almost as soon as the flood had succeeded in establishing its permanence. And after death came decay, as always; only, as regards the timber-trees under such circumstances, the decay commenced not at the bottom nor at the top, but just where the water-line of the destroying flood ringed the trunk. It was there that fungus and rot and insect were most busily and most effectively at work, and it was there that the consequent weakness of the great strong trunk first showed itself;[1] and when

---

[1] This is a well-ascertained fact; the instances in which it has been illustrated are literally innumerable. Some of the cases recorded as occurring in the coal-measures are of singular interest, as tending to prove not only the general fact stated in the text, but as proving also that, although all the wood proper from the interior of the stumps left in the ground had decayed away, yet the bark itself had remained standing and firm, and with sufficient consistency to reveal its nature to the observant eyes which were noting it. And it had been the same in this swampy piece I was draining, when poor Ditchburn began his unlooked-for and unwelcome descent towards the lower world. It was the bark which was left in its consistency, and had formed the tub in which he had taken his entirely undesired bath. Indeed, I saw the life-destroying energies of water on living trees, under the circumstances noted, well illustrated in the course of the formation of the North Yorkshire and Cleveland line of railway. A little short of the Lealholm Bridge Station, on its west side, is a very heavy embankment, underneath which runs a small stream called Park Head Beck. To permit the proper passage of this stream a culvert was built, but the mason-work put in had not been strong enough to

the pressure of storm and tempest bore heavily upon them, it was there that the resisting strength first gave way. The tree broke off short, and as it fell, there it lay, anchored by its branches, until at last, in the course of time, all fashion as of a tree had fleeted away, and the woody constituents of its ancient substance had gone to form indistinguishable ingredients in the soil of the "black land."

That is the history of the black land as it is read in the unfaltering, undeceiving, and as yet indelible records of God's earth; and the black land lies all over the dales, and even in many places where one would not have thought of looking for it, for here and there it creeps up the slopes at the foot of the moor, up steeply-ascending moor-banks, or rather hill-sides. , And wherever one finds the black land, there may usually be found too ample evidence to testify to the fact of primæval woody growth there. No doubt there are variations in the application of this general rule, and one of these variations is, that the lower the level, or, in other words, the nearer the level of the main system of the drainage of the dales themselves, the more numerous and the more impressive become the black-land-covered forest growths. One of my oldest acquaintances in the parish—dead a few months ago only—told me that, having occasion to drive a very deep drain through a part of his property not very far distant from the banks of the stream running along the length of Danby Dale, he had to "cut through three forests." There they lay, one above the other, at three different and distinct, but severally, perfectly continuous and well-defined levels. Three slow and gradual growings of the trees, three cataclysms, three periods of decay and falling, and mouldering and becoming "bogwood"; and then time for the conversion of the stagnant pool enveloping the still standing butts into bog first,

bear the superincumbent pressure, and the culvert failed; consequently the waters of the stream were headed back, and a pool of some dimensions on the higher side of the embankment formed. The work of reconstructing the culvert, and allowing the pent-back waters to run off, was one of difficulty and time; and consequently several ash and other trees growing on the verge of the little stream interfered with had from two to four feet of their trunks (nearest the ground) under water for the time—a period of three or four months or more. Every such tree was killed, and has long since been removed.

2 G

into swamp next, into carr-land last, with a consistency which was
that of the "earth above" rather than that of the "waters beneath
the earth."

For all this peaty soil that constitutes the upper two to three,
or from that to five or six, feet of the black-land fields has taken
its origin in this way. Water-plants of various sorts and water-
mosses have grown up and died down year by year, forming thin
layers, as each successive season rolled on its way; and these layers
were permeated by the roots of other plants and mosses, and the
slow process of growth and accretion narrowed the skirting margins
first, and raised the shallower portions of the bottom nearer the
surface, and so what was in a sense dry land began to appear, but
land that almost all the way through, from margin to margin and
from bottom to surface, was of vegetable growth that had blackened
with decay, and had had its hues further intensified by chemical
action. The "Moss-litter Companies" may bring us brown peats
of superficial and comparatively recent formation, but our black
earth took longer to form, and the hue is distinctly black, and not
brown, not even a dark brown.

The fact is, there are trunks of trees lying about at from just
level with the surface to eight, ten, or twelve feet below it in all
directions, and to an extent that is hardly suspected by not a few
among those who are supposed to know something about such
matters; and the dimensions of these trees are such as to open
the eyes of those who see the present growths of timber in the
dales, and have come to have their notions modified by what they
have thus observed. For instance, some fifteen or eighteen years ago
I was far up in Danby Head one day on some parish errand, and I
chanced to hear the sound of hard and continued chopping in a
direction which I could only associate with an area of ploughed
fields, separated each from the other by stone walls in lieu of
hedges, and totally innocent of bushes and much more of timber.
I went a little out of my way to see what it could be that was
being chopped. It turned out that the woodman was one of my
old friends, the small farmers living in the Dale-head; and as soon
as I entered the field in which he was at work—it was one of the
blackest of black-land fields, even in that black-land part of my
parish—I saw him, with his plough-team and bright-breasted

plough, all idle and vacuous, close by, hacking away with mighty strokes at something not rising up from the ground but laid within it; for there was nothing whatever visible to strike at, as I saw him, on the palpable surface. On going up to him I saw it was a bit of a great black tree he was hacking at. The fact was that by reason of the gradual settlement of the soil through drainage and other agricultural causes, the tree had come to be in the way of the plough, and he was chopping the intrusive part away. " You see, sir," was his explanation to me, " thoase au'd tree-trunks *will* work oop." And so he had bared about ten or twelve feet of its length—for it lay slopingly in the ground, and as it grew thicker it was seen to lie deeper—and was hacking with might and main to remove so much of it as was actually within scraping distance of his plough-sole. Now that tree, where the farmer was cutting it through towards its upper part, was still eighteen inches in diameter, and allowing only six inches for the waste occasioned by decay, what a tree it must have been, with such a diameter at, probably, at least five-and-twenty feet above the point at which it had first decayed and then broken short off.

Another specimen I saw taken out of the ground in a field in Fryup Head. This was little more than the six-inch-thick shell of less than the longitudinal half of a tree which, in its decayed condition, attested a diameter of at least four feet. It was more than twenty feet in length, and, shell as it was, it took two horses to "snig" it—that is, to trail or drag it along the ground by aid of a chain and other tackle. The diameter of that tree where it broke across must have been nearly or quite six feet, and the length—who shall even estimate it?

Another, and of hardly inferior dimensions, was partly bared by the action of a small black stream on the moors, about a mile north of Danby or Dale End. More and more of it was disclosed from year to year during the first decade of my residence in the parish ; and, first and last, I saw fully forty feet of it laid bare. What the total dimensions were I failed to ascertain ; for one fine day some enterprising person cleared it out, or, at least, as much of it as he could get ; but from what I saw of it, it must have been originally some sixty or seventy feet from the ground before it ceased to be timber that might be squared.

All three of the trees thus mentioned were firs of some sort—
I believe, Scotch pines.

As to the oaks I have seen taken out of these repertories of great
trees, not a few of them showed signs of having formed portions of
fine, well-grown, even if not magnificent, specimens of forest growth ;
but they were, almost invariably, very much more decayed than
the pines, and it was difficult to meet with blocks of such size and
quality as to admit of being put to any practical use.

But the noble trunk I mentioned as occurring in the course of a
small moorland stream was far from being an isolated instance of
the former growth of trees on what is now, and long has been,
bare and treeless moor. To mention but one case : in the peat-
moor used by the Lealholm community there used to be, and
probably are still, large quantities of the stumps of fir-trees, affording a close analogy to that one which gave the black bath to my
luckless drainer, except that they were so much more recent that
the woody character had by no means entirely forsaken them ; on
the contrary, they were hacked up for fuel by such as went to the
pits to cut peat.

It is indeed entirely impossible to define exactly the proportion
of what has long been treeless moor, which in remote times has
been demonstrably under wood at some period ; but I believe the
space is enormously larger than is usually allowed for or even
suspected. And if so, what with the testimony of the black land in
the bosoms of the dales ; what with the forest-clothed slopes of every
moor-bank in the district down to less than a century and a half ago ;
and what with the hundreds and hundreds of acres of the " thwaits,"
" launds," " lawns," or scrubby wood pastures, of the seventeenth
century,—what is the reasonable conclusion as to the extent of forest
and swamp throughout the whole district called Danby now that
must have presented itself on all sides in even slightly prehistoric
times ?

APPENDIX H

I AM able now to add a little further information touching these primitive dwelling-houses and their successive developments. In three out of the one hundred and thirty-eight Conveyances, all dated in 1656, to which reference is made in the Section on the "Old Oak Chest" (p. 295), I find these bits of technical or legal description:—"All that Messuage or Tenement conteyninge one Fire-house being one roome "; "A Messuage or Tenement commonly called Brooke Rigg Farm, conteyninge the Antient Fire-house "; and " All that Messuage or Tenement conteininge two Fire-houses under one roofe, commonly called Mythe Slacke Farme." The expression "Fire-house" perplexed me a little at the time I was busy abstracting or copying the said Conveyances ; but in my present view, and after further examination of the old wrecks of houses already referred to, and careful investigation amid the remnants that were left of another previously unnoticed by me, much, if not all, of the said perplexity may be looked upon as removed. The house last adverted to had been known to me inside and outside from the earliest period of my residence here. But it was last year's removal of the thatch and complete exposure of the old rafters, previously to the total demolition of the antique end of the dwelling, which enlightened me considerably ; and what I had failed to discover there, had been revealed to me by further researches carried out when the "infinite and majestic nettles " of my description on p. 24 had died down. For it then became apparent, with respect to these old habitations, not only that previously to 1656 no chimney whatever had been extant, but that the fireplaces and chimneys eventually holding place in them had been the result of distinct but not immediate after-thought.

But the nettle-begrown building will serve the purpose of illustration best. From measurements made quite recently, the total length, within the rafters or "forks," is 17 ft. 6 in. ; the total breadth at the floor-level (on which the forks still rest) is 16 ft. 10 in. ; which, at 5 ft. 6 in. above the floor, diminishes to 14 ft. 4 in. To the apartment thus limited an addition of about six feet in width has been subsequently made at the south end ; and, apparently at the same time, arrangements had been made at the other end for the insertion of a fireplace and the necessary chimney. The former was provided for by the insertion of vertical slabs, reaching up to about four feet and a half from the floor, and from two feet and a half to three feet wide, with an interspace of about, or nearly, five feet. A foot or two above these, other flat stones were inserted, projecting from the wall rather less than a foot, and about the same distance apart, in order to form the chimney, which expanded below so as to project across the width of the fireplace, as well as to some distance over it in front, and into the room itself ; and it may be added that several of these hooded chimneys —or rather fireplaces—are yet extant in the dale, and I have seen not a few (notably one in the Castle) which projected forward from four to five feet, or even more.

But in the old dwelling particularly under notice, the chimney, thus provided and engineered, necessarily passed over the surface of the tie-beam which connected and strengthened the pair of forks standing at that end of the building ; and to obviate the danger of ignition thus originating, or rather made inevitable, a length of about three feet of the said tie-beam had been cut away ; and, to obviate the structural weakness thus entailed, a pro-tie-beam was introduced just a little in the rear of the hood of the chimney. And there it is to this day ; and the post placed beneath in order to support it at about six feet from the east wall of the house, now hangs, suspended from the beam through decay of its lower end, showing some rather rough ornamental carving on its inner face. From this support to the gable wall, or by the side of the fireplace, so as to shut in and shelter, or rather help to create, a "chimney-neukin," there was a panelled screen, such as to shut off some of the draught entering the house through the door which opened in the said gable wall within a foot or two of the side or eastern wall.

In the next place, and again evidently as an after-thought, this one living-room of 17 ft. 6 in. × 16 ft. 10 in. had been chambered over; the massive stone stairs leading to the chamber still remaining *in situ*. As regards the time at which this was done, I connect the accruing of the additional space at the south end (already noticed) with the epoch of this chambering; for the upper room was continued over it also. And it is noticeable that the insertion of the stone staircase either exacted or utilised an already existing "inserted" protrusion of about twenty-two to twenty-four inches in depth from the east wall—in the substance of which wall, be it remembered, the one of the original pair of forks still remains imbedded.

Whether contemporaneous with, or somewhat subsequent to, this creation of chambers above I am not able, from the extant testimony, to say, a further addition was made to the capacity of the dwelling in the form of an additional room at the north end of the house, separated from the earlier part by a passage, to which entrance was gained by a door through the continuation of the original east wall, into which, for the future, what was originally the external doorway through the north gable end more comfortably opened.

Thus enabled, as we are, to trace the introduction of the fireplace and its chimney into what was—not the primary, perhaps even not the secondary, but rather—the tertiary phase or development of the dwelling, the force and meaning of the term "Firehouse" in the Conveyances referred to above is not so much vividly set before us as is the establishment of the fact that the original structure with the thatched roof (resting what should have been its eaves upon the actual surface of the ground), as artificially warmed at all, was warmed by aid of a fire burning on the floor: besides which, the presumption is encouraged that, even after the erection of the side walls and the consequent bestowal of eaves to the roof, the case continued to be the same.

Thus the two entries " a Fire-house, being one roome," and " the Messuage, Tenement or Farmeholde conteining the antient Firehouse," seem sufficiently explained both as to what they imply, and in the double connection of their infrequent occurrence, and of the fact that in one case at least the fire-house was not a new thing altogether; but possibly a word or two on what seems, with the said connection still kept in mind, the sufficiently remarkable fact that one of the Messuages or Tenements which changed hands in 1656 " conteined two fire-houses under the same roofe," may be anything rather than uncalled-for or out of place. Fortunately the absolute identification of this " farmeholde " is not difficult. From the names of the fields specified in the body of the Conveyance there can be no possible doubt that the farmhold called " Mythe Slacke" in 1656 is the Wild Slack of the nineteenth century. But equally beyond doubt the Wild Slack Messuage or Tenement is on, or close upon, the site of the *manerium* or *mansio* of 1086 called Crumbeclive. And here comes in a somewhat happy reminiscence. One day some twenty years ago (or upwards), walking with a practical and practising architect, the presence of portions of a newel-stair and other stones bearing the impress of mediæval architectural features were discovered by us in the dry-stone walls serving as the fences enclosing some of the fields close to this very farmhouse. The architect said, "There has been a house of some pretension—a mansion—here or near by, in former days." The local antiquary said, "The Crumbeclive *manerium* must have been in the closest vicinity ; for there is Crunkley (Crumbeclive) Gill just in the rear of the existing farmhouse and its various farm-buildings."

Granted these premises, there is not much wonder that in 1656 this Crunkley Gill Messuage—Wild Slack, identical with the old Mythe Slacke—should have " two fire-houses under one roofe."

The contrast between the smoke-darkened and begrimed hovels of the early and middle part of the seventeenth century and the probably dilapidated mansion-house of Crumbeclive, with its two apartments still retaining their fireplaces and chimneys, is sufficiently striking rather than merely marked. But what about the contrast suggested by thoughts of the kitchen of the fourteenth baronial mansion, now known as Danby Castle, with its two fire-places nearly opposite each other, only twenty-five feet apart, and each with an opening extending to no less than fourteen feet and a half in fire-containing width ? And this, too, besides the two capacious ovens opening into the same apartment.

APPENDIX I

CALF-BURYING

FIVE instances of the performance of the calf-burying ceremony, occurring within this district during the last few years, have been communicated to me since the publication of the present book. The same observances as those noted in the text (p. 62) appear to have been strictly adhered to in either case. A correspondent has suggested that the burial of the calf might have originally been made with sanitary objects in view. The idea seems to me to be too superficial to need much consideration. Burials of dead stock, for sanitary ends only, never have been and never are made in, nor even near, the cowhouse, or any other building the end and purpose of which is the housing of live stock. The trouble of removing and replacing the threshold, whether of wood or stone, would be ridiculously gratuitous on such a supposition ; and the care taken to place the calf on its back with its legs and feet extended upwards a still greater absurdity. As a matter of fact, animals buried with a sanitary end in view are, as a rule (often enforced by authority emanating from the Justices in Quarter Session), buried at a distance from the public road as well as the cow-byre, besides being made at a sufficient depth below the surface. Moreover, a calf laid on its back, with its legs sticking up, would require an excavation far deeper than mere sanitary considerations would suggest. In fact, if you take away the "overtrow" explanation of the observance in question, there is no other available that is not simply inconsistent with common experience, not to say common sense.

APPENDIX K

As a pendant to the notice of our Dales weddings and some of their accompaniments given at p. 205 *et seq.*, the following anecdotes may be given as being not entirely without pertinence. Within the last half-dozen years, being myself the officiating minister at a wedding, when I asked the formal question, "Who giveth this woman to be married to this man?" the father of the bride—a personage who, in the very large percentage of cases, is just the one "person or party" who does *not* "give away the bride," being indeed very rarely present at the ceremony at all—made ready answer, "Ah dis"; and then ignoring, as usual, the positive direction of the rubric, addressing himself to the bridegroom he added, "Tak' her. She's a guid an'!"

Another and rather startling innovation on the prescribed ritual in the "celebration of holy matrimony," occurring, it is true, before my time, was related to me very soon after my coming into the district. The ceremony was proceeding, when, in what, it seems to me, may rightly be termed the license permitted on such occasions some fifty years ago and upwards, a gun was fired from the entrance through the basement of the church-tower (which serves as porch) into the nave of the church. As it was a very dark day in November, the flash of the gun lighted up the building as vivid lightning might have done, and, together with the loud report reverberating under the low roof, entirely startled the wedding group, minister included. He, however, recovered himself first, and addressing the bridegroom—I tell it in the words in which it was told to me; and the telling was corroborated by the very bridegroom himself, not long before he died, some ten years ago—he said, "Weel, Tommy, nowther thou nor I's shotten. I think we'll gan on." "Tommy" assured me these were the *ipsissima verba.*

APPENDIX L

DANBY CASTLE; ITS PERIOD AND PLAN

It is curious that, writing as I did (p. 283 *supra*) of the
"dilapidated condition of (the original) Danby Castle" in 1242
and onwards to 1271, and the continuance at Kilton of the
"baronial residence" of the Thwengs after the intermarriage of
Marmaduke de Thweng with Lucia de Brus, it should have totally
escaped my notice that I had, neither there nor in any other place
in the book, adverted to the building of the second and still extant
Danby Castle; to the manner in which such building became
incumbent on the possessor of the barony of Danby; to the identity
and time of the said possessor; to any particulars of plan, structure,
architectural style or peculiarities, or anything else (save only its
existence) connected with the baronial residence concerned. But so
it is; and I propose to remedy the oversight as far as I can in the
present section in the Appendix.

The reader will have noticed that at p. 285 it is stated that
Marmaduke de Thweng, by his wife Lucia de Brus, had an eldest
son Robert and a second son Marmaduke; that Robert, by his
marriage with Matilda Hansard, became the father of a daughter
named Lucia, the only issue of the match; and that, in consequence
of his early death, the headship of the family and the inheritance
of the most of the family lands devolved upon his brother Marmaduke. Robert's daughter Lucia, however, heiress of the Danby
estate (which had been part of her grandmother's portion of the
Brus inheritance), was married in 1296 to William le Latimer the
younger, being then seventeen years of age. It is elsewhere recorded
that, being born in 1279, she was in 1285 *in custodia Regis* as a
minor; which means of course that her father was already dead,

and consequently that Kilton Castle and manor were in the hands
or possession of her uncle Marmaduke de Thweng. In other words,
Kilton Castle was no longer a manor-house or residence available
to the heiress of the Danby manors, and the others associated with
them in her grandmother's share of the Brus patrimony.

No doubt the Latimers had manor-houses or residences elsewhere;
but it was, on the face of it, scarcely reasonable—perhaps, indeed,
scarcely possible or permissible—that so extensive and important a
manor as that of Danby, with its great extent, its ancient Forest
and Chace, and with the mineral treasures it contained—we remember there were seven furnaces "in blast" when Peter de Brus
III died in 1271—should be left permanently without a manorial
seat or *caput*. And in point of fact, it was not so left. The still
extant Danby Castle was built, and has ever since occupied the
status or position so indicated.

It may not be possible to specify the positive or exact date of its
erection; but it is very possible to give a close approximate date.
William le Latimer, as has been said, married the heiress (being yet
a minor) in 1296. It is likely no such great building operation as
that implied in the erection of the Castle would be undertaken
during the continuance of her minority : but still the Castle, almost
beyond the admission of a doubt, must have been completed before
1305. The presence of the armorial bearings of both her father-
in-law and her husband, side by side (the latter distinguished by
the presence of the label) on the north wall of the Castle towards
its eastern limit, seems to be amply sufficient to warrant that
conclusion. And William le Latimer senior, the said father-in-law,
died, says Dugdale (no doubt rightly), in 1304 or 1305. And thus
we have the date of the building of Danby Castle (if not, as I conceive, its completion) laid certainly between 1296 and 1305 ;
possibly, if not probably, between 1300 and the later date. So
much for the date of the building.

As to the manner or fashion of the building, or the general plan
or design of the structure, there are a variety of particulars well
worthy of notice. I made an attempt to describe it nearly twenty
years ago in my then forthcoming History of Cleveland, and in
what follows I, for the most part, transcribe what I wrote then,
merely adding or altering as further or more accurate knowledge

dictates. "The original design of the building has been that of an oblong block with rectangular towers projecting diagonally at each angle, but with this notable peculiarity that the amount of projection on the north and south faces was but from seven to eight feet, while on the east and west it was not less than twenty-four. The total length of the oblong block (or without noticing the projection of the corner towers), inclusive of the thickness of the walls —five to six feet—has been 117 feet, and the breadth from east to west 81 feet. Within this block of building was a court the measurements of which eventually, if not originally, were fifty-four feet by not quite twenty." [1]

As will very likely have been, from what has been said, anticipated, the Castle has undergone very considerable alterations, and it is not altogether easy to decide from the existing remains what the original arrangements or proportions internally were. Certainly, there is no difficulty in making out where the kitchen was. Its site is attested by the presence of two great fireplaces, neither of them much under fourteen feet in width, on opposite sides of an apartment occupying a considerable proportion of the central part of the north side of the Castle ; and so is the manner of the daily provision required at the hands of the cook ; for besides the fireplaces, the position of two ovens is clearly to be distinguished.

In a line with the south wall of the kitchen, as arranged at first

---

[1] In the book quoted from I have made reference to the misleading account of the Castle given in Murray's *Yorkshire Handbook*. The first misstatement is that the Castle was founded by Robert de Brus. Then "the Castle, which the Bruces specially valued"—all of them having been in their graves more than a hundred years before the first stone of it was laid—"from the wild and free hunting-ground which surrounds it, stands finely with a wide view over Danby Dale " ; the fact being that what view there is, fine enough in strict truth, is over the Esk Valley, Danby Dale itself not being so much as visible from any point near the Castle. "Its plan seems to have been a long parallelogram, with square blocks projecting at the angles. All is apparently of one date " ; the real truth, however, being that the attentive eye is smitten with the clearest evidences of divers diversities of date. The account then proceeds: "There were two courts, divided by a strong wall," the object of dividing even a fairly large court into two by a strong wall not being apparent, while such a court as this at Danby Castle, of 54 feet by 20, would surely neither require nor admit of division at all. But this is the way in which local history is too often written or compiled.

(if only we may trust the apparent indications), was the north end of the great hall, a noble apartment of some fifty feet by twenty-eight and a half, occupying nearly the entire eastern wing of the building. It was lighted by four windows, of two lights each under a square hood-moulding, sixteen and a half feet in height, and opening on to the court inside.

Originally, as it would seem from the plinth and other features on the outside of the northern wall of the hall, this must have been an exterior wall; although subsequently corbels were introduced (or inserted) above for the purpose of supporting either a roof, or a floor, covering an apartment of twenty-one feet by twenty, abutting on the east end of the kitchen. From this room, as well as from the apartment in the base of the north-eastern angular projection or block, doors opened into the hall. Another door into the hall gave upon the north-east angle of the court, close to the entrance to the kitchen; and a fourth would seem to have opened either immediately, or indirectly through the medium of a lobby, upon a vaulted staircase near the other end of the west side, which gave access to the upper floor in the south wing of the Castle; and no doubt there was another at the north-east angle of the hall, admitting to the winding stair which conducted to the upper floor in the north-east block, and all along the north wing or front by a passage in the thickness of the wall.

Nothing is left of the hall now but the west wall, with its doorway and remains of windows. A barn and threshing-floor occupy no small part of the area of the court, and the driving-gear of the machine is in a shed reared in its northernmost part, abutting on the south side of the kitchen. West of the kitchen, as already noted, were ovens; and beyond them in the base of the north-west projecting tower a room twenty-four feet by eighteen and a half, dimly lighted by two slits looking south-west, about sixteen inches wide, with deep embrasures, and with a fireplace between them.

The corresponding room in the north-east tower was similarly warmed and lighted, but the windows were on opposite sides.[1]

---

[1] It is not so very easy to convey an idea of the way in which the angular blocks or towers named in the text are united with the main block or building of parallelogram form; and less still one of the curious consequences accruing in respect of the ground-plan so far as the utilising of the angular

It is quite impossible now to make out what the upstair arrangements were in any part of what remains of the northern side of the Castle.

The great gate or main entrance must necessarily have been on the west side or front ; and the remaining skew-table or roof-line on the still existing part of the south (or exterior) side of the south wall of the kitchen and its prolongation towards the west shows that the buildings on that side, and probably on either side, of the gateway, were covered with a lean-to roof. No remains of the gateway, nor of the walls or buildings on either side of it, are now in being, save only parts of the ground table or plinth of the outer wall, and parts also of the foundation or ground-work of the inner walls. A second turret-stair, moreover, existed in the north-west angle, abutting on the junction of the corner tower with the same western face or front.

All that remains of the southern front with the south-east angular projection, except the external or southern wall of the former, and parts of the basement story, have been greatly altered,—

spaces created by the meeting of the converging lines of the main building and the—so to speak—angularly intruded lesser parallelograms, which the corner towers really are as to their ground-plan. If any reader desires to form some sort of a notion of what is meant, it may be done by taking a sheet of notepaper of, say, "commercial" size, and laying it open on a desk or table ; the next step being to take a card half the size of an ordinary postage-card. Then superimpose this card on the left-hand corner of the sheet in such manner that, with one angle of the card exactly on the left edge of the sheet with the longer side of the card projecting from it at an obtuse angle, the lower angle of the paper shall coincide with a point in the parallel longer side of the card, just a third of its own length from the angle opposite to that resting on the edge of the paper. In this way it becomes apparent at once that, if the square of the intruded angular block is maintained, and also the square of the apartments along the line of the wall represented by the lower edge of the note-sheet, a triangular space is left between the line of the intruded wall and that of the apartment in the main building lying to the right of it. These triangular spaces are utilised by the formation of very peculiarly shaped rooms, vaulted above, and with massive ribs in the vaulting, and five-sided, no two sides being of equal widths. The one at the north-east angle has no light whatever from the outside ; while the one at the north-west angle, having had its shape a little modified by the arrangements needed in connection with one of the ovens above named, is less decidedly five-sided in shape, and is lighted by a narrow slit giving upon the north.

although still in comparatively remote times, dating probably well on into, if not late in, the fifteenth century. Then the, as assumed, original nearly square angular towers seem to have been made to give place to longer and narrower projections, which, although still built at the same angle to the general block of the Castle, were so added as to lengthen the east and west fronts by not less than 17 to 18 feet, and to shorten the south front to 48 or 50 feet in place of 75. Of the south-west projection nothing is left save the ground-work of the outer wall, and a fragment or two, of a few feet high, close to the angle of junction.

Some of the rooms on the upper floor of the south front and south-east projection still remain, and in one of them, in actual use as a sleeping-room, is a very fine fireplace; while another is still lined with dark oak wainscoting. The so-called dungeon is curious, and shows a very fine example of a ribbed and vaulted roof. This, it is hardly necessary to say, is coeval with the first foundation of the Castle, and it is not easy to say what the original purpose of it may have been.

On the westernmost end of the south side is a shield of arms with supporters, which may fairly be described as peculiar. The Nevilles, Lords Latimer, whose arms they are, usually had two griffins, and not a lion and a griffin (as here), for supporters, and either a black roundel or a black annulet as the difference. It may be, it was suggested to me many years ago by an heraldic friend, "that this is 'the shield of peace' of Lord Latimer, and that he wore the saltire of his house as a badge, surmounting it with the Tudor rose, as befitted a loyal subject."

As may be well conceived, there is much that is left to unsatisfactory surmise, alike as to the nature, extent, and date of the successive alterations to which the original structure has been subjected. But I think it is fairly safe to assume that the nobleman who built the Castle Bridge (as what is now called Duck Bridge used to be designated up to less than a century and half ago), placing his arms on the west battlement, so as to enable us both to attribute and date it correctly, and who also left another like and very conspicuous memorial of himself, as just noticed, on the Castle itself, may be regarded as the author of no small or unimportant part of the most evident as well as noteworthy alterations and enlargements which are now under notice. What is left of the roof of that part of the edifice which is specially marked by the affixing of the shield of arms in question is anything but inconsistent with such a conclusion ; indeed, is such as to add probability, if not confirmation.

But when we proceed in the direction of the elongated offshoot or prolonged corner-projection, and note the fine, though not highly ornamented hammer-beam roof, there extant, we seem to become aware of further alteration, if not addition, belonging to a date later by some half century at least than that of the first Neville, Lord Latimer ; while within the spacious apartment covered by the said roof we see evident tokens of yet further and later modifications and changes. What I specially refer to is the cutting away of part of the tie-beam at the south-east end of the roof in order to admit of the construction of the chimney, applied to, rather than built within, the wall, which is remarked upon in the note at the foot of p. 24.

Whether Richard, Lord Latimer, or his son John (who was the last lord of this branch) ever resided at Danby, it is quite impossible to assert. But it would seem from the architectural survivals about different parts of the Castle, many of which are not inconsistent in point of date with the affirmative conclusion, and besides are of a nature to indicate that the place was kept up as, at least, an occasional residence of the manorial lord was likely to be,— from such tokens and inferences it is not unreasonable to conclude that such a residence was at least possible.

But it is a far leap from such a halting surmise as this to the alleged residence here of the Lady Latimer who became the last of Henry the Eighth's wives. The simple historical facts that the king married Katherine Howard in July 1540 ; that he was actually at York in the following year ; but that the accusations made against his wife were not made until the November of that year ; and that she was not executed until 12th February 1542,—would seem to be enough to show the flimsy foundation on which the Stormy Hall legend rests ; even if it had not been known that Henry never travelled north of York on the occasion of his visit to that city.

2 H

INDEX

Burial customs—
  necessity of passing over church road, 130, 220, 230
  singing at a burial, 232
Burial places, Quakers', 223
  speech at a Quaker's, 225
By, its meaning, 264

CALF, burial of an abortive, 62, 132, 456
Carucate, variations in the, 407
Castle, date of the present, 460, 461 *n.*, 464, 465
  design of, 461-463
  dungeon so-called, 464
  erection of, 460
  fireplaces at, 461, 464
  remains of, 462
Celt (bronze) found in Glaisdale, 254
Celtic Britain quoted, 258 *n.*
Charm against a witch, 95, 104, 106
Charm for bewitched land, 238
Church, baptisms not solemnised in the, 45 *n.*
  hats worn in, by mourners, 225
  want of reverence in, 44, 45
Church rates, payment of, by Quakers, 224
Churchway, coffins conveyed only by the, 130, 220, 230
Churchyard, charcoal found in, 214 ; its purpose, 219, 221, 432
  flint found in, 157
  pottery found in, 213, 221
Class differences, absence of, 5, 12
Clay beds, structure of, 190, 193, 395
Cleveland, Danish names in, 263, 265
  whinstone dike in, 148
Climb, a toilsome, 220
Common rights, 10, 307
  encroachment on, 307
Congregations in winter, 352, 360, 365
Conveyances of Danby lands, 306, 391
Coums, Danby, description of, 194, 196
  subsidence at, 195
"Country, a devil of a," 190, 191
Coursing witches, 83, 85
Crag wood at Danby, 181
Crops, rotation of, 9
Crunkley or Crumbeclive, 185, 439, 456

DALES, configuration of the, 185, 396, 399

Dales, scenery, 42, 185, 372, 400
  the, apparently submerged, 188
  wedding, a typical, 205
Dalesmen, thrift of the, 112
Danby, area of district of, 184, 405
  changes at, 4, 5
  political, 17
Danby, condition of, at the Conquest, 266, 391, 402, 408
  configuration of the district around, 182, 185
  Danes, marks left by the, at, 263, 425, 429, 432
  earls of, 293, 294, 299
  early settlers at, 260, 425
  first piano in, 14
  how I came to, 37
  my first ride to, 38
  site of the ancient vill of, 387, 429
  the name, 264, 265
  Agricultural Show, origin of the, 11
   speech at the first, 112 *n.*
  Beacon, 38 *n.*, 40, 161, 375
  Botton, 397
  Castle, destruction of the old, 279
   jury-room at the present, 295
   old materials of, possibly used for the church, 281
   old, strength of, 270, 271, 311, 441
  Church, condition of, 44, 45
  Forest, extent of, 404, 409
  Lords of—
   Brus, Adam de, deprived of part of his lands, 273-275
    Peter de, 274, 390 *n.*
    lands restored to, 275
    Robert de, 269
   Danvers, Sir Henry, 293
    Sir John (Dauntsey), 293
    Sir John (Chelsea), 297-300
    sale of estate by, 298, 301-303
   FitzBaldric, Hugh, 266-269, 402
   Latimer, William le, 286, 460
    jun., 289, 460
   Nevill, John, Lord, 292
    jun., 293
    Richard, 293
   Orm, 266, 434
   Thweng, Marmaduke de, 283
    Robert de, 285, 444
Dawnay, John, purchase of lands at Danby by, 304-306

Printed by R. & R. CLARK, *Edinburgh*

Printed in the United Kingdom
by Lightning Source UK Ltd.
130326UK00001B/104/A